Vector Optimization

Series Editor

Johannes Jahn, Department of Mathematics, University of Erlangen-Nürnberg, Erlangen, Germany

The series in Vector Optimization contains publications in various fields of optimization with vector-valued objective functions, such as multiobjective optimization, multi criteria decision making, set optimization, vector-valued game theory and border areas to financial mathematics, biosystems, semidefinite programming and multiobjective control theory. Studies of continuous, discrete, combinatorial and stochastic multiobjective models in interesting fields of operations research are also included. The series covers mathematical theory, methods and applications in economics and engineering. These publications being written in English are primarily monographs and multiple author works containing current advances in these fields.

Kesra Nermend

Multi-Criteria and Multi-Dimensional Analysis in Decisions

Decision Making with Preference Vector Methods (PVM) and Vector Measure Construction Methods (VMCM)

Springer

Kesra Nermend
Institute of Management
University of Szczecin
Szczecin, Poland

ISSN 1867-8971 ISSN 1867-898X (electronic)
Vector Optimization
ISBN 978-3-031-40537-2 ISBN 978-3-031-40538-9 (eBook)
https://doi.org/10.1007/978-3-031-40538-9

Translation from the Polish language edition: "Metody wielokryterialnej i wielowymiarowej analizy we wspomaganiu decyzji" by Kesra Nermend, © Polish Scientific Publishers PWN 2020. Published by Polish Scientific Publishers PWN. All Rights Reserved.

This Springer imprint is published by the registered company Springer Nature Switzerland AG
The registered company address is: Gewerbestrasse 11, 6330 Cham, Switzerland

Paper in this product is recyclable.

Preface

In the era of new challenges of modern scientific economy, it is indispensable to use methods and techniques which support their solutions. In order to acquire various types of goods and services related to everyday functioning, e.g., while buying a trip, choosing an insurance company, the consumer needs the right method to make the right choice based on many criteria. Consumers are manipulated by producers and sellers in majority of the cases which makes it difficult for them to make rational decisions. The usage of publishing methods in making decisions and help the consumers to make a choice which will be more rational.

There are two main areas under decision support: multi-criteria analysis and multidimensional comparative analysis. Two schools dealing with decision-making methods can be distinguished within the first area which are "a European school" (including national schools) and "an American school." The founders of these schools were B. Roy (French), J. Brans (Belgian), and T. Saaty (American). As part of the French school, for example, a group of ELECTRE methods was developed (they are described in more detail in [43, 66, 91, 124, 162, 206]). The Belgian school, supported by French, is known for the PROMETHEE method [183], Methods from America are AHP [173]and ANP [176]. Whereas the representatives of the Polish school can be considered by the professors: Korzeniewska-Gubała, Trzaskalik, Slavinski, Kacprzyk, Kaliszewski, Nowak, Szapiro, Michałowski, and others. Within this school methods such as: BIPOLAR [44], GRIP [50], INSDECM [143], WINGS [122], and MARS [160].

Multidimensional Comparative Analysis (*Multidimensional Comparative Analysis*—MCA) is associated mainly with representatives of the Polish schools, which focuses on taxonomic methods, mainly used to rank objects. Polish taxonomy was initiated in 1909 by Prof. J. Czekanowski, and in 1957 by Prof. Fierich returned to the Czekanowski method. Then taxonomy was developed by Jan Zdzisław Hellwig, particularly in the field of linear ordering of objects method. The pioneering work in the field of application and development of taxonomy in economic sciences should be considered by the work from 1968 entitled: "Application of the taxonomic method to the typological division of countries due to their level of development and the resources and structure of qualified staff" [73].

MCA methods are dedicated mainly to study the socio-economic development of regions and countries [10, 16, 17, 21, 32, 33, 41, 63, 100, 127, 128, 130, 141, 192], to assess the financial attractiveness of stock exchanges, [99, 197, 199], to examine the effectiveness of banks [220], to evaluate the activities of enterprises [151], and in the similar areas.

In this book, the main focus is on proprietary solutions derived from the Hellwig method [74]. A discussion was started on their location in the field of multidimensional/multi-criteria methods. The original applications of MCA methods (rankings), with minor modifications, can be extended towards multi-criteria decision support. By definition, these methods are methodically less complex, patches and implementations, provide the less opportunities in the context of solving decision related problems. They allow considering a large number of decision variants, by taking many criteria into account and will minimize the decision-maker's participation in the calculation process. As the author observes, a new area is emerging into which a certain group of methods can be qualified which have the characteristics of multi-dimensional comparative analysis and multi-criteria decision-making analysis. These are methods such as: TMAI, VMCM, TOPSIS, VIKOR, or PVM (Preference Vector Method). They can be used to make multi-criteria decisions; however, the decision-maker's participation in the decision-making process is relatively small, e.g., just the selection of diagnostic variables or expert judgment (which is one of the features of multi-dimensional comparative analysis). With this approach, decision making can be more automated and it becomes more objective.

In order to fully use the MCA methods to solve the multi-criteria problems, we must adapt, customize, and naming for methodological purposes. Instead of the terms used in MCA methods regarding the nature of diagnostic variables: stimulant, destimulant, and nominator, the concepts of desirable, undesirable, motivating, demotivating, and natural criteria have been introduced. The author's solutions were also compared with other selected methods of multidimensional comparative analysis and multi-criteria decision making.

This monograph is addressed to the scientific community from various fields of science (social, technical, etc.) and managers and persons managing various institutions, i.e., wherever dealing is necessary with multi-criteria decision-making issues. In addition to proprietary solutions, the knowledge contained in this book also gathers and organizes scientific achievements in various areas of decision support, i.e., MCDM (*Multiple Criteria Decision-Making*), MCDA (*Multi Criteria Decision Analysis*), and MCA methods. The numerous examples contained in the book (mainly in the field of economics) constitute purposeful and deliberate action to facilitate understanding of the characteristics of individual methods, identify areas of their application, and improve the implementation in the form of computer programs. This form of presenting the content of the monograph enables interested persons (scientists, decision-makers) to verify the applicability of methods and obtain practical recommendations on their selection for specific decision problems.

The book consists of three parts and six chapters. The first chapter, which was deliberately separated from the whole book, is an introduction to the problems of multi-criteria and multidimensionality in decision support. Based on the proposed classification, the concepts of decision and decision process are approximated, and the procedure for making decisions and solving decision problems in the area of multidimensional comparative analysis and multi-criteria decision analysis has been characterized. The problem of decision support, model problems as well as preferential situations and relations between obsessions (variants) was presented. The classification of problems of multi-criteria decision support was made, followed by MCDM/MCDA methods, and more significant multi-criteria methods and selected methods of multidimensional comparative analysis were briefly characterized. It was also proposed to isolate a group of methods (using reference points) that have features from both MCA and MCDM/MCDA methods.

Part I—"Multidimensional Comparative Analysis Method"—consists of two chapters (Chaps. 2 and 3). Chapter 2 provides a general description procedures for obtaining and analyzing data for the purposes of solving problems of decision-making. The principles of selection of variables have been discussed, with particular focus on their quality and compliance with the adopted research assumptions. The guidelines for determining the validity of criteria were presented, followed by the rules for normalizing their validity. By changing the standardization base (e.g., standard deviation, max, min, median) and other normalization parameters (e.g., min, average, median) in the general normalization formula, examine the properties of the resulting special cases of this formula. The research was carried out in terms of susceptibility of normalization formulas to noise, sensitivity to missing objects, sensitivity to atypical objects, and sensitivity to change the location of one of the objects.

In Chap. 3, the construction methods of aggregate measures (standard and non-standard) have been characterized in detail, their properties were examined, and the considered methods were compared. The methods of the Polish school of decision-making MCA were analyzed, such as Hellwig, orthographic projection, and GDM. In addition, the author's VMCM (*Vector Measure Construction Method*) was described in detail, and then compared with other methods of the same nature.

Part II—"Multi-criteria Decision Support Methods"—comprises three successive chapters. Chapter 4 is devoted to the review of selected multi-criteria methods derived from the European school (family of methods ELECTRE and PROMETHEE), based on the escalation relationship. These methods were subjected to detailed analysis; algorithms of their operation were described and illustrated by examples. For the purposes of these methods, preferences for the character (desirable, undesirable, motivating, demotivating, natural) of individual types of criteria (true, semi-criteria, interval, pseudo-criteria) were examined. The aim of this research was to obtain the basis for comparing these methods with the proprietary PVM method. Chapter 5 describes selected methods based on the utility function (AHP, ANP, REMBRANDT, DEMATEL). Algorithms of their operation and examples of practical use in business are presented similar to the previous chapter. A detailed description of these methods is also an attempt to enrich Polish literature in the theory and practice of these methods. Chapter 6 contains the theoretical foundations of the author, multi-criteria PVM decision support method.

Selected methods, commonly used in the world, using reference points, such as VIKOR or TOPSIS, were also discussed. Practical case studies of using the PVM method in various areas of the economy have been shown. The results of comparing this method with other multi-criteria methods described in Chaps. 3, 4, and 5 are also presented.

List of Major Markings

General Markings

K	Criteria
k_i	i-th criterion
W	Variants
W_i	i-th variants
w	Weight
w_i	i-th weight
$\mathbb{C}$	Complete set of complex numbers
$\mathbb{N}$	Complete set of natural numbers
$\mathbb{Q}$	Complete set of rational numbers
$\mathbb{R}$	Complete set of real numbers
$\mathbb{Z}$	Complete set of integers
$\times$	Cartesian product
$\bigwedge$	For everyone
$0 \bigvee$	There
$\|X\|$	Vector norm X
(X, Y)	Scalar product of X and Y vectors
WW	Own vector
ww_i	i-th element of the eigenvector
λ	Eigenvalue
p	Quantile order
pozKw_p	Quantile position of order p
V_{x_i}	Significance factor of the feature x_i
I	Unit matrix
.*	Multiplication of element matrix by element

TOPSIS

$v_{i j}$	Value of the i-th criterion for the j-th object after normalization and multiplication by weight (TOPSIS)
v_j^+	j-th coordinate of the positive ideal solution (TOPSIS)
v_j^-	j-th coordinate of the negative ideal solutions (TOPSIS)
d_j^+	Distance of the j-th object from positive ideal solution (TOPSIS)
d_j^-	Distance of the j-th object from negative ideal solution (TOPSIS)
S_j	Measure value for the j-th object in the TOPSIS method

VIKOR

S_j	Average value of the j-th object by the VIKOR method
R_j	Value of the maximum measure for the j-th object by the VIKOR method
Q_j	Value of the comprehensive index for the j-th object by the VIKOR method
q	Parameter of the VIKOR method specifying the share of the mean value and maximum measure
$r_{i j}$	Value of th i-th variable for the j-th object after normalization and "reflection mirror" in the VIKOR method

ELECTRE

Υ_i	i-th matrix of pair comparisons (of the ELECTRE method, PROMETHEE, AHP, REMBRANDT)
$v_{i,j,k}$	Element of the j-th row, k-th column, i-th matrix of comparison (of the ELECTRE method, PROMETHEE, AHP, REMBRANDT)
C	Preference matrix (of the ELECTRE method, AHP)
$c_{i,j}$	i-th element of j-th row, preference matrix (of the ELECTRE method, PROMETHEE, AHP)
CW_i	i-th matrix of outranking indicators (ELECTRE III)
W_j	j-th decision variant (of the ELECTRE method, PROMETHEE, AHP)
$g_i\left(W_j\right)$	Value of the i-th criterion for the j-th decision variant (ELECTRE III, PROMETHEE, AHP)
q_i	Indifference threshold for the i-th criterion (of the ELECTRE method, PROMETHEE, AHP)
q_i'	Preference threshold of the i-th criterion (of the ELECTRE method, PROMETHEE, AHP)

PROMETHEE

CK	Matrix of comparison of criteria pairs (AHP, PROMETHEE)
ck_i	i-th element of the matrix of comparison pairs of criteria (AHP, PROMETHEE)
Υ_i	i-th matrix of pair comparisons (of the ELECTRE method, PROMETHEE, AHP, REMBRANDT)
$\upsilon_{i,j,k}$	Element of j-th row, k-th column, i-th matrix of comparison pairs (of the ELECTRE method, PROMETHEE, AHP, REMBRANDT)
$c_{i,j}$	i-th element of j-th row, preference matrix (of the ELECTRE method, PROMETHEE, AHP)
W_j	j-th decision variant (of the ELECTRE method, PROMETHEE, AHP)
$g_i\left(W_j\right)$	Value of the i-th criterion for the j-th decision variant (ELECTRE III, PROMETHEE, AHP)
q_i	Indifference threshold for the i-th criterion (of the ELECTRE method, PROMETHEE, AHP)
q_i'	Preference threshold i-th criterion (of the ELECTRE method, PROMETHEE, AHP)
F_i	Preference function i-th criterion (PROMETHEE)
p	Desirable value (of the ELECTRE method, PROMETHEE, AHP)
np	Non-desirable value (of the ELECTRE method, PROMETHEE, AHP)

AHP,ANP

CU_i	i-th normalized matrix of pair comparisons (AHP)
$cu_{i,j,k}$	The element of i-th row, j-th column, k-th normalized matrix of pair comparisons (AHP)
$c'_{i,j}$	j-th the element of i-th preference matrix (AHP)
MZ	Matrix of the compliance measure (AHP)
mz_i	i-th the element of matrix the compliance measure (AHP)
$mzs_{i,j}$	j-th component i-th element of matrix the compliance measure (AHP)
CK	Matrix of comparison of criteria pairs (AHP, PROMETHEE)
ck_i	i-th element of the matrix of comparison pairs of criteria (AHP, PROMETHEE)
Υ_i	i-th matrix of pair comparisons (of the ELECTRE method, PROMETHEE, AHP, REMBRANDT)
$\upsilon_{i,j,k}$	The element of j-th row, k-thj column, i-th matrix of pair comparisons (of the ELECTRE method, PROMETHEE, AHP, REMBRANDT)
C	Preference matrix (of the ELECTRE method, AHP)
$c_{i,j}$	i-th the element of j-th row, preference matrix (of the ELECTRE method, PROMETHEE, AHP)
W_j	j-th decision variant (of the ELECTRE method, PROMETHEE, AHP)

$g_i\left(W_j\right)$ The value of i-th criterion for the j-th decision variant (ELECTRE III, PROMETHEE, AHP)
CK' Criterion preference matrix (AHP)
ck' i-th the element of criterion preference matrix (AHP)
q_i Indifference threshold for the i-th criterion (of the ELECTRE method, PROMETHEE, AHP)
q_i' Preference threshold of the i-th criterion (of the ELECTRE method, PROMETHEE, AHP)
K_i i-th main criterion (AHP)
$K_{i,j}$ j-th sub-criterion of the i-th main criterion (AHP)
CI Consistency Index (AHP)
CR Consistency Ratio (AHP)
K_i i-th main criterion (ANP)
$K_{i,j}$ j-th sub-criterion i-tego main criterion (ANP)
W_i j-th decision variant (ANP)
p Desirable value (of the ELECTRE method, PROMETHEE, AHP)
np Non-desirable value (of the ELECTRE method, PROMETHEE, AHP)

REMBRANDT

Υ_i i-th matrix of pair comparisons (of the ELECTRE method, PROMETHEE, AHP, REMBRANDT)
$\upsilon_{i,j,k}$ The element of j-th row, k-th column, i-th matrix of pair comparisons (of the ELECTRE method, PROMETHEE, AHP, REMBRANDT)
R_i i-th matrix of pair comparisons after transformation to a geometric scale in the REMBRANDT method
$r_{i,j,k}$ The element of j-th row, k-th column, i-th matrix of pair comparisons after transformation to a geometric scale in the REMBRANDT method
$rK_{j,k}$ The element of j-th row, k-th column matrix of pair comparisons after transformation to a geometric scale in the REMBRANDT method
RK Matrix of pair comparisons after transformation to a geometric scale in the REMBRANDT method
γ Constant in the REMBRANDT method
V_j Preference values matrix for variants j-th criterion (REMBRANDT)
$\upsilon_{i,j}$ Preference value for i-tego obiektu j-th criterion (REMBRANDT)
V_j' Normalized preference values matrix for variants for j-th criterion (REMBRANDT)
$\upsilon_{i,j}'$ Normalized preference values for i-th object j-th criterion (REMBRANDT)
VK Matrix of preference values for criteria (REMBRANDT)
υK_i Preference value for i-th criterion (REMBRANDT)
CK Normalized matrix of preference values for criteria (REMBRANDT)

$c\mathrm{K}_i$ Normalized preference value for i-th criterion (REMBRANDT)
$C\mathrm{P}$ Priority matrix for decision variants (REMBRANDT)
$c\mathrm{p}_i$ Priority value for i-th decision variant (REMBRANDT)

DEMATEL

$\widehat{B}$ Indirect influence matrix between a factors and events (DEMATEL)
$\widehat{b_{i,j}}$ Indirect influence value between of the i-th and j-th factors, events (DEMATEL)
T Total influence matrix between factors and events (DEMATEL)
$t_{i,j}$ Total influence value between i-th and j-th factor, events (DEMATEL)
$B\mathrm{N}$ Normalized direct influence matrix between a factors and events (DEMATEL)
$b\mathrm{N}_{i,j}$ Normalized direct influence matrix between i-th and j-th factor, events (DEMATEL)
λ Matrix divider B during normalization (DEMATEL)
T^+ Matrix meaning indicator (DEMATEL)
t_i^+ Meaning indicator i-th(DEMATEL)
T^- Matrix of relationship indicators (DEMATEL)
t_i^- Relationship indicators i-th factor (DEMATEL)
Z_i i-th factor, events (DEMATEL)
B Direct influence matrix between a factors and events (DEMATEL)
$b_{i,j}$ Direct influence value between of the i-th and j-th factor, events (DEMATEL)

PVM

pozKwI Position of the first quartile
pozKwII Position of the second quartile (median)
pozKwIII Position of the third quartile
$\overrightarrow{\Psi}$ Motivating preference vector
ψ_i i-th coordinate of the motivating preference vector
$\overrightarrow{\Psi'}$ Normalized motivating preference vector
ψ_i' i-th coordinate of the normalized motivating preference vector
$\overrightarrow{\Phi}$ Demotivating preference vector
$\overrightarrow{\Phi'}$ Normalized demotivating preference vector
ϕ_i i-th coordinate of the demotivating preference vector
ϕ_i' i-th normalized coordinate of the demotivating preference vector
$\overrightarrow{\mathrm{T}}$ Preference vector

τ_i	i-th coordinate of the preference vector
$\overrightarrow{\mathrm{T}}$	Normalized preference vector
$\overrightarrow{\Psi'} - \overrightarrow{\Phi'}$	Difference between normalized motivating preference vector and normalized demotivating preference vector
τ_i'	i-th coordinate normalized preference vector
X_i Q1	Value of the first quartile for i-th criterion
X_i Q2	Value of the second quartile for i-th criterion
X_i Q3	Value of the third quartile for i-th criterion
Ω_v	Set of criteria indexes X_i being motivating and demotivating criteria
Ω_d	Set of criteria indexes X_i being desirable and non-desirable criteria
N_v	Number of motivating and demotivating criteria
N_d	Number of desirable and non-desirable criteria
w_i	Weight for i-th criterion
r_j v	Measure value for j-th object for motivating and demotivating criteria
r_j d	Measure value for j-th object for desireble and non-desirable criterion
r_j	Measure value fo j-th object
C_i	i-th matrix of pair comparisons (PVM)
$\mathrm{c}_{i,j,k}$	The element of j-th row, k-th column, i-th matrix of pair comparisons (PVM)
K	Determination of the criterion in the PVM method
nom_i	Nominants i-th variable
D	Decision matrix
$\mathrm{d}_{i,j}$	The element of i-th row, j-th column of the decision matrix
k_i	i-th category
I	Indifference
P	Outranking
P	Strong preference
S	Weak preference
N	Incomparabilities
C_i, D_i	Relation matrix for i-th variable (generalized correlation coefficient)
$c_{i\,j,k}$, $d_{i\,j,k}$	Elements of the relation matrix for i-th variable and j-th i k-th object (generalized correlation coefficient)

Contents

Chapter 1
The Issue of Multi-criteria and Multi-dimensionality in Decision Support

1.1 Decision-Making Process

Making important decisions is usually a difficult and complicated task. In each enterprise, the people are responsible for its development in making a huge number of decisions regarding the economic process. Decision-making is an essential factor in many important problems at the level of an organization. Similarly, every person, regardless of the situation, must make different decisions in life. In such circumstances, the question arises about possible variants (alternatives). What could we gain and what could we lose by making these or other decisions? This question is important because each decision has its specific effects. In the case of businesses, this could be, for example, the financial benefits gained as a result of making the right investment decisions, or, for example, the lost opportunities to attract a new customer after being offered excessive prices for the products offered. When people decide to buy a car, an apartment, choosing a school for children or even shopping in a supermarket are considered as possible variants of their choice. In such situations, it is usually impossible to indicate one best answer to our questions. If that were the case, then running a business would be easy and the life of an average person would be much easier. Answering questions related to the choice of a variant at the time of making the decision is usually difficult to provide, and it may be possible to assess the relevance of this choice in retrospect, when its effects can be assessed. The risk in making decisions, whether related to business or other spheres of life, is that we do not know the answers to these questions.

The decision-making process can potentially be enriched by various less formal factors. One of them is experience that allows making choices based on situations that have happened before. Also, intuition, common sense, or developed practical principles are used in many decision-making situations. Problems of the rules of the brain's operation and mechanisms of human thinking, including the role of intuition and experience in decision-making, have been the subject of detailed research, which Daniel Kahneman (2002 Nobel Laureate) conducted with his associates [39],

K. Nermend, *Multi-Criteria and Multi-Dimensional Analysis in Decisions*, Vector Optimization, https://doi.org/10.1007/978-3-031-40538-9_1

including Elliot Aronson [4]. These studies show that choices and decisions made by people depend on thinking mechanisms, the so-called fast thinking (unconscious, automatic) and slow thinking (controlled). Fast thinking does not require effort because it is based on mental patterns (life experience) or heuristics (the so-called short thinking, automatic reactions to stimuli from the environment). Fast thinking allows you to make specific decisions almost immediately, but it comes with the risk of not analyzing the situation. In the case of slow thinking, or controlled by man, considerable intellectual effort is required to analyze the information available. It boils down to verifying fast (automatic) thinking and taking control over emerging choices. Informal decision support techniques can also include a coin toss, fairy, or astrologer predictions, although these are not ways that are of great practical importance. All these approaches can be helpful, but they cannot replace reliable analysis, which allows more detailed consideration of decision alternatives and their assessment due to specific preferences of decision-makers.

While initializing to analyze the decision-making process, it is necessary to clarify the concepts associated with it. The basic term here is decision. Thinkers in ancient times have already wondered about the concept of a decision and its meaning. Philosophers such as Aristotle, Plato, and Thomas Aquinas considered human possibilities and predispositions to decide. Some of them claimed that our ability to make decisions in complicated situations is the main feature that distinguishes us from animals [48]. Deciding, or making decisions, is associated with a conscious, non-accidental, non-random choice. It is an action, an activity that leads to a change in reality. The decision is the final goal of this action [36, 158]. The term "decision" comes from the Latin word *decisio*, which means resolution. In the literature on the subject, you can find various definitions of decisions, which, however, in most cases come down to the determination of decisions, precisely as a non-random selection of a given action. And so, A. Koźmiński [105] defines a decision as a conscious, non-random choice of one of the possible, recognized variants of future action. Similarly, J. Ruńskiński [172] defines a decision as a conscious, precise choice of one of the variants, which is preceded by an analysis of possible variants of behavior. Refraining from choosing is also a decision. A. Czermiński and M. Czapiewski [36] also use a similar definition of a decision, specifying it as a conscious choice (or lack of choice) of one of many possible actions at a given moment. Generally, it can be assumed that the decision is a formal or informal act on the basis of which in a conscious way made, to select (or not made) one of the available variants.

Different categories can be classified depending on the adopted decision criteria. For example, it may be a division due to the decision-making environment (private and professional decisions), reflection time (impulsive, factual), repeatability (routine, non-routine), time horizon (short term, medium term, long term), position hierarchical (strategic, tactical, operational, implementation), level of conditions stability (decisions taken in conditions of certainty and risk), decision-making entity (group, one man), decision context (one stage, multi-stage), etc. [95, 156, 157]. In terms of decision-making, one of the most common classifications in the literature is the number of assessment criteria that is the one that takes into account. There are single-criteria and multi-criteria decisions. In practice, most problems are multi-criteria, where the choice is a compromise, and different points of view are taken into account. We are dealing here with compromise solutions that are the decision-maker preferences, as well as an analysis of benefits and losses in relation to the adopted assessment criteria is taken into account.

When considering the concept of a decision, one can often find a rational decision. Each action taken produces certain effects that can be assessed positively, negatively, or indifferently (neutrally). While describing rationality, it should be understood as the choice of a variant of action that ensures the best relationship between the positive and negative effects of evaluating this action. Therefore, making rational decisions requires the decision-maker to be fully aware of the possible effects of selecting actions and assessing the anticipated effects of these actions [67, 148, 193]. The decision should be distinguished from the decision problem. I. Kaliszewski [90] defines a decision problem as the choice of a variant for which the criteria value vector is the most preferred, assuming certainty of the decision-making environment of the problem. The problem occurs when there is a gap, a mismatch, between what actually exists and what should exist. Solving a problem is a process of developing ways to solve situations that close a gap. A feature of the problem is that there is usually no one way to solve it, to give one correct answer. Solving the problem is related to making a decision, but this decision only applies to one of the possible solutions. If you choose another way to solve the problem, the decisions may be different. This is due to the fact that decisions are often made in conditions of uncertainty [28].

In the literature on the subject, you can find various ways and procedures to describe the decision-making process. This area is the responsibility of many scientific disciplines, such as computer science, cognitive science, decision theory, psychology, management, economics, sociology, political science, statistics, and others [14, 45, 71, 120, 219]. Each discipline deals with slightly different aspects of decision-making, but they all have their origin in the processes of taking place in the human brain. In this context, decision-making is considered as one of 37 basic cognitive processes modeled in the layered brain reference model [215, 216]. Generalizing and reducing to real situations based on one's own preferences, it can be assumed that decision-making is a process whose goal is to choose a favorable solution or course of activities from a set of variants based on established criteria or adopted strategies [215, 217].

Based on scientific knowledge in the field of operational research and decision theory, decision-making gains the ability to predict, describe, and control decision-making [52]. Various, often complex internal and external conditions are very significant to take into account during the process of making decisions. It is related to the fact that the experience and intuition are insufficient to make accurate decisions because the decision-maker does not have perfect (complete) information about the phenomenon under consideration, including its environment (there is an information gap) [218]. The minimization of this gap is possible by improving the process of obtaining valuable information, its quality, quantity, and appropriate processing [38].

Decision-making problems can be described by using the mathematical language and captured in the form of models to reflect real phenomena. Methodologies in this area are derived from econometrics and its derived scientific disciplines, such as statistics (analysis and data processing that reflects reality) and operational research (decision optimization). For operational research, participants in the decision-making process (decision-makers) are put in the center of attention. They assess decision-making situations (subjective point of view) where the set of adopted assessment criteria is taken into account. They face a decision-making problem in which various conflicting goals should often be considered. Such a situation, defined as a multi-criteria decision problem, is therefore characterized by the subjectivity of defining the problem, objectives, defining assessment criteria, and assessing their effects [39]. This approach is supported by multi-criteria decision support methods. However, in the case of using the statistical apparatus for a multidimensional description of reality referred to as multidimensional comparative analysis, there is the possibility of a relatively objective and automated analysis and solution of the considered problem [136]. The decision-maker's participation is limited to the minimum. Although both approaches enable the analysis of decision problems and can be used for similar purposes, e.g., for grouping or ordering decision variants, the methodologies differ significantly, and the analytical perspective of both approaches is different. Depending on the approach used, different concepts and methodologies are used to solve decision problems.

Procedures are also different, although some stages are similar. The procedure of proceedings in the multidimensional comparative analysis depends on the specifics of the problem under consideration, but it can specify stages (sub-tasks) that occur or may occur in each case. They are shown in Fig. 1.1. The basis for multidimensional comparative analysis is the observation matrix, whose structure has a decisive impact on the correctness of final results [65].

The structuring of the decision problem is the first level of the procedure in the multidimensional comparative analysis. It includes such activities as: analysis of the research problem environment, determination of the scope of research, stage of data collection, analysis of this data, and determination of diagnostic variables (features).

The analysis of the environment of the research problem concerns observation and analysis of the environment, which should result in a better understanding and identification of the problem and consideration of the limitations and uncertainties related to the issues raised. The result of these analyses is the formulation of the purpose of the study and the adoption of preliminary research hypotheses.

The next stage concerns the definition of the scope of research in terms of content, territorial, and temporal. Elements of the set of objects and output variables are selected here, and the measurement scales are determined [211]. The selection of diagnostic variables consists in reducing the pre-adopted set of variables so that the remaining ones are characterized by the greatest diagnostics. The advantage of possibility related to elimination regarding the quantities that provide random and too detailed information is that the numerical description of the considered objects can be significantly simplified [147].

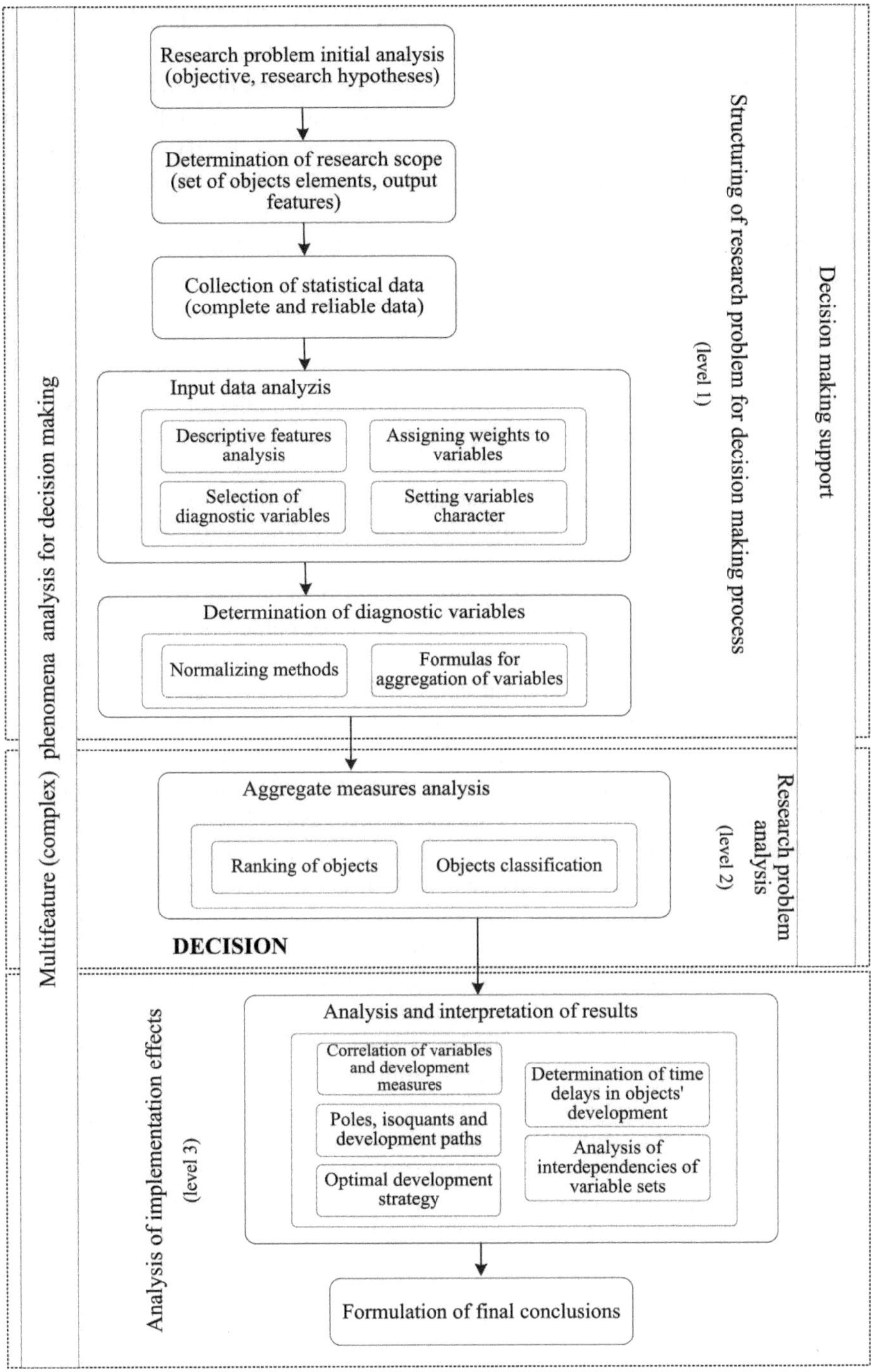

Fig. 1.1 The procedure of proceedings in the multidimensional comparative analysis

The source of statistical data is usually generally available databases developed, among others by the Central Statistical Office (GUS), Eurostat (European Statistical Office), OECD (Organization for Economic Cooperation and Development, Organization for Economic Cooperation and Development), or the World Bank (World Bank database, World Development Indicators—WDI). Along with the development of information technologies, new possibilities of acquiring behavioral data have appeared, such as the use of webtracking, EEG (electroencephalography, electroencephalogram), GSR (galvanic skin response), etc. A more detailed description of data acquisition is provided in Sect. 2.1.

Input data analysis is an important stage in the structuring of a research problem in multidimensional comparative analysis. It consists of four steps, covering such activities as: selection of diagnostic variables, analysis of descriptive parameters, determination of the nature of variables, and determination of variable weights. The analysis of descriptive parameters is associated with the determination and analysis of parameters of the distribution of data variability, such as: mean, standard deviation, maximum, and minimum (stretch mark). The purpose of this action is to determine the significance of variables based on the calculation of the coefficient of variation of diagnostic variables.

The next step of the procedure in multidimensional comparative analysis is the selection of diagnostic variables, which can be implemented in two ways, namely, using an approach related to substantive and logical selection and an approach related to elimination, e.g., those variables that are characterized by a high degree of collinearity [116]. The criteria for selecting diagnostic variables are described in detail in the literature, e.g., [65], as well as later in this work. They define what such variables should characterize, e.g., capture the most important properties of the phenomena under consideration, should be precisely defined, logically related to each other, measurable (directly or indirectly), expressed in natural units (in the form of intensity indicators), contain a large load of information, should be characterized by high spatial variability, should be highly correlated with non-diagnostic variables and a synthetic variable, and not be highly correlated with each other, etc. The procedure for selecting diagnostic variables is associated with various statistical analyses, during which many different criteria are taken into account.

Determining the diagnostic variables character refers to assigning diagnostic variables to one of three groups, namely stimulants, destimulants, and nominants. Stimulants are such variables, which have greater values, which means the higher level of development of studied processes, e.g., considering the quality of life, there will be: the number of GPs, cars, residential area per person, etc. Destimulants are such variables that have smaller values, which means the higher level of development, for instance, considering the standard of living, there will be: inflation, unemployment, etc., while nominants are such variables whose desired values are within a specific range (e.g., natural growth, lending rate, etc.). An adverse situation for the nominator is a state in which they are higher than the upper limit of the compartment and lower than the lower limit of the compartment. In the literature on the subject, one can often find such a fairly constant assignment of specific variables to a given group, such as unemployment, inflation—

destimulants, average life expectancy, living space per person—stimulants, etc. Variables have reservations for such a way of classification, however, because in given conditions of economic development, not necessarily some of the indicators usually referred to as, for example, destimulants or stimulants should be. A better approach would be to classify them as nominants. For example, are very low unemployment rates (below the unemployment rate) as a destimulant and high deflation, or are the average life expectancy of 160 years actually stimulants? Certainly not in some situations. So there is a big challenge for theoreticians and practitioners of business life. One should consider (conduct research) on the development of sets of nominants and determining the lower and upper ranges of their ranges in which a given indicator should fall. Approaching these ranges or exceeding them by a given indicator should be a signal to economic development managers about unfavorable changes that must be reacted to. For the Polish economy, the boundaries of at least some indicators should be established on the basis of a comparison with similar indicators of developed, stable, and prosperous global economies. Sets of nominants developed in this way can have high substantive value for people who are managing the Polish economy, both at the macro- and micro-levels.

Determining the character of variables is based on an analysis of the direction of their impact on the process under consideration [199]. This should be done by taking substantive (non-statistical) considerations into account [65].

In order to take the unequal impact of diagnostic variables on the synthetic measure into account, weight systems are constructed. Two approaches are used to set variable weights. The first uses non-statistical information, in which the weights are most often determined by the method of expert assessment, and these are called substantive scales. The second approach is related to the use of information derived from various types of statistical materials, obtained using various statistical tools. In this case, we are talking about statistical weights [199]. In practice, weights are more often determined by using the second approach, based on statistical resources [65]. Nevertheless, regardless of the system adopted, the balances should undergo a standardization process. Due to the essence of this stage in the multidimensional comparative analysis procedure, these issues are discussed in detail in Sect. 2.2.

Standardization and aggregation of variables are activities that must be carried out as part of the diagnostic variable determination stage. Before the variable aggregation stage, standardization of variables should be taken, whose main goal is to bring diagnostic variables to comparability and standardize their measurement units [146]. The effect of such transformation is to lead to mutual comparability of the analyzed variables, unification of the character of variables, elimination of non-positive values, and replacement of varied ranges of variability of these variables with a fixed range [65].

Aggregation of diagnostic variables is carried out according to formulas, which in most cases can be classified into one of two groups, namely non-reference and reference. In the case of non-reference methods, normalized variable values are averaged taking into account the adopted weighting factors. Various forms of average value are used here, such as arithmetic or geometric mean. The reference methods determine the distance of objects from the adopted reference object. For this purpose, for example, distance formulas are used, such as: Minkowski, Clark, Bray–Curtis, or Jeffreys–Matusita distance [65]. For more information on the activities related to the diagnostic variable determination stage, see Sect. 2.1.

The next level (analysis of the research problem) in the multidimensional comparative analysis procedure covers the issues of rank of objects and their division into classes (grouping). The result of these actions is a decision.

The ranking of objects is related to the linear ordering of objects from the best to the worst or from the worst to the best in terms of aggregate characteristics.

Division of objects into classes (grouping) is, however, performed in order to create groups of objects that will contain relatively homogeneous objects with a similar internal structure of variables characterizing them. The grouping process should meet the requirements related to maintaining homogeneity (similarity of objects within individual groups) and heterogeneity (no similarity of objects belonging to different groups). Grouping can take place by using one of many existing grouping methods (e.g., diagram methods, dendrite division, closest group, Wrocław and Kraków methods) [146]. One of the most commonly used is the method that uses two parameters of the taxonomic measure of development, namely the arithmetic mean and standard deviation, and divides the objects into four groups.

The analysis of the effects of the solution implementation is the last (third) level in the multidimensional comparative analysis. It includes stages such as: analysis and interpretation of results and formulation of final conclusions. Various dependency measures (e.g., correlation coefficient) can be used to check for the existence of significant relationships between the obtained aggregate measure values and the level of development of the tested objects. You can analyze development trends, examine delays between individual objects, or consider different development strategies.

The procedure for proceeding in multi-criteria decision-making analysis (derived from operational research), where many assessment criteria were taken into account, has a different methodological approach than in the case of multidimensional comparative analysis. In the environment of a multi-criteria decision problem, there are several elements that have a fundamental impact on the decision-making process, namely [225]:

- Subject of the decision, decision-maker (person with influence on the decisions taken, responsible for planning)
- The purpose of the decision (the situation sought by solving the decision problem)
- Decision problem
- Consciousness and autonomy (the ability to make decisions regarding the principles adopted and the established area of operation)
- Choice (making decisions based on specific criteria of different implementation options)
- Decision-making environment (surroundings)

The complexity of the decision-making process and the need to perform a range of activities before the final decision is made, and the whole process is broken down into stages. In the literature on the subject, there is a great variety of defining stages and their content, which is somewhat from different points of view. In the context of operational research, regardless of the area considered and the degree of complexity of the process, there are always several common characteristics that allow it to be modeled [29]. The most general approach to the decision-making process sets out only two stages, namely the preparation stage and the decision-making stage [109]. Some authors talk about three stages of this process, which consists of phases: recognition (describing the decision problem), design (defining variants), and choice (indicating the best solutions) [53, 186]. Sometimes these stages are worded differently and differ in the actions to be taken. For example, W. Kieżun [95] divides the decision-making process into the preparation phase (defining and describing the problem, defining decision variants), choice (initial selection and final decision-making), and implementation (decision implementation, effect analysis, and eventual correction). Others, in turn, indicate that there should be four stages: formulation of a decision problem, identification and characterization of possible options for action, evaluation of individual options according to set goals and preferences, and the final phase of decision implementation [8, 58]. Five stages are often specified but are defined differently. For example, they may include: determining the problem, obtaining information, determining the possibility of obtaining an appropriate result, setting criteria, and making a choice [37]. The five-step decision-making process also presents the PrOACT approach, whose name comes from the first letters of the English names of individual stages, (*Problem*, *Objectives*, *Alternatives*, *Consequences*, *Tradeoffs*), namely:

- Defining and presenting a decision problem
- Definition of the objectives to be achieved
- Determining possible decision options (ways to solve the decision problem)
- Analysis and impact assessment of each of the decision options
- Choice of solution (decision variant)

Sometimes three additional stages are added to the PrOACT approach, including uncertainty, risk tolerance, and linked decisions. They are considered in the decision-making process under sensitive or evolving conditions [70]. The PrOACT procedure is universal enough that it is also used in defining the negotiation problem [189].

Another five-stage decision-making process often referred to in the literature is the following steps [3, 157]:

- Identification of the decision problem
- Determination of possible solutions (variants)
- Definition of criteria
- Assessment of variants
- Choosing the best solution

At this point, the differences between the decision-making process and the decision-making problem solving process should be signaled. The latter concept is more comprehensive, which covers the stages detailed in the decision-making process, and also contains additional steps such as:

- Implementation of the selected solution
- Assessment of the effects of the implementation and recognition of whether the problem has been resolved

As points out R.I. Levin [113] is an equally important stage of decision-making, and often overlooked is the analysis of the environment of the decision problem, consisting of thorough research and observations of the environment in which the given problem is considered. The seven-step decision problem solving procedure proposed by Anderson [3] and other authors of decision-making can be supplemented with this initial stage (analysis of the decision problem environment). Graphic representation of it, detailing the main levels, stages, and relationships between them, is presented in Fig. 1.2.

The decision problem solving procedure sets three important levels: structuring a decision problem, analyzing a decision problem, and implementing a solution.

The structuring of a decision problem is also the first and basic level of the decision-making process. Within it, actions should be carried out covering four stages: analysis of the decision problem environment, formulation of the problem, determination of variants, and determination of criteria. The correct implementation of these activities can be verified on the basis of the CAUSE (*Criteria*, *Alternatives*, *Uncertainties*, *Stakeholders*, *Environment*) [40].

The first stage (environmental analysis of the decision problem) is related to, among others with research and observations of the environment, whose purpose is to better understand and identify the problem. It should be borne in mind that all decisions are made under certain conditions, with various types of restrictions and uncertainties. The decision-maker should be fully aware of the environment, tasks, methods of operation, and the scope of the impact of possible effects on making a rational decision [35, 113].

The stage of formulating the decision problem is the activities related to determining the subject of the decision and setting the goal. Each problem can be formulated in different ways and can be considered from different perspectives. The formulation of the goal takes place in the context of the chosen perspective. The decision-making goal (main) is the overriding criterion and should answer the question about the method and the final solution of the decision problem. In this way, the preferred course of action is obtained [157]. Before starting work on formulating a problem, verify that the information describing the problem is reliable. On this basis, it is possible to identify an information gap and assess whether the difference between the current situation and the target situation can be considered important. It may turn out that this difference is not significant, and it is not worth describing the problem in a formal way. Good understanding and formulation are so important that in the event of an incorrect description can focus on the wrong area or take the wrong approach. Sometimes, these types of errors can be detected and modified in

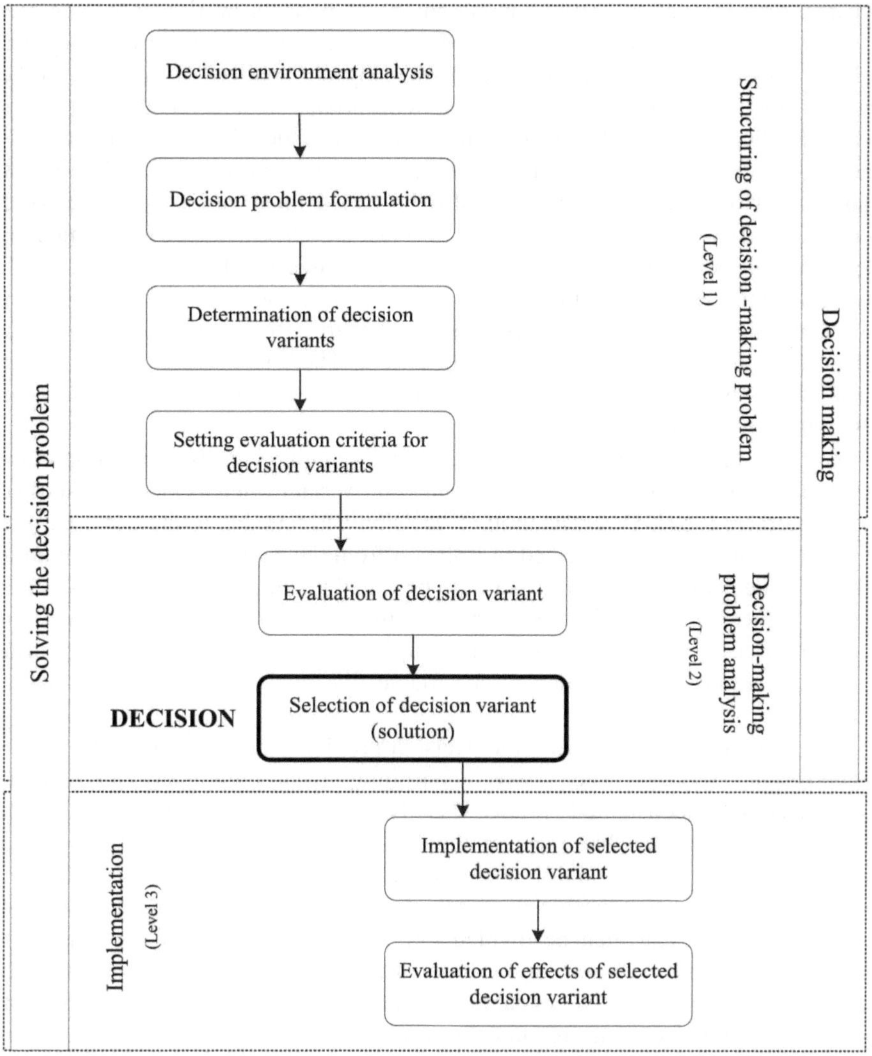

Fig. 1.2 The decision problem solving procedure [3, 106, 113, 157]

further stages of the procedure. However, if the error is not detected, as a result of the decision problem solving procedure, the best solutions cannot be obtained, and thus the problem will not be solved [67].

The determination of decision variants (alternatives, options, possibility) is associated with the decision-making person in choosing one of at least two elements. Roy [164] defines a variant as a representation of a possible component of a global decision, which, taking into account the state of the decision-making process, can be considered independently and can be a point of application for decision support (characterize the variant). Roy has classified the variants into several categories. The first of them included the so-called reality variants, occurring in completely refined projects, and fictitious for underdeveloped (idealized) projects. Another category includes real and unreal variants. Real variants are associated with a project whose application is absolutely possible, while unrealistic when it can, for example, meet contradictory objectives and provide a basis for discussion. Fictitious variants can be real or unreal, but they can also be called ideal variants, i.e., in which they are exactly as described. Potential variants are also distinguished, which can be both real and fictitious variants, provisionally assessed by at least one of the participants in the decision-making process as real. In the context of multi-criteria problems, the definitions of effective variants that are associated with optimality are also encountered, from the perception of Pareto. There is also concept of utopian variants, i.e., more preferred (dominant) than all other criteria, usually an additional concept of the ideal variant [90].

Roy also introduces the concept of a global variant when its application eliminates other variants (applies to models) and a sub-variant when its inclusion does not exclude others [164]. Determination of decision variants due to the complexity of the issues cannot be implemented in isolation from the analyzed decision situation. The set of decision variants will therefore be called the finite set of solutions, which will be subjected to analysis and then assessment carried out during the decision-making process. This set can be permanent, i.e., one that does not change during the decision-making procedure, or a variable that evolves, is subject to change [203, 209].

The final stage of structuring the decision problem is related to setting criteria for assessing variants. They allow determining local preferences, i.e., mutual dominance of the considered options. Usually, decision options are assessed on the basis of many criteria, while in exceptional situations, the assessment can be based on one of them. We are talking about single-criteria decisions. While describing more complex decision problems, a set of criteria defined as criterion space is used [201]. They can then be divided into superior criteria and sub-criteria, to which the analyzed variants can be ordered in more detail in the context of the implementation of the decision goal [97]. When assessing on the basis of more than one criterion, it must be ensured that the criteria used are independent of each other and do not overlap. Otherwise, using two different criteria (related to cause and effect relationships) to evaluate the same variants, the calculations will be performed twice. It is therefore necessary to decide on one of these criteria in favor of the more important one. The large number and complexity of criteria have become the basis for the concept of multi-criteria or multidimensional decisions [146]. The number of criteria taken into account should be limited by the possibilities of analyzing and processing a large amount of information, but you can also find limitations due to the possibilities of human perception. In order to ensure maximum effectiveness of the assessment process and solution of the decision problem, there is a small number of criteria used (7 ± 2), their quantitative character, and a specific direction of preference [93, 182]. However, every good decision-making criterion should meet two basic conditions, namely [67]:

1. Should express a decision-making goal, or at least part of it.
2. It must clearly indicate which variants are assessed.

When defining the set of criteria, it should be strived for it to meet the requirements related to the exhaustiveness of the assessment (completeness of the decision problem under consideration), its consistency (mutual validity of the criteria), and non-redundancy (uniqueness of the range of meaning criteria) [164].

Decision problem analysis is the second level in the decision-making process and includes two stages: assessment of variants and choice of solution (Fig. 1.2). At this level, there is a selection of appropriate techniques and methods to support decision-making. The choice of method is related to many factors taken into account, including adaptation to the information needs of the decision-maker. It should be remembered that the results (choice of solution) may differ depending on the adopted method [200]. When analyzing decision support methods, it should be remembered that they have various types of limitations, and the method of achieving the goal should be adapted to the specificity of the decision-making situation [157]. A general review of multi-criteria decision support methods is conducted in the next Sect. 1.2, and selected methods are discussed in more detail in the following chapters of this book.

Decision-making, i.e., the selection of a specific solution (decision variant), is the last stage of the level of decision problem analysis.

When considering the issue of decision support, it can be seen that practically most decision-making situations boil down to the problem of choosing the best solution from a finite set of variants $W = \{W_1, W_2, W_3, \ldots, W_m\}$, evaluated based on a set of criteria $K = \{k_1, k_2, k_3, \ldots, k_n\}$. Individual criteria usually have different significance, which gives them the appropriate weights $w = \{w_1, w_2, w_3, \ldots, w_n\}$. The values of these weights are usually assigned in a subjective way, reflecting the preferences of the decision-maker or in such a way as to reconcile the often conflicting interests of participants in the decision-making process [97]. Any multi-criteria decision problem (situation) can be presented in the form of the so-called decision matrix D, which contains assessments of the value of decision variants against individual criteria:

$$D = \begin{bmatrix} d_{1,1} & d_{1,2} & d_{1,3} & \cdots & d_{1,n} \\ d_{2,1} & d_{2,2} & d_{2,3} & \cdots & d_{2,n} \\ d_{3,1} & d_{3,2} & d_{3,3} & \cdots & d_{3,n} \\ \vdots & \vdots & \vdots & \ddots & \vdots \\ d_{m,1} & d_{m,2} & d_{m,3} & \cdots & d_{m,n} \end{bmatrix}. \tag{1.1}$$

The decision matrix can also be presented in tabular form, in which the rows of the matrix correspond to individual decision variants and the columns to the criteria. Additionally, a normalized weight vector w should be taken into account, fulfilling the condition that the sum of all elements of this vector is 1 [9]. This vector assigns

Table 1.1 Generalized form of the decision matrix (based on [97])

	Decision criterion			
	Criterion k_1	Criterion k_2	Criterion k_3	Criterion k_4
Variant W_1	$d_{1,1}$	$d_{1,2}$	$d_{1,3}$	$d_{1,4}$
Variant W_2	$d_{2,1}$	$d_{2,2}$	$d_{2,3}$	$d_{2,4}$
Variant W_3	$d_{3,1}$	$d_{3,2}$	$d_{3,3}$	$d_{3,4}$
Variant W_4	$d_{4,1}$	$d_{4,2}$	$d_{4,3}$	$d_{4,4}$
Weighting coefficients	w_1	w_2	w_3	w_4

a numerical weight value to each criterion, defining its importance, i.e., the degree of influence on the final decision (Table 1.1).

The selection of the best solution (variant) is usually carried out on the basis of a synthetic assessment of variants as a result of aggregation of partial assessments, but there are also alternative methods for selecting the most advantageous solution.

The last level in the procedure for solving the decision problem includes the stage of implementing the decision variant and the stage of assessing the effects of its implementation. However, these steps are not considered in this book.

The procedure for solving the decision problem, including decision-making, proposed in Fig. 1.2, is a methodological and typical indication of every decision situation. As noted by A. Prusak and P. Stefanów [157], all activities related to decision support are carried out according to algorithms, which are most often a connection, combination, extension, or simplification of this procedure.

Obtaining effective (optimal in the Pareto sense) solutions, as well as ensuring their objectivity, can be disturbed regardless of the methodological approach used. This is due to the fact that the models used are only a simplified picture of reality, and it is often impossible to take into account all the conditions of the decision-making process and to obtain reliable data. In addition, the human factor is also of great importance and related to it, e.g., subjective assessment of model elements, largely conditioned by individual preferences.

When considering the decision-making process, it is impossible to ignore the human aspect. The key role in choosing a decision is always played by the human who is the last and most important element of this process. The use of tools supporting the decision-making process and computerization of these processes will not eliminate or replace a human being. The result of this process should be a decision in line with the preferences of the person or persons participating in it. Making a decision cannot be reduced to automatic generation by the IT system of the final decision, although in case of simple decision problems where such a situation can be imagined. Generally, the decision problem is related to the processing of information, using quantitative methods to assess the problem, but with the active participation of human. This participation may vary, depending on the issues and the degree of decision-making procedures used.

Roy [164] defines the participants in the decision-making process (defined after Boudon [22]) as interveners, pointing out that they may be guided by different goals and may have different value systems. It is difficult to define one model that will be beneficial for all participants in the decision-making process. Therefore, one intervener is usually distinguished, which can be a single person or a group (team) of people. Such an intervener is called a decision-maker. The decision-maker, as an individual, plays the main role in the decision-making process and expresses common goals and preferences. In the case of a set of people, he is their spokesperson and carries out an assessment of decision-making possibilities and the results obtained. Roy [164] lists two other categories among participants in the decision-making process, namely analysts and principals. The analyst is usually a specialist in a given field, who may be a collaborator of the decision-maker or come from outside the circle of people cooperating with him, e.g., from other institutions. The analyst's task is to present the model, show the possibility of using it to obtain results, explain to the decision-maker the effects of a given procedure, as well as provide suggestions for specific actions or the choice of methodology. However, the client is responsible for commissioning a case study and providing funds for its implementation. He usually presents the problem to the analyst, assists him in acquiring knowledge in the field of the analyzed issues, and assesses his work in the aspect of correct formulation of the problem. In the context of the above considerations, it should be noted that the decision-maker may or may not act directly as analyst (no direct contact). Similarly, the principal may play the role of analyst or decision-maker but may also not perform these roles.

Prusak i Stefanów [157] proposed the division of decision-makers, classify them on the basis of their competences, into:

- Experts (advisers) and analysts (substantive competences)
- Sponsors (material competences)
- Principals (formal competences)

Experts are responsible for preparing decisions. Analysts support experts in expressing the opinion of decision-makers, modeling, and implementation of the analytical phase of the decision support procedure. Sponsors are responsible for financing and providing infrastructure, while principals make the final decision.

When considering the issue of supporting decision-making, it is important to emphasize the significant role of models constituting the simplification of the analyzed phenomenon, a fragment of reality. Identifying and verbally presenting the decision problem is the basis for a formal description of the decision situation in the form of mathematical formulas, i.e., the development of the model. When constructing a model of a certain class of phenomena, one should strive to obtain a model as close as possible to the objective [78]. Such a model is characterized by the fact that:

- It is an impartial representation of the described class of phenomena (the area of issues under consideration).
- It provides an impartial basis for research, including communication (The class of phenomena is taken into consideration and the way it is separated from the environment, context).

Formulating a fully objective model is not an easy task, however, because there are a number of typically technical and human factors in the environment of the analyzed phenomena, which have a significant impact on these phenomena. As Roy [164] notes, it is practically impossible to take technical factors into account, such as the definitions of all assumptions for building the model, their specificity, the study of interrelationships, consideration of inaccuracies, uncertainties, or their indeterminacy. In the area of factors related to the human aspect, objectivity of decision-making encounters other problems. They are associated with such human traits such as, e.g., emotional sensitivity, psychosensory sensitivity, or subconscious integrating abilities. By taking all restrictions into account, the construction of the model should go in the direction of correct deduction and unadulterated description of the facts, and not to preserve the objectivity of the model in accordance with its definition.

Decision support should therefore be understood as a conscious action of a human who uses models (not necessarily completely formalized structures) and obtains answers to the questions posed [165]. Decision support is a recommendation or distinction of an action that gives the best results in the context of the adopted goals and expectations of the decision-maker. However, it is not necessary for this process to be formalized [166]. Decision support, whose bases originate from operational research (behavioral, soft, hard), is implemented using techniques and methods by covering areas from various sciences and fields. Specific approaches to problem solving have been developed for specific areas. Economic methods deal with aspects of optimal resource allocation and maximization of benefits for the decision-maker, e.g., humanities, analysis of behavioral manifestations of making choices, or factors affecting the definition of preferences of decision-makers. In the case of technical sciences, we deal with techniques of modeling reality, as well as effective selection of the best variant based on available data.

Decision support should be implemented based on developed schemes. Roy [164] proposes such a scheme (methodology) that includes four main levels:

1. Defining the subject of the decision, including determining the scope of the analyst's activities (presentation of the form of decision modeling, selection of decision variants)
2. Analysis of the consequences of decisions and the development of criteria for comparing decision variants (examining the impact of possible decisions on process evolution, formalizing the consequences, determining the impact of decisions on factors of inaccuracy, constructing and testing the usefulness of criteria in assessing options)
3. Modeling the global preferences of the decision-maker and developing ways to aggregate grades (analysis of the use of criteria to describe participants' preferences, selection of a method for aggregating variant assessment in relation to various criteria)
4. Selection of research procedures and presentation of appropriate recommendations (the use of formalized procedures for gathering and processing information in order to obtain detailed solutions, such as, e.g., selection, allocation, or classification procedures)

The levels of decision support proposed by Roy are a proven methodological guide to the procedure in which the order of occurrence of individual stages is not rigidly defined, i.e., they do not have to be consecutive.

Considering the decision problem in the aspect of decision-making support, it is important to correctly assign the problem to a given category, formulate the correct assumptions, or correctly focus on the research. Also the choice of decision support method should be considered in the context of the type of information needs and the nature of the problem [68]. Four model issues are identified in the area of decision support [164]:

1. Choice
2. Sorting
3. Ordering
4. Description

The problem of choice (P.α) consists in putting the decision problem in terms of choosing one best variant, i.e., optimum (searching for the least numerous subset A' of set A, in this case one element is considered). If it is not possible to select the optimum, a possibly reduced set of variants A' is sought, which, however, does not constitute the selection of the optimal variant, and the elements from the set A', i.e., *satisfecum* (Fig. 1.3).

The sorting issues (P.β) are related to putting the problem of allocating variants from set A into predefined categories (division of set A into categories k_1, k_2, ..., k_n). Each variant is assigned to only one category (Fig. 1.4).

Ordering issues (P.γ) consists in the problem of isolating decision variants (all or some) from set A and arranging them in subsequent classes of variants (creating a ranking). The row of classes obtained in this way allows total or partial ordering of variants according to preferences (Fig. 1.5).

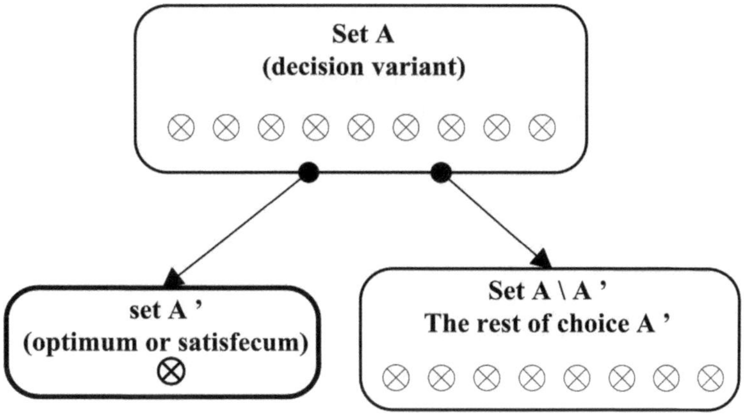

Fig. 1.3 Problems of choice [164]

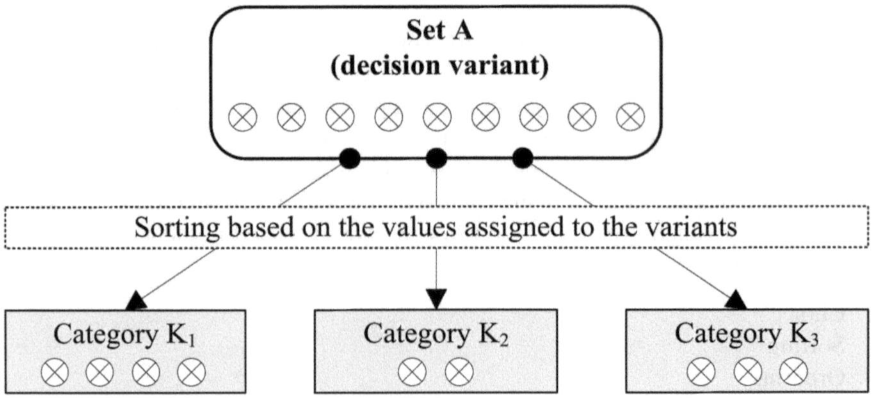

Fig. 1.4 Sorting issues [164]

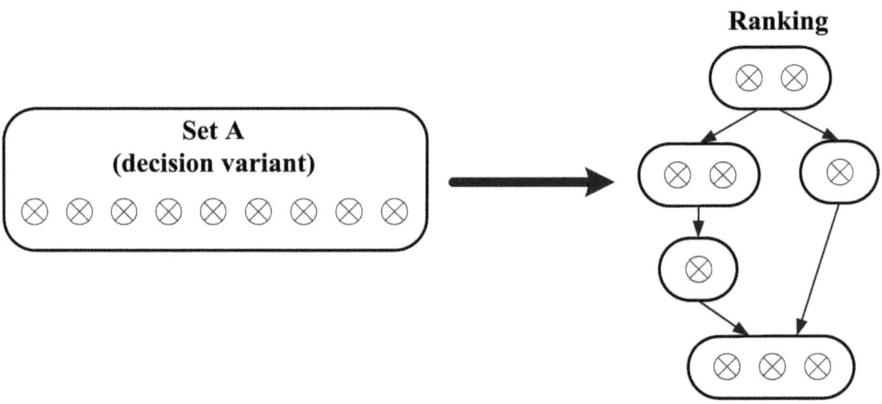

Fig. 1.5 Ordering issues [164]

Description problems (P.δ) is associated with providing a description of decision variants from set A, in order to better understand them by the decision-maker, understand, and evaluate. As a result of such studies, information on potential variants should be disclosed.

The adopted issues may relate to one of four reference problems (or some limited scope of one of them), a combination of two or more reference problems, or a mixed one (other combinations) [164].

Regardless of the adopted model issues, decision variants are compared with each other according to certain principles, and preferences depend on participants in the decision-making process. These comparisons may be consistent, e.g., with identical scoring systems, or may not be compatible. Generally, two types of preferences can be distinguished [97]:

1. Local (they concern the assessment of individual decision options in relation to subsequent criteria)
2. Global (related to the assessment of the significance of the considered options)

When considering how to aggregate preferences, we can list the two most common models [194]:

1. Based on usability function
2. By using outranking relation

Multi-attribute utility theory (associated with the so-called American school) assumes the existence of a utility function whose values allow the assessment of individual decision variants. According to this theory, the considered variants (e.g., variant *a* and variant *b*) may be in relation to each other in two relationships, i.e., the equivalence of the compared variants and the prevalence of one variant over the other (Table 1.2).

The degree of outranking can be determined by using a scale of comparisons, e.g., the Likert or Saaty scale [174, 205].

In the context of the so-called European school, decision support preferences are aggregated by using outranking relationships. The possibility of incomparability of the indifferent variants' consideration is allowed here when the decision-maker is not able to indicate a better option or when he cannot consider the options as comparable. Therefore, four preferential situations are possible in the context of the considered decision variants: equivalence, strong preference, weak preference, and incomparability (Table 1.3) [164, 209].

In relation to the classical theory of decision-making (Table 1.2), the preferential situations presented in Table 1.3 have been extended to include the possibility of

Table 1.2 Preferential situations for the model based on the utility function [97]

Preferential situation	Description	Mark
Indifference	Variant *a* is indifferent variant *b*	*a*I*b*
Outranking	Variant *a* is outranks on variant *b*	*a*P*b*
	Variant *b* is outranks on variant *a*	*b*P*a*

Table 1.3 Preferential situations for the model using the outranking relation [164]

Preferential situation	Description	Mark
Indifference	Variant *a* is indifferent variant *b*	*a*I*b*
Strong preference	Variant *a* is strong preferred on variant *b*	*a*P*b*
	Variant *b* is strong preferred on variant *a*	*b*P*a*
Weak preference	Variant *a* is weak preferred on variant *b*	*a*S*b*
	Variant *b* is weak preferred on variant *a*	*b*S*a*
Difference	Variant *a* is noun different with variant *b*	*a*N*b*

Table 1.4 Characteristics of binary relations [164]

Type of relation	Description	Designation
Symmetrical	Occurs when (it is fulfilled), when the order of writing the variants *a* i *b* is irrelevant	$a\text{I}b \Rightarrow b\text{I}a$
Reflexive	Occurs when (it is fulfilled) the variants under consideration are identical	$a\text{I}b$
Asymmetric	Occurs when (it is fulfilled), when the order of writing the variants *a* i *b* is relevant	$a\text{P}b \Rightarrow b\text{P}a$
Transitive	A relation that, if it occurs for the first (*a* i *b*) and the second one (*b* i *c*) a pair of variants, this also applies to the third (*a* i *c*) a pair of variants	$a\text{I}b \wedge b\text{I}c \Rightarrow a\text{I}c, a\text{P}b \wedge b\text{P}c \Rightarrow a\text{P}c$

weak preferences and incomparability. Additional options for comparing variants become desirable when the assessment cannot be clearly resolved, and the assessor cannot solve it or does not want to [164]. Describing the relationships between objects (variants) is possible using a binary relation. There are four types of these relationships: symmetrical, reflexive, asymmetrical, and transitive (Table 1.4).

Referring to four basic preferential situations (Table 1.3) can assign them the appropriate binary relations:

- Equivalence situation—relation I (symmetrical feedback)
- Situation of strong preference—relation P (asymmetric reverse)
- Situation of occurrence of weak preferences—relation Q (asymmetric reverse)
- Situation of incomparability—relation R (symmetrical inverse)

I, P, Q, R relationships form the basic preference relational system by which can describe the decision-maker preferences. There is also a grouped preference relational system that allows five additional binary relations. More information on the topic of preference modeling can be found in Roy's study [164].

Summarizing, the multidimensional comparative analysis finds application mainly in making socio-economic decisions regarding the community, e.g., administrative, production units, or groups of people. Methods in this area make it possible to conduct comparative analysis, e.g., between the considered objects, the analyzed object, and a non-existent object (artificial pattern), or to examine the relationship of the state of a given object with its past condition. The effect of comparative analysis is usually the classification or ordering of objects described by means of variables. The final result of such comparisons can be, for example, a diagnosis of the state of socio-economic units (objects) and the relationships that occur between them [131]. The construction of aggregate measures for the purposes of analyzing the level of development of objects is important here, which due to its complexity (specificity and usually a large number of considered objects) may be a problem in carrying it out. Multidimensional comparative analysis is supported by an extensive methodological apparatus in the field of statistics and mathematics, enabling the construction of aggregates using measures of similarity or vector projection, such as: Euclidean, urban, Minkowski, correlation, Clark measure, etc. [131]. One of the most important stages of multidimensional comparative analysis is the selection of diagnostic variables to describe socio-economic objects. This selection for the classification of objects can be considered in the context of the application of the statistical approach, substantive approach (use of expert knowledge), or both. In the first case, the set of decision variables should be based on the substantive knowledge, choose those that have the most important characteristics of the objects in question. In the second approach, the selection of variables occurs as a result of processing and analysis of statistical data in accordance with existing formal procedures. A two-step variable selection procedure is also used, which is a combination of both approaches, which can be the most effective solution. The set of diagnostic variables should be defined in such a way that it characterizes the phenomenon as much as possible, which ultimately translates into the accuracy of the decisions made [141] (a detailed description of the selection of variables and determination of their nature is provided in Sect. 2.1). In multidimensional comparative analysis, expert knowledge is actually limited to the stage of selection of diagnostic variables, or defining the character of these variables. The remaining stages of the procedure in the multidimensional comparative analysis do not require the active participation of the decision-maker. It is possible to automate and objectify the process of analyzing the problem under consideration. This is the basic difference from multi-criteria decision-making analysis, in which the decision-maker's participation is significant. The decision-maker sets out a set of criteria there, expressing his preferences directly. Information obtained from the decision-maker about the validity of the criteria is subjective, which shows that none of the choices made is better or worse than the others. Decision-makers with the same set of objective (generally available) information can make different decisions. In the case of multi-criterion decisions, subjectivity is an immanent feature [185]. The decision-maker's participation in multi-criteria decision-making problems analyzed by using multi-criteria decision support methods is therefore important.

1.2 Review of Decision Support Methods

Multi-criteria decision support and its development have been carried out for many decades by numerous groups of scientists around the world. The issue of multi-criteria decisions and applied methods derives directly from the scientific discipline, which is operational research. They are closely related to mathematical programming and decision-making theory. Mathematical programming deals with the problems of algorithms for solving optimization problems. Operational research deals with building models for various decision-making situations, whereas the theory of decision-making includes issues of developing decision rules based on the analysis of the properties of various decision-making models [185]. The beginnings of multi-criteria decision support are considered to be the development by Koopmans (1951) of the concept of functional vector (non-dominated solution), which laid the foundations for today's theory of multi-criteria decision support [101]. The methods used in multi-criteria decision support, based on the methodology developed from operational research, allow the determination of a set of acceptable solutions, and then the search for an optimal solution (in the Pareto sense). This is done by assessing the considered solutions using a defined set of criteria. These methods belong to the group of multi-criteria optimization methods in which there is a finite set of sizes [51]. This issue in the literature is referred to as *Multiple Criteria Decision-Making*, MCDM or *Multi-criteria Decision Analysis*, MCDA. The International Society on (*International Society on Multiple Criteria Decision-Making*) as a field of research dealing with the study of methods and procedures that, taking into account many often conflicting criteria, support decision-making processes [81]. The main purpose of multi-criteria decision support is to provide decision-makers with tools that will facilitate to solve decision problems in situations where different criteria for assessing decision variants exist. MCDM is associated with the so-called American trend, which assumes the existence of a multi-attribute utility function by providing synthetic assessments of the analyzed decision variants. MCDA is combined with the so-called French or, more generally, a European school. This trend is based on the occurrence of outranking relations, in which the aggregation of partial assessments is carried out on the basis of a set of conditions at which the global outranking relation occurs [123, 149].

Usually, MCDM/MCDA problems are divided into two main categories, MADM (multiple attribute decision-making) and MODM (*multiple attribute decision-making*). This division takes the variety of goals and different types of data used in the multi-criteria decision-making process into account [69, 80, 123, 149].

MADM, also called multi-criteria discrete methods, usually occurs in cases where there is a limited number of decision variants, a set of specific criteria will not necessarily be quantifiable, and a discrete description of preferences. MODM, on the other hand, covers decision problems in which the area of admissible decisions is a continuous set, and the number of possible variants of the solution can be infinite. The decision is made on the basis of an analysis of a group of quantifiable goals narrowed by a set of restrictions on the values of decision variables [202]. Decision-making can take place as a result of consideration (research) of decision variants by individual decision-makers or their groups. Group assessment is one way to objectify it. Multi-criteria decision support can therefore be considered due to the criterion of the number of decision-makers (experts) [118].

In real situations, we also meet fuzzy decision-making problems related to goals, dimensions, criteria, and variants. In these cases, MCDM/MCDA problems, taking the fuzzy environment into account and based on the division of MADM and MODM, are classified into two groups: fuzzy (*fuzzy multiple attribute decision-making*, FMADM) and (*fuzzy multiple objective decision-making*, FMODM) [118].

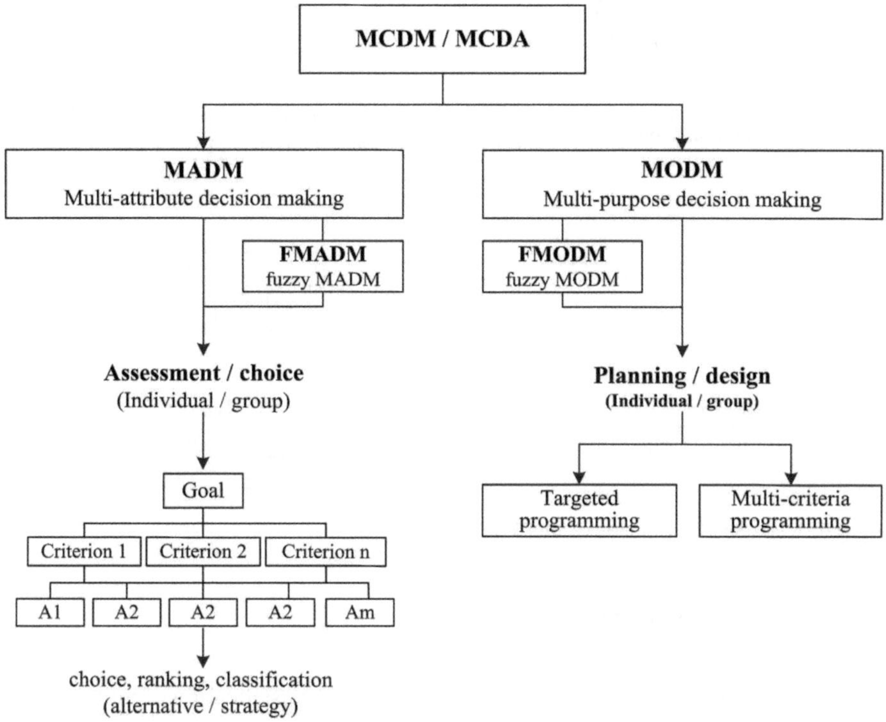

Fig. 1.6 Classification of MCDM problems, based on [5, 69, 92]

The classification of multi-criteria decision support issues, as described above, is presented in Fig. 1.6.

Multi-criteria decision support methods can be grouped according to various criteria. In the subject literature, one can encounter various division methods, which results from the adopted assumptions regarding the classification made [155, 209]. In the simplest assumption, it can be assumed that multi-criteria methods are classified into two basic groups: methods focused on solving discrete and continuous problems. Discrete tasks are those where there is a finite set of variants and a finite set of criteria on the basis of which the variants are assessed. Kodikara (2008) talks about five categories [1], but most often in the literature, there are two groups, namely a group of methods based on:

- Outranking relation
- Utility function

The division of multi-criteria methods into 5 groups can also be found in the study of T. Trzaskalik (2014). These are groups of methods [203]:

- Using the utility function
- Based on outranking relation
- Using reference points

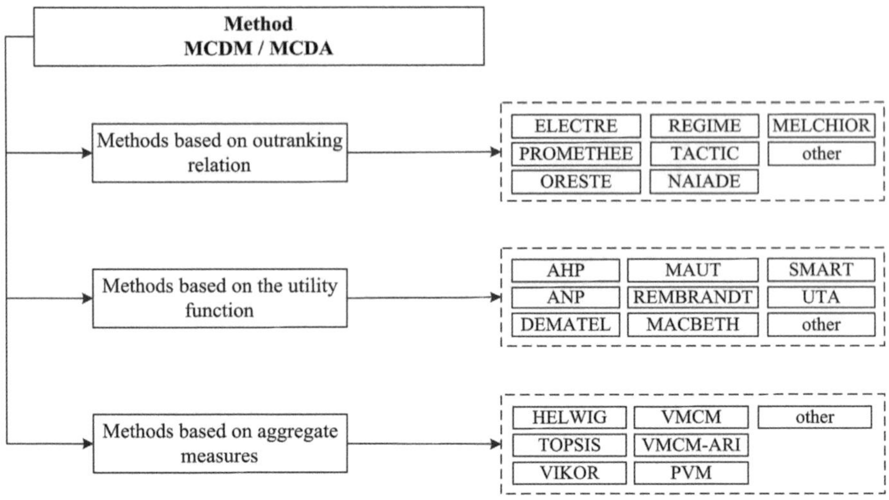

Fig. 1.7 Classification of methods MCDM/MCDA

- Based on pairwise comparisons
- Interactive

In turn, J. Żak (2005) adopted more criteria for the classification of multi-criteria methods and included them in them [228]:

- The purpose of the decision-making process
- Defining a set of decision variants
- The type of information available and processed
- How to define local preferences
- A method of synthesizing global preferences
- Time variability of considered decision problems
- Accuracy of the solutions obtained

Another possible way of dividing the MCDM/MCDA methods is the one that was used in this chapter and is presented in Fig. 1.7.

Multi-criteria methods based on the outranking relation are characterized by the occurrence of an outranking relation that relates to the relationship between decision variants and which represents specific preferences of the decision-maker. The most important and the most popular methods from the group of methods based on the relation of outranking are methods from the ELECTRE family, methods PROMETHEE, ORESTE, REGIME, TACTIC, NAIADE, or, e.g., MELCHIOR.

The ELECTRE method (*ELimination Et Choix Traduisant la REalité, ELimination and Choice Expressing REality*) [13] includes the methods ELECTRE I [59, 162], ELECTRE Iv [121, 170], ELECTRE Is [2, 171], ELECTRE II [167, 168], ELECTRE III [163], ELECTRE IV [114, 170], and ELECTRE TRI [124]. ELECTRE I, ELECTRE Iv oraz ELECTRE Is methods are used where

Table 1.5 ELECTRE method [97]

ELECTRE method	Kind of problem	Indifference threshold and preference	Weight	Vito
ELECTRE I	Choice	No	Yes	No
ELECTRE Iv	Choice	No	Yes	Yes
ELECTRE Is	Choice	Yes	Yes	Yes
ELECTRE II	Ranking	No	Yes	Yes
ELECTRE III	Ranking	Yes	Yes	Yes
ELECTRE IV	Ranking	Yes	No	Yes
ELECTRE TRI	Sorting	Yes	Yes	Yes

there is a problem of choice. They can also be used to organize decision variants in the order from the best to the worst. These methods differ in the context of the assumptions made regarding the types of criteria and methods of analysis discordance [203]. The ELECTRE methods together with the type of problems in which they are used are presented in Table 1.5.

The ELECTRE I method allows you to choose the optimal decision variant without ranking the variants under consideration. Preference relation is included, but there is no demarcation between them for weak and strong preference relation (there are no preference and indifference thresholds). Depending on the preferences adopted, each evaluation criterion is assigned an appropriate weight. It is assumed that all criteria are true and are evaluated on the same scale. After defining the preferences and determining the compliance coefficients for each pair of variants, the difference and indifference conditions are checked, and then the difference and indifference sets are determined. The next stage of the procedure is to determine the outranking relation. The algorithm of the ELECTRE I method ends with determining the graph of the outranking relation [59, 162, 203].

The ELECTRE Iv method is a development of the ELECTRE I method, by eliminating its imperfections related to the unacceptability of differences between decision variants within one criterion. It introduces a veto threshold that allows you to specify the amount by which the values of the criteria may differ between the compared variants (the veto threshold is defined separately for each criterion). This threshold can be defined as a constant value or as a function whose value depends on the criterion value of a given variant [203]. Exceeding this threshold means one decision variant is better than the other and it is independent of the value in the preference matrix [121, 170]. The computational procedure is similar to that of the ELECTRE I method. However, by modifying the method of creating the graph of the exceedance relation, the final result is a ranking of decision variant [97].

The ELECTRE Is method, however, introduces pseudo-criteria instead of true criteria and also uses indifference and preference thresholds. The difference of indifference is also checked differently. In addition, the calculation algorithm is similar to the ELECTRE I method [2, 171, 203]. However, the ELECTRE Is method did not find much practical application [97].

The ELECTRE II, III, and IV methods are used in situations where it is required to organize decision variants and create a ranking (ordering issues). There are no preference and indifference thresholds in ELECTRE II method. For difference tests (weak, sufficient, strong) and for tests of indifference (sufficient, strong), weak and strong preference is distinguished. There are true criteria here. The calculation procedure of the ELECTRE II method is very similar to the ELECTRE Iv method (calculating the outranking degrees matrix of preference, creating a set of constraints, constructing the graph of the outranking relation) [167, 168].

The ELECTRE III method is the most popular method from ELECTRE II, III, IV. Method. It uses preference and indifference thresholds, takes into account veta thresholds, weighting factors, and is based on the concept of a pseudo-criterion. The calculation procedure consists of four main stages. In the first stage, the indifference set is determined based on the calculated indifference factors for each pair of variants. The next step involves determining a set of incompatibilities, where for each pair of variants indifference indexes are determined for individual criteria. Subsequently, based on indifference indexes, the outranking relation is determined, and this is done for the next pair of variants. The last stage involves the creation of a final ranking of variants (in descending and ascending distillation procedures) with the simultaneous possibility of outranking, indifference, or difference relation between them [97, 163].

The ELECTRE IV method is similar to the ELECTRE III procedure. In contrast to ELECTRE III, there are no weighting criteria because of their equality. They are therefore of equal importance in determining global relations. The final ranking of decision variants is determined on the basis of study made by Lima and Roy B. et al. [114, 170].

The ELECTRE TRI method, as the only one from the ELECTRE method, allows you to solve problems related to sorting decision variants. These variants are assigned to previously defined categories, determined on the basis of the so-called border profiles. The assignment of variants to individual categories is carried out on the basis of designated compliance and reliability coefficients, and the classification is carried out using an optimistic or pessimistic procedure. The method is used especially where there are many decision variants [124, 202].

A more detailed analysis of the ELECTRE method carried out in Sects. 4.1 and 4.2 of this book.

PROMETHEE methods (*Preference Ranking Organisation METHod for Enrichment Evaluations*) are another group of methods that are used for the outranking relation. The most well-known PROMETHEE methods are PROMETHEE I [24, 26, 203] and PROMETHEE II [24, 26, 203], which were developed in 1982 by Brans.

PROMETHEE I makes it possible to determine the partial ranking of decision variants, which is created on the basis of a procedure involving the determination of an aggregated preference index (for individual pairs of variants) and the calculation of positive and negative escalation flow for each variant. The final ranking results from the intersection of these flows [24, 26, 202, 203].

The PROMETHEE II method allows you to obtain an overall ranking, and the procedure is similar to that of the PROMETHEE I method. The aggregated preference index, positive and negative outranking flows, and net outranking flow are determined. The final ranking is created as a result of arranging in descending order of the value of net flows [24, 26, 202].

Further methods from this group, namely PROMETHEE III, IV, V, VI, were developed by Brans and Mareschal. The PROMETHEE III method allows you to determine the ranking based on time steps, PROMETHEE IV applies to the case of continuous time, and the PROMETHEE V methods (problems with additional segmentation restrictions) and VI (used when the decision-maker is unable to define constant weight values for variants but can define truth intervals for these weights) are an extension of the PROMETHEE III and IV methods. The group of these methods also includes PROMETHEE GDSS (group decision-making), PROMETHEE & GAIA (analysis support and graphic representation), PROMETHEE TRI (sorting issues), and the PROMETHEE CLUSTER method (nominal classification) [26].

Methods from the PROMETHEE group have been characterized in more detail in Sect. 4.3.

The ORESTE method (*Organisation Rangement Et Synthése de donées relationelles*) was created to solve problems in which decision variants should be ordered according to individual criteria. It enables obtaining independent rankings for each of the assessment criteria and independent rankings for decision variants in relation to each of the adopted criteria. Usually, it is used in decision-making situations in which variants are assessed on the basis of criteria using different measuring scales [161].

The REGIME method uses the so-called dominance matrix, which is obtained as a result of pairwise comparison of decision variants in the multi-criteria assessment table. Rows of this matrix (dominance vectors) allow the determination of an ordered ranking of variants. The indifference matrix is built from compliance coefficients calculated on the basis of weights for the assessment criteria and created domination vectors [79].

The TACTIC method uses the true criteria and pseudo-criteria to which the relevant significance weights are assigned to evaluate the decision variants. Using the condition of indifference, the preference for a given decision option over another is determined, and in the presence of additional pseudo-criteria, the non-objection condition is used [207].

The NAIADE method (*Novel Approach to Imprecise Assessment and Decision Environment*) is a discrete multi-criteria method developed in 1995 by G. Munda, in which matrix elements can assume mixed assessment values, i.e., sharp, stochastic, or fuzzy. Some information may be provided on a quantitative or qualitative scale, and the estimation of assessment criteria in the form of traditional weights is not used jest dyskretną metodą wielokryterialną opracowaną w 1995 r. [89, 126].

The MELCHIOR method (*Méthode d'ELimination et de Choix Incluant les relation d'ORdre*) is an extension of the ELECTRE IV method. It uses pseudo-criteria and a mutual order relation to determine the relative importance of the criteria "is at least as important as ..." does not use global criteria weights [112].

The most common methods of the second group, based on the utility function, include the following methods: AHP, ANP, DEMATEL, MAUT, REMBRANDT, MACBETH, SMART, and UTA.

The AHP (*Analytic Hierarchy Process*) method—hierarchical analysis of decision problems—is one of the simplest and most popular multi-criteria methods. The slightly complicated calculation algorithm and publicly available tool support (method implementation) which means it is widely used to solve decision problems in various aspects of life. In this method, the vector of the scale is obtained by comparing pairs of decision variants in the context of individual criteria and comparing assessment criteria with each other. The vector components of the scale allow the order of variants to be obtained and thus the best to be indicated. The pairwise comparison process uses a nine-grade rating scale called the Saaty scale or corresponding verbal description. In the hierarchical structure to describe the decision problem, the main goal is at the very top, the next level includes assessment criteria (the criteria can be divided into sub-criteria), and the considered decision variants are at the bottom of this hierarchy. The calculation procedure of the AHP method involves four main stages: development of a hierarchy of goals, creation of a matrix of comparisons of significance of criteria, construction of a matrix of comparison of variants for individual criteria, and synthesis of the importance of criteria and preferences of variants in relation to criteria [173, 180]. A detailed description of the AHP method is provided in Sect. 3.1.

The ANP (*Analytic Network Process*) method—an analytical network process—is a development of the AHP method by taking the relationships between criteria and the links between variants and criteria into account. Hierarchical structure is used to describe the decision problem, similarly to the AHP method, but in the ANP method, there may be horizontal links between the assessment criteria and feedback links between the criteria and decision variants. The criteria can be combined into the so-called components, whose components may be elements of the type criteria and decision variants. The occurring dependencies between components are depicted in the form of a dependency network [176, 179, 203]. A detailed description of the ANP method is provided in Sect. 5.2.

The DEMATEL (*DEcision MAking Trial and Evaluation Laboratory*) method makes it possible to solve decision problems using a direct influence graph, which makes it possible to study the impact of the analyzed objects on each other in identifying cause and effect relationships [55]. Details of the DEMATEL method can be found in Sect. 5.4.

MAUT (*Multi-attribute Utility Theory*) is a method that finds application primarily in the analysis of decision variants regarding the selection of different locations. Multi-attribute utility theory consists of two main steps. The first concerns the determination of the partial utility of variants in relation to each of the criteria, while the second involves the determination of global utility on the basis of a multi-attribute utility function. The utility functions defined in this method (e.g., additive, multiplicative form) are used to assess the quality of decision variants, and the purpose of the function is to aggregate criteria into one value. This makes it possible to create a ranking of variants where the best variant is the one for which the value of the utility function is the highest [68, 93].

REMBRANDT (*Ratio Estimation in Magnitudes or deci-Bells to Rate Alternatives which are Non-DominaTed*) is a method similar to the AHP method, but it eliminates imperfections related to the nine-grade (1–9) grading scale and the method of evaluation of variants is obtained. The Saaty rating scale has been replaced by a logarithmic scale, while the method of determining scale vectors (Perron–Frobenius) by the logarithmic least squares method. The structure of the description of the decision problem in the REMBRANDT method is three level and includes the main objective, assessment criteria, and considered decision variants [117, 203]. A more detailed description of the method is provided in Sect. 5.3.

In the MACBETH (*Measuring Attractiveness by a Categorical Based Evaluation TecHnique*) method, similar to the AHP method, pairs of elements being criteria or decision variants are made, and users express their preferences only through qualitative assessments. The assessment of the consistency of comparisons is carried out on the basis of the resulting matrix of pairwise comparisons. The elements of the hierarchy compared by the decision-maker are assessed by determining the differences in their attractiveness. After obtaining consistency of comparisons, weights for criteria and numerical assessments of variants are obtained [7].

In the SMART (*Simple Multi-attribute Ranking Technique*) method, the assessment of decision variants is carried out in the context of individual criteria, by assigning them values in the range of 0–100. For the qualitative criteria, the variants are ordered from the best to the worst, and then rated 100 and 1, respectively, and the other options selected from the range (0–100). After determining the assessment of decision variant, weights for individual criteria are determined. Each variant is assigned a final grade, which is interpreted as the global utility of the variant. After ordering the decision variants according to the values of their global utilities, the ones with the highest usability are the best solutions [210].

The UTA method calculates the global utility function based on the partial utility functions for each of the criteria, which are determined by using linear programming methods [83]. UTA forms a group of differing methods, which include UTASTAR, UTADIS, UTADIS I, UTADIS II, or UTADIS III [187].

The methods based on aggregate measures are the third group of MCDM/MCDA methods (Fig. 1.7). Generally, these methods come from a group of taxonomic methods that are used in ordering and classifying complex and heterogeneous multidimensional objects. They can be used to carry out studies of complex economic and economic process. They are mainly dedicated to create rankings, and patterns are often used in their creation. The last decade has been the wide application of these methods in multi-criteria decision-making, which results, among others, due to their low complexity. Methods in this group include, for example, TOPSIS, VIKOR, HELWIG, as well as proprietary VMCM, VMCM-ARI, and PVM methods.

The TOPSIS (*Technique for Order Preference by Similarity to Ideal Solution*) method is used to order (sort) decision variants in terms of their similarity to the pattern, i.e., the most desirable variant in the TOPSIS method is to determine the positive and negative ideal solutions. It is to identify the positive ideal alternative (extreme performance on each criterion) and identify the negative ideal alternative (reverse extreme performance on each criterion). The ideal positive solution is the solution that maximizes the benefit criteria and minimizes the cost criteria, whereas the negative ideal solution maximizes the cost criteria and minimizes the benefit criteria. Between each variant and the ideal and anti-ideal standard are calculated distances, on the basis of which the value of the measure is determined. It allows creating the final order [80]. The data types considered determine different versions of the TOPSIS method: classic, interval (interval), or fuzzy. In the classical version, the features of the objects in question are described by using known real values [80]. The interval variation of the TOPSIS method assumes that the values of the features of the objects are interval numbers, i.e., the beginning of the interval determines the minimum value of the feature and its end determines the maximum value [85]. In case of the fuzzy version of the method, the values of the object features are not precisely defined, and they can be described by using a linguistic variable that covers one of three levels of assessment: negative (pessimistic), intermediate (most likely), or positive (optimistic) [84].

The VIKOR method (serb. *VIsekrzterijumska Optimizacija i Kompromisno Resenje*) enables the ranking of decision variants and the selection of a compromise alternative, taking conflicting assessment criteria into account. The evaluation of solutions (variants) is based on their distance from an ideal point and an anti-ideal point. The weighted average distance from the ideal solution is determined for individual decision variants, the maximum weighted distance from this point, and the so-called comprehensive indicator. Based on the values obtained in this way, the variants are arranged in order to obtain three rankings. The proposed compromise solution is a decision variant with the lowest value of the comprehensive indicator, but only when the conditions of acceptable advantage and acceptable decision stability are met. If one or both of these conditions are not met, the compromise solution is an appropriate set of variants [144, 145].

The Hellwig method is derived from the name of the authors method Zdzisław Hellwig, one of the creators of multidimensional comparative analysis, included in the discipline of science called taxonomy. The proposed method enables linear ordering and grouping of socio-economic objects based on an aggregate measure developed according to many features (criteria). Z. Hellwig for the construction of aggregate measures gives the criteria the character of stimulants (variables for which the highest values are desired) and destimulants (variables with the lowest values) [73]. There is also a third character of the criteria proposed by T. Borys, referred to as nominants, where a specific value or values that are derived from a certain numerical range are desired [20]. To group objects, Hellwig uses the arithmetic mean and standard deviation. This measure is used to rank the objects that are taken into consideration [73].

The VMCM (*Vector Measure Construction Method*) was developed in 2008 by K. Nermend. VMCM uses the properties of a vector calculus to build a vector aggregate measure (based on the definition of a scalar product) without referring to the distance measure. This approach makes it possible to eliminate the limitations known from the HELLWIG method regarding the possibility of considering objects better than the defined pattern. In addition, the VMCM method allows to add objects outside of the sample without having to rebuild the pattern as well comparative and multi-criteria decision-making analysis is more sensitive to the dynamics of change and allows its analysis [132, 138]. A detailed description of the VMCM method is provided in Sect. 3.3.

A variation of the VMCM method is the VMCM-ARI (*Vector Measure Construction Method and ARithmetic of Increments*) method developed by M. Borawski and described in detail in Sect. 3.3. Compared to the VMCM method, it has been modified in the area of using the arithmetic properties of increments to study the time and spatial homogeneity of socio-economic objects. In the construction of the aggregate measure, an ordered pair was used, which consists of an average value and an increase in the standard deviation. As a result, additional information on time and spatial homogeneity of socio-economic objects was obtained for each measure value [19].

The group of methods based on aggregate measures also includes the proprietary PVM preference vector method developed by K. Nermend (described in Chap. 6). The research procedure for this method comprises six stages: selection of criteria, assessment of the nature of criteria, normalization of criteria values, determination of the preference vector based on a motivating and demotivating preference vector, and construction of a ranking of considered decision variants [136].

Summing up the considerations on supporting decision-making in the aspect of multi-criteria and multidimensionality, one can notice some similarities as well as conceptual and methodological differences of both approaches. In addition to the differences in the terminology itself used in multivariate comparative analysis and multi-criteria decision-making analysis (e.g., objects—variants, variables—atrybuty, itp., attributes, etc.), there are various applications of the methods from these two areas, but the scope of the decision-maker's participation in decision-making process. In multi-criteria methods of decision support, the participation of the decision-maker at individual stages of this process is much greater, and the associated assessment is subjective, and the decision-making process is difficult to automate. However, one can distinguish a certain group of methods that has common features of methods in the field of multidimensional comparative analysis and multi-criteria decision analysis (Fig. 1.8).

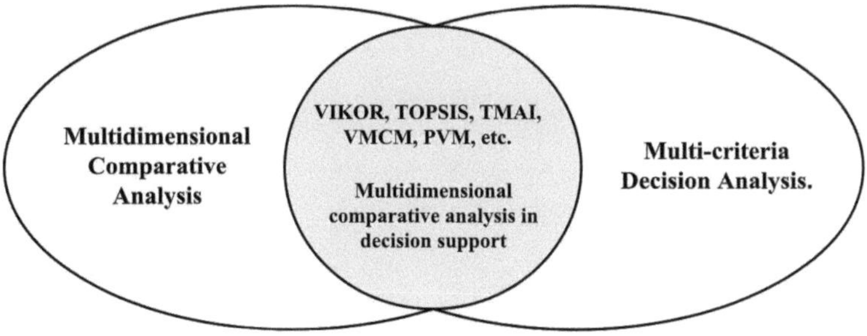

Fig. 1.8 A common area of two approaches: multidimensional comparative analysis and multi-criteria decision-making analysis

The essence of building these methods is to strive for the possibility of limiting interaction with the decision-maker to the minimum necessary. For example, in the PVM method, the presence of a decision-maker does not have to be large (a feature of multivariate comparative analysis), or it can be significant (a feature of multi-criteria decision analysis). In the first case, the decision-maker determines his preferences, defines criteria, and provides them character. Then it is calculated by motivating and demotivating preference vector (for motivating and demotivating criteria). Based on these vectors, the criteria weights are automatically determined, and an artificial preference vector is calculated. This approach can be considered as an objective solution to the decision problem, as the participation of the decision-maker is low here. In the second case, the decision-maker determines his preferences by defining criteria, gives character to these criteria, determines the weight of criteria, and provides criteria values in the form of two vectors (motivating and demotivating preference vector). Based on these vectors, the preference vector is calculated according to the decision-maker preferences. In this approach, the decision-maker's participation is much larger, so the assessment becomes more subjective. One should consider whether it is worth to introduce a new term for the highlighted common area of two approaches: multidimensional comparative analysis and multi-criteria decision analysis. The proposal for this area is a *Multidimensional Comparative Analysis Decision-Making* (MCADM).

Part I
Multidimensional Comparative Analysis Methods

The initiation of taxonomy can be considered the development of plant and animal systematics by Charles Linnaeus in the eighteenth century. It was a qualitative approach. Quantitative methods for taxonomy were first introduced (beginning of the twentieth century) by Jan Czekanowski (the so-called Lviv taxonomic school). He developed a measure of similarity between objects in multidimensional space (the so-called Czekanowski distance) and a method of ordering distance matrices by the diagraph method (Czekanowski diagram) [154]. Continuation of these studies was conducted by the so-called Wrocław school of taxonomy, initially by K. Florek, J. Łukaszewicz, J. Perkal, H. Steinhaus, and S. Zubrzycki and further developed by Z. Hellwig. The Wrocław taxonomy (dendritic method) consists in the development of dendrite, i.e., such a broken branching line that connects all objects from the classified set. The distances between individual pairs of objects are the length of dendrite ligaments, on the basis of which it is possible to order nonlinear objects. The smaller the dendrite length, the better the ordering of the given set of objects [54]. The development of taxonomy in economic sciences was initiated in 1968 by Z. Hellwig, who published the results of his research in the work "Application of the taxonomic method to the typological division of countries by level of their development and the resources and structure of qualified staff" [73]. He proposed a synthetic measure of economic development for linear ordering and grouping of economies due to homogeneous sets [116]. This method—ordering objects in a multidimensional space of features—called the multidimensional comparative analysis allows the ranking of objects in this space to be created on the basis of the criteria adopted for ordering [154]. In this method, Hellwig used the arithmetic mean and standard deviation to build a synthetic measure and introduced the concepts of stimulant and destimulant as the nature of diagnostic variables. He also proposed two approaches to ordering socio-economic objects, namely reference and without reference ordering [73, 116, 154]. In the following years, the synthetic measure of economic development of Z. Hellwig was subject to numerous modifications by various scientific communities. Among others, various distance measures were used [214], a new character of diagnostic variables [21] was introduced, different methods of normalizing variables [20], different ways of determining the development pattern [98, 192], or the use of fuzzy sets to create a synthetic measure [87]. In turn, generalized distance measure (GDM) used to determine the distance between multidimensional objects, respectively, with the adopted measuring scale, was presented by M. Walesiak [213]. On the other hand, M. Kolenda proposed orthogonal projection to determine the aggregate measure, allowing the introduction of a pattern that does not necessarily have to be the best in the sample (as in the original Hellwig method) [98]. As part of the so-called Krakow school, research work was initiated in 1957 by J. Fierich, who indicated the applications of the Czekanowski method in the field of socio-economic sciences [47]. During this period, a monograph of J. Steczkowski was also created, presenting the use of taxonomic methods to select features describing multidimensional objects ("dual" approach) [190]. Other scientists of the Krakow center also brought various improvements to the assumptions made by the so-called Wroclaw school. This is, among others, T. Grabiński [64], who enriched the existing methods with hierarchical and agglomeration solutions, such as the King method, Prima dendrite, or time consideration. J. Pociecha developed an algorithm for measuring the compliance of qualitative features [153]. The development of taxonomy toward new methods and procedures, including the significant contribution of the Wrocław and Kraków centers, resulted in the creation of a new research area known as multidimensional comparative analysis (MCA) [116]. The eighties of the twentieth century was a period of popularization of MCA methods, as well as their increasing use in the field of socio-economic sciences [64, 223]. The author's own contribution to the development of multidimensional comparative analysis methods is the proposed VMCM (*Vector Measure Construction Method*), which uses the properties of a vector calculus to build a vector aggregate measure (based on the definition of a scalar product) without referring to the distance measure. VMCM complements the Hellwig's method with the possibility of including objects better than the defined pattern. In the original Hellwig approach, the synthetic measure used somewhat limits the assumption that the pattern must be the best object in every respect. This excludes the use of real patterns, for which, as a rule, not all coordinates in the feature space are larger than the other objects. This approach causes that the aggregate measures being built become sensitive to the appearance in the set of examined objects of units with unusually large coordinate values that can significantly affect the ranking results. This method has been described in [129, 132]. Implementing the properties of increment arithmetic to the VMCM method enables the study of time and spatial homogeneity of socio-economic objects. This method was developed by M. Borawskii and named as VMCM-ARI (*Vector Measure Construction Method and ARithmetic of Increments*) [19]. Determining in this way the aggregate measure gives a chance to introduce into the calculations a factor that may provide additional information useful for the interpretation of the result [19, 138]. This information may be an increase in standard deviation. Depending on the method of calculating the increase in the standard deviation, it may contain information about the homogeneity of the set of socio-economic objects (making up the analyzed object), information about the impact of the diversity of real objects (on the basis of which the pattern was calculated) on the location of the examined objects in the ranking, and information about dynamics of measure value changes over the years.

Chapter 2
Initial Procedure for Data Analysis

2.1 Selection and Definition of the Character of Variables

The selection of appropriate variables is a very important stage because it directly affects the results of the research. Inadequate selection of variables may lead to the results that misrepresent the analyzed research area. It can be considered in two aspects: their quality and reliability and compliance with the adopted research assumptions. In order for the obtained result to properly depict the research area, it is necessary to have both adequate quality data and the appropriate selection of variables representing the studied reality.

The following factors affect data quality [62, 107]:

1. Credibility. Data must have a certain error range, and there must be no values that have an abnormally high error value. They should be burdened with systematic error as little as possible, which means that there should be no "one-way" deviation of the data value.
2. Adequacy. Reported variables should be consistent with their definitions, which should be precise enough to prevent misinterpretation by data entry persons (in the case of surveys also by the responders).
3. Comparability. The set of measured variables and their definitions should be identical throughout the period considered and the entire area under consideration. Unfortunately, in the case of research covering large areas or long periods of time, this demand cannot always be met.
4. Data completeness. Periods or objects for which some data is undefined cannot exist. Usually, the lack of data makes it necessary to calculate them on the basis of other known data, which reduces the reliability of the results of tests carried out on their basis.

K. Nermend, *Multi-Criteria and Multi-Dimensional Analysis in Decisions*, Vector Optimization, https://doi.org/10.1007/978-3-031-40538-9_2

Kordos J. [102] lists three other factors influencing the quality of data (especially, in the context of their external acquisition and research objectives):

1. Fitness. The data does not always have to exactly match the recipient's needs. Sometimes this forces you to replace inaccessible data with others that you have access to. It may result in lowering the quality of obtained test results.
2. Timeliness. As a rule, in research we are interested in knowing the current state and predicting future states. Therefore, data must be as fresh as possible, while the concept of timeliness of data depends on the character of the phenomena and objects studied. In some analyses, data from the last year is considered current, while in others, for example, when analyzing stock market trends from the last few hours.
3. Accuracy. Data accuracy can be understood as its compliance with true values. Accuracy, like timeliness, is a relative concept and depends on the character of the analyzes performed and expectations as to the accuracy of their results.

Two factors affect data accuracy: accidental (random) and systematic (non-random) errors. Systematic errors can be statistical or non-statistical. "Systematic errors of a statistical character most often occur in a situation of a heterogeneous general population, the wrong general population, in the case of an insufficient sample or the wrong method of its selection, an inappropriate sampling frame, etc." [42]. These errors can be largely eliminated by the proper collection of data, and hence it is often assumed that their value is negligible. Systematic errors of a non-statistical character may arise in the process of data processing. Their size and occurrence is difficult to capture. Due to the non-statistical character and the associated difficulty in their analysis, despite the possible considerable values of these errors are also often overlooked.

Systematic errors can be removed if we are able to find out their relationship with the measured values. Generally, the detection and removal of these errors is made through [42]: pilot testing (to pretest research methods), the use of methods using interpretation subtasks and replicas, comparison of results with the results obtained by other methods, repetition of tests, use relations between phenomena.

The second element to consider when choosing variables is the correct representation of the aspect of reality being studied. The selected variables are a description of the phenomena and objects studied, and they must represent their properties that are relevant to the research being carried out. The choice of variables determines which properties of phenomena and objects are relevant and which are irrelevant What is more, in the case of many methods, the number of variables describing individual properties will have a significant impact on the result obtained. If a number of variables are assigned to each significant property of an object or a phenomenon, those with the greater number of variables will be more important. Therefore, to eliminate the impact of the number of variables on the importance of properties, specific variables are assigned specific weights.

Variable selection can be supported by variable elimination methods. The character of some variables may disqualify them in the context of research. The most important technical problem when choosing them is to distinguish between variables that carry important information and those that contain mainly informational noise. Some random factors are associated with each recorded data. The very character of microscale physical phenomena is chaotic. While in the macroscale one can predict the movement of physical objects and their behavior with high accuracy, in the microscale, at the atomic level, these predictions are burdened with a very large error. Many economic processes have a similar character. The smallest objects that can be considered in economic research are people or small family businesses, often employing one or two people. When such objects are considered in large numbers, certain regularities associated with these objects can be determined. In some situations, some objects may behave in a manner inconsistent with existing regularities. This may be due to various factors, such as misinterpretation of the information received, fatigue, accidents, diseases, etc. When variables describe many objects at the same time, such behavior (incompatibility with regularities), due to the low frequency of occurrence, will be negligible affect their values. However, if such objects are considered in small groups, they will cause "distortions" of variable values.

Economic processes are usually closely related, and individual objects interact with each other. Therefore, irrational behavior (wrong decisions, mistakes, etc.) of some objects affects others. This can cause changes in the variable values describing not only one object but also many others associated with them. In this way, the effect of irrational behavior is strengthened, and they are usually incidental and thus cause short-term changes in the variable values. This generates a significant part of the information noise contained in variables describing the objects.

Another reason for information noise is errors in determining variable values. Often, data on objects, when we consider a large number of them, are collected on the basis of some selected representatives—samples. Therefore, one cannot expect that the obtained value defining some property of objects is accurate. It is always burdened with a certain error, often negligibly small, and the very form of the record generates informational noise. Therefore, an appropriate form of entry should be adopted, which boils down to determining the smallest distinguished value. If a variable describes the weight of manufactured goods, the question should be asked: with what accuracy, in what units should it be recorded (in tonnes, in kilograms). Adopting a certain accuracy results in the need for a rounding procedure, which in turn generates information noise.

For most variables, the existence of this noise can be ignored because its low value does not affect the result of the analysis in any way. This is the case with variables for which the property described by the variable is somehow differentiated. This causes considerable differences in the values of the variable for individual objects, which are much larger than the differences resulting from the existence of information noise. Therefore, this noise will not affect the test results. However, if in the examined set of objects, the property described by the variable does not change much or even is the same, then the differences in the variable values resulting from the differences in properties will be comparable or smaller than the differences resulting from the information noise. When creating aggregate measures, as well as for classifying, variables are subjected to normalization, aimed at harmonizing their ranges. This equates the amplitude of the variability of the describing variable with other variables. It also results in a significant increase in the amplitude of the information noise, which can affect the results of the analysis.

In besides to information noise, the variable may disqualify small variations in value. If it is not large, then the significance of this type of variable is also not too large and should not significantly affect the result of the analysis. However, standardization procedures may increase the scope of its fluctuations, which in turn leads to an increase in its significance This can be prevented by eliminating this type of variable because its impact on the result should not be significant anyway. Another way to solve this problem is to introduce variable weighting and give them a low enough weight.

Determining whether a given level of variation of a variable for different objects is associated with significant differences in the level of analyzed property is a very difficult task and requires careful analysis of the character of the property. If the oscillations of the fluctuations do not take place around zero, but around a certain value, which is the average of a given variable, then the significance of these fluctuations can be determined on the basis of the ratio of the standard deviation of the fluctuations to the average value. This is the coefficient, which is called the coefficient of variation [107]:

$$V_i = \frac{\sigma_i}{\bar{x}_i}, \tag{2.1}$$

where

x_i—i-th variable,
σ_i—standard deviation of the i-th variable,
$\bar{x}_i$—mean value of the i-th variable,

whereas

$$\bar{x}_i = \frac{\sum_{j=1}^{n} x_{i_j}}{n}, \tag{2.2}$$

where

x_{i_j}—value of the i-th variable for the j-th object,
n—number of objects,

and

$$\sigma_i = \sqrt{\frac{\sum_{j=1}^{n} \left(x_{i_j} - \bar{x}_i \right)^2}{n-1}}. \tag{2.3}$$

In [107, 188], it was determined that the variables whose values of coefficients of variation are in the range of $\langle 0; 0.1 \rangle$ are quasi-constant variables and should be eliminated from the set of variables.

When choosing variables, it is assumed that the postulate of their non-negativity should be met. However, it should be noted that in some specific cases the coefficient of variation may take negative values, e.g., natural increase. This is often the case in well-developed countries. The standard deviation of the variable describing the natural increase is always positive, but the average value usually depends on the sign of the natural increase of most objects. Therefore, the sign of the coefficient of variation will depend on the sign of the mean value. One should ask what will happen if the variable has a negative value of the variation coefficient close to zero. This variable will also be a quasi-constant variable, but with a negative sign. It is therefore necessary to extend the range that classifies variables as quasi-constants by negative values: $\langle 0; 0.1 \rangle$.

Table 2.1 contains values indicating the rate of population growth for Polish regions in 2010. The values in this table will be treated as the variable for which the coefficient of variation will be determined. The average value will be

$$\bar{x} = \frac{0.2 + 0.9 + 0.3 + 2.0 + (-0.2) + 2.2}{6} = \frac{5.4}{6} = 0.9. \tag{2.4}$$

The numerator of the formula (2.3) which calculates standard deviation is

$$[0.2 - 0.9]^2 + [0.9 - 0.9]^2 + [0.3 - 0.9]^2 + [2.0 - 0.9]^2 + \\ + [-0.2 - 0.9]^2 + [2.2 - 0.9]^2 = 4.59, \tag{2.5}$$

and therefore the standard deviation is equal to

$$\sigma = \sqrt{\frac{4.59}{6-1}} = \sqrt{0.918} \approx 0.958. \tag{2.6}$$

The coefficient of variation will be

$$V_{x_i} = \frac{0.958}{0.9} \approx 1.065. \tag{2.7}$$

Table 2.1 Natural population growth for Polish regions in 2007 (source: Eurostat)

Region	Birth rate
Central	0.2
South West	−0.2
South	0.9
North-West	2.0
North	2.2
Eastern	0.3

Its value is out of the range: $\langle 0; 0.1 \rangle$, and for this reason, the analyzed feature is not a quasi-constant variable.

K. Kukuła proposes to use an additional measure of differentiation called the relative amplitude of fluctuations [107]:

$$A_i = \frac{\max_j x_{ij}}{\min_j x_{ij}}, \tag{2.8}$$

where $\min_j x_{ij} \neq 0$.

It should be noted that the coefficient of relative amplitude of fluctuations given by the formula (2.8) is determined for positive variable values. Its value for this type of variables is always greater than one. If there are negative values of the variable, it is possible to obtain any of its values. Due to the unification of interpretations for negative variables, it should be used in the form:

$$A_i = \frac{\max_j \left| x_{ij} \right|}{\min_j \left| x_{ij} \right|}, \tag{2.9}$$

where

$\min_j \left| x_{ij} \right| \neq 0.$

K. Kukuła further proposes to use the coefficient of relative amplitude of fluctuations as a complement to the coefficient of variation. A variable should be eliminated when

$$|V_i| \leqslant c_1, \tag{2.10}$$

and at the same time

$$|A_i| \leqslant c_2, \tag{2.11}$$

where c_1 and c_2 are appropriately selected constants. c_1, as previously stated, should be 0.1, while c_2 should be only slightly above one, e.g., 1.2 [107]. Only the fulfillment of both conditions at the same time can result in rejection of the variable. Continuing the example, the value of the coefficient of relative amplitude

Table 2.2 Value of variable emission of gaseous pollutants

County	Emissions of gaseous pollutants $[t/r]$
Białogard county	58,301
Drawsko county	30,672
Kołobrzeg county	87,559
Gryfino county	3,948,566
⋮	⋮
Szczecinecki county	395,412
Sławno county	11,253
Koszalin county	11,536

of fluctuations was calculated for the rate of natural growth:

$$A_i = \frac{\max\{|0.2|\,;\,|0.9|\,;\,|0.3|\,;\,|2.0|\,;\,|-0.2|\,;\,|2.2|\}}{\min\{|0.2|\,;\,|0.9|\,;\,|0.3|\,;\,|2.0|\,;\,|-0.2|\,;\,|2.2|\}} = \frac{2.2}{0.2} = 11. \tag{2.12}$$

As you can see, this value significantly exceeds 1.2 and at the same time is not a quasi-constant variable, and therefore it meets both conditions qualifying it for further research.

Another example would be determining the significance of variable gaseous emissions for counties of the West Pomeranian province. This variable was examined in terms of its variability. Data were obtained from the Central Statistical Office (2005). The variable is marked by X. Table 2.2 contains a partial implementation of this variable in 7 counties and the calculations are made for all 21 counties of the West Pomeranian province ($i = 1; 2; \ldots; 21$). The coefficient of variation was calculated according to the formulas (2.1)–(2.3) and its value was 2.25. Then the coefficient of relative amplitude of fluctuations was calculated according to formula (2.8), where its value was 350.89. According to the adopted assumption about the values of both coefficients, the considered variable can be included in further studies.

It may happen many times that a variable containing a single implementation strongly differing from the others is not rejected, even though this is indicated by the coefficient of variation. However, it should be emphasized that this variable may cause problems in further calculations. It will depend on the methods chosen. It will depend on the methods chosen. A particular attention should be paid to choosing standardization methods that do not cause the unusually large value will differ significantly from other large values of the other variables. When creating aggregate measures and with many grouping methods, this situation will increase the importance of this variable for a given object. In extreme cases, it may lead to disregarding the values of other variables.

There are methods that partially automate the selection of variables by calculating specific coefficients. An example can be the methods proposed by S. Bartosiewicz [11], Z. Hellwiga [76, 77], W. Plutę [150], and E. Nowaka [139]. A comprehensive review of variable selection methods can be found in [60].

In the parametric method proposed by Z. Hellwiga [77], at the beginning an initial list of variables is created. Some of them may be so correlated that they form local clusters. In this case, to create an aggregate measure of clusters, it is not necessary to use all the variables and only use one of them as a representative of the other. The whole procedure in the parametric method aims to eliminate some variables and leave only representatives and variables that do not form clusters. For this purpose, it uses the correlation matrix R calculated for all variables, and its elements can be determined from the following formula:

$$r_{i,k} = \frac{\sum_{j=1}^{n}\left(\underset{j}{x_i} - \bar{x}_i\right)\left(\underset{j}{x_k} - \bar{x}_k\right)}{\sqrt{\sum_{j=1}^{n}\left(\underset{j}{x_i} - \bar{x}_i\right)^2 \sum_{j=1}^{n}\left(\underset{j}{x_k} - \bar{x}_k\right)^2}}, \tag{2.13}$$

where

n—number of objects.

The parametric method requires a parameter specifying the limit value of the correlation coefficient. If two variables have this coefficient greater than the limit value, they are assumed to belong to the same cluster. This coefficient is called the critical value of the correlation coefficient and its value is always in the range of $\langle 0; 1\rangle$.

The first step in this method is to calculate the sum of correlations in each correlation matrix for each column [140]:

$$rsum_k = \sum_{j=1}^{n} \left|r_{j,k}\right|. \tag{2.14}$$

Next, the variable for which the correlation coefficient value is the largest [140] (whose $rsum_p$ satisfies the following equation) is

$$rsum_p = \max_k \{rsum_k\}. \tag{2.15}$$

The variable indicated by the p index is considered to be a cluster representative. In the column with index p, all elements satisfying inequality are selec [140]:

$$\left|r_{q,p}\right| \geqslant r^*, \tag{2.16}$$

where

r^*—critical value of the correlation coefficient.

Variables with indexes q satisfying the above inequality and not representing clusters are deleted from the list of variables. Then all activities are repeated until the condition (2.16) is not satisfied.

Another way to select variables is the method proposed by E. Nowaka [139], which is a modification of the method of information capacity indicators by Z. Hellwiga [75]. These indicators are the criterion for accumulating information in specific combinations of variables and are determined for all possible combinations without repetition.

Individual modified information capacity indicators can be determined from the following formula [140]:

$$\underset{s}{h_l} = \frac{\left(\underset{s}{\bar{r}_l}\right)^2}{1 + \sum\limits_{\substack{k=1 \\ k \neq l}}^{n_s} |r_{l,k}|}, \tag{2.17}$$

where

s—combination number,
l—analyzed variable number,
n_s—number of variables in a combination.

At the same time, the numerator of the above formula contains the arithmetic mean of the modules of the correlation coefficients of the variable with the number l [140]:

$$\underset{s}{\bar{r}_l} = \frac{1}{n - n_s} \sum_{p=1}^{n-n_s} |r_{l,p}|, \tag{2.18}$$

where

$n - n_s$—number of variables that are not a part of the combination.

Integral modified information capacity indicators for each combination can be determined on the basis of the formula [140]:

$$\underset{s}{H} = \sum_{l=1}^{n_s} \underset{s}{h_l}. \tag{2.19}$$

The $\underset{s}{h_l}$ and $\underset{s}{H}$ coefficients are the higher the variables are less correlated with each other in a given combination and more strongly correlated with variables that are not part of this combination. The values of these indicators are always in the range of ⟨0; 1⟩. The best combination of variables is characterized by the highest value of the integrally modified indicator of information capacity $\underset{s}{H}$.

The selection of variables can also be performed with the use of grouping methods [140], whereby not objects are grouped, but variables. For this reason, each variable is one object, and the individual values of those variables are taken as coordinates. After grouping, a representative is selected for each created class. Representatives of all classes create a set of variables that can be used for further research.

After selecting the variables, it is important to define the measurement scale on which the data is expressed, as this determines the choice of methods that can be used for data processing. A measurement scale is a classification proposed to describe the character of the information contained in numbers assigned to objects. It refers to the level at which data characteristics can be mathematically modeled [96]. The most commonly used classification is the one developed in 1946 by S.S. Stevens [191]. It includes four measurement scales: nominal, ordinal, interval, and ratio (Table 2.3).

In a nominal scale, it is only possible to determine if two objects are similar to each other or different. It is not possible to determine that one object is better than another. Operations on data expressed on this relate to counting similar and dissimilar objects. The use of this classification in ranking objects is limited by the inability to determine which of the two objects is better. For data about objects expressed on this scale, it is possible to create similarity rankings, but they do not need to be described with numbers.

In the ordinal scale, apart from determining similarity, it is possible to determine whether a given object is better than another, what allows ordering rankings to be made—from the best to the worst. Operations on data in this scale relate on counting similar and dissimilar objects and the number of majority and minority relations. An

Table 2.3 Basic properties of measuring scales [56]

Scale type	Mathematical transformation allowed	Acceptable relations	Allowed arithmetic operations
Nominal	$z = f(x)$, $f(x)$—any transformation mutually unambiguous	Equality $x_A = x_B$, diversity $x_A \neq x_B$	Counting the number of equality and difference relations
Ordinal	$z = f(x)$, $f(x)$—any strictly monotonic function	Above and most $x_A > x_B$ and minorities $x_A < x_B$	Counting the number of equality, diversity, minority, and majority relations
Interval	$z = bx + a$, for $b > 0$ i $x, z \in \mathbb{R}$	Above and the equality of diversity and ratio $x_A - x_B = x_C - x_D$	Above and addition and subtraction
Ratio	$z = bx$, for $b > 0$ i $x, z \in \mathbb{R}_+$	The above and equal ratio $\frac{x_A}{x_B} = \frac{x_C}{x_D}$	Above and multiplication and division

example of their description on this scale is the assessment of the product: 1—very good, 2—good 3—average, and 4—weak. They do not need to be described by numbers.

The interval scale allows you to determine whether objects are similar if a single object is better than the other and to what extent (how many times) it is better. The same operations on data like on the ordinal scale are allowed and also addition and subtraction. Objects must be described with real numbers.

The ratio scale allows you to determine whether objects are similar if a single object is better than the other and to what extent it is better and how many times. Operations on data like on the interval scale are allowed and additionally multiplication and division. Objects must be described with the real, positive numbers.

The measurement scales are ordered by determining that the nominal scale is the weakest, the ordinal scale—stronger, the interval scale—even stronger, and ratio scale—the strongest. If data is on different measurement scales, transformation from the stronger to the weaker scales is possible but never the other way around. Methods used on the weaker ones can be used on the stronger ones [56].

Determining the character of the variables is very important while creating aggregate measures. An aggregate measure is a result of aggregation of many variables, from which some may be positively or negatively correlated with it. High values of some variables should determine high values of an aggregate measure and others low. Therefore, in [73], Hellwig proposed to introduce a classification into stimulants and destimulants. *Stimulants* are variables whose large values influence the high rating of tested objects, while *destimulants* are variables, whose low values influence the high rating. In addition, there are also variables called nominants. A term of nominant was introduced by Boris [20]. *Nominant* is a variable, whose values from a specific range affect the high rating of objects, while values outside this range, both greater and lesser, are non-desirable values.

The selection of variables involves their unification. In the case of aggregate measures, depending on the character of a method applied in creation, these variables should meet the following conditions of uniformity:

1. Strong. The variables can be only stimulants or only destimulant.
2. Weak. The values cannot be nominants.

A strong condition is required for aggregate measures based on the arithmetic mean or weighted average. Combining destimulants and stimulants will cause that both high stimulant and destimulant values will determine high measure values. In practice, it should be so that if high values of stimulants affect a high value of a measure, high values of destimulants should lower their value of the aggregate measure.

In order to meet the strong demand, it is necessary to introduce transformations of stimulants into destimulants (or vice versa). As a rule, if most of the variables are stimulants, then destimulants are converted into stimulants. Conversely, if a majority of variables are destimulants, then stimulants are transformed into destimulants. There are many of such transformations, most of which can be attributed to

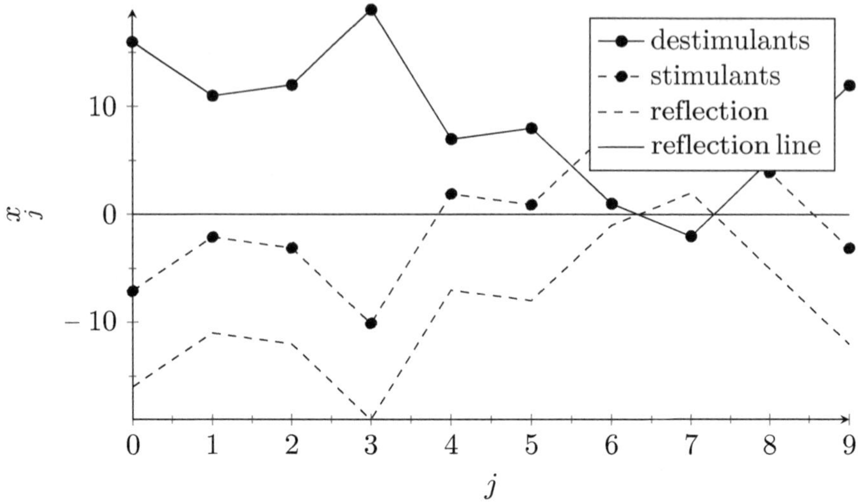

Fig. 2.1 Zamiana destymulanty na stymulantę

either of the two groups: reverse or inverse transformations. As a part of reverse transformations, the value of a variable is "mirrored" over some value. This is presented in Fig. 2.1.

The reverse transformation can be described by the formula [98]

$$\underset{j}{x'_i} = a - \underset{j}{x_i}, \tag{2.20}$$

where

$\underset{j}{x'_i}$—value of i-th variable for j-th object after transformation,
a—parameter.

The variable is reflected in relation to OX axis and then shifted by the value of the parameter a. Depending on its value, one can distinguish transformations that perform reflection relative to zero value, maximum value, doubled mean value, the value of one, and the value of 100.

Reflection in relation to zero value [98] is

$$\underset{j}{x'_i} = -\underset{j}{x_i}. \tag{2.21}$$

Change of sign in all values to opposite ones.

Reflection in relation to the maximum value [98, 107] is

$$x'_{ij} = \max_j \left(x_{ij} \right) - x_{ij}. \tag{2.22}$$

After transformation, with the assumption of a positive value, the maximum value will not be exceeded.

Reflection in relation to a doubled mean value [98] is

$$x'_{ij} = 2\bar{x}_i - x_{ij}. \tag{2.23}$$

The mean value after transformation is kept.
Reflection in relation to 1 [107]

$$x'_{ij} = 1 - x_{ij}. \tag{2.24}$$

Keeps the range for variables from the interval $\langle 0; 1 \rangle$.

Reflection in relation to parameter a equal 100

$$x'_{ij} = 100\% - x_{ij}. \tag{2.25}$$

Keeps the range for variables expressed in percentage terms, which maximum value do not exceed 100%.

The selection of an appropriate reflection point may significantly affect obtained results. This depends, however, on the selected normalization method and calculation of a measure. In case of a measure calculated based on the weighted mean value, it affects the measure value but not the ordering of objects. This, however, does not change the distance between objects. This is illustrated in Table 2.4.

Three variables were selected to determine a measure, out of which the first two were stimulants and the last one indexed with three was a destimulant. Firstly, the value of a measure was calculated by converting a destimulant into stimulant, according to the formula (2.21) and then according to the formula (2.22). Determined measure values differ by the same value equal to two. For this reason,

Table 2.4 Determination of the aggregate measure for various reflection points

x_1	x_2	x_3	m_{s1}	m_{s2}
1	2	2	0.33	2.33
2	3	3	0.67	2.67
1	4	4	0.33	2.33
2	5	5	0.67	2.67
3	6	6	1	3
2	7	2	2.33	4.33

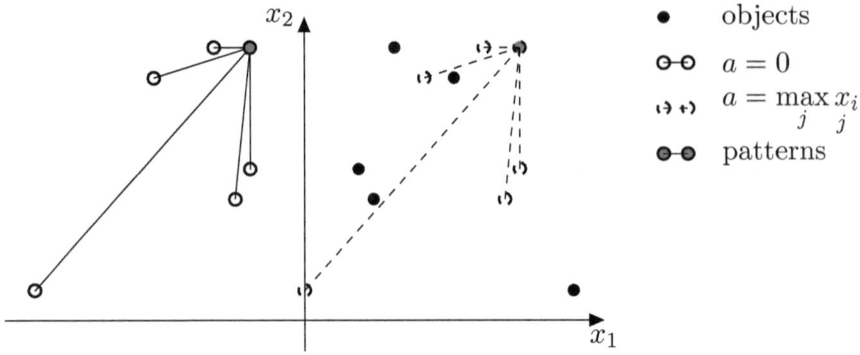

Fig. 2.2 Difference in values of the objects' projections depending on the applied transformation method to convert a destimulant to a stimulant

the selection of a reflection point does not affect the ordering of objects. This applies to a measure calculated under the weighted mean value.

In calculation of the aggregate measure based on the distance from a pattern, the selected method of transformation of destimulant into stimulant affects the location of this pattern. If a measure of distance applied to determine an aggregate measure is a shift invariant, then a method of conversion of destimulant into stimulant is of no importance. The Euclidean distance is an example of such a measure. For this measure, displacement of two objects at the same time, by the same distance, and in the same direction does not affect the distance between them. When applying each of formulas (2.21)–(2.25), the result will be exactly the same (Fig. 2.2).

For measures that are not shift invariants, the selection of a transformation method to convert a destimulant into stimulant will affect the value of a measure. The distance between the objects for these measures depends on their location in space. This will result from the applied transformation method, and unless it results in displacement of objects beyond the accepted range of space, for majority of methods this will not affect the ordering of objects. However, gaps between the objects may significantly change and not similarly for all. In case they are allocated to a specific class according to an aggregate measure value, this can make a change in classification of objects located on borderlines between classes.

In projection, a choice of transformation method is of no importance unless a vector to which a projection is done is determined under the difference between the coordinates of a pattern and an antipattern (Fig. 2.3).

The second important factor affecting the choice of transformation method of destimulant into stimulant is the applied normalization method. The use of any normalization method that brings the mean value to zero or reduces the extreme values to levels established in advance eliminates displacement in the data values resulting from the assumed reflection point. All the opposite transformations have exactly the same effect in this case.

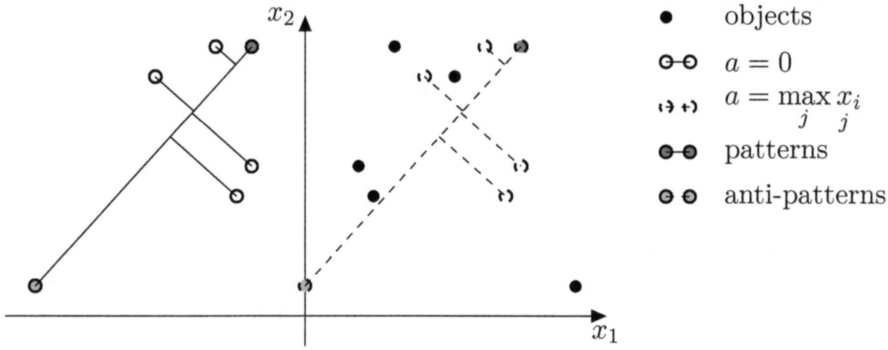

Fig. 2.3 Difference in values of the objects' projections depending on the applied transformation method to convert a destimulant to a stimulant

When choosing the most appropriate transformation from the group of opposite transformations, the simplest one should be selected, assuming that the applied normalization method eliminates the choice of a reflection point or the method of determining an aggregate measure is insensitive to its location. In this case, the appropriate is transformation according to the following formula (2.21). In situations, where you can expect the selected transformation to affect the measure value, a transformation that causes the least object displacement should be used. This can be obtained by conversion according to the following formula (2.23). In most cases, reflection relative to the mean value guarantees the least displacement of objects.

The second large group of transformations that convert destimulants into stimulants is inverse transformations. They can be described by the formula [98]

$$x'_{\underset{j}{i}} = \frac{a}{x_{\underset{j}{i}}}, \tag{2.26}$$

where

$x_{\underset{j}{i}} \neq 0.$

The value of the parameter a determines the type of an inverse transformation. The following formulas can be obtained for different inverse transformations at a equal to

1. One [98, 107]:

$$x'_{\underset{j}{i}} = \frac{1}{x_{\underset{j}{i}}}. \tag{2.27}$$

2. Nominal value [98, 107]:

$$x'_{\substack{i\\j}} = \frac{\min\limits_{j}\left(x_{\substack{i\\j}}\right)}{x_{\substack{i\\j}}}. \tag{2.28}$$

Inverse transformations cause non-linear change in a "gap" between objects. Those at the one end of the scale are moved to the opposite end, and at the same time their density changes. The effect is that in majority of methods conversion from destimulants to stimulants (or stimulants to destimulants) may cause the change in the objects' order. The exception is aggregate measures that are created on the basis of determining a distance from the pattern using distance measures that are invariants of the scale.

The invariance of measures with respect to the shift and the scale does not occur for one measure at the same time. Due to the character of invariance, the opposite transformations are predisposed to be used with measures that are a shift invariant, while inverse transformations are predisposed to be used with measures that are scale invariants.

Table 2.5 illustrates the example for transformation of destimulant to stimulant using an opposite and inverse transformation. It is clearly visible that in case of inverse transformation values have been significantly decreased, and however none of the positive values were converted to a negative one.

For most methods of creating aggregate measures, it is not necessary to convert variants being stimulants to destimulants and vice versa. It is only required by a measure calculated using the weighted arithmetic mean. The situation is different for nominants. The assumption about the existence of a value or a range of values which characterizes the best objects means that for practically every method of creating a measure it is necessary to convert a nominant to stimulant or destimulant. The exceptions are measures created on the basis of a distance from a pattern, but this

Table 2.5 Conversion of destimulant into stimulant

County	Emission of gaseous pollutants $\left[t/km^2\right]$ annually	$x'_j = \frac{1}{x_j}$	$x'_j = 2\bar{x} - x_j$
Białogardzki county	69	0.0145	662.5
Drawski county	17.38	0.0575	714.12
Kołobrzeski county	120.6	0.0083	610.89
Gryfinski county	2111.53	0.0005	−1380.04
⋮	⋮	⋮	⋮
Szczecinecki county	223.03	0.0045	507.46
Sławienski county	10.78	0.0928	720.72
Koszalinski county	6.91	0.1447	724.58

requires a special method of its selection. There are two basic ways to convert a nominant into stimulant [107, 211]:

$$x'_{ij} = \begin{cases} x'_{ij} - c_i \text{ for } x'_{ij} \leqslant c_i, \\ c_i - x'_{ij} \text{ for } x'_{ij} > c_i \end{cases} \tag{2.29}$$

and [107, 211]

$$x'_{ij} = \begin{cases} \frac{x'_{ij}}{c_i} \text{ for } x'_{ij} \leqslant c_i, \\ \frac{c_i}{x'_{ij}} \text{ for } x'_{ij} > c_i, \end{cases} \tag{2.30}$$

where

c_i—the most desirable value of a variable.

The formula (2.29) transforms a nominant so that its largest value is zero. Therefore all values of a variable can only be negative or equal to zero. While the formula (2.30) transforms the values of positive nominants into the range from zero to one. No value can be greater than one. By analogy, formulas can be given for changing a nominant to a destimulant:

$$x'_{ij} = \begin{cases} x'_{ij} - c_i \text{ for } x'_{ij} > c_i, \\ c_i - x'_{ij} \text{ for } x'_{ij} \leqslant c_i, \end{cases} \tag{2.31}$$

and

$$x'_{ij} = \begin{cases} \frac{x'_{ij}}{c_i} \text{ for } x'_{ij} > c_i, \\ \frac{c_i}{x'_{ij}} \text{ for } x'_{ij} \leqslant c_i. \end{cases} \tag{2.32}$$

In the first formula, the nominants are changed into positive values. The least value determines the best object. In the second formula, the best object is determined by one. All others have values greater than one, with the assumption that a nominat was described by positive values.

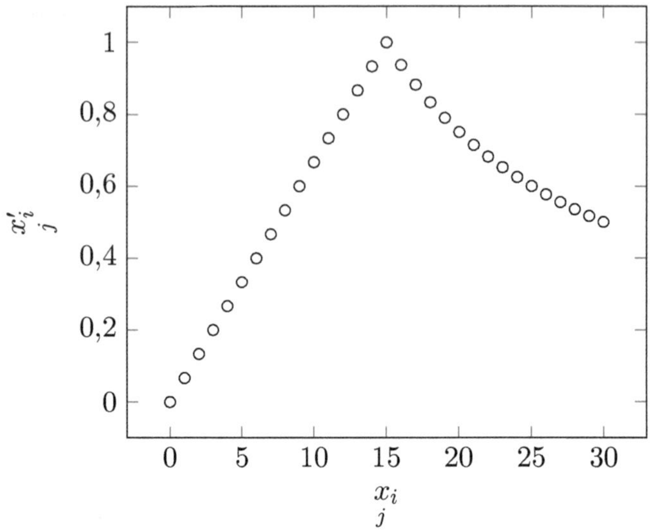

Fig. 2.4 The conversion of a nominant into a stimulant at nom = 15

Another way tp change a nominat to a stimulant is illustrated by a formula [213]:

$$x'_{\substack{i\\j}} = \frac{\min\left\{\text{nom}_j;\, x_{\substack{i\\j}}\right\}}{\max\left\{\text{nom}_j;\, x_{\substack{i\\j}}\right\}}, \tag{2.33}$$

where

nom_j—a nominat of the j-th variable.

Figure 2.4 illustrates the result of nominant into stimulant conversion when nominal value equals 15. If the values of a variable are positive, then after conversion values in the range from zero to one are obtained. The value of one is obtained when the converted value is equal to a nominal value.

The conversion of nominants to stimulants and destimulants according to formulas (2.29)–(2.32) is done with the assumption that the best nominat value is determined. Sometimes, not the best but the worst value of a nominat can be determined, that is, the least possible value for the worst object. In such a case, formulas (2.29) and (2.30) determine the method of transformation of a nominant into destimulant while (2.31) and (2.32) into stimulant.

2.2 Determination of Weights of Variables

In the linear ordering methods, weighting of variables can be applied what results in determining their effect on the established aggregate measures of objects. The measure of a relative information value can be applied for this purpose [147]:

$$w_i = \frac{V_i}{\sum\limits_{i=1}^{m} V_{x_i}}. \tag{2.34}$$

Values w_i can be considered as variable weights "*variable weight*". The variable will have the greater impact on the value of a measure, the greater the value of wi is, i.e., the greater the variability of a given variable for the analyzed set of objects. Weights can also be discretionary, based on our knowledge. Generally, in this case, the knowledge of experts is utilized to assign specific numerical values to variables. However, we should remember that weights assigned by experts should be positive and meet the following condition:

$$\sum_{i=1}^{m} w_i = 1. \tag{2.35}$$

If weights do not meet this condition, they can be recalculated with the following formula [140]:

$$w_i = \frac{\overset{\mathrm{e}}{w}_i}{\sum\limits_{i=1}^{m} \overset{\mathrm{e}}{w}_i}, \tag{2.36}$$

where

$\overset{\mathrm{e}}{w}_i$—weigh of i-th variable assigned by an expert.

Weights $\overset{\mathrm{e}}{w}_i$ can also be scores assigned by an expert to individual variables. In the case of a greater number of experts, $\overset{\mathrm{e}}{w}_i$ may be the sum of points assigned to individual variables. With a large number of variables, they can be grouped and scored within individual groups (by different experts). The following formula can be applied to determine weights:

$$w_i = \frac{\overset{\mathrm{g}}{w}_k \overset{\mathrm{ge}}{w}_{kg}}{\sum\limits_{k=1}^{\overset{\mathrm{g}}{m}} \overset{\mathrm{g}}{w}_k \sum\limits_{g=1}^{\overset{\mathrm{ge}}{m}_k} \overset{\mathrm{ge}}{w}_{kg}}, \tag{2.37}$$

where

$\overset{g}{w}_k$—weight of the k-th group,
$\overset{ge}{w}_{kg}$—weight of the k-th variable of g-th group,
$\overset{g}{m}$—number of groups,
$\overset{ge}{m}_k$—number of variables of the k-th group,

where i represents the i-th variable of the k-th group with a g-th number in this group.

When conducting research, variables can be assigned to specific groups. For example, when creating an aggregate measure that describes communes, variables can be divided into four groups: demographic and social, socio-economic, infrastructural, and ecological. Each of them may contain a different number of variables, which will cause that the importance of a group depends on the number of variables assigned to them. After introducing a double system of weights, the weight of the $\overset{g}{w}_k$. group of variables will depend only on the assigned weight. Similarly to groups, weights can be assigned to variables belonging to particular groups. This is important as some of the variables may be considered more and other less significant. By assigning a separate weight to variables in groups, changing their weights will not change the significance of the entire group.

Sometimes, determining weights can be difficult. In such a situation, it is advisable to assume the same weights for all variables:

$$\bigwedge_{i=1,2,\ldots,m} w_i = \frac{1}{m}. \tag{2.38}$$

In the case of a double weigh system, the equal weights can be applied for each group:

$$\bigwedge_{i=1,2,\ldots,n_g} w_k' = \frac{1}{n_g} \tag{2.39}$$

and equal weight values within each group:

$$\bigwedge_{k=1,2,\ldots,n_g} \bigwedge_{i=1,2,\ldots,n_k} w_{ki} = \frac{1}{n_k}. \tag{2.40}$$

In [98], it was proposed to interpret the formula for ranking according to a variable given by the formula:

$$\underset{j}{\mathrm{m_s}} = \sum_{i=1}^{m} w_i \underset{j}{x_i'}, \tag{2.41}$$

as the orthogonal projection. The coordinates of objects as well as their weights can be treated as vectors, but the vector of weights must have non-negative coordinates and be a unit vector.

The vector of weights can be selected using the method of sum of variables with equal weights. In this method, due to the fact that vector of weights must be a unit vector, the values of weights are different from one by M and [98]

$$\bigwedge_{i=1,2,\ldots,m} w_i = \frac{1}{\sqrt{m}}. \tag{2.42}$$

The sum of weights is not equal to 1, but

$$\sum_{i=1}^{m} w_i = \frac{m}{\sqrt{m}}. \tag{2.43}$$

Formally, the orthogonal projection becomes a scaled mean value, which makes an aggregate measure dependent on the number of variables and does not guarantee that a scale of variables will be preserved. If the values of variables fall within the range from zero to one and the number of variables is four, the values of the measure will be in the range from zero to two, and the range will increase as the number of variables increases.

A similar problem appears in the sum of variables method with different weights. The weights are calculated using the following formula [98]:

$$\bigwedge_{i=1,2,\ldots,m} w_i' = \frac{w_i}{\sqrt{\sum_{i=1}^{m} w_i^2}}, \tag{2.44}$$

where

w_i—typical weights,
w_i'—new values of weights.

The change in weights is of no substantial importance [98]. In practice, it causes a change in the measure range and makes it dependent on the number of variables. Both methods of determining weights should be used when the calculated value of an aggregate measure is not the purpose of calculations, but some indirect result within the framework of calculations in the vector space.

Another method for defining weights proposed in work [98] is the method of the first principal component. It is a method that automatically determines a vector of weights, adjusting it to the characteristics of the set of points representing studied objects. In this method, based on the eigenvector with the highest eigenvalue, the main direction of the variability of the set of points is determined. The coordinates of this vector can therefore be taken as weight values. Most algorithms for computing

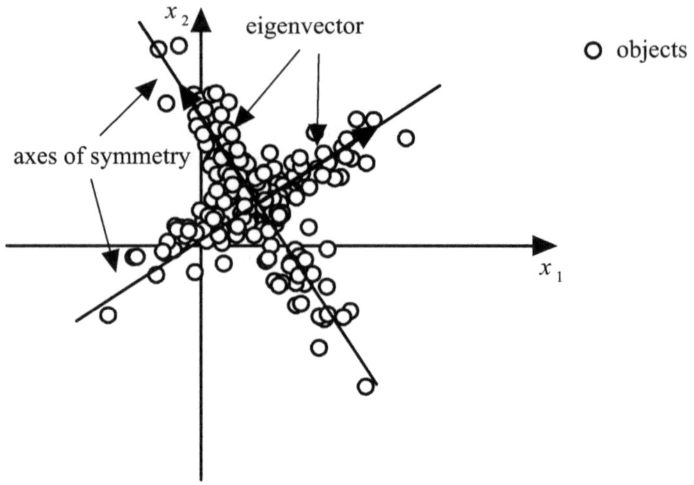

Fig. 2.5 Wektory własne o podobnych wartościach własnych

eigenvalues and eigenvectors automatically reduce eigenvectors to unit vectors. However, this does not need to be so, and in such cases, it is necessary to reduce a weight vector to a unit vector. This method has two major disadvantages. In [98], attention was drawn to the fact that eigenvector coordinates can be negative, so according to the assumption (3.68) such vectors cannot be used as weight vectors.

In some situations, the local density of points representing objects may be symmetrical about perpendicular axes of symmetry. An example of such a set of points is an isosceles cross in a two-dimensional space (Fig. 2.5), a hypersphere with a constant density of points, or an n-dimensional normal distribution. For this type of objects, the eigenvalues are similar in terms of value. Small changes in the set of studied objects may affect the selection of an eigenvector. Because all eigenvectors are orthogonal, each of them represents a completely different part of variability. This means that a slight change in the set of features can completely change the measure values for individual features. Therefore, when using this method, it is necessary to check that the largest eigenvalue is significantly different from the rest.

Both of the abovementioned disadvantages strongly limit the first component method as a method of creating a weight vector. The chance that all eigenvectors will be greater than zero decreases in proportion to the increase in the number of variables. With a larger number of variables, this condition is very difficult to meet.

The formula (2.41) can be interpreted not only as the orthogonal projection but also as the projection of a vector representing objects onto a unit vector of weights. There is no limit with regard to the positivity of all coordinates. To calculate the value of a variable, you can use eigenvectors also with negative coordinates. As a rule, numerical algorithms give unit vectors as eigenvectors. As a rule, numerical algorithms give unit vectors as eigenvectors. However, you should remember that the eigenvector is any vector that is parallel to a determined eigenvector. Its direction can be any, and therefore the direction of an eigenvector does not have to be aimed at the best objects. For this reason, it is necessary to determine from the ranking of objects whether high values of the measure indicate the best or the worst ones. One drawback of aggregate measures determined on the basis of eigenvectors is the fact that they do not have a uniform range of values, as it will depend on the character of the set of points.

In summary, the calculation of the aggregate measure based on the first eigenvector should be performed in the following steps:

1. Determination of eigenvalues and eigenvectors.
2. Search for the greatest eigenvalue.
3. Check whether the largest eigenvalue is significantly different in value from the others.
4. Calculate the measure for the eigenvector corresponding to the highest eigenvalue.
5. Check if the greatest values of a measure correspond to the best objects, and if not, multiply all the eigenvector coordinates by minus one and recalculate the measure.

2.3 Normalization of Variables

Variables involved in the creation of aggregate measures or used in clustering are often expressed in various units of measure, for example, people per square kilometer, in zloty. Such variables are incomparable. They can also have the same measurement units but be incomparable due to a different range of values. An example would be the average monthly income per person and the average monthly amount spent on culture (cinema, theater, etc.). Both variables are comparable, and however, due to the higher values of the average monthly income per person, this variable will dominate. Its importance will be significantly greater than the importance of the average amount spent on culture, and therefore, the latter will only slightly affect the value of the aggregate measure and the results of clustering.

In order to have variables comparable, the variable normalization procedure is applied. It brings the variables into a more or less similar range of values. Normalization methods can be divided into two large groups [107]:

1. Rank methods.
2. Methods using the quotient transformation.

In ranking methods, variables are assigned numerical values (usually natural numbers) resulting from the location of the "old" values on the number line. In the simplest case, the values of variables are ordered from the smallest to the largest, assuming its ordinal number in the sequence as the "new" value of a variable. Another method of ranking is ranking by class. In this case, the entire range of variables is divided into ranges and assigned sequential numbers. The "new" value of a variable is created by replacing the "old" value with the number of the range to which the value has been assigned.

The ranking methods change the spacing between the values of variables. If they are not evenly distributed in the considered range, then an uneven increase in the distance between individual values arises. This method should not be used to create aggregate measures that require not only the ordering of values but also the spacing between them. For this reason, the most popular are normalization methods that use the quotient transformation.

In general, the variable normalization formula can be presented as follows [62]:

$$x''_{\substack{i\\j}} = \left(\frac{x'_{\substack{i\\j}} - A_i}{B_i}\right)^p, \tag{2.45}$$

where

$x''_{\substack{i\\j}}$—value of the i-th variable for the j-th object after normalization,
B_i—normalization base of the i-th variable ($B_i \neq 0$),
A_i—displacement of normalized values relative to zero,
p—parameters.

Value p increases or decreases the ratio of a space between small and large values of a variable. For p equal to one, this ratio does not change. If p is greater than one, the space between small values will decrease and between large values will increase. Conversely, for p less than one and greater than zero, a space between small values will increase and between large values will decrease. The latter case is particularly interesting when variables describe objects of various scales, for example, enterprises employing both several dozen and several thousand employees. The economies of scale mean that if objects are divided into classes based on the value of a measure, all small enterprises will fall into one class. The analysis of their diversity will be difficult. In such a situation, adopting the p coefficient as less than one will increase the space between small values and decrease between large values, so in the presented example distinguishability of small enterprises will improve.

In some cases, the total independence from the objects' scale might be important, so that a space between objects was considered depending on the objects' scale. In such a case, a scale invariant can be used as transformation. An example of such transformation is logarithm. The formula (2.45) including logarithm can be described as follows:

$$x''_{\substack{i\\j}} = \log_a\left(\frac{x'_{\substack{i\\j}} - A_i}{B_i}\right), \tag{2.46}$$

where the base of a logarithm can be either, while the following condition must be satisfied:

$$\frac{x'_{\substack{i\\j}} - A_i}{B_i} > 0. \tag{2.47}$$

It follows that only quotient transformations that give values greater than one can be applied here. In the case of multiple quotient transformations, to satisfy the condition (2.47), the following formula can be applied:

$$x''_{\substack{i\\j}} = \log_a \left[\frac{x'_{\substack{i\\j}} - A_i}{B_i} - \min_j \left(\frac{x'_{\substack{i\\j}} - A_i}{B_i} \right) + c \right], \tag{2.48}$$

where c jest is a positive constant close to zero.

In the methods that use ratio transformations, the problem is to determine what the range of values for which the variables are reduced to comparability should be determined with. The reference point is defined by the appropriate determination of the normalization base. In the case when the values of the variables are similarly distributed, the normalization procedure effectively brings the variables to comparability, most often regardless of the chosen normalization base. The problem is, however, in case of variables for which the values are distributed differently. An example may be variables with several values that differ significantly from the others. In this case, the value of the aggregate measure will strongly depend on the selected value of the normalization base.

Most often, the value of the standard deviation of a variable is taken as the value of the normalization base [107]:

$$B_i = \sqrt{\frac{\sum_{j=1}^{n} \left(x'_{\substack{i\\j}} - \bar{x}'_i \right)^2}{n-1}} \tag{2.49}$$

or the range [140]

$$B_i = \max_j \left(x'_{\substack{i\\j}} \right) - \min_j \left(x'_{\substack{i\\j}} \right). \tag{2.50}$$

In the first case, standardization methods are referred to, and in the second—unitization methods. A characteristic feature of standardization methods is bringing down the standard deviation of the normalized variables to the value equal to one. Unitization methods are more sensitive to extreme values. Excluding or adding extreme objects with abnormally great values can strongly affect a normalization result. In the case of standardization methods, the impact is not so strong.

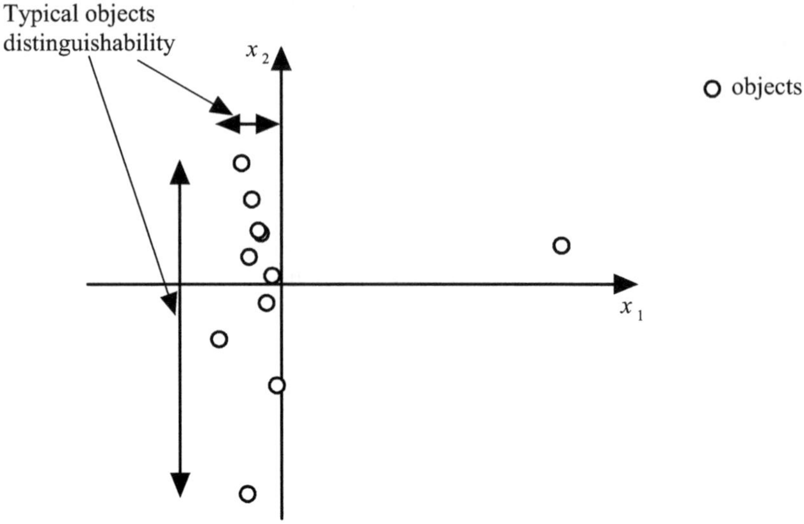

Fig. 2.6 Rozróżnialność obiektów typowych po standaryzacji

The appearance of objects with unusually large values of variables in the examined set is a serious problem. These objects, during standardization, "compact" the remaining values into a certain, small range of values. In the case of unitarization, the "compaction" is even much stronger. Both during clustering and when creating aggregate measures, this effect causes weak distinguishability of objects due to the variable within which such atypical objects exist. In the extreme case, there may be a situation in which for this variable it will only be possible to distinguish atypical objects from others, without the possibility of differentiating typical objects (Fig. 2.6).

After standardization, atypical objects obtain a very high value of this variable, for which they have atypical value. Consequently, the value of this variable will depend mainly on the value of an aggregate measure for a given object. The problem of atypical objects in the case of standardization can be somewhat mitigated by using instead of the standard deviation given by the formula (2.49) the weighted standard deviation of a sample:

$$B_i = \sqrt{\frac{\sum_{j=1}^{n} w_j \left(x'_{i_j} - \frac{\sum_{k=1}^{n} x'_{i_k}}{n} \right)^2}{\left(1 - \frac{1}{n}\right) \sum_{j=1}^{n} w_j}}, \tag{2.51}$$

where

$\underset{j}{w}$—value of a weight for the j-th object,

or population:

$$B_i = \sqrt{\frac{\sum_{j=1}^{n} \underset{j}{w} \left(\underset{j}{x_i'} - \frac{\sum_{k=1}^{n} \underset{k}{x_i'}}{n} \right)^2}{\sum_{j=1}^{n} \underset{j}{w}}}. \tag{2.52}$$

The formula (2.51) by $\underset{j}{w} = \frac{1}{n}$ is equal to (2.49). By entering the formula (2.51) $\underset{j}{w} = \frac{1}{n}$ and then $\sum_{j=1}^{n} \underset{j}{w} = 1$, the result is

$$\sqrt{\frac{\sum_{j=1}^{n} \frac{1}{n} \left(\underset{j}{x_i'} - \sum_{k=1}^{n} \frac{\underset{k}{x_i'}}{n} \right)^2}{\left(1 - \frac{1}{n}\right)}} = \sqrt{\frac{\frac{1}{n} \sum_{j=1}^{n} \left(\underset{j}{x_i'} - \bar{x}_i' \right)^2}{\left(1 - \frac{1}{n}\right)}} = \sqrt{\frac{\frac{1}{n} \sum_{j=1}^{n} \left(\underset{j}{x_i'} - \bar{x}_i' \right)^2}{\frac{1}{n}(n-1)}}. \tag{2.53}$$

The above derivation shows that the weighted and unweighted measures coincide.

The appropriate use of weights allows to reduce the influence of outliers on the value of deviation. Observations far from the mean value are assigned weights smaller than observations close to the mean value. In the simplest case, zero–one weighting system can be applied in standardization

$$\underset{j}{w} = \begin{cases} 1 \text{ for } \left| \underset{j}{x_i'} - \bar{x}_i' \right| \leqslant p, \\ 0 \text{ for } \left| \underset{j}{x_i'} - \bar{x}_i' \right| > p. \end{cases} \tag{2.54}$$

This weighting system assigns weights the value of one, if the absolute difference between an observation and mean value is smaller or equal to a given threshold p, and zero, if it is greater.

Atypical objects are quite rare in the population, often two or three times for a set of one hundred elements containing both typical and atypical objects. It follows that the value of the p threshold can be made dependent on the predicted probability of the occurrence of atypical objects. For example, it can be assumed that the probability of an atypical object occurrence is less than 5%. So, if we presume that a distribution of the variable is normal, then the threshold value p can be assumed as approximately equal to $2\sigma_{x_i'}$. In the general case, when a distribution is unknown, but there is a standard deviation for it, to obtain a similar probability, one should approximate $p = 5\sigma_{x_i'}$. However, one should remember that the given probability of the occurrence of atypical value is the highest possible probability. If the unknown distribution turned out to be a normal distribution, the actual probability would be only about 0.0000006%. Due to the fact that summing the distributions (brings them closer) to the normal distribution, most of the distributions of variables are close to it. The value of the threshold with a slight error can therefore be estimated based on the assumption that the distribution is normal. Thus the threshold value of p can be assumed as $2\sigma_{x_i'}$.

Mean absolute deviation can also be used instead of standard deviation [104]:

$$B_i = \frac{\sum\limits_{j=1}^{n} \left| x_{i\,j}' - \bar{x}_i' \right|}{n - 1}. \tag{2.55}$$

Due to the fact that the values of differences are not squared, it is not as sensitive to atypical observations as standard deviation. Disadvantage of the applied formula (2.55) is that in case of standardization of variables the value of the standard deviation after standardization not always equals zero. In contrast, the weighted standard deviation ensures that for typical objects after standardization, the standard deviation is equal to one.

There are also methods to reduce the impact of atypical objects on unitization. Zeroed unitarization is particularly sensitive to atypical objects, and at the same time it is one of the few methods that allow to reduce the range of values to a predetermined one. It ensures that the values after normalization will be exactly in the range $\langle 0; 1 \rangle$. It is of great importance in the case of ranking methods that require the index values to be within a predetermined range. Hence, in the case of atypical objects, it is necessary to search for alternative methods, less sensitive to these objects. Unfavorable properties of zeroed unitarization result from its use of extreme coordinate values for displacing and scaling a set of objects. The process of zeroed unitarization consists of two stages: displacement of a set and changing a scale. In Fig. 2.7, points representing objects before zeroed utilization are marked with white color. In the first stage of this unitarization, the points are displaced so that the smallest value of the objects' coordinates is zero. Displaced points are marked in light gray. After displacement, the coordinates are rescaled in such a way that their largest values are equal to one. Points representing objects after scaling are presented in dark gray (Fig. 2.7b).

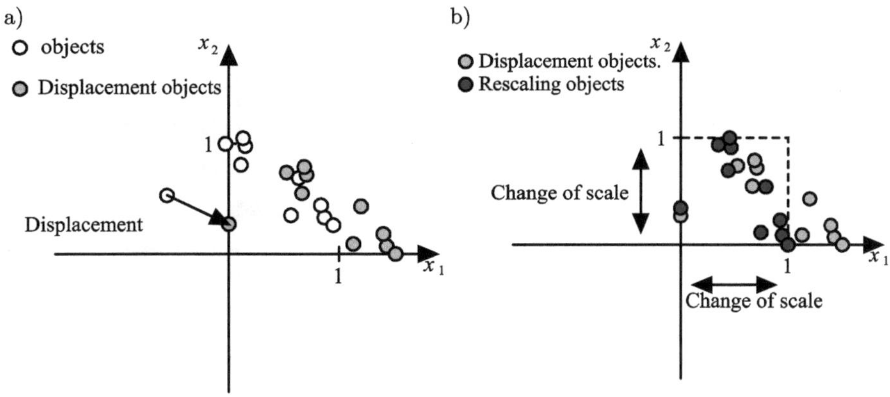

Fig. 2.7 Zeroed unitization: (**a**) set of objects displacement and (**b**) change of scale

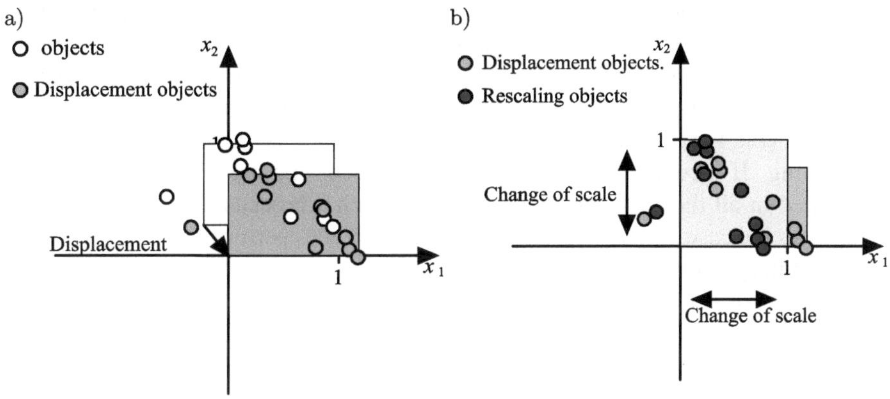

Fig. 2.8 Displacement and rescaling objects using area where majority of objects is placed: (**a**) displacement of a set and (**b**) change of a scale

The extreme values of the coordinates can be replaced by the boundaries of area where most objects are located. In Fig. 2.8, such an area is marked with a rectangle filled with white. In the presented example, the size of the rectangle was determined under the standard deviation, where its sides were assumed as 1.28155 of the standard deviation of coordinates' values. This ensures that at normal distribution 80% of possible values of the coordinates are within the ranges determined by the sides of this rectangle. The set of points representing objects was displaced so that its lower left vertex was at the origin of the coordinate system. After moving, the rectangle was marked as filled in with light gray color. Figure 2.8b presents the effect of scaling of the set of points representing objects. Rescaling was made so that the rectangle representing the area in which most of the objects are located becomes a square with the sides equal to one.

Fig. 2.9 Correction of the extreme objects placement

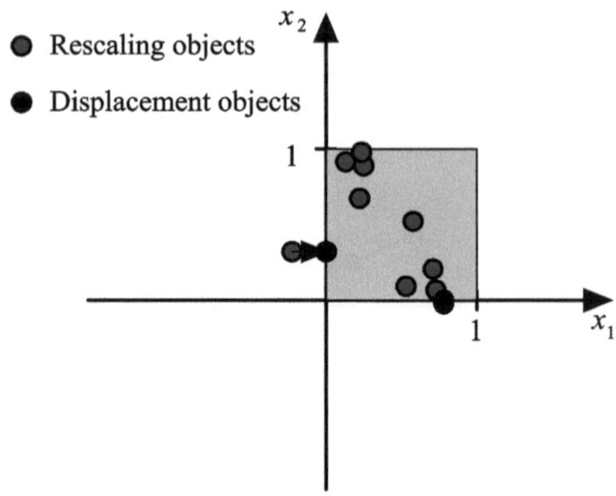

After scaling, some objects outside the highlighted area have coordinates greater than one or less than zero. Their coordinates should be corrected by reducing the coordinates greater than one to one and increasing the coordinates less than zero to zero. In Fig. 2.9, points representing objects with corrected coordinates are marked in black. This type of operation reduces the influence of large coordinate values on ranking. If a researcher is interested in objects that are relatively uniformly developed in all the analyzed indicators, then such a procedure is beneficial. This eliminates the case where objects with very low indices perform very well with one or two indices with very large values.

You can correct the coordinates by using the formula:

$$x''_{\substack{i\\j}} = \begin{cases} 0 \text{ for } \acute{x}_{\substack{i\\j}} < 0, \\ \acute{x}_{\substack{i\\j}} \text{ for } \acute{x}_{\substack{i\\j}} \in \langle 0; 1 \rangle, \\ 1 \text{ for } \acute{x}_{\substack{i\\j}} > 1, \end{cases} \tag{2.56}$$

where

$\acute{x}_{\substack{i\\j}}$—value of the i-th variable for the j-th object, following displacement and scaling of the set of points but before the coordinates correction.

There are many options for determining the area where most objects lie. For this purpose, for example, the standard deviation can be applied. In such a case, A_i coefficient can be calculated under the following formula:

$$A_i = \bar{x}'_i - w_\sigma \sigma_{x'_i}, \tag{2.57}$$

where

w_σ—parameter defining the size of the area accepted for that where the most objects are placed.

Coefficient B_i can be calculated under the formula:

$$B_i = 2w_\sigma \sigma_{x_i'}. \tag{2.58}$$

Knowing the distribution of the coordinate values a can be selected so that the specified percentage of the coordinate values is in the range $\left\langle \bar{x}_i' - w_\sigma \sigma_{x_i'}; \bar{x}_i' + w_\sigma \sigma_{x_i'} \right\rangle$.

It is also possible to use percentiles to delineate area where most of the objects lie. In this case, coefficient Ap_i can be calculated as follows:

$$A_i = \underset{j}{\text{percentyl}}_{100\% - \frac{w_p}{2}} \left(\underset{j}{x_i'} \right), \tag{2.59}$$

where

w_p—is a percentage of the coordinate population that belongs to the designated area ($w_p \leqslant 100\%$).

Coefficient B_i can be calculated under the following formula:

$$B_i = \frac{\underset{j}{x_i'}}{\underset{j}{\text{percentyl}}_{\frac{w_p}{2}} \left(\underset{j}{x_i'} \right) - \underset{j}{\text{percentyl}}_{100\% - \frac{w_p}{2}} \left(\underset{j}{x_i'} \right)}. \tag{2.60}$$

Percentile defines a value below which the given percentage of a coordinate value is placed. Coefficient w_p allows to define the limits of a range, where $w_p\%$ coordinate values are placed. The lower limit of this value is percentile $\underset{j}{\text{percentyl}}_{\frac{w_p}{2}} \left(\underset{j}{x_i'} \right)$, while the upper limit is percentile $\underset{j}{\text{percentyl}}_{100\% - \frac{w_p}{2}} \left(\underset{j}{x_i'} \right)$.

To define limits of the area where most of the coordinates are, the brightness and contrast correction method used in some devices for automatic printing and in digital cameras can be applied. The problem that occurs while image processing is similar to variables normalization. A certain range of values is used to save the images, most often ⟨0; 255⟩. However, as soon as it is captured, the image has a much larger range of values that must be narrowed down to the target value. In the simplest case, zeroed unitarization (in image processing called normalization) can be used, the value of which is multiplied by the target maximum value, usually 255. However, there is a problem of atypical values related to the large number of pixels in the image. This causes most of the values to be cumulated over a small fraction of the target range. As a consequence, the image does not appear to be very contrasting. To increase the contrast, normalization does not use extreme values, but two threshold values—left and right—determined under the special algorithm, most often based on histogram analysis.

A similar solution can be adopted for normalization of variables. Threshold values can be taken as a normalization base:

$$B_i = x'_{\mathrm{P}_i} - x'_{\mathrm{L}_i}, \tag{2.61}$$

where

x'_{P_i}—left threshold of the i-th variable,
x'_{L_i}—right threshold of the ith variable.

Threshold values, like for images, can be determined on the basis of the frequency histogram, but in the case of variables it is necessary to use the frequency histogram calculated for the value ranges. Such a histogram is determined for a predetermined number of intervals or their width, where the first case is so much more convenient that it is possible to determine what their minimum number should be approximately. Ideally, it should be of such a value that there are on average less than ten objects per one interval:

$$n_{\mathrm{P}} \leqslant \frac{n}{10}, \tag{2.62}$$

where

n_{P}—number of intervals.

In the first step of determining the frequency histogram, the range of values is determined by subtracting the minimum value from the maximum value:

$$\mathrm{zakr} = \max_j \left(x'_{i \atop j} \right) - \min_j \left(x'_{i \atop j} \right). \tag{2.63}$$

The range of values is the basis for calculating the width of intervals:

$$\mathrm{szer} = \frac{\mathrm{zakr}}{n_{\mathrm{P}}}. \tag{2.64}$$

It allows us to define the limits of individual intervals:

$$\begin{cases} g_{\mathrm{L}k} = \mathrm{szer}\,(k-1)\,, \\ g_{\mathrm{P}k} = \mathrm{szer}\,k, \end{cases} \tag{2.65}$$

where

$g_{\mathrm{L}k}$—left limit of the k-th interval,
$g_{\mathrm{P}k}$—right limit of the k-th interval.

The limits calculated in this way define the intervals, where one interval is always closed on both sides, and the remaining ones can be closed on the left side:

$$\left\langle g_{L1}, g_{P1}\right), \left\langle g_{L2}, g_{P2}\right), \ldots, \left\langle g_{Ln_p}, g_{Pn_p}\right\rangle \quad (2.66)$$

or right side

$$\left\langle g_{L1}, g_{P1}\right\rangle, \left(g_{L2}, g_{P2}\right\rangle, \ldots, \left(g_{Ln_p}, g_{Pn_p}\right\rangle. \quad (2.67)$$

The choice of the method of closing intervals when the number of objects is large does not have a significant impact on the result of variable normalization. For each interval, the number of the variable's values that belong to it is determined. This creates a frequency histogram whose bar heights depend on the number of all objects and the number of intervals. The more the objects, the higher the bars are. Whereas the more the intervals are, the more detailed the histogram illustrates the structure of a variable. In order to make the level of detail of the histogram independent from the number of objects and the number of intervals, they are rescaled:

$$\mathrm{h}_k = \frac{n_p \mathrm{h}_{cz\ k}}{n}, \quad (2.68)$$

where

$\mathrm{h}_{cz\ k}$—k-th element of the frequency histogram,
h_k—k-th element of the rescaled frequency histogram.

The rescaled frequency histogram is the basis for determining the left and right thresholds which are entered to the formula (2.61). The distribution of the values of variables is characterized by the presence of a certain area of accumulation of the most of values (Fig. 2.10). Outside this area, there are atypical values of a variable, which are quite rare. Due to the random occurrence of atypical values, they can be ignored when determining the left and right thresholds. The left and right thresholds can be taken as the limits of the accumulation of values. The first left-hand interval for which the minimum number of elements on the left side has been exceeded (prg_{Li}) is assumed as the left limit. Similarly, the first right-hand interval for which the minimum number of right-hand elements (prg_{Pi}) has been exceeded is taken as the right limit. Ultimately, x'_{Li} and x'_{Pi} will be the centers of intervals thus determined.

Values x'_{Li} i x'_{Pi} can also be determined as values of the fist and the third quartile. This method of determining is much simpler than the previous one, but it does not adapt exactly to the shape of the area in which points representing objects with typical variable values occur.

The effectiveness of using the histogram determines the size of the objects' set. In a small size sets, the effectiveness of the method presented above drops significantly, or it is even impossible to apply.

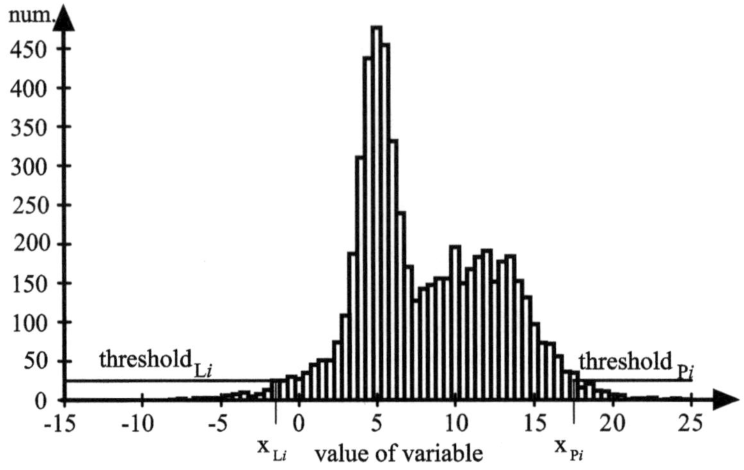

Fig. 2.10 Determination of x'_{Li} i x'_{Pi}

A certain variety of unitization methods are methods that use the maximum value of a variable as the normalization basis [140]:

$$B_i = \max_j \left(\begin{matrix} x'_i \\ j \end{matrix} \right), \tag{2.69}$$

or minimum [140]:

$$B_i = \min_j \left(\begin{matrix} x'_i \\ j \end{matrix} \right). \tag{2.70}$$

In the first case, the distance from the maximum value to zero is reduced to one, and in the second case, the distance from the minimum value to zero is reduced to one. Because absolute values are not taken into account, the obtained range of result in both cases should be considered depending on whether a variable takes negative values. For reasons of simplifications, we can assume that $p = 1$ i $A_i = 0$. In the simplest case, when the variable takes only positive values, taking the maximum value as the normalization basis, the obtained values will be in the range of $\langle 0; 1 \rangle$, where the occurrence of value equal to one is "guaranteed." This value is certain to occur, while the lower value of the range will depend on the minimum value of a variable and it will be less than zero.

If the minimum value is adopted as the normalization basis, the occurrence of a value equal to one is also guaranteed, but it is the minimum value. The maximum value can be either—greater than or equal to one. It will depend only on the value of a variable. When a variable can only have negative values, or positive and negative values, these ranges change (this is illustrated in Table 2.6).

Table 2.6 Dependence of the possible variable range after normalization on the presence of negative and positive values (for the normalization basis equal to the maximum and minimum value of the variable and $p = 1$ i $A_i = 0$)

B_i	Value of a variable before normalization Only positive	Only negative	Positive and negative
$\max_j \left(x'_{ij} \right)$	$\langle 0; 1 \rangle$	$\langle 1; \infty)$	$(-\infty; 1\rangle$
$\min_j \left(x'_{ij} \right)$	$\langle 1; \infty)$	$\langle 0; 1 \rangle$	$(-\infty; 1\rangle$

Table 2.7 The dependence of the possible variable range after normalization on the presence of negative and positive values (for the normalization basis equal to the maximum and minimum absolute value of the variable and $p = 1$ i $A_i = 0$)

B_i	Value of a variable before normalization Only positive	Only negative	Positive and negative
$\max_j \left| x'_{ij} \right|$	$\langle 0; 1 \rangle$	$\langle -1; 0 \rangle$	$\langle -1; 1 \rangle$
$\min_j \left| x'_{ij} \right|$	$\langle 1; \infty)$	$(-\infty; -1\rangle$	$(-\infty; -1\rangle$ i $\langle 1; \infty)$

Due to problems with changing the range of values, normalization bases equal to maximum and minimum values should not be applied if the values of a variable might be negative, but this is not certain. In such a case, normalization bases can be calculated under the following formulas:

$$B_i = \max_j \left| x'_{ij} \right|, \tag{2.71}$$

and:

$$B_i = \min_j \left| x'_{ij} \right|. \tag{2.72}$$

The range of values calculated under the formula (2.72) is discrete (Table 2.7). The distance of the smallest possible absolute value from zero is extended (or narrowed) to one. Therefore, there is a gap between values not less than two. Referring to the distance of the smallest value from zero is very disadvantageous in the situation where a variable can naturally assume values very close to zero. Population growth could be such an example. In this case, values significantly different from zero can take very high values. As a result, this can cause significant variations in the variable ranges. In the case of many aggregate measures, this may indicate the dominance of a variable with high value.

The range of values obtained according to formula: (2.71) is from minus one to one. This method, in terms of character, is similar to unitarization. If, due to the way in which an aggregate measure is created, it is necessary that it takes values from zero to one, the range of values can be easily reduced to one:

$$B_i = \frac{\max_j \left| x'_{i_j} \right|}{2}. \tag{2.73}$$

Assigning A_i parameter, the value of 0.5 will finally make the range from zero to one. This method also resembles unitization a bit, and the important difference here is that the minimum value is not taken into account and no "guarantee," is granted that the extreme values will occur. In the case of unitarization, the occurrence of extreme values is "guaranteed," while in this method the occurrence of only one extreme value is certain. If, for some reason, the left range of values is random, it seems more appropriate to use the absolute maximum value as the basis for the normalization, instead of the unitarization formula. An example of such a situation may be the presence of a very limited number of objects with values close to zero (assuming the positivity of a variable), as to which their occurrence in the studied population is not certain.

When it is important to keep the ratio of variability to mean values, the mean value can be used as the normalization base [140]:

$$B_i = \frac{\sum_{j=1}^{n} x'_{i_j}}{n}. \tag{2.74}$$

Standardization and unitization change the spectrum of variability, bringing them to a similar range. Sometimes the range of variation can be important in creating an aggregate measure. An example could be monthly household expenses. Expenditures on individual groups of articles depend on their average price. However, some expenses cannot be avoided, and therefore some costs are incurred at a similar level by different households, while the part of expenses depends on the level of wealth of individual households. The application of standardization or normalization would equalize the ranges of variability. In the case of necessary expenses, their minor differences, depending mainly on the random factor, would gain the same weight as differences for other expenses. This would cause the value of a measure to change, distorting the picture of reality to some extent. In this situation, the reference to the mean value is more favorable as it does not increase the importance of low volatility variables excessively. The mean value as the normalization basis makes the importance of a variable dependent on the ratio of variability to the mean value.

However, the use of a mean value can be very "dangerous" when the values of a variable fluctuate around zero. As a consequence, these values after normalization may be many times, even several thousand times higher than before normalization. In this way, variables oscillating around zero will have many importance times greater than other variables. This importance may be so great that practically the other variables will not affect the value of a measure. To overcome this inconvenience, the mean of absolute values can be used instead of the arithmetic mean:

$$B_i = \frac{\sum_{j=1}^{n} \left| x'_{i\,j} \right|}{n}. \tag{2.75}$$

This mean, even for values oscillating around zero, does not take values close to zero.

An alternative to the mean value can be the root mean square [140]:

$$B_i = \sqrt{\frac{\sum_{j=1}^{n} x'^2_{i\,j}}{n}}. \tag{2.76}$$

It is more sensitive to great values of variables than the mean value. Similarly, the mean value of absolute values, even for those oscillating around zero, does not give a value close to zero. Sometimes a problem can arise when using an average value and the variables have significantly different values. This is illustrated in Table 2.8. Two variables were normalized. The first one is where twelve objects have values approximately equal to one and three around ten. The second one, for the first twelve objects, has values equal to the first variable, and the next three are the values of the first variable minus eight.

After normalization with the mean value (for the objects with the highest values), the first variable on average obtained values 2.2 times greater than the second one. This means that this variable will have more weight for these objects than the others. After using the quadratic mean value, the first variable has an average value of 1.44 times greater than the second one. It follows that for these objects its importance in relation to other variables has decreased. Normalization by means of the quadratic mean can be applied wherever it is important that variables which differ from the others do not have too much influence on the measurement values of objects. However, this only applies to objects defined with high values of a variable. Unfortunately, a significant disadvantage of this normalization basis is that for objects with small values of a variable, it significantly reduces the share of a variable in creating the aggregate measure.

In the literature, you can also find the following normalization basis [107]:

$$B_i = \sqrt{\sum_{j=1}^{n} x'^2_{i\,j}}. \tag{2.77}$$

Table 2.8 Normalization with the use of mean and quadratic mean

		Base normalization			Base normalization	
Objects	x_1'	Mean value	Mean quadratic	x_2'	Mean value	Mean quadratic
Object 1	0.83	0.30	0.17	0.83	0.73	0.62
Object 2	0.61	0.22	0.13	0.61	0.54	0.46
Object 3	1.48	0.54	0.30	1.48	1.30	1.10
Object 4	0.78	0.29	0.16	0.78	0.69	0.58
Object 5	1.24	0.45	0.25	1.24	1.09	0.92
Object 6	0.52	0.19	0.11	0.52	0.46	0.39
Object 7	0.88	0.32	0.18	0.88	0.78	0.66
Object 8	0.57	0.21	0.12	0.57	0.51	0.43
Object 9	0.71	0.26	0.15	0.71	0.63	0.53
Object 10	1.38	0.50	0.28	1.38	1.22	1.03
Object 11	1.43	0.52	0.29	1.43	1.26	1.07
Object 12	0.74	0.27	0.15	0.74	0.66	0.55
Object 13	9.58	3.50	1.97	1.58	1.39	1.17
Object 14	10.35	3.79	2.12	2.35	2.07	1.75
Object 15	9.90	3.62	2.03	1.90	1.67	1.41
Mean value	2.73			1.13		
Mean						
Quadratic	4.87			1.34		

It is a variation of the quadratic mean and is equally sensitive to large variable values. Its value depends on the number of objects under studies, which makes the results incomparable when comparing the value of the measure from different tests. Such a comparison is possible only for vector aggregate measures and measures based on a weighted average. In the methods based on the distance from the pattern, such a comparison is not possible due to the very character of measure. With a large number of objects, this normalization basis results in obtaining the variable values of very small sizes. For the aggregate measure using the weighted average, it also results in very small values of the aggregate measure, which is unfavorable due to the presentation of the results. For vector aggregate and distance-based measures and for most distance measures, this normalization basis can be used interchangeably with the quadratic mean value. The results obtained for both standardization bases will be identical.

Factor A_i in the formula (2.45) accounts for displacement of normalized values in relation to zero. In the simplest case, where [98]

$$A_i = 0, \tag{2.78}$$

values of the normalized variables will be scaled in such a way that their distance from zero will decrease proportionally to the normalization basis (at $p = 1$). It is important that the level of normalized variables should be considered when creating an aggregate measure.

The mean value is often several times or greater than the volatility measures. Thus, when creating an aggregate measure, its weight will be many times greater than the weight of the volatility measure. This means that the value of the measure will be influenced mainly by the mean values of variables, causing the value of the measure to oscillate slightly around a certain value. For this reason, value levels are most often removed during normalization. For example, this can be done by assigning [98]

$$A_i = \frac{\sum_{j=1}^{n} x'_{ij}}{n}. \tag{2.79}$$

This causes the normalized values to oscillate around zero. If, for methodological reasons, it is unacceptable for a normalized variable to assume negative values, then the minimum values should be used [98]:

$$A_i = \min_j \left(x'_{ij} \right). \tag{2.80}$$

This is important for some distance measures used to create aggregate measures based on the distance from a pattern, for example, Clark's measure or Jeffreys–Matusit's measure. By using a minimum value, the values will always be greater than or equal to zero, with the "guaranteed" occurrence of zero. The disadvantage of this approach is that all values of the variable depend on the extreme minimum. In this case, the value of the measure will be influenced by adding or not including the objects with the lowest value of the variable in the set of objects under studies.

In situation, when B_i is calculated under the formula (2.61), as value A_i can be

$$A_i = x'_{\mathrm{L}i}. \tag{2.81}$$

As a result, the lower limit of the cumulative value of variable will be zero, and the upper will be one. It means, however, that a normalized variable can assume values less than zero and greater than one. If it is important that the values of a variable fall between zero and one, you can assign all values less than zero to zero and greater than one.

So far, methods of normalizing the variables have been presented. The value of each variable creates the coordinate of examined objects in a space with as many dimensions as there are objects under consideration. It is also possible to normalize the coordinates of objects using the formula:

$$x''_{\substack{i\\j}} = \frac{x'_{\substack{i\\j}}}{\sqrt{\sum_{i=1}^{m} x'^2_{\substack{i\\j}}}}, \tag{2.82}$$

where

$$\sum_{i=1}^{m} x'^2_{\substack{i\\j}} > 0$$

This normalization causes that the Euclidean distance of a point from the origin of the coordinate system will be equal to one. Distance-to-reference methods should use the Euclidean distance measure. If the objects are treated not as points but as space vectors, the normalization can be expressed as follows:

$$\underset{j}{X''} = \frac{\underset{j}{X'}}{\sqrt{\left(\underset{j}{X'}, \underset{j}{X'}\right)}}, \tag{2.83}$$

where

$$\left(\underset{j}{X'}, \underset{j}{X'}\right) > 0$$

$\underset{j}{X'}$—vector representing the j-th object,
$\underset{j}{X''}$—vector representing the j-th object after normalization.

where $\left(\underset{j}{X'}, \underset{j}{X'}\right)$ should be understood as the dot product of the vector $\underset{j}{X'}$ on itself Mostly,

$$\left(\underset{j}{X'}, \underset{j}{X'}\right) = \sum_{i=1}^{m} x'^2_{\substack{i\\j}}. \tag{2.84}$$

For this reason, the formula (2.83) is expressed as follows: (2.82). The vectors representing the objects thus become unit vectors.

After normalization, all points representing objects will be located on the surface of the sphere with the center at the origin of the coordinate system and the radius equal to one. Such an operation will result in bringing all objects to the same scale (understood as a geometric scale, not a measurement scale). For example, a household may have a different number of people. Spending on individual products will depend on the number of people in a household. If on a single-person household certain amounts are spent on certain food items, then on a two-, three-, or more-person household, two, three, or more times will be spent on these items, respectively. By standardizing the coordinates, this scale effect will be leveled and the variables for these farms will take the same values.

By normalizing the coordinates, the objects are reduced to one scale. The value of variables ceases to be important, but only their mutual relations. The normalization of coordinates does not require the reference of indicators that later create variables to the area, the total population, or other such reference points, making the values independent of the scale, because the scale of objects is removed. This is especially useful where the reference of the scale is difficult to determine. If indicators independent of the scale of objects are used as variables, then the use of this type of normalization is not necessary. It can be used in parallel with other normalization methods.

Different variables can have different meanings for the decision-maker, and therefore, after normalizing, they can be multiplied by weights:

$$\underset{j}{x''_{\mathrm{w}\,i}} = \mathrm{w}_i \underset{j}{x''_i}, \tag{2.85}$$

where

$\mathrm{w}_i > 0$
$\underset{j}{x''_{\mathrm{w}\,i}}$—the weighted value of variable.

The higher the w_i, weighted value, the greater the influence of the variable on the value of the aggregate measure.

2.3.1 Studies on A_i Properties

Most normalization methods perform two operations: move the set of points and change the coordinate scale of the points. In order to thoroughly examine the properties of individual normalization methods, it is possible to isolate these two operations and examine them separately. Hence, it is possible to examine the influence of A_i and B_i on normalization results separately. For research purposes, test sets were generated consisting of 6, 16, 66, 150, 380 and 700 objects. The values 6, 16, 66 and 700 roughly correspond to the number of territorial units for each NUTS in Poland. The coordinates of the points of these sets have normal distribution. They were generated so that they had mean values of approximately 2 for x_1 and 1 for x_2 and x_3. The standard deviation of the coordinates of the points is approximately 1 for x_1 i x_3 and 2 for x_2. An example set of 66 elements is presented in Fig. 2.11.

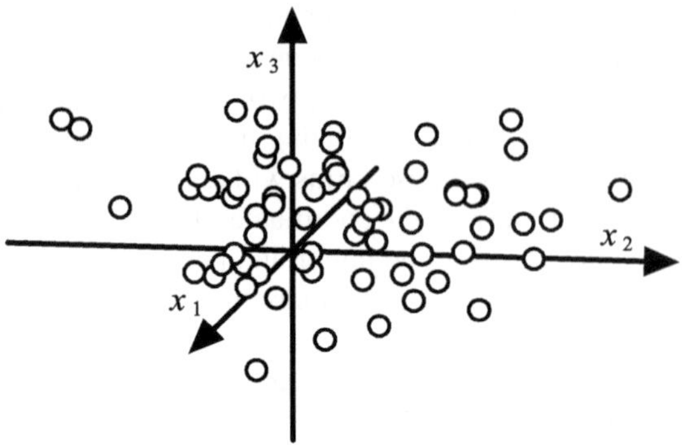

Fig. 2.11 Sample test set of 66 elements

A_i is responsible for displacement of the set of points. However, some factors may interfere with the correct determination of the A_i value. These factors include noise, incompleteness of the set of objects, the appearance of atypical objects in the set, and displacement of objects resulting from the use of outdated data. In order to check the susceptibility of A_i of individual normalization methods to these factors, a coefficient ${}_p\overset{k}{w}_A$ was defined. It determines how the values of the coordinates of the points differ after normalizing coordinates themselves and coordinates on which a certain operation was performed with k parameter for the p-th randomly selected set of objects:

$$ {}_p\overset{k}{w}_A = \frac{\sum_{j=1}^{n}\sum_{i=1}^{m}\left|\mathrm{norm}\left({}_p\underset{j}{x_i'}\right) - \mathrm{norm}\left({}_p\overset{k}{\underset{j}{\hat{x}_i'}}\right)\right|}{nm}, \tag{2.86} $$

where

norm—normalization function,
${}_p\underset{j}{x_i'}$—i-th coordinate of the j-th object from the p-th, selected set,
${}_p\overset{k}{\underset{j}{\hat{x}_i'}}$—$i$-th coordinate of the j-th object from the p-th, selected set, on which some operation was performed with the parameter k.

Operations performed on coordinates will simulate factors that may interfere with the correct determination of A_i value. Value of three was taken as m Value of three was taken as B_{ij} and one as. As a result, changes in coordinate values to which objects are subjected will not affect B_i. As a result, the normalization formula is reduced as follows:

$$ \underset{j}{x_i''} = \mathrm{norm}\left(\underset{j}{x_i'}\right) = \underset{j}{x_i'} - A_i. \tag{2.87} $$

Seven types of A_i coefficients were tested:

1.
$$A_i = \bar{x}_i'. \tag{2.88a}$$

2.
$$A_i = \min_j \left(\begin{matrix} x_i' \\ j \end{matrix} \right). \tag{2.88b}$$

3.
$$A_i = \max_j \left(\begin{matrix} x_i' \\ j \end{matrix} \right). \tag{2.88c}$$

4.
$$A_i = \operatorname{median}_j \left(\begin{matrix} x_i' \\ j \end{matrix} \right). \tag{2.88d}$$

5.
$$A_i = \bar{x}_i' - w_\sigma \sigma_{x_i'}. \tag{2.88e}$$

Values of the normalizing function smaller than zero are converted to 0 and greater than $2w_\sigma \sigma_{x_i'}$ to $2w_\sigma \sigma_{x_i'}$. The value of w_σ has been taken as 1.64485, which with normal distribution ensures that 90% of observations are in the main range.

6.
$$A_i = \underset{j}{\operatorname{percentile}}_{100\% - \frac{w_p}{2}} \left(\begin{matrix} x_i' \\ j \end{matrix} \right). \tag{2.88f}$$

Values of the normalizing function smaller than zero are converted to 0, while greater than

$\underset{j}{\operatorname{percentile}}_{\frac{w_p}{2}} \left(\begin{matrix} x_i' \\ j \end{matrix} \right)$ to $\underset{j}{\operatorname{percentile}}_{\frac{w_p}{2}} \left(\begin{matrix} x_i' \\ j \end{matrix} \right)$. The value of 90 has been taken as w_p, which means that 90% of observations are within the main range.

7.
$$A_i = 0. \tag{2.88g}$$

As the result of research for each method and each value of k parameter a series of ${}_{p}\overset{k}{w}_{A}$ coefficients will be created, which can be presented on the chart. Due to the size of tests carried out, the number of the resulting charts would be very large. For one test it would be 14 methods that would need to be multiplied by 6 test sets of different size, resulting in 84 charts. The analysis of such a number would be difficult. Therefore, based on ${}_{p}\overset{k}{w}_{A}$, coefficient is calculated ${}_{p}\overline{w}_{A}$:

$$
{}_{p}\overline{w}_{A} = \frac{\sum\limits_{k \in \{k_1, k_2, \ldots, k_{m_k}\}} {}_{p}\overset{k}{w}_{A}}{m_k}, \tag{2.89}
$$

where

$k_1, k_2, \ldots, k_{m_k}$—tested values of parameters,
m_k—number of tested parameters.

${}_{p}\overline{w}_{A}$ is the mean value of ${}_{p}\overline{w}_{A}$ coefficients in the scope of analyzed parameters $k_1, k_2, \ldots, k_{m_k}$. This allows for a simple comparison of the analyzed methods. The lower the ${}_{p}\overline{w}_{A}$ value for a given method, the better the properties of a method. Because a set of objects was selected randomly, its distribution in space changed. The effect is that ${}_{p}\overline{w}_{A}$ may vary depending on objects distribution in space. On the basis of ${}_{p}\overline{w}_{A}$, coefficient for different distribution of objects in space two coefficients can be calculated:

$$
\overline{\overline{w}}_{A} = \frac{\sum\limits_{p=1}^{m_p} {}_{p}\overline{w}_{A}}{m_p}, \tag{2.90}
$$

where

m_p—number of test sets of equal size (in all studies $m_p = 10{,}000$),

and

$$
\zeta_{{}_{p}\overline{w}_{A}} = \frac{\sqrt{\dfrac{\sum\limits_{p=1}^{m_p} \left({}_{p}\overline{w}_{A} - \overline{\overline{w}}_{A}\right)^2}{m_p}}}{\overline{\overline{w}}_{A}}, \tag{2.91}
$$

where $\overline{\overline{w}}_{A}$ defines how much, on average, the points of coordinates differ after the normalization of coordinates and coordinates on which a certain operation was performed. $\zeta_{{}_{p}\overline{w}_{A}}$ shows a research experiment, to what extend ${}_{p}\overline{w}_{A}$ depends on the distribution of objects in space.

The first study in which A_i coefficients mentioned above were analyzed was the determination of susceptibility to noise. Recorded data are usually overlapped by certain information noise, which may be the effect of measurement errors, errors in estimating the values of indicators, incorrect estimation of data by experts, measurement of indicators' values at a specific point in time when data is subject to cyclical or seasonal fluctuations, etc. The existence of this noise means that a certain part of the indicator value depends on the case. Therefore, it is necessary to answer the question, to what extent will this noise affect the normalization process?

In the carried out study, the coordinates of the test set of points were changed using two approaches. In the first one, the randomly selected value was added to each coordinate of the individual set of points. These values were normally distributed with a mean value of zero and a constant standard deviation (in a given study):

$$ {}_{p}\overset{k}{\underset{j}{\hat{x}'_i}} = {}_{p}\underset{j}{x'_i} + k \,\mathrm{randn}_{0;1}, \tag{2.92} $$

where

$\mathrm{randn}_{0;1}$—a randomly selected value (a normal distribution with a mean value equal to zero and standard deviation equal to 1).

The above method of ${}_{p}\overset{k}{\underset{j}{\hat{x}'_i}}$ determination maps the situation, where several factors affect the value of the indicator, one of which is random. In the study, the value of k was changed from 0.1 to 0.5 in step of 0.01. The determined values of $\overline{\overline{w}}_A$ coefficient are presented in Fig. 2.12. With a very small number of objects, the one that uses the mean value turned out to be the best method. As the number of objects increases, the advantage of this method decreases, and when the number of objects is large, the percentile method turns out to be the best. The worst are the methods based on the minimum and maximum, and with a very small number of objects, also the method that takes into account the standard deviation. The weakness of the methods based on the minimum and maximum results from the fact that the displacements of the entire set of points depend in this case on one extreme object. The other methods calculate the displacement of the objects based on the entire set of coordinates values. The effect of normally distributed information noise is being reduced because the noise values cancel each other out when considering a larger number of objects. Hence it follows the similarity of the results of the other methods and the similarity to the case when the set of objects is not moved. Big differences occur only with small numbers of the set of objects.

In the second approach, the randomly selected value was also added to each coordinate of all set points. They had a normal distribution with a mean value of

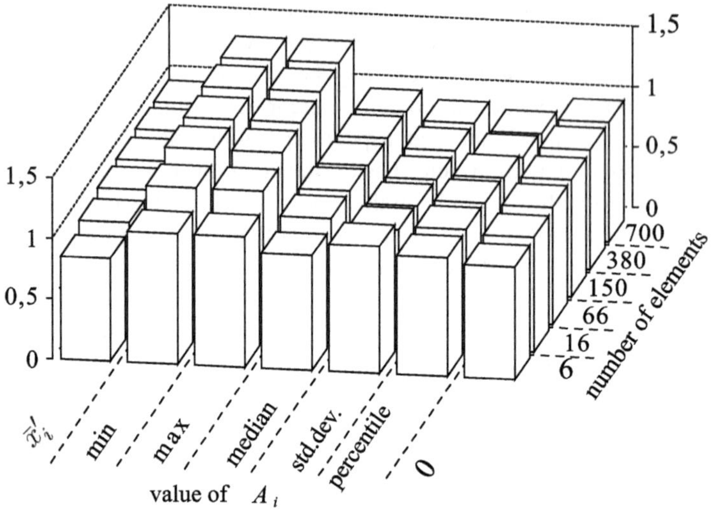

Fig. 2.12 Testing susceptibility to noise independent of the coordinate value

zero and a standard deviation depending on the coordinate value:

$$\underset{j}{{}_{p}\overset{k}{\hat{x}}{}'_{i}} = \underset{j}{{}_{p}x'_{i}} + k\,\underset{j}{{}_{p}x'_{i}}\mathrm{randn}_{0;1}, \tag{2.93}$$

where

$\mathrm{randn}_{0;1}$—a randomly selected value (a normal distribution with a mean value equal to zero and standard deviation equal to1).

This maps the situation where the random value results from inaccuracy in determining the level of indicator. If an expert estimates an indicator value, the estimation error will depend on the range of the estimated value. Some measurement methods introduce the similar error. In the study, the value of k was being changed from 0.1 to 0.5 in steps of 0.01. The determined values of the $\overline{\overline{w}}_A$ coefficient are presented in Fig. 2.13. The obtained values were very similar to the previous ones. The main difference is the very poor results for methods using maximum. This is because the objects with the largest coordinate values have the greatest noise amplitude.

When conducting research, we are not always able to guarantee a full set of objects. For example, when making rankings of European Union countries, it very often turns out that data is not available for some countries. In this case, the objects for which data is missing must be removed from the set. However, this data may appear over time. Then, the question arises, how can the exclusion of an object from the set affect the normalization results? For this purpose, a test set was selected randomly, and then in the next steps objects were taken out one by one until 25% of

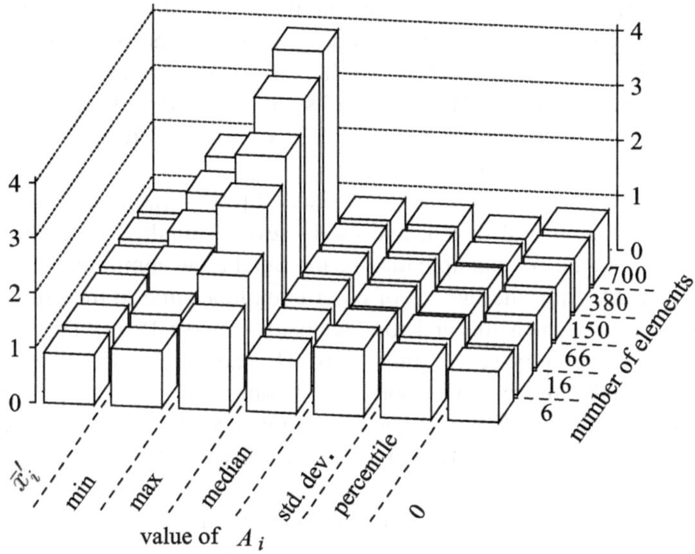

Fig. 2.13 Testing of susceptibility to noise depending on the coordinate value

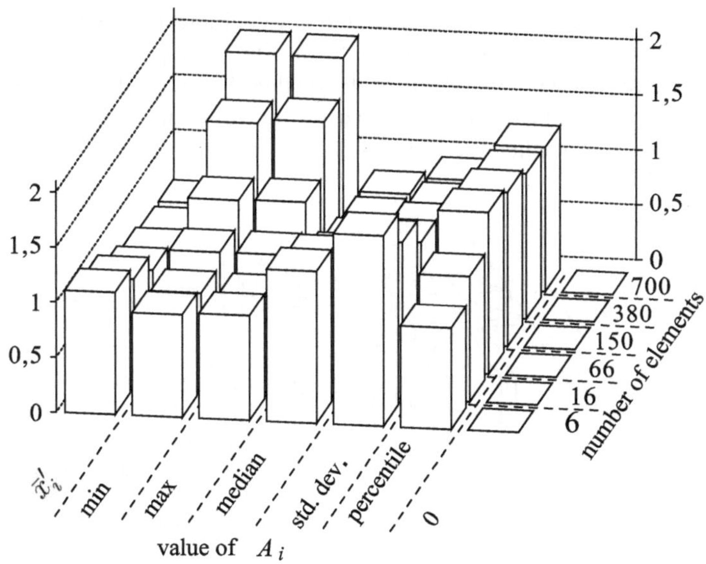

Fig. 2.14 Testing sensitivity to missing objects

all objects were removed. The determined values of $\overline{\overline{w}}_A$ coefficient are presented in Fig. 2.14.

When reducing objects, the method using the mean value turned out to be the most universal. For a small number of objects, it is only slightly worse than the maximum, minimum, and percentile methods. As the size of the set of objects increases, the method using the mean value gives better and better results, and for medium and large sets it is the best. In the case of the minimum and maximum methods, the case is reverse. The best results are achieved with a small number of objects in a set. As their number increases, worse and worse results appear, and the deterioration is very significant.

Sometimes the research includes atypical objects, which may usually have several, sometimes several dozen, and rarely several hundred times higher index values than the others. An example may be the Bełchatów commune, whose indices differ significantly from the indices of other communes due to the presence of the Bełchatów Brown Coal Mine and the Bełchatów Power Plant. They change the indices related to ecology very significantly. This adversely affects its position in ranking while analyzing economic potential of communes (despite high incomes).

The aim of the next study was to check the influence of atypical objects on the Ai coefficient. For this purpose, one of the objects was moved along the OX axis. The standard deviation of the set of objects along this axis was 2. Displacement began and ended at the distance of 8 along the OX axis from the center of the set of objects. The determined values of $\overline{\overline{w}}_A$ coefficient are presented in Fig. 2.15. Because $\overline{\overline{w}}_A$ takes very large values for some A_i, the figure does not show the full height of the bars representing $\overline{\overline{w}}_A$. They are marked with crosses.

The analyzed methods of determining the $\overline{\overline{w}}_A$ coefficient show that the one that used the median turned out to be the least sensitive to atypical objects. Close but slightly worse results were obtained for the method based on the mean value. The worst results were obtained by the method using the minimum and maximum, where in extreme cases $\overline{\overline{w}}_A$ reached the value of 60–80.

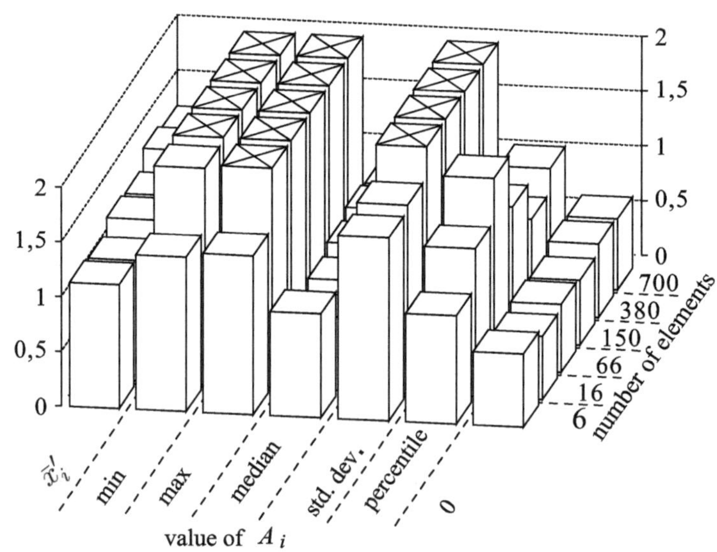

Fig. 2.15 Testing sensitivity to atypical objects

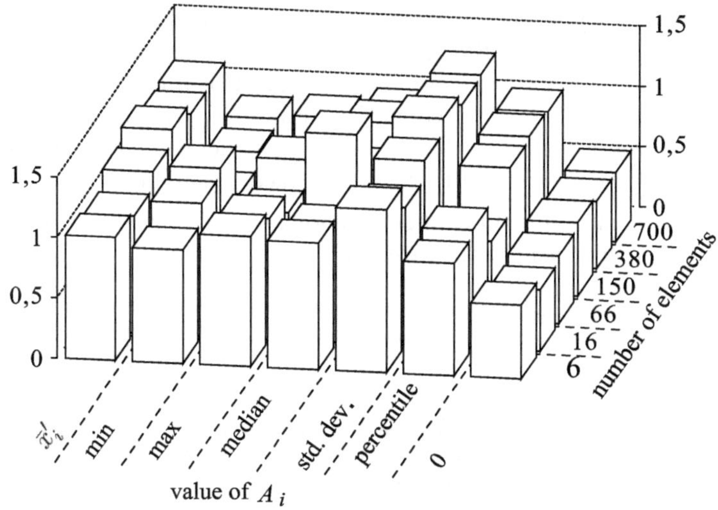

Fig. 2.16 Testing susceptibility to changing the position of one of the objects

Objects evaluate over time. Therefore, the values of their indicators also change over time, which entails a change in their position. However, this should not affect the position of other objects. Due to the fact that during normalization a set of objects is displaced based on a value calculated on the basis of coordinates of all objects, a change in the position of one of them will affect the coordinates of the other objects. To check the degree of this influence, one of the set of objects is selected randomly and then moved to a randomly chosen place in space. The determined values of the $\overline{\overline{w}}_A$ coefficient are presented in Fig. 2.16.

The tested methods are characterized by more or less similar sensitivity to change the location of one of the objects. The method that uses standard deviation is slightly more sensitive, but the difference between this method and other methods is unimportant.

2.3.2 Studies on B_i Properties

Some aggregate measures are insensitive to displacement of the set of points, and therefore A_i value is irrelevant for them. This applies to measures whose values are counted in relation to a reference point determined on the basis of a data set provided to them. An example may be aggregate measures constructed according to Hellwig's method, where the reference point is a pattern established based on data (from the observation matrix, from a finite sample).

The B_i value is responsible for the scale change that is performed to eliminate the influence of measurement units and the size of value levels on the ranking. For example, if a ranking includes two indicators *income per capita* and *the percentage of people with higher education*, then in the case of pattern measures, the latter indicator will have a very small impact on ranking. This is due to its much smaller values. Therefore, the correct selection of the scale change factor is very important. To test normalization methods in terms of their properties related to the scale change the change of coordinates coefficient was defined specifying how the values of coordinates of points ${}_{p}\overset{k}{w}_{B}$, differ after the normalization of coordinates themselves and coordinates on which a certain operation was performed:

$$
{}_{p}\overset{k}{w}_{B}=\frac{\sum_{j=1}^{n}\sum_{i=1}^{m}\left[1-\min\left\{\left|\frac{\operatorname{norm}\left({}_{p}\underset{j}{x'_{i}}\right)}{\operatorname{norm}\left({}_{p}\underset{j}{\overset{k}{\hat{x}'_{i}}}\right)}\right|;\left|\frac{\operatorname{norm}\left({}_{p}\underset{j}{\overset{k}{\hat{x}'_{i}}}\right)}{\operatorname{norm}\left({}_{p}\underset{j}{x'_{i}}\right)}\right|\right\}\right]}{nm}. \tag{2.94}
$$

Operations on coordinates will simulate factors that may interfere with the correct determination of B_i. Value of three was taken as m and zero as A_i. As the result, changes in coordinate values to which objects are subjected will not affect B_i. As a result, the normalization formula is reduced as follows:

$$
\underset{j}{x''_{i}}=\operatorname{norm}\left(\underset{j}{x'_{i}}\right)=\frac{\underset{j}{x'_{i}}}{B_{i}}. \tag{2.95}
$$

Fourteen types of $B_i$coefficients were subject to the research:

1.

$$
B_{i}=\sigma_{x'_{i}}. \tag{2.96a}
$$

2.

$$
B_{i}=\bar{x}'_{i}. \tag{2.96b}
$$

3.

$$
B_{i}=\min_{j}\left(\underset{j}{x'_{i}}\right). \tag{2.96c}
$$

4.

$$
B_{i}=\max_{j}\left(\underset{j}{x'_{i}}\right). \tag{2.96d}
$$

5.

$$B_i = \max_j \left(x'_{i_j} \right) - \min_j \left(x'_{i_j} \right). \tag{2.96e}$$

6.

$$B_i = \operatorname*{median}_j \left(x'_{i_j} \right). \tag{2.96f}$$

7.

$$B_i = \operatorname*{percentile_{25\%}}_j \left(x'_{i_j} \right). \tag{2.96g}$$

8.

$$B_i = \operatorname*{percentile_{0.75\%}}_j \left(x'_{i_j} \right). \tag{2.96h}$$

9.

$$B_i = \operatorname*{percentile_{75\%}}_j \left(x'_{i_j} \right) - \operatorname*{percentyl_{25\%}}_j \left(x'_{i_j} \right). \tag{2.96i}$$

10.

$$B_i = \sqrt{\sum_{j=1}^{n} \left(x'_{i_j} \right)^2}. \tag{2.96j}$$

11.

$$B_i = \sqrt{\frac{\sum_{j=1}^{n} \left(x'_{i_j} \right)^2}{n}}. \tag{2.96k}$$

12.

$$B_i = 2w_\sigma \sigma_{x'_i}. \tag{2.96l}$$

Values of the normalizing function less than $\acute{\bar{x}}_i - 0.5$ are converted to $\acute{\bar{x}}_i - 0.5$, while greater than $\acute{\bar{x}}_i + 0.5$ to $\acute{\bar{x}}_i + 0.5$. $\acute{\bar{x}}_i$ is the mean value of i variable after normalization. Like before, 1.64485 was taken as w_σ .

13.

$$B_i = \underset{j}{\text{percentile}_{\frac{w_p}{2}}}\left(\begin{matrix} x_i' \\ j \end{matrix}\right) - \underset{j}{\text{percentile}_{100\%-\frac{w_p}{2}}}\left(\begin{matrix} x_i' \\ j \end{matrix}\right). \tag{2.96m}$$

Values of normalizing function less than $\underset{j}{\text{percentile}_{100\%-\frac{w_p}{2}}}\left(\begin{matrix} \acute{x}_i \\ j \end{matrix}\right)$ are converted to $\underset{j}{\text{percentile}_{100\%-\frac{w_p}{2}}}\left(\begin{matrix} \acute{x}_i \\ j \end{matrix}\right)$, while greater than $\underset{j}{\text{percentile}_{\frac{w_p}{2}}}\left(\begin{matrix} \acute{x}_i \\ j \end{matrix}\right)$ to $\underset{j}{\text{percentile}_{\frac{w_p}{2}}}\left(\begin{matrix} \acute{x}_i \\ j \end{matrix}\right)$. Like before, 90% was taken as w_p .

14.

$$B_i = 1. \tag{2.96n}$$

Based on determined ${}_p\overset{k}{w}_B$, coefficients like it was in the case of study on A_i, the following coefficient is calculated:

$${}_p\overline{w}_B = \frac{\sum\limits_{k\in\{k_1,k_2,\ldots,k_{m_k}\}} {}_p\overset{k}{w}_B}{m_k}, \tag{2.97}$$

and

$$\overline{\overline{w}}_B = \frac{\sum\limits_{p=1}^{m_p} {}_p\overline{w}_B}{m_p}. \tag{2.98}$$

It is also possible to determine the following coefficient:

$$\zeta_{{}_p\overline{w}_B} = \frac{\sqrt{\frac{\sum\limits_{p=1}^{m_p}\left({}_p\overline{w}_B - \overline{\overline{w}}_B\right)^2}{m_p}}}{\overline{\overline{w}}_B}. \tag{2.99}$$

Analogous method like for A_i coefficient was applied in the analysis. For research purposes, test sets consisting of 6, 16, 66, 150, 380, and 700 objects were generated. The values 6, 16, 66, and 700 roughly correspond to the number of territorial units for individual NUTS in Poland. The coordinates of the points of these sets have normal distribution. They were generated so that they had mean values of approximately 2 for x_1 and 1 for x_2 and x_3. The standard deviation of the coordinates of points is approximately 1 for x_1 and x_3 and 2 for x_2.

The first study in which B_i coefficients mentioned above were tested was the susceptibility to noise. At the beginning, to each of coordinates of all points, the randomly selected value according to the formula (2.92) was added. Initially, the value of k was changed from 0.1 to 0.5 in step of 0.01. The determined values of $\overline{\overline{w}}_B$ coefficient are presented in Fig. 2.17. Most methods achieve similar results. For an average and small number of objects, the methods using the minimum and the first quartile are relatively weak. For a very small number of objects, poor results are also obtained for the method that takes into account the difference of quartiles.

In the second study, the randomly selected value, depended on the variable according to the formula (2.93), was also added to each coordinate of individual set of points. In the research, the value of k was changed from 0.1 to 0.5 in a step of 0.01. The determined values of $\overline{\overline{w}}_B$ coefficient are presented in Fig. 2.18. The best results are obtained with the quadratic mean method and the root of the sum of squares. They have a very similar method of determining, and they obtain very similar results. Methods using the third quartile and standard deviation also perform well (2.961). For sets of very small size, the method based on the difference of quartiles is the worst. For medium and large size, methods using the minimum,

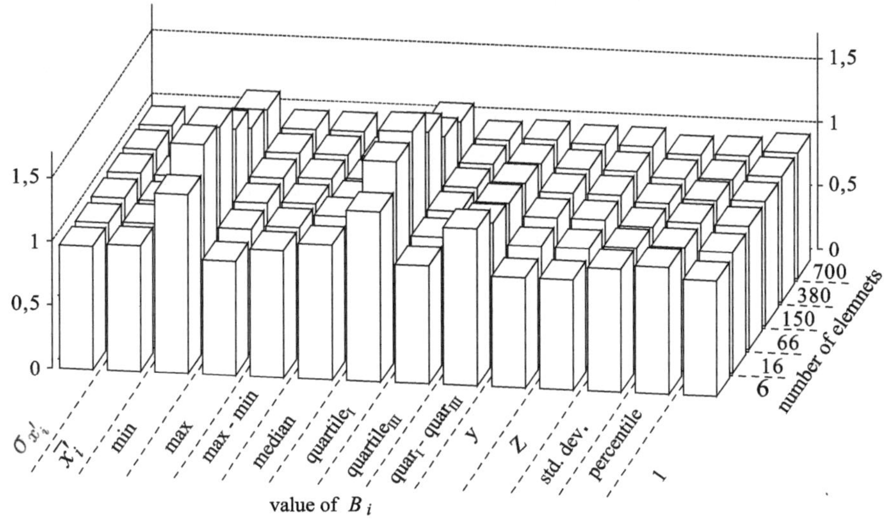

Fig. 2.17 Testing susceptibility to noise independent of the coordinate value

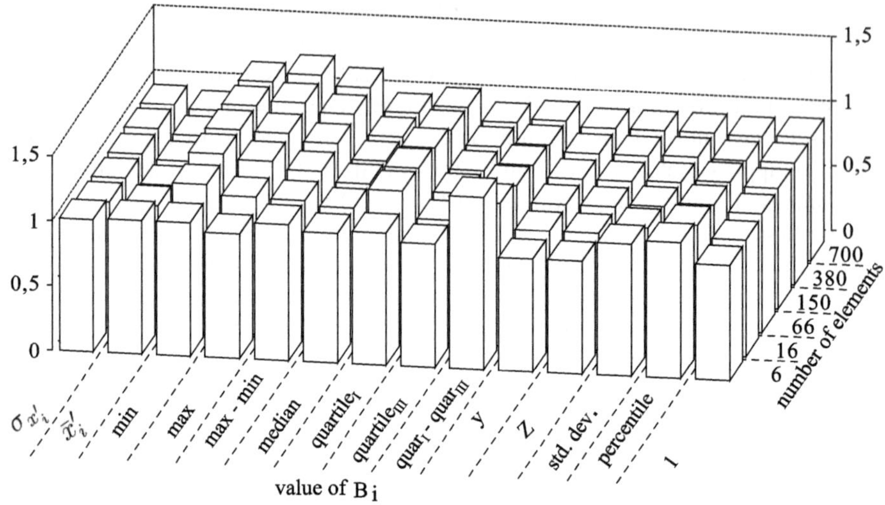

Fig. 2.18 Testing susceptibility to noise depending on the level of the coordinate value

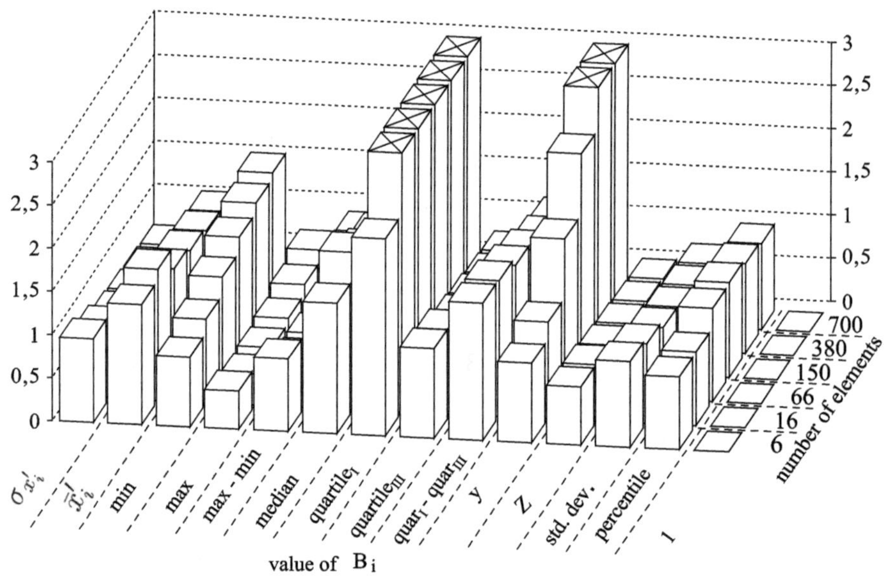

Fig. 2.19 Testing sensitivity to missing objects

maximum, and the difference between the maximum and the minimum are slightly worse.

In order to test the sensitivity to missing objects, a test set was randomly selected, and then in the next steps one object was eliminated until 25% of all objects were removed. The determined values of the $\overline{\overline{w}}_A$ coefficient are presented in Fig. 2.19. The methods using the maximum and the quadratic mean turned out to be the best.

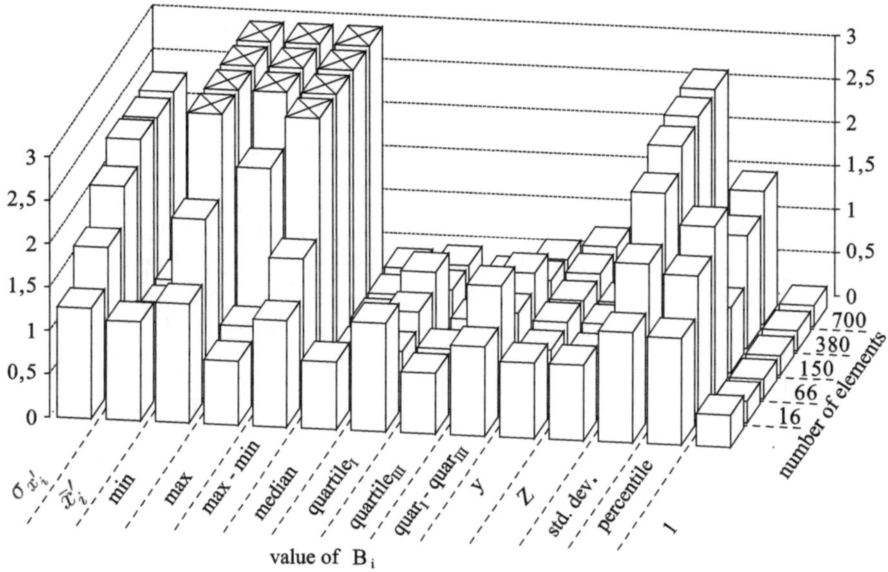

Fig. 2.20 Testing sensitivity to atypical objects

For larger reductions, the method based on the III quartile and the standard deviation also performs well. With medium and high reduction of objects, the method using the I quartile and the root of the sum of squares is very poor.

The aim of the next study was to check the influence of atypical objects on normalization results. One of the objects was moved along the OX coordinates axis. The standard deviation of the set of objects along this axis was 2. The move started at 8 along the axis OX from the center of the set of objects and also ended at the same distance. The object shifted as it moved through the set of objects. The test results are presented in Fig. 2.20. Methods that use the median, third quartile, root of the sum of squares and quadratic mean give the best results. For a medium and large number of objects, the worst results were obtained for the methods using the minimum, maximum, and the difference between the maximum and minimum. The obtained results practically disqualify these methods from being used in collections of medium and large numbers, when these sets include atypical objects.

The last test was to check the sensitivity to change the location of one of the objects. Due to the fact that one of the objects moves, the coefficient $\overline{\overline{w}}_B$ does not have a zero value even at B_i equal to zero. This is the limit case and it is not possible to go below the value of this coefficient. The determined values of $\overline{\overline{w}}_B$ coefficient are presented in Fig. 2.21. The methods using the root of the sum of squares and the quadratic mean also performed well. The poor performance gave methods based on the I quartile, the median, and the III quartile. With small displacements, the methods using the minimum, I quartile, and III quartile achieved worse results.

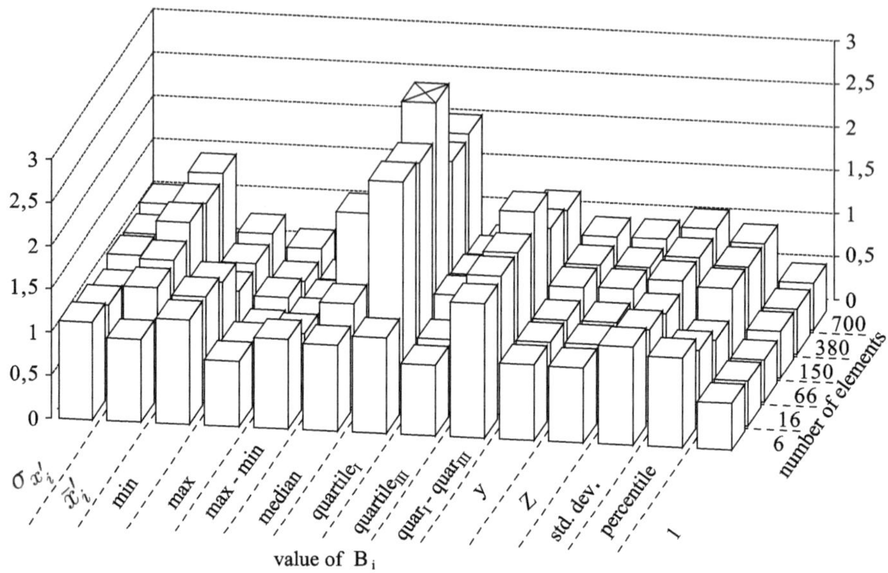

Fig. 2.21 Testing susceptibility to changing the position of one of the objects

When building an aggregate measure, with some methods it is necessary to change the character of the variables from a destimulant, a nominant to a stimulant. Replacing a destimulant with a stimulant in accordance with the formula (2.21)–(2.25) is necessary when building an aggregate measure using the weighted arithmetic mean. For the other discussed methods, for example, Hellwig's and VMCM methods, there is no need to perform such a conversion. The choice of a formula is important when calculating the aggregate measure using the weighted arithmetic mean, while the order and distance between the objects does not change. This is of particular importance when the researcher determines the scope of a measure. For example, the range can be zero to one or zero to one hundred. In the first case, the variables should also be in the range from zero to one (formula 2.24). While, in the second, when the variables are given as percentages, the formula (2.25) should be used in the range from zero to one hundred. For the methods that use the similarity measures, any of the formulas (2.21)–(2.25) can be applied. The method of its selection is not important for measures that are invariants of displacement (for example, Euclid measure, square of Euclid, city, Bray–Curtis [131]).

The choice of a normalization method may have a significant influence on the selection of conversion from a destimulant to a stimulant. For example, for all normalization methods that remove the mean value and bring the extreme values to a predetermined level, the choice of any of the formulas (2.21)–(2.25) will not affect the result.

Table 2.9 presents a comparison of various A_i and B_i coefficients. The given results are summarized for a different number of objects. The letter r means that

Table 2.9 Comparison of normalization methods

	6 objects	16 objects	66, 150 objects	380, 700 objects
A_i—impact of noise type 1 on test results				
r	$\bar{x}_i'$, 0	$\bar{x}_i'$, 0	Std. dev., $\bar{x}_i'$	Percentile, std. dev.
nr	Max, min	Max, min	Max, min	Max, min
B_i—impact of noise type 1 on test results				
r	$\sqrt{\sum_{j=1}^{n}\left(x_i'\right)_j^2}$, $\sqrt{\frac{\sum_{j=1}^{n}\left(x_i'\right)_j^2}{n}}$	$\sqrt{\sum_{j=1}^{n}\left(x_i'\right)_j^2}$, $\sqrt{\frac{\sum_{j=1}^{n}\left(x_i'\right)_j^2}{n}}$	Std. dev., $\sqrt{\sum_{j=1}^{n}\left(x_i'\right)_j^2}$, $\sqrt{\frac{\sum_{j=1}^{n}\left(x_i'\right)_j^2}{n}}$	Std. dev., $\sqrt{\sum_{j=1}^{n}\left(x_i'\right)_j^2}$, $\sqrt{\frac{\sum_{j=1}^{n}\left(x_i'\right)_j^2}{n}}$
nr	Min, quartile I	Min, quartile I	Min, quartile I	Min, quartile I
A_i—impact of noise type 2 on test results				
r	$\bar{x}_i'$, 0	0, $\bar{x}_i'$	Percentile, 0	Percentile, std. dev.
nr	Max, std. dev.	Max, min	Max, min	Max, min
B_i—impact of noise type 2 on test results				
r	$\sqrt{\sum_{j=1}^{n}\left(x_i'\right)_j^2}$, $\sqrt{\frac{\sum_{j=1}^{n}\left(x_i'\right)_j^2}{n}}$	$\sqrt{\sum_{j=1}^{n}\left(x_i'\right)_j^2}$, $\sqrt{\frac{\sum_{j=1}^{n}\left(x_i'\right)_j^2}{n}}$	1, $\sqrt{\frac{\sum_{j=1}^{n}\left(x_i'\right)_j^2}{n}}$	Std.dev. $\bar{x}_i'$
nr	Quartile difference, percentile, max–min	Quartile I, min	Min, max	Min, max
A_i—testing sensitivity to missing objects				
r	0, percentyl	0, max	0, $\bar{x}_i'$	0, $\bar{x}_i'$
nr	Std. dev., median	Std. dev. median	Percentile, max	Max, min
B_i—testing sensitivity to missing objects				
r	1, max	1, max	1, max	1, $\sqrt{\frac{\sum_{j=1}^{n}\left(x_i'\right)_j^2}{n}}$
nr	Quartile I, quartile difference	Quartile I quartile difference	Quartile I, $\sqrt{\sum_{j=1}^{n}\left(x_i'\right)_j^2}$	Quartile I, $\sqrt{\sum_{j=1}^{n}\left(x_i'\right)_j^2}$

(continued)

Table 2.9 (continued)

	6 objects	16 objects	66, 150 objects	380, 700 objects
A_i—testing sensitivity to atypical objects				
r	0, median	0, median	0, median	0, median
nr	Std. dev., max	Max, min	Max, min	Max, min
B_i—testing sensitivity to atypical objects				
r	1, quartile III	1, median	1, quartile III	1, quartile III
nr	Min, std. dev.	Min, std. dev.	Min, max-min	Min, max-min
A_i—Ai—testing sensitivity to changing the position of one object				
r	0, percentile	0, median	0, median	0, min
nr	Std. dev., max	Std. dev., min	Std. dev., $\bar{x}_i'$	Std. dev., $\bar{x}_i'$
B_i—testing sensitivity to changing the position of one object				
r	1, max	1, max	1, max	1, max
nr	Quartile difference, min	Quartile I, quartile difference	Quartile I, quartile difference	Quartile I, $\bar{x}_i'$

the coefficient is recommended for a given number of objects and the number—not recommended, while normalization of variables the researcher should not use non-recommended coefficients.

Chapter 3
Methods of Building the Aggregate Measures

3.1 Patternless Reference Methods

The normalized values of features are the base for calculating the measure describing a studied object. Depending on the selected variables, this measure may determine, for example, the competitiveness of an enterprise, the development of a region, investment attractiveness, etc. It is called an aggregate measure, and usually, based on the value of this measure, objects can be ordered linearly. Hence, measurement construction methods are often called linear ordering methods. These methods are divided into patternless and pattern—referenced methods. The patternless methods include three varieties of the average value [56]: arithmetic mean, harmonic mean, and geometric mean.

Calculations are performed on the normalized values of variables. If the value of a measure is to be in the range of $\langle 0; 1\rangle$, use the normalizing formula given by the formula (2.45), with the coefficient p equal to one, A_i equal to the minimum value of a variable, and B_i is being the difference between the maximum and minimum values of a variable. An alternative may be to use the standard deviation or percentiles according to the procedure described in Sect. 2.3. Ideally, all variables should be stimulants. If there is a destimulant and a nominant present, they can be converted into stimulants. Weights can be determined in three ways [56]: by the expert method, with the use of computational algorithms, utilizing information contained in the variables themselves, and by methods that are a combination of both methods.

After normalizing the variables, the weighted arithmetic mean can be used to determine the aggregate measure value [56]:

$$\underset{j}{\mathrm{m_s}} = \frac{1}{m}\sum_{i=1}^{m} \mathrm{w}_i \underset{j}{x_i''}, \tag{3.1}$$

K. Nermend, *Multi-Criteria and Multi-Dimensional Analysis in Decisions*, Vector Optimization, https://doi.org/10.1007/978-3-031-40538-9_3

gdzie:

$\underset{j}{\mathrm{m_s}}$—value of the synthetic feature for the j-th object

$\underset{j}{x_i''}$—normalized value of the i-th variable for the j-th object

w_i—weight of the i-th variable

In the literature, to calculate the value of an aggregate measure, another form of weighted arithmetic mean called ranking according to the synthetic feature can be found [98]:

$$\underset{j}{\mathrm{m_s}} = \sum_{i=1}^{m} \mathrm{w}_i \underset{j}{x_i''}. \tag{3.2}$$

The weights determine the "importance" of individual variables, and the greater it is for a given variable, the greater share of a given variable in creating an aggregate measure. In the simplest case, the weights can be equal to each other. If it is assumed that each of the weights is equal to the reciprocal of the number of variables, then formula (3.2) changes into the ordinary arithmetic mean.

Most often, the sum of weights is assumed to be equal to one [98]:

$$\sum_{i=1}^{m} \mathrm{w}_i = 1. \tag{3.3}$$

This condition is assumed to ensure a range of measure values approximately equal to the range of variables. So if, for example, the values of normalized variables are in the range of zero to one, the values of the measure will also fall in this range. Equation (3.2) can be reduced as follows:

$$\sum_{i=1}^{m} \mathrm{w}_i \underset{j}{x_i''} - \underset{j}{\mathrm{m_s}} = 0. \tag{3.4}$$

This is the equation of the hyperplane in $m + 1$ dimensional space, where $\underset{j}{x_i''}$ and $\underset{j}{\mathrm{m_s}}$ are unknown, and w_i are equation coefficients. Each object can be presented as a point on this hyperplane (Fig. 3.1). Therefore, it consists of all possible values of the normalized variables and the corresponding values of a measure. Because for all variables equal to zero the aggregate measure is also equal to zero, the hyperplane always passes through the origin of the coordinate system.

Ranking by synthetic feature assumes that all variables are stimulants. Thus, for all variables greater than zero, the measure value is also greater than zero. The ranking can also be performed with the simultaneous use of a stimulant and a destimulant. In this case, negative weight values should be used for destimulants.

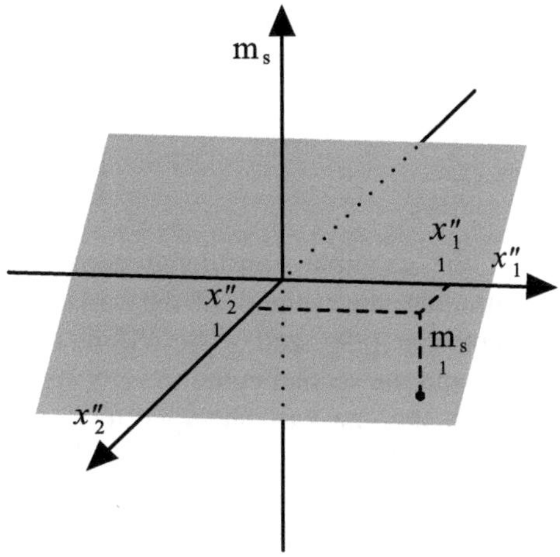

Fig. 3.1 Geometric interpretation of ranking according to the synthetic feature

If the possibility of negative weight values is assumed, then using condition (3.3) it is not possible to provide a range of weights similar to the variable range.

The following example can be given. Let us assume the weight values be ten for the first variable and minus nine for the second variable. So the sum of them is one. Variables are normalized in the range from zero to one. For some object, the value of the first variable is one and the second is zero. The value of the measure is therefore ten. If the situation changes and the first variable is zero and the second variable is one, the value of the measure will be minus one. So the range is minus nine to ten. To keep the range of measure values limited to zero from the bottom, and to any value from the top, the measure value should be calculated following the formula:

$$\underset{j}{\mathrm{m_s}} = \frac{\mathrm{z_g}}{2} + \sum_{i=1}^{m} \begin{cases} \dfrac{n_\mathrm{s}}{n_\mathrm{s}+n_\mathrm{d}} \mathrm{w}_i^+ \underset{j}{x_i''} & \text{for stimulants,} \\ \dfrac{n_\mathrm{d}}{n_\mathrm{s}+n_\mathrm{d}} \left(-\mathrm{w}_i^-\right) \underset{j}{x_i''} & \text{for destimulants,} \end{cases} \tag{3.5}$$

where:

$\mathrm{z_g}$—upper range of variables.
w_i^+—positive object weights.
w_i^-—negative object weights.
n_s—the number of stimulants.
n_d—the number of destimulants.

The range of all variables must be the same as the target range of a measure. Additionally, the following conditions have to be met:

$$\begin{cases} \sum_{i=1}^{n_s} \mathrm{w}_i^+ = 1, \\ \sum_{i=1}^{n_d} \mathrm{w}_i^- = 1. \end{cases} \tag{3.6}$$

In the example considered above, where there is only one stimulant and destimulant, the weights of the variables should be equal to one and minus one, respectively, $\frac{n_s}{n_s+n_d}$ and $\frac{n_d}{n_s+n_d}$ will be equal to 0.5. Then for the first variable equal to one and the second equal to zero, the measure value will be $0.5 + 0.5 + 0 = 1$. Then for the first variable equal to zero and the second variable equal to one, the measure will be $0.5 + 0 - 0.5 = 0$. Thus, the range is between zero and one.

For variables whose range is symmetric around zero (in order to maintain this range), the following formula can be used to calculate the measure (3.2). However, the condition that has to be met by weights will be as follows:

$$\sum_{i=1}^{m} |\mathrm{w}_i| = 1. \tag{3.7}$$

It is visible that the use of weights is much simpler for variables with negative values and symmetric range relative to zero. Let us assume the range of variables from minus one to one for one stimulant and one destimulant with weights 0.5 and −0.5, respectively. Then the measure will get the maximum value for the first variable equal to one and the second equal to minus one. The obtained result is $0.5 * 1 - 0.5 * (-1) = 1$. The smallest value can be obtained for the first variable equal to minus one, and the second equal to one: $0.5 * (-1) - 0.5 * 1 = -1$. So the range is as expected and stays from minus one to one.

An alternative to the weighted mean can be the weighted harmonic mean [56]:

$$\underset{j}{\mathrm{m_s}} = \frac{m}{\sum_{i=1}^{m} \frac{\mathrm{w}_i}{\underset{j}{x_i''}}}, \tag{3.8}$$

and the geometric mean [56]:

$$\underset{j}{\mathrm{m_s}} = \left[\prod_{i=1}^{m} \left(\underset{j}{x_i''} \right)^{\mathrm{w}_i} \right]^{\frac{1}{m}}. \tag{3.9}$$

In the case of the weighted harmonic mean, it is possible to use weights that satisfy the condition (3.3). Then the formula (3.8) can be reduced as follows:

$$\underset{j}{m_s} = \frac{1}{\sum_{i=1}^{m} \frac{w_i}{\underset{j}{x''_i}}}. \tag{3.10}$$

The main advantage of ranking with the use of patternless measures is the uncomplicated construction of a measure based on a very simple formula. There is no need to define the pattern like it is in reference methods.

3.2 Distance Reference Pattern-Based Methods

Distance reference pattern-based methods are a large group of methods. Z.Hellwig developed the methodological foundations of these methods in [73]. He proposed the concept of the so-called taxonomic measure of development, which is understood as the ordering of the studied units depending on the distances achieved by them from a certain, artificially constructed point called the development pattern. The taxonomic measure of development is an aggregate value that is the resultant of all variables defining the units of a studied group. Therefore, it is used for the linear ordering of the elements of a given group.

W. Tarczyński used the following set of features to estimate the Taxonomic Measure of Investment Attractiveness (TMAI) ratio of hypothetical profit to net profit, dynamics of net profit, rate of return, risk of rate of return, beta ratio, current liquidity ratio, quick liquidity ratio, profitability, debt rate, receivables turnover, inventory turnover, liability turnover, efficiency of fixed assets, and return on equity. This made it possible to build a portfolio of securities based on a criterion resulting from an aggregate measure [195, 196, 198].

Another example of the use of the aggregate measure is the method of determining the standard of leaving in European countries presented in [61]. It is calculated on the basis of seven diagnostic variables from the demographic, economic, and technical infrastructure areas, using the linear ordering method. This enabled the assessment of Poland's delay compared to other European countries in the years 1960, 1970, 1980 and forecasting for 1990.

In distance reference methods, the value of a measure is determined based on the distance from an accepted standard (Fig. 3.2). The main issues affecting the value of the measure are: appropriate selection of the normalization method, selection of the pattern, and selection of the distance measure.

The pattern can be selected on a discretionary basis by selecting one of the objects considered to be the best based on knowledge and expert opinion. This method of selecting a standard is rarely used because it assumes that all variables are nominants with optimal values equal to the standard coordinate (Fig. 3.3).

In practice, it is often the case that it is not possible to distinguish one pattern, but several, each of which has some variables with desired values and others with

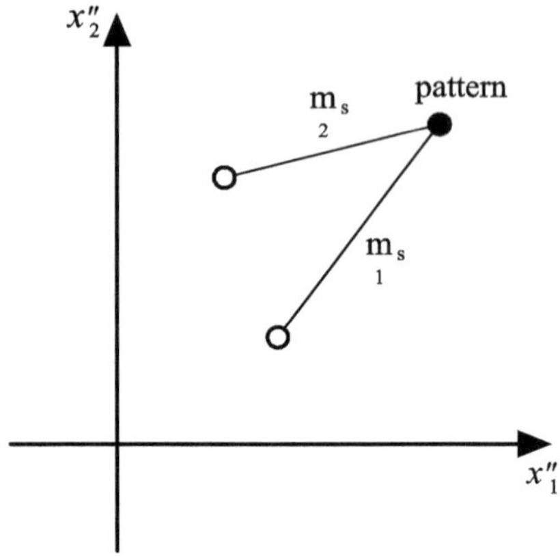

Fig. 3.2 Geometric interpretation of distance reference pattern-based methods

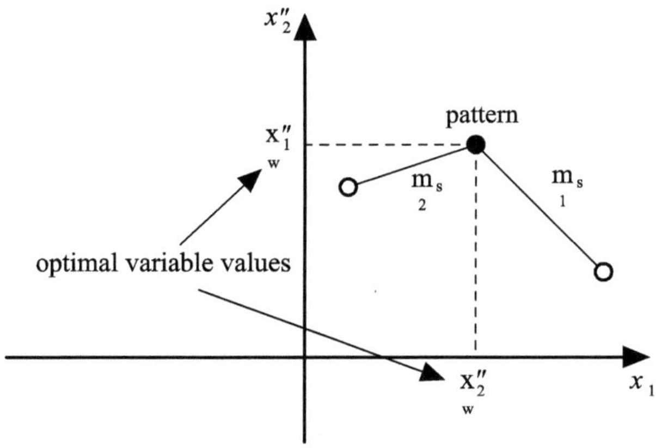

Fig. 3.3 Optimal variables values

average values. In this situation, the choice of any of these patterns as the measure standard will result in the optimal measure value being the coordinates of the measure. Even if the values of the variables higher than the measure standard are more desirable, the measure will "treat" them as worse, because they are not equal to the optimal values.

The inconvenience of a need to determine optimal values of variables is removed by creating an ideal pattern, not necessarily having an equivalent in reality. The variables here are divided into stimulants, destimulants, and dominants. For stimulants, the highest value of the variable for all objects is taken as the coordinate of a pattern, for the destimulants—the lowest value, and for nominants—the optimal value:

$$\underset{\mathrm{w}}{x_i''} = \begin{cases} \max_j x_{ij}'' & \text{for stimulants,} \\ \min_j x_{ij}'' & \text{for destimulants,} \\ \mathrm{o}_i & \text{for nominants,} \end{cases} \tag{3.11}$$

where:

$\underset{\mathrm{w}}{x_i''}$—$i$-th coordinate of a pattern.
o_i—optimal value of the i-th feature.

In case of nominants for which optimal values fall within a certain range $\langle \mathrm{o}_{\mathrm{d}i}; \mathrm{o}_{\mathrm{g}i} \rangle$, the coordinates of a pattern change dynamically depending on the coordinate values of the object for which the measure value is calculated:

$$\underset{\mathrm{w}}{x_i''} = \begin{cases} 0 \ \text{for} & \underset{\mathrm{w}}{x_i''} \in \langle \mathrm{o}_{\mathrm{d}i}; \mathrm{o}_{\mathrm{g}i} \rangle, \\ \mathrm{o}_i \ \text{for} \ \underset{\mathrm{w}}{x_i''} < \mathrm{o}_{\mathrm{d}i} \vee \underset{\mathrm{w}}{x_i''} > \mathrm{o}_{\mathrm{g}i}. \end{cases} \tag{3.12}$$

Thanks to the application of an ideal pattern, the measurement values can be calculated based on stimulants, destimulants, and nominants. However, it makes each study "limited." At the beginning of the study, a set of analyzed objects is defined and cannot be extended. If tests are not carried out once, but periodically, it will be a considerable inconvenience. When it is necessary to compare the test results from different periods, a common pattern should be established for data on objects from individual cycles. In practice, this means that in each subsequent period in which calculations are performed, a new pattern must be determined and all calculations for the previous time cycles must be performed again. It is not possible to use aggregate measures that have been calculated earlier.

An aggregate measure is calculated for each object as its distance from the pattern. Therefore, there is a need to adopt a specific measure. Due to their comparative nature, they should meet the following strong postulates:

1. There must be a value for the maximum similarity that can only occur when an object is compared to itself.
2. The similarity of object A to B should be the same as object B to A (symmetry).

Failure to meet the first postulate leads to the appearance of lines or curves along which the measure of similarity is zero. The distance from objects depends on their location in space. The measure of similarity must be very well suited to the nature of the compared objects. Comparing is possible here, but the measure of similarity practically must be created specifically for a given type of objects, or adjusted to the objects by regulating appropriate parameters. It is an extremely difficult task and the measures are not universal.

Failure to meet the second postulate is possible only in the case of assigning objects to given classes, when the pattern is imposed in advance. In the case of grouping algorithms in which the division into classes is automatic, this can lead to assigning objects to classes depending on the order in which the algorithm processes them.

Additionally, to increase the compliance of similarity measures with our intuition, and thus facilitate the interpretation of the results, two weak postulates can be imposed:

1. The measure should be a metric.
2. Increase in difference between any coordinates of objects should increase the measure and decrease in difference of coordinates—decrease the measure.

The construction of aggregate measures is the creation of a certain comparative indicator that tells about the degree of objects development. It is created from a comparison with a certain pattern, but the goal is not to compare with that pattern, but to compare objects with each other. Such an assumption causes the postulates for aggregate measures to change. Strong postulates as such cannot be formulated here due to the fact that we compare all objects only with a pattern that is constant for a given study. However, we can distinguish a few weak postulates:

1. Increasing the difference between any coordinates of objects should increase the measure, and decreasing the coordinates—decrease the measure.
2. The measure cannot be limited in any way, neither from the bottom nor from the top.
3. Changing the scale of the compared objects should not affect the value of the measure.
4. The measure should not impose any restrictions on the coordinate values of objects.

The first postulate has to be satisfied only if we are interested in coordinate values, and not in their relations. Let us assume that an object is a very small poviat for which the variable value of administrative area i 400 km^2, and the population 50 K. We compare it with a much larger poviat whose area is equal to 1600 km^2 and population 200 K. It is clearly visible that despite the large difference in the variable values, they are very similar poviats because their population density is the same. In fact, we are not interested in the values of the coefficients themselves, but in their mutual relations.

The second postulate contradicts the strong postulate for the similarity measures mentioned before. This is due to the fact that the character of a pattern here is slightly different. It is a unit of measurement, i.e., its nature resembles a one-meter standard. The value of the similarity measure of a pattern with itself is here the limit that divides objects into better and worse than the pattern. We are never sure if there will be an object worse than the worst we know now, and we are never sure if there will be an object better than the best known to us. Thus, the measure cannot be limited in any way, either from the bottom or from the top.

The variables that are used to create an aggregate measure have different scales of values. An example would be an area of thousands and a population as much as hundreds of thousands. From this, the third postulate follows. If it is not satisfied, it causes a strong dominance of variables with large values. Measures that meet this postulate are not so susceptible to this domination.

Measures should not impose restrictions on the possible variable values, as this limits their application to specific issues. Of course, it is possible to reduce the variables to the required range, but this may cause the scale of values to change and the mean value to shift. In some situations, this may affect the results of subsequent comparisons.

One feature that can be attributed to measures is invariance with respect to geometric transformations. Invariance means that a given transformation does not affect the measure value, i.e., performing a given transformation on a set of points will not change the measure value. There are three types of transformations with respect to which invariance can be considered: shift, scale change, and rotation. Considering the last of these transformations—rotation—usually does not make sense in the context of coordinates that are variables describing the parameters of socio-economic objects.

Invariance with respect to displacement means that moving all points by any identical vector will not change the distance between them. For measures of such type, any value can be taken as A_i. In the formula (2.45) for measures that are scale invariants, Bi parameter is not important. Regardless of its value (excluding zero), the value of the measure will be the same. Thus it can be assumed that $A_i = 0$.

Scale invariance means that multiplying the coordinates by any value will not change the distance between them. In the formula (2.45) for measures that are scale invariants, B_i. Regardless of its value (excluding zero), the value of the measure will be the same. Thus it can be assumed that $B_i = 1$.

Invariance with regard to scale is important especially when very large and very small objects are included in one study. For example, these may be enterprises employing several people and several thousand. The use of ordinary distance measures will cause that very small objects will have very similar measurement values, which in turn will make it difficult to distinguish between them. A measure that is invariant to the scale will cause the spacing between objects to also depend on the size of their coordinates. For “small” objects will be larger than for the normal measure, and for “large” objects smaller. As a result, it is possible to distinguish between objects with small and large values quite well.

In practice, the problem of different scales of objects is eliminated by creating indicators related to certain parameters determining the scale of objects. For example, the coordinates that define the enterprise can be divided by the number of employees, and the coordinates that define the commune by its area or population. As a result, the use of distance measures that are invariant to the scale is not necessary.

In some situations, however, the use of these measures may be appropriate. An example may be a study in which a certain size of an object is considered optimal, and at the same time very “small” and very “large.” Objects occur next to each other. Objects that are too large can be considered inappropriate as well as objects that are too small. The use of indicators causes that the information about the scale is irretrievably lost, while the measures that are scale invariants only result

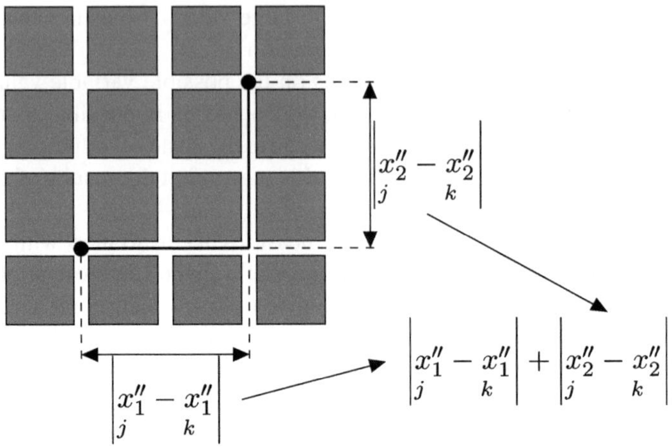

Fig. 3.4 City metrics

in greater distinguishability of objects with small coordinate values. Therefore, in the presented example, it is necessary to use this type of measures.

An illustration of measures that are invariants of displacement can be Minkowski's measures [211]:

$$\mathrm{d}\left(\underset{j}{X''}, \underset{k}{X''}\right) = \sqrt[p]{\sum_{i=1}^{m} \left|\underset{j}{x''_i} - \underset{k}{x''_i}\right|^p}, \tag{3.13}$$

where:

$\mathrm{d}\left(\underset{j}{X''}, \underset{k}{X''}\right)$—distance between points $\underset{j}{X''}$ and $\underset{k}{X''}$.
$\underset{j}{x''_i}, \underset{k}{x''_i}$—coordinates of points $\underset{j}{X''}$ and $\underset{k}{X''}$.
p—parameter that is a non-zero positive number.
m—the number of space dimensions.

These measures are metrics. For $p = 1$, a measure called the city metric is created [211]:

$$\mathrm{d}\left(\underset{j}{X''}, \underset{k}{X''}\right) = \sum_{i=1}^{m} \left|\underset{j}{x''_i} - \underset{k}{x''_i}\right|. \tag{3.14}$$

The name of the measure comes from the method of determining the distance that must be covered in cities where all streets intersect at right angles (Fig. 3.4). Due to the fact that buildings interfere with moving in a straight line, the road can only be passed along horizontal or vertical streets.

In formula (3.13) at $p = 2$, one of the most frequently used metrics is obtained, the Euclidean metric [211]:

$$d\left(\underset{j}{X''}, \underset{k}{X''}\right) = \sqrt{\sum_{i=1}^{m}\left(\underset{j}{x''_i} - \underset{k}{x''_i}\right)^2}. \tag{3.15}$$

Its popularity is due to an intuitive understanding of how it measures distances. It is a metric of the surrounding reality as seen on the human scale. The distance between points is taken along the straight line joining two points. The extreme case of Minkowski's measures is the Chebyshev metric, for which $p \to \infty$ [211]:

$$d\left(\underset{j}{X''}, \underset{k}{X''}\right) = \max_i \left|\underset{j}{x''_i} - \underset{k}{x''_i}\right|. \tag{3.16}$$

In this metric, the distance is taken as the greatest absolute difference between two coordinates.

Minkowski's metrics meet both strong and weak postulates of similarity measures. They enable easy interpretation of the obtained results but do not meet all the postulates of aggregate measures. They are limited from the bottom, and the minimum measure value is always zero. As a consequence, this leads to a situation where a pattern must always be the best.

An example of a measure invariant to scale is the Clark's measure [211]:

$$d\left(\underset{j}{X''}, \underset{k}{X''}\right) = \sqrt{\frac{1}{m}\sum_{i=1}^{m}\left(\frac{\underset{j}{x''_i} - \underset{k}{x''_i}}{\underset{j}{x''_i} + \underset{k}{x''_i}}\right)^2}. \tag{3.17}$$

The Clark measure should only be used for variables with positive values. The value of the maximum similarity of a measure is zero, and the value of maximum similarity is one. Clark's measure achieves maximum dissimilarity in two cases: when one of the compared points has all coordinates equal to infinity or when all coordinates are equal to zero.

Another example of a measure invariant to scale is the Canberra measure [211]:

$$d\left(\underset{j}{X''}, \underset{k}{X''}\right) = \sum_{i=1}^{m}\frac{\left|\underset{j}{x''_i} - \underset{k}{x''_i}\right|}{\underset{j}{x''_i} + \underset{k}{x''_i}}. \tag{3.18}$$

This measure has similar properties to the Clark's measure and should only be used for positive variables. The value of the maximum similarity of the measure is zero, while the value of the maximum similarity is m (the number of variables). The Canberra measure reaches the maximum dissimilarity in two cases: when one of the compared points has all coordinates equal to infinity or when all coordinates equal zero. Canberra can be normalized to a range between zero and one:

$$d\left(\underset{j}{X''}, \underset{k}{X''}\right) = \frac{1}{m}\sum_{i=1}^{m}\frac{\left|\underset{j}{x''_i} - \underset{k}{x''_i}\right|}{\underset{j}{x''_i} + \underset{k}{x''_i}}. \tag{3.19}$$

Due to the way the measure is determined, the Clark's measure is equivalent to the Euclidean metric and the Canberra measure is the city metric. However, they are not invariant with regard to displacement.

In addition to distance measures, a measure that compares directions and the level of correlation is sometimes used [211]:

$$d\left(\underset{j}{X''}, \underset{k}{X''}\right) = \frac{\sum_{i=1}^{m}\left(\underset{j}{x''_i} - \underset{j}{\bar{x}''}\right)\left(\underset{k}{x''_i} - \underset{k}{\bar{x}''}\right)}{\sqrt{\sum_{i=1}^{m}\left(\underset{j}{x''_i} - \underset{j}{\bar{x}''}\right)^2}\sqrt{\sum_{i=1}^{m}\left(\underset{k}{x''_i} - \underset{k}{\bar{x}''}\right)^2}}. \tag{3.20}$$

This measure is invariant to the displacement and independent of the scale of the object's value. If you multiply all the coordinates of the object by the same value, it will not affect the result of comparison. However, if you multiply the value of one of variables of all objects by the same value, the value of the measure will be affected. This measure is only a partial invariant of the scale. Hence, when normalizing the variables for this measure, the value of B_i in formula (2.45) is important, while the value of A_i is irrelevant. It is one of the few measures that is a shift invariant and at the same time a partial scale invariant.

The value of the correlation coefficient is one or minus one when features are similar and zero when they are dissimilar. A value of minus one means the same direction, but the opposite head of vectors. For time series, the correlation compares vectors representing a data variable component. It is marked in Fig. 3.5 as A_{zm}. Because A_{sr} vectors representing the constant portion of data are always perpendicular to the vectors representing the variable portion of data, this reduces the space in which the comparison is performed by one dimension. The effect is that in two-dimensional space it can only reach the value of one or minus one because all vectors of the variable's value always have the same direction, and they can only have the opposite head (Fig. 3.5b). It follows that as a measure of comparison with the pattern, when creating an aggregate measure of correlation, you can only use the number of variables greater than two.

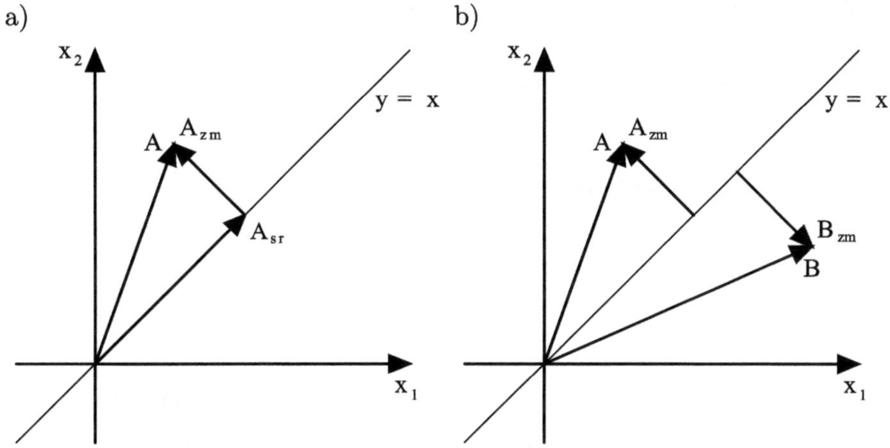

Fig. 3.5 Comparison of vectors by means of correlation: (**a**) division of a vector into a vector representing a constant and a variable component [18]; (**b**) comparing two vectors in a two-dimensional space

The values of the measures of the distance between the objects and the reference objects can be considered as the values of the aggregate measure:

$$\underset{j}{\mathrm{m_s}} = \mathrm{d}\left(\underset{j}{X}, \underset{\mathrm{w}}{X}\right), \tag{3.21}$$

where:

$\underset{j}{\mathrm{m_s}}$—value of the aggregate measure: for the j-th object.
$\underset{j}{X}$—a vector representing the j-th object.
$\underset{\mathrm{w}}{X}$—a vector representing a pattern.

If the values of distance measures do not allow obtaining values in the range from zero to one, then the values of the aggregate measure are normalized to this range [150]:

$$\underset{j}{\mathrm{m'_{sn}}} = \frac{\underset{j}{\mathrm{m_s}}}{\mathrm{m_{s0}}}, \tag{3.22}$$

where $\underset{j}{\mathrm{m'_{sn}}}$ is the normalized value of $\underset{j}{\mathrm{m_s}}$. The value of $\mathrm{m_{s0}}$ can be calculated under the formula [150]:

$$\mathrm{m_{s0}} = \overline{\mathrm{m}}_{\mathrm{s0}} + 2\sigma_{\mathrm{m_{s0}}}. \tag{3.23}$$

$\overline{\mathrm{m}}_{\mathrm{s0}}$ is the mean value of the aggregate measure [150]:

$$\overline{\mathrm{m}}_{\mathrm{s0}} = \frac{1}{n}\sum_{j=1}^{n} \underset{j}{\mathrm{m_s}}, \tag{3.24}$$

and $\sigma_{\mathrm{m_{s0}}}$ its standard deviation [150]:

$$\sigma_{\mathrm{m_{s0}}} = \sqrt{\frac{1}{n}\sum_{j=1}^{n}\left(\underset{j}{\mathrm{m_s}} - \overline{\mathrm{m}}_{\mathrm{s0}}\right)^2}. \tag{3.25}$$

The $\underset{j}{\mathrm{m'_{sn}}}$ development measure is non-negative and only with a probability close to zero exceeds the value of one. A given unit is at the higher development level, the more the value of the development measure approaches zero.

The measure of development constructed in this way is usually used in a modified form [150]:

$$\underset{j}{\mathrm{m_{sn}}} = 1 - \frac{\underset{j}{\mathrm{m'_{sn}}}}{\mathrm{m_{s0}}}. \tag{3.26}$$

It is interpreted as follows: the individual is the more developed, the closer the value of the measure of development approaches to one. The value obtained is always less than one. If the distribution of the measure values is normal, then a value less than zero is obtained with a probability of less than 5%. This makes it possible to easily identify objects with a very low level of development. The number of objects for which the measure value is negative can be adjusted by changing the multiplier with the standard deviation in the formula (3.23). If it is one, about 32% of the objects will get negative values, and if it is equal to 3, then there will be less than 1%. The latter multiplier is used when we want to limit the range of measure to positive values. Then the occurrence of a negative value of the measure for a not too large set of test objects is very unlikely.

Generalized Distance Measure GDM

An alternative to the correlation coefficient can be a generalized correlation coefficient [94]:

$$\Gamma_{c,d} = \frac{\sum_{j=1}^{m}\sum_{k=1}^{m} c_{j,k}\, d_{j,k}}{\sqrt{\sum_{j=1}^{m}\sum_{k=1}^{m} c_{j,k}^2 \sum_{j=1}^{m}\sum_{k=1}^{m} d_{j,k}^2}}, \tag{3.27}$$

where:

$c_{j,k}$, $d_{j,k}$—matrices of relations between objects for variables c and d.

This factor can be calculated when variables are given as ranking values expressed in any measurement scale. This distinguishes it from the Pearson correlation coefficient that can only be calculated for variables expressed in a ratio scale. The relation matrix is built for a specific variable, and it is a square matrix that has as many rows and columns as objects (rows and columns correspond to successive objects). Exemplary relation matrix:

$$C = \begin{bmatrix} 0 & 1 & -2 \\ -1 & 0 & -3 \\ 2 & 3 & 0 \end{bmatrix}. \tag{3.28}$$

This matrix presents the relationship between objects. A value of zero means that the objects are identical with each other. On the main diagonal, there are results of comparing objects with themselves; therefore, they take the value of zero. A value of one in the first row of the second column explains that the first object is better than the second object by the value of 1. A minus three in the second row of the third column explains that the second object is inferior to the third object by value of 3. The relation matrix is the asymmetric matrix:

$$\bigwedge_{j,k} c_{j,k} = -c_{k,j}, \tag{3.29}$$

that is,

$$C = \begin{bmatrix} 0 & c_{1,2} & c_{1,3} & \cdots & c_{1,m} \\ -c_{2,1} & 0 & c_{2,3} & \cdots & c_{2,m} \\ -c_{3,1} & -c_{3,2} & 0 & \cdots & c_{3,m} \\ \vdots & \vdots & \vdots & \ddots & \vdots \\ -c_{m,1} & -c_{m,2} & -c_{m,3} & \cdots & 0 \end{bmatrix}. \tag{3.30}$$

Taking advantage of the fact that the relation matrices are asymmetric, the generalized correlation coefficient between the i-th and j-th variables can be noted as [213]

$$\Gamma_{i,l} = \frac{\sum_{j=2}^{m}\sum_{k=1}^{j-1} c_{i\,j,k}\, c_{l\,j,k}}{\sqrt{\sum_{j=2}^{m}\sum_{k=1}^{j-1} c_{i\,j,k}^2 \sum_{j=2}^{m}\sum_{k=1}^{j-1} c_{l\,j,k}^2}}. \tag{3.31}$$

$c_{i\,j,k}$ is an element of the relation matrix C_i, created for the i-th variable. Having the values of the variables expressed in a quotient or interval scale, the relation matrices for the variables can be created using the formula [94]:

$$c_{i\,j,k} = x'_{i\,j} - x'_{i\,k}. \tag{3.32}$$

When the variables are expressed in an ordinal scale, the relation matrices are constructed as follows [213]:

$$c_{i\,j,k} = \begin{cases} 1 & \text{if } x'_{i\,j} > x'_{i\,k}, \\ 0 & \text{if } x'_{i\,j} = x'_{i\,k}, \\ -1 & \text{if } x'_{i\,j} < x'_{i\,k}. \end{cases} \tag{3.33}$$

Table 3.1 presents data on cars' fuel consumption in liters per hundred kilometers, prices in PLN, and the appearance expressed using the ordinal scale (10—the most beautiful car, and 1—the ugliest). The correlation between fuel consumption and appearance will be determined.

First, a relation matrix is created for the fuel consumption variable. This is the asymmetric matrix. Therefore, it is enough to calculate only the values above the main diagonal:

$$c_{1\,1,2} = \begin{cases} 1 & \text{if } x'_{1\,1} > x'_{1\,2}, \\ 0 & \text{if } x'_{1\,1} = x'_{1\,2}, \\ -1 & \text{if } x'_{1\,1} < x'_{1\,2}. \end{cases} \tag{3.34}$$

Table 3.1 Przykład—dane dotyczące samochodów

Car	Fuel consumption	Appearance	Price
Opel	8	5	110,000
Audi	9	7	140,000
BMW	10	8	150,000
Mazda	7	6	130,000

The value of 8 is less than 9; therefore, $c_{1 \atop 1,2}$ totals -1. Values above the main diagonal of the c_1 matrix will be the following:

$$C_1 = \begin{bmatrix} 0 & 1 & 1 & -1 \\ -1 & 0 & 1 & -1 \\ -1 & -1 & 0 & -1 \\ 1 & 1 & 1 & 0 \end{bmatrix}, \tag{3.35}$$

while of c_2 matrix will be

$$C_2 = \begin{bmatrix} 0 & 1 & 1 & 1 \\ -1 & 0 & 1 & -1 \\ -1 & -1 & 0 & -1 \\ -1 & 1 & 1 & 0 \end{bmatrix}. \tag{3.36}$$

In the formulas, elements to be used in further calculations are highlighted in gray color. The other values cannot be enumerated, and they are later replaced with signs (−). To determine a numerator in the formula (3.31), you must multiply an element of matrix c_1 by an element of matrix c_2:

$$C_1 .* C_2 = \begin{bmatrix} - & 1 & 1 & -1 \\ - & - & 1 & -1 \\ - & - & - & -1 \\ - & - & - & - \end{bmatrix} .* \begin{bmatrix} - & 1 & 1 & 1 \\ - & - & 1 & -1 \\ - & - & - & -1 \\ - & - & - & - \end{bmatrix} = \begin{bmatrix} - & 1 & 1 & -1 \\ - & - & 1 & 1 \\ - & - & - & 1 \\ - & - & - & - \end{bmatrix}. \tag{3.37}$$

The numerator in the formula (3.31) is the sum of all elements of the matrix calculated above and it is equal to 4. To find a denominator in this formula, take the square of all elements in matrix c_1:

$$C_1 .* C_1 = \begin{bmatrix} - & 1^2 & 1^2 & (-1)^2 \\ - & - & 1^2 & (-1)^2 \\ - & - & - & (-1)^2 \\ - & - & - & - \end{bmatrix} = \begin{bmatrix} - & 1 & 1 & 1 \\ - & - & 1 & 1 \\ - & - & - & 1 \\ - & - & - & - \end{bmatrix}, \tag{3.38}$$

and find their sum, which in this case is 6. Similar calculations should be made for matrix c_2. As the result, the obtained value is also 6. Finally, the denominator is equal to

$$\mathrm{m} = \sqrt{6 * 6} = 6. \tag{3.39}$$

The correlation value is

$$\Gamma_{1,2} = \frac{4}{6} = \frac{2}{3}. \tag{3.40}$$

M. Walesiak proposed a distance measure based on the generalized correlation coefficient [213]. Miara ta nosi nazwę uogólnionej miary odległości GDM (*Generalized Distance Measure*) This measure is called the generalized distance measure GDM and can be calculated under the formula [213]:

$$\mathrm{d}\left(\underset{j}{X'},\underset{k}{X'}\right)=\frac{1}{2}-\frac{\sum_{i=1}^{n}\underset{j,k}{c_i}\,\underset{k,j}{c_i}+\sum_{i=1}^{n}\sum_{\substack{l=1\\ l\neq j,k}}^{m}\underset{j,l}{c_i}\,\underset{l,k}{c_i}}{2\sqrt{\left(\sum_{i=1}^{n}\underset{j,k}{c_i^2}+\sum_{i=1}^{n}\sum_{\substack{l=1\\ l\neq j,k}}^{m}\underset{j,l}{c_i^2}\right)\left(\sum_{i=1}^{n}\underset{k,j}{c_i^2}+\sum_{i=1}^{n}\sum_{\substack{l=1\\ l\neq j,k}}^{m}\underset{l,k}{c_i^2}\right)}}. \tag{3.41}$$

The above entry can be presented in the more simple form [213]:

$$\mathrm{d}\left(\underset{j}{X'},\underset{k}{X'}\right)=\frac{1}{2}-\frac{\sum_{i=1}^{n}\underset{j,k}{c_i}\,\underset{k,j}{c_i}+\sum_{i=1}^{n}\sum_{\substack{l=1\\ l\neq j,k}}^{m}\underset{j,l}{c_i}\,\underset{l,k}{c_i}}{2\sqrt{\left(\sum_{i=1}^{n}\sum_{l=1}^{m}\underset{j,l}{c_i^2}\right)\left(\sum_{i=1}^{n}\sum_{l=1}^{m}\underset{l,k}{c_i^2}\right)}}. \tag{3.42}$$

The matrix c_i is asymmetric, the values on the main diagonal are zero, and hence, $\underset{j,j}{c_i}=0$. Then,

$$\mathrm{d}\left(\underset{j}{X'},\underset{k}{X'}\right)=\frac{1}{2}-\frac{\sum_{i=1}^{n}\underset{j,k}{c_i}\,\underset{k,j}{c_i}+\sum_{i=1}^{n}\sum_{l=1}^{m}\underset{j,l}{c_i}\,\underset{l,k}{c_i}}{2\sqrt{\left(\sum_{i=1}^{n}\sum_{l=1}^{m}\underset{j,l}{c_i^2}\right)\left(\sum_{i=1}^{n}\sum_{l=1}^{m}\underset{l,k}{c_i^2}\right)}}. \tag{3.43}$$

Also, $\underset{j,k}{c_i}=-\underset{k,j}{c_i}$, that:

$$\mathrm{d}\left(\underset{j}{X'},\underset{k}{X'}\right)=\frac{1}{2}+\frac{\sum_{i=1}^{n}\underset{j,k}{c_i^2}+\sum_{i=1}^{n}\sum_{l=1}^{m}\underset{j,l}{c_i}\,\underset{k,l}{c_i}}{2\sqrt{\left(\sum_{i=1}^{n}\sum_{l=1}^{m}\underset{j,l}{c_i^2}\right)\left(\sum_{i=1}^{n}\sum_{l=1}^{m}\underset{l,k}{c_i^2}\right)}}. \tag{3.44}$$

Notations (3.42) and (3.44) are equivalent, but the latter form is easier to implement in programming languages that support matrix operations.

For variables measured in a quotient and interval scale, the substitution (3.32) is used. Then the notation (3.42) takes the form [213]:

$$d\left(\underset{j}{X'}, \underset{k}{X'}\right) = \frac{1}{2} - \frac{\sum_{i=1}^{n}\left(\underset{j}{x'_i} - \underset{k}{x'_i}\right)\left(\underset{k}{x'_i} - \underset{j}{x'_i}\right) + \sum_{i=1}^{n}\sum_{\substack{l=1\\ l\neq i,k}}^{m}\left(\underset{j}{x'_i} - \underset{l}{x'_i}\right)\left(\underset{k}{x'_i} - \underset{l}{x'_i}\right)}{2\sqrt{\left[\sum_{i=1}^{n}\sum_{l=1}^{m}\left(\underset{j}{x'_i} - \underset{l}{x'_i}\right)^2\right]\left[\sum_{i=1}^{n}\sum_{l=1}^{m}\left(\underset{k}{x'_i} - \underset{l}{x'_i}\right)^2\right]}}. \tag{3.45}$$

The above formula can also be recorded differently:

$$d\left(\underset{j}{X'}, \underset{k}{X'}\right) = \frac{1}{2} + \frac{\sum_{i=1}^{n}\left(\underset{j}{x'_i} - \underset{k}{x'_i}\right)^2 - \sum_{i=1}^{n}\sum_{l=1}^{m}\left(\underset{j}{x'_i} - \underset{l}{x'_i}\right)\left(\underset{k}{x'_i} - \underset{l}{x'_i}\right)}{2\sqrt{\left[\sum_{i=1}^{n}\sum_{l=1}^{m}\left(\underset{j}{x'_i} - \underset{l}{x'_i}\right)^2\right]\left[\sum_{i=1}^{n}\sum_{l=1}^{m}\left(\underset{k}{x'_i} - \underset{l}{x'_i}\right)^2\right]}}. \tag{3.46}$$

For the ordinal scale, relation matrices determined by the formula (3.33) are used. It is possible to calculate the GDM measure for the nominal scale based on the formula (3.41) and substitute as follows:

1. For the compared objects j and k (factor $\sum_{i=1}^{n} \underset{j,k}{c_i}\ \underset{k,j}{c_i}$ in formula (3.41)) [212]:

$$\underset{j,k}{c_i}\ \underset{k,j}{c_i} = \begin{cases} 1 & \text{for } \underset{j}{x'_i} = \underset{k}{x'_i} \wedge j \neq k, \\ 0 & \text{for } \underset{j}{x'_i} = \underset{k}{x'_i} \wedge j = k, \\ -1 & \text{for } \underset{j}{x'_i} \neq \underset{k}{x'_i} \wedge j \neq k. \end{cases} \tag{3.47}$$

The case, where $j = k$ and $\underset{j}{x'_i} \neq \underset{k}{x'_i}$, cannot occur because then $\underset{j}{x'_i} \neq \underset{j}{x'_i}$.

2. For other objects $l = 1, 2, \ldots m \wedge l \neq j \wedge l \neq k$ (element of $\sum_{i=1}^{n}\sum_{\substack{l=1\\ l\neq j,k}}^{m} \underset{j,l}{c_i}\ \underset{l,k}{c_i}$ formula (3.41)):

$$\underset{j,l}{c_i}\,\underset{l,k}{c_i} = \begin{cases} 1 \text{ for } \underset{j}{x'_i} = \underset{k}{x'_i}, \\ -1 \text{ for } \underset{j}{x'_i} \neq \underset{k}{x'_i}. \end{cases} \tag{3.48}$$

For the nominal scale, the formula (3.41) can be simplified by noting the element $\sum_{i=1}^{n} \underset{j,k}{c_i^2}$ as follows:

$$\sum_{i=1}^{n} \underset{j,k}{c_i^2} = \sum_{i=1}^{n} \underset{j,k}{c_i}\,\underset{j,k}{c_i}. \tag{3.49a}$$

Two cases should be considered here. In the first one, an object is compared to itself, and then $j = k$, that is, $\underset{j,k}{c_i}\,\underset{j,k}{c_i} = \underset{j,j}{c_i}\,\underset{j,j}{c_i}$. Referring this to the formula (3.47): $j = k$, $\underset{j,j}{c_i}\,\underset{j,j}{c_i} \Rightarrow \underset{j}{x'_i} = \underset{j}{x'_i}$, hence $\underset{j,j}{c_i}\,\underset{j,j}{c_i} = 0$, that is,

$$\sum_{i=1}^{n} \underset{j,j}{c_i^2} = 0. \tag{3.49b}$$

In the second case, different objects are compared, then $j \neq k$, but $\underset{j,k}{c_i}\,\underset{j,k}{c_i} \Rightarrow \underset{j}{x'_i} = \underset{j}{x'_i}$, hence, $\underset{j,k}{c_i}\,\underset{j,k}{c_i} = 1$, that is,

$$\sum_{i=1}^{n} \underset{j,k}{c_i^2} = n. \tag{3.49c}$$

Element $\sum_{i=1}^{n} \sum_{\substack{l=1 \\ l \neq j,k}}^{m} \underset{j,l}{c_i^2}$ can be noted as follows:

$$\sum_{i=1}^{n} \sum_{\substack{l=1 \\ l \neq j,k}}^{m} \underset{j,l}{c_i^2} = \sum_{i=1}^{n} \sum_{\substack{l=1 \\ l \neq j,k}}^{m} \underset{j,l}{c_i}\,\underset{j,l}{c_i}. \tag{3.49d}$$

Referring $\underset{j,l}{c_i}\,\underset{j,l}{c_i}$ to the formula (3.48): $\underset{j,l}{c_i}\,\underset{j,l}{c_i} \Rightarrow \underset{j}{x'_i} = \underset{j}{x'_i}$, and then $\underset{j,l}{c_i}\,\underset{j,l}{c_i} = 1$. In this case, two situations should be considered as well. The first one, where $j = k$, that is,

$$\sum_{i=1}^{n} \sum_{\substack{l=1 \\ l \neq j}}^{m} \underset{j,l}{c_i^2} = n\,(m-1). \tag{3.49e}$$

The value $(m-1)$ results from that l cannot be equal to j. Likewise in the case of $j \neq k$, the result is

$$\sum_{i=1}^{n} \sum_{\substack{l=1 \\ l \neq j,k}}^{m} \underset{j,l}{c_i^2} = n\,(m-2)\,. \tag{3.49f}$$

Putting together the obtained results for $j = k$, we will get

$$\sum_{i=1}^{n} \underset{j,j}{c_i^2} + \sum_{i=1}^{n} \sum_{\substack{l=1 \\ l \neq j}}^{m} \underset{j,l}{c_i^2} = 0 + n\,(m-1) = n\,(m-1)\,, \tag{3.49g}$$

and for $j \neq k$, we will get

$$\sum_{i=1}^{n} \underset{j,k}{c_i^2} + \sum_{i=1}^{n} \sum_{\substack{l=1 \\ l \neq j,k}}^{m} \underset{j,l}{c_i^2} = n + n\,(m-2) = n\,(m-1)\,. \tag{3.49h}$$

Entering the obtained results into the formula (3.41), we will obtain a simplified formula for a nominal scale:

$$\begin{aligned} \mathrm{d}\left(\underset{j}{X'}, \underset{k}{X'}\right) &= \frac{1}{2} - \frac{\sum_{i=1}^{n} \underset{j,k}{c_i}\,\underset{k,j}{c_i} + \sum_{i=1}^{n} \sum_{\substack{l=1 \\ l \neq j,k}}^{m} \underset{j,l}{c_i}\,\underset{l,k}{c_i}}{2\sqrt{n\,(m-1)\,n\,(m-1)}} \\ &= \frac{1}{2} - \frac{\sum_{i=1}^{n} \underset{j,k}{c_i}\,\underset{k,j}{c_i} + \sum_{i=1}^{n} \sum_{\substack{l=1 \\ l \neq j,k}}^{m} \underset{j,l}{c_i}\,\underset{l,k}{c_i}}{2n\,(m-1)}\,. \end{aligned} \tag{3.50}$$

The GDM measure makes a distance between two objects dependent on the alignment of a set of all points that represent objects. Figure 3.6 shows the dependence of a position of one object on another marked with a circle. The locations of points representing the objects are marked with triangles and the measurement values with level lines. You can see that the measure values change quickly as we move away from the object marked with the circle toward the center of the set, while when moving in other directions, the rate of change is much slower. Values greater than 0.7 are obtained when the objects between which the distance is measured are on opposite sides of the set of points representing the objects. It is also possible to obtain a measure value greater than 0.7 in other cases, but both objects must be far away from each other.

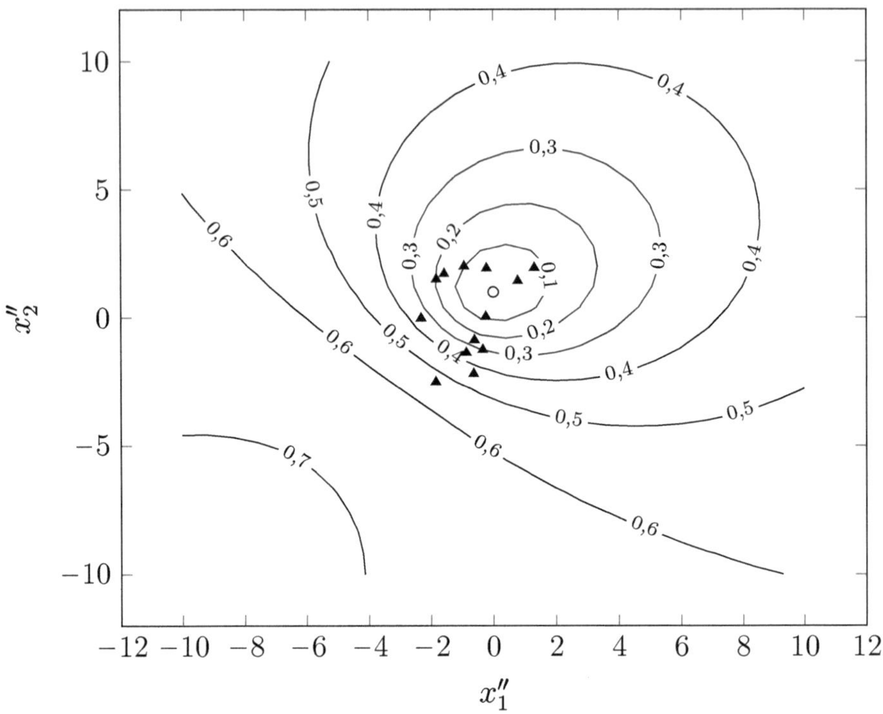

Fig. 3.6 The values of the GDM measure depending on a position in relation to the pattern

The above-mentioned properties of the distance measure have their advantages and disadvantages. The advantage is that it can be applied to various measurement scales and that the distinguishability of objects is the best in the area of the center of the set of points, i.e., in the place of most interest to the researcher. The disadvantage is that each study is finite. Adding a new object to the set of existing ones will change the values of the aggregate measure (calculated based on GDM) for all objects. Thus, for objects counted in one time period, these values cannot be referenced to an aggregate measure value from another period of time. The exception is when one set is made of points representing objects in both periods of time. Moreover, Fig. 3.6 shows that the GDM measure is non-invariant with respect to the displacement and that the k-times distance of the objects from each other will not k-times change the value of the measure. This means that the differences in the value of the aggregate measure calculated on the basis of the GDM measure do not translate into a proportional difference in the values of indicators representing the objects.

The mentioned disadvantages of the GDM distance measure are not always significant. For example, when this measure is used in the Hellwig's method, which has similar disadvantages, it does not negatively affect the result of the Hellwig's method. The arrangement of the pattern in the Hellwig's method is such that the results obtained with the use of the GDM measure are very similar to those obtained

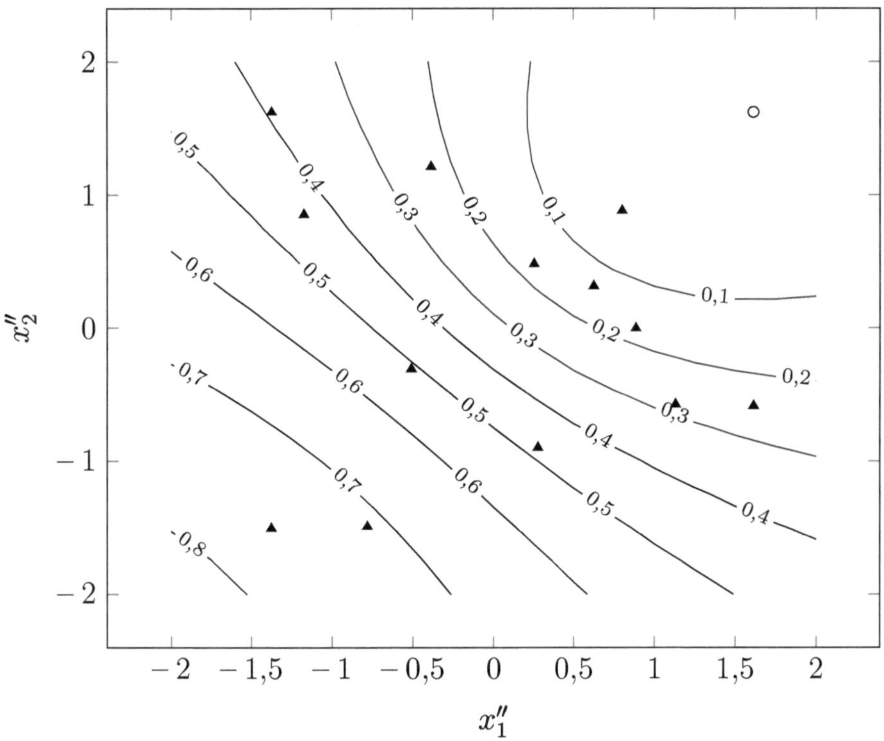

Fig. 3.7 The values of the GDM measure depending on the position in relation to the pattern defined as the maximum values of the coordinates

by the measures in which the differences in the values of the aggregate measure translate into a proportional difference in the values of the indicators representing the objects. This is presented in Fig. 3.7. In this drawing, the coordinates of the reference object from which the distances are calculated have been determined as the maximum values of all objects belonging to the set under consideration. Object coordinate values have been normalized according to the formula (2.45), with A_i determined as the mean value (2.79) and B_i as the standard deviation (2.49). The figure shows that the values of GDM measure have very similar character to the Euclidean measure (similar system of level lines). They differ in their variable density mainly near the pattern object.

The data from Table 3.1, were used to illustrate calculations, for which the GDM distance between Opel and Audi will be determined. To do this, you need to compute the relation matrices. Matrices C_1 and C_2 have been already determined—formulas (3.35 and 3.36). Matrix C_3 will be as follows:

$$C_3 = \begin{bmatrix} 0 & 1 & 1 & 1 \\ -1 & 0 & 1 & -1 \\ -1 & -1 & 0 & -1 \\ -1 & 1 & 1 & 0 \end{bmatrix}. \tag{3.51}$$

There are two elements in the numerator of the formula (3.44). The first one is

$$\sum_{i=1}^{3} \underset{1,2}{c_i^2} = \underset{1,2}{c_1^2} + \underset{1,2}{c_2^2} + \underset{1,2}{c_3^2} = 1^2 + 1^2 + 1^2 = 3. \tag{3.52}$$

The second element is the sum of the products of the rows (or columns) in the relation matrix corresponding to the specified objects. These rows are shown in gray and dark gray:

$$\begin{bmatrix} 0 & 1 & 1 & -1 \\ -1 & 0 & 1 & -1 \\ -1 & -1 & 0 & -1 \\ 1 & 1 & 1 & 0 \end{bmatrix}, \begin{bmatrix} 0 & 1 & 1 & 1 \\ -1 & 0 & 1 & -1 \\ -1 & -1 & 0 & -1 \\ -1 & 1 & 1 & 0 \end{bmatrix}, \begin{bmatrix} 0 & 1 & 1 & 1 \\ -1 & 0 & 1 & -1 \\ -1 & -1 & 0 & -1 \\ -1 & 1 & 1 & 0 \end{bmatrix}. \tag{3.53}$$

This element for selected objects will be as follows:

$$\begin{aligned} \sum_{i=1}^{3}\sum_{l=1}^{4} \underset{1,l}{c_i}\,\underset{2,l}{c_i} =\; & \underset{1,1}{c_1}\,\underset{2,1}{c_1} + \underset{1,2}{c_1}\,\underset{2,2}{c_1} + \underset{1,3}{c_1}\,\underset{2,3}{c_1} + \underset{1,4}{c_1}\,\underset{2,4}{c_1} + \\ & \underset{1,1}{c_2}\,\underset{2,1}{c_2} + \underset{1,2}{c_2}\,\underset{2,2}{c_2} + \underset{1,3}{c_2}\,\underset{2,3}{c_2} + \underset{1,4}{c_2}\,\underset{2,4}{c_2} + \\ & \underset{1,1}{c_3}\,\underset{2,1}{c_3} + \underset{1,2}{c_3}\,\underset{2,2}{c_2} + \underset{1,3}{c_3}\,\underset{2,3}{c_3} + \underset{1,4}{c_3}\,\underset{2,4}{c_3}. \end{aligned} \tag{3.54}$$

By substituting values, the result will be as follows:

$$\begin{aligned} \sum_{i=1}^{3}\sum_{l=1}^{3} \underset{1,l}{c_i}\,\underset{2,l}{c_i} =\; & 0\cdot(-1) + 1\cdot 0 + 1\cdot 1 + (-1)\cdot(-1) + \\ & 0\cdot(-1) + 1\cdot 0 + 1\cdot 1 + 1\cdot(-1) + \\ & 0\cdot(-1) + 1\cdot 0 + 1\cdot 1 + 1\cdot(-1), \end{aligned} \tag{3.55}$$

that is,

$$\sum_{i=1}^{3}\sum_{l=1}^{4} \underset{1,l}{c_i}\,\underset{2,l}{c_i} = 0+0+1+1+0+0+1-1+0+0+1-1 = 2. \tag{3.56}$$

The denominator also has two elements. The first is the sum of the squares of the rows (or columns) in the relation matrix corresponding to the first object (in 3.53 marked in light gray):

$$\sum_{3=1}^{n}\sum_{l=1}^{4} c_{i\,1,l}^{2} = c_{1\,1,1}^{2} + c_{1\,1,2}^{2} + c_{1\,1,3}^{2} + c_{1\,1,4}^{2} + c_{2\,1,1}^{2} + c_{2\,1,2}^{2} + c_{2\,1,3}^{2} + c_{2\,1,4}^{2} + c_{3\,1,1}^{2} + c_{3\,1,2}^{2} + c_{3\,1,3}^{2} + c_{3\,1,4}^{2}. \tag{3.57}$$

Further, substituting the values, we get

$$\sum_{i=1}^{3}\sum_{l=1}^{4} c_{i\,1,l}^{2} = 0^2+1^2+1^2+(-1)^2+0^2+1^2+1^2+1^2+0^2+1^2+1^2+1^2=9. \tag{3.58}$$

The second element is the sum of the squares of the rows (or columns) of the relation matrix (in 3.53 zaznaczone kolorem ciemnoszarym):

$$\sum_{i=1}^{3}\sum_{l=1}^{4} c_{i\,2,l}^{2} = 9. \tag{3.59}$$

Finally, GDM value is

$$d\left(\underset{1}{X'}, \underset{2}{X'}\right) = \frac{1}{2} + \frac{3+2}{2\sqrt{9\cdot 9}} = \frac{1}{2} + \frac{5}{18} = \frac{14}{18} \approx 0.7778. \tag{3.60}$$

In another example, for the data in Table 3.2, the first student was compared to himself and to the second one. For this purpose, the values of the GDM measure were determined GDM. For $j = 1$ and $k = 1$, value $\sum_{i=1}^{n} \underset{j,k}{c_i}\, \underset{k,j}{c_i}$ was

$$\sum_{i=1}^{n} \underset{j,k}{c_i}\,\underset{k,j}{c_i} = \sum_{i=1}^{3} \underset{1,1}{c_i}\,\underset{1,1}{c_i} = \overset{x'_1=x'_1}{\underset{1,1}{c_1}\,\underset{1,1}{c_1}} + \overset{x'_2=x'_2}{\underset{1,1}{c_2}\,\underset{1,1}{c_2}} + \overset{x'_3=x'_3}{\underset{1,1}{c_3}\,\underset{1,1}{c_3}} = 0+0+0=0, \tag{3.61}$$

Table 3.2 Example—data of students

Student	Place of residence	Gender	Faculty
Student 1	zachodniopomorskie	Female	Economics
Student 2	mazowieckie	Female	Economics
Student 3	mazowieckie	Male	Mechanics
Student 4	pomorskie	Male	Mechanics
Student 5	pomorskie	Male	Political science

while $\sum_{i=1}^{n}\sum_{\substack{l=1\\l\neq j,k}}^{m} \underset{j,l}{c_i}\,\underset{l,k}{c_i}$ is equal to

$$\begin{aligned}\sum_{i=1}^{n}\sum_{\substack{l=1\\l\neq j,k}}^{m} \underset{j,l}{c_i}\,\underset{l,k}{c_i} &= \sum_{i=1}^{3}\sum_{\substack{l=1\\l\neq 1}}^{5} \underset{1,l}{c_i}\,\underset{l,1}{c_i} = \sum_{i=1}^{3} \underset{1,2}{c_i}\,\underset{2,1}{c_i} + \underset{1,3}{c_i}\,\underset{3,1}{c_i} + \underset{1,4}{c_i}\,\underset{4,1}{c_i} + \underset{1,5}{c_i}\,\underset{5,1}{c_i} = \\
&= \overset{x'_1=x'_1}{\underset{1,2}{\overset{1}{c_1}}\,\underset{2,1}{\overset{1}{c_1}}} + \overset{x'_1=x'_1}{\underset{1,3}{\overset{1}{c_1}}\,\underset{3,1}{\overset{1}{c_1}}} + \overset{x'_1=x'_1}{\underset{1,4}{\overset{1}{c_1}}\,\underset{4,1}{\overset{1}{c_1}}} + \overset{x'_1=x'_1}{\underset{1,5}{\overset{1}{c_1}}\,\underset{5,1}{\overset{1}{c_1}}} + \overset{x'_2=x'_2}{\underset{1,2}{\overset{1}{c_2}}\,\underset{2,1}{\overset{1}{c_2}}} + \overset{x'_2=x'_2}{\underset{1,3}{\overset{1}{c_2}}\,\underset{3,1}{\overset{1}{c_2}}} + \overset{x'_2=x'_2}{\underset{1,4}{\overset{1}{c_2}}\,\underset{4,1}{\overset{1}{c_2}}} + \overset{x'_2=x'_2}{\underset{1,5}{\overset{1}{c_i}}\,\underset{5,1}{\overset{1}{c_i}}} + \\
&+ \overset{x'_3=x'_3}{\underset{1,2}{\overset{1}{c_3}}\,\underset{2,1}{\overset{1}{c_3}}} + \overset{x'_3=x'_3}{\underset{1,3}{\overset{1}{c_3}}\,\underset{3,1}{\overset{1}{c_3}}} + \overset{x'_3=x'_3}{\underset{1,4}{\overset{1}{c_3}}\,\underset{4,1}{\overset{1}{c_3}}} + \overset{x'_3=x'_3}{\underset{1,5}{\overset{1}{c_3}}\,\underset{5,1}{\overset{1}{c_3}}} = \\
&= 1+1+1+1+1+1+1+1+1+1+1+1 = 12.
\end{aligned} \tag{3.62}$$

The value of the GDM measure when comparing the first student with himself will be

$$d\left(\underset{1}{X'}, \underset{1}{X'}\right) = \frac{1}{2} - \frac{\sum_{i=1}^{n} \underset{1,1}{c_i}\,\underset{1,1}{c_i} + \sum_{i=1}^{n}\sum_{\substack{l=1\\l\neq 1}}^{m} \underset{1,l}{c_i}\,\underset{l,1}{c_i}}{2n\,(m-1)} = \frac{1}{2} - \frac{0+12}{2\cdot 3\,(5-1)} = \frac{1}{2} - \frac{1}{2} = 0. \tag{3.63}$$

When comparing the first student with the second ($j = 1$ and $k = 2$), value of $\sum_{i=1}^{n} \underset{j,k}{c_i}\,\underset{k,j}{c_i}$ will be equal to

$$\sum_{i=1}^{n} \underset{j,k}{c_i}\,\underset{k,j}{c_i} = \sum_{i=1}^{3} \underset{1,2}{c_i}\,\underset{2,1}{c_i} = \overset{x'_1\neq x'_1}{\underset{1,2}{\overset{1}{c_1}}\,\underset{2,1}{\overset{2}{c_1}}} + \overset{x'_2=x'_2}{\underset{1,2}{\overset{1}{c_2}}\,\underset{2,1}{\overset{2}{c_2}}} + \overset{x'_3=x'_3}{\underset{1,2}{\overset{1}{c_3}}\,\underset{2,1}{\overset{2}{c_3}}} = -1+1+1 = 1, \tag{3.64}$$

while $\sum_{i=1}^{n}\sum_{\substack{l=1\\l\neq j,k}}^{m} \underset{j,l}{c_i}\,\underset{l,k}{c_i}$:

$$\begin{aligned}
\sum_{i=1}^{n}\sum_{\substack{l=1\\ l\neq j,k}}^{m} \underset{j,l}{c_i}\,\underset{l,k}{c_i} &= \sum_{i=1}^{3}\sum_{\substack{l=1\\ l\neq 1,2}}^{5} \underset{1,l}{c_i}\,\underset{l,2}{c_i} = \underset{1,3}{c_i}\,\underset{3,2}{c_i} + \underset{1,4}{c_i}\,\underset{4,2}{c_i} + \underset{1,5}{c_i}\,\underset{5,2}{c_i} = \\
&= \overset{x'_1\neq x'_1}{\underset{1,3}{\overset{1}{c_1}}\,\underset{3,2}{\overset{2}{c_1}}} + \overset{x'_1\neq x'_1}{\underset{1,4}{\overset{1}{c_1}}\,\underset{4,2}{\overset{2}{c_1}}} + \overset{x'_1\neq x'_1}{\underset{1,5}{\overset{1}{c_1}}\,\underset{5,2}{\overset{2}{c_1}}} + \overset{x'_2=x'_2}{\underset{1,3}{\overset{1}{c_2}}\,\underset{3,2}{\overset{2}{c_2}}} + \overset{x'_2=x'_2}{\underset{1,4}{\overset{1}{c_2}}\,\underset{4,2}{\overset{2}{c_2}}} + \overset{x'_2=x'_2}{\underset{1,5}{\overset{1}{c_i}}\,\underset{5,2}{\overset{2}{c_i}}} + \\
&+ \overset{x'_3=x'_3}{\underset{1,3}{\overset{1}{c_3}}\,\underset{3,2}{\overset{2}{c_3}}} + \overset{x'_3=x'_3}{\underset{1,4}{\overset{1}{c_3}}\,\underset{4,2}{\overset{2}{c_3}}} + \overset{x'_3=x'_3}{\underset{1,5}{\overset{1}{c_3}}\,\underset{5,2}{\overset{2}{c_3}}} = \\
&= -1 - 1 - 1 + 1 + 1 + 1 + 1 + 1 + 1 = 3.
\end{aligned} \tag{3.65}$$

The value of the GDM measure when comparing the first student with the second will be

$$\begin{aligned}
d\left(\underset{1}{X'}, \underset{1}{X'}\right) &= \frac{1}{2} - \frac{\sum_{i=1}^{n} \underset{1,2}{c_i}\,\underset{1,2}{c_i} + \sum_{i=1}^{n}\sum_{\substack{l=1\\ l\neq 1,2}}^{m} \underset{1,l}{c_i}\,\underset{l,2}{c_i}}{2n\,(m-1)} \\
&= \frac{1}{2} - \frac{1+3}{2\cdot 3\,(5-1)} = \frac{1}{2} - \frac{1}{6} = \frac{1}{3}.
\end{aligned} \tag{3.66}$$

3.3 Vector Reference Methods

Vector reference methods are based on determining the value of an aggregate measure on the basis of a pattern with the participation of elements of vector calculus. The weighted arithmetic mean given by the formula (3.2) can be interpreted as an orthogonal projection of the point $\underset{j}{x''}$ onto a straight line in the direction determined by weights (w), which can be treated as a direction vector of a straight line. This is presented in Fig. 3.8. Such an interpretation is possible as long as a weight vector satisfies the following conditions [98]:

$$\sum_{i=1}^{m} \mathrm{w}_i^2 = 1, \tag{3.67}$$

it is a unit vector and [98]:

$$\bigwedge_{i=1,2,\ldots,m} \mathrm{w}_i > 0. \tag{3.68}$$

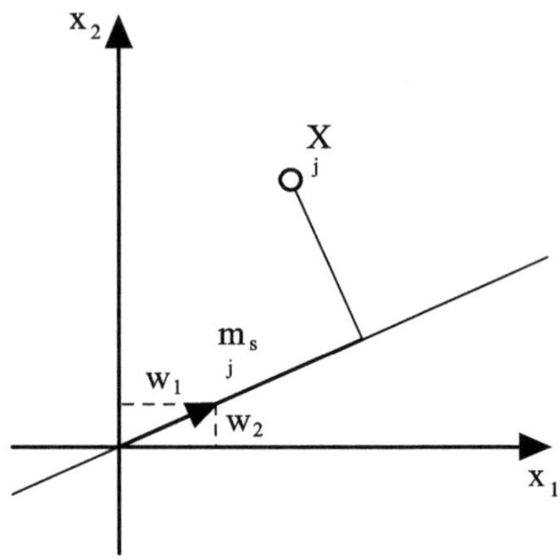

Fig. 3.8 Orthogonal projection on the line determined by the directional vector of weights

a) b)

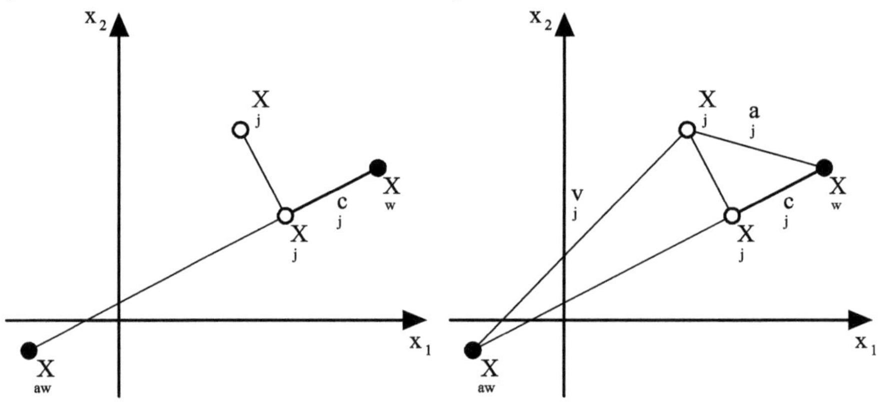

Fig. 3.9 Determining the aggregate measure according to the distance of the orthogonal projection of a point on the straight line from the pattern and anti-pattern [98]: (**a**) geometric interpretation; (**b**) distances between points

Moreover, feature values must be normalized in such a way that arithmetic means of features are equal to zero [98].

There are several methods of selecting weights, of which the work [98] lists the following: the method of the first main component, the sum of features with the same weights, the sum of features with different weights, and I and II methods of the Hellwig's development path. The first three will be covered later in this book.

Method I of the development path is described in [98] as the method proposed by Hellwig. Method II [98] is based on the orthogonal projection of a point on the point-pattern and point-anti-pattern connecting point (Fig. 3.9a). The maximum values of variables are taken as the pattern and minimum values as the anti-pattern.

The value of the aggregate measure is determined based on the distance between the projection of a point and a pattern [98]:

$$\underset{j}{c} = \frac{\underset{j}{a}^2 + o^2 - \underset{j}{v}^2}{2o}, \tag{3.69}$$

where:

$\underset{j}{c}$—Euclidean distance of the point $\underset{j}{X'''}$, which is the projection of the point $\underset{j}{X''}$ from a pattern $\underset{\text{w}}{X''}$ (Fig. 3.9b).

$\underset{j}{a}$—Euclidean distance of a point $\underset{j}{X''}$ from a pattern $\underset{\text{w}}{X''}$.

$\underset{j}{v}$—Euclidean distance of a point $\underset{j}{X''}$ from an anti-pattern $\underset{\text{aw}}{X''}$.

o—Euclidian distance of a pattern $\underset{\text{w}}{X''}$ from an anti-pattern $\underset{\text{aw}}{X''}$.

The distance of a point projection from a pattern is a positive value, for which objects closest to a pattern are close to zero. The smallest value is zero, and the largest one depends on a method of variable normalization. To normalize a synthetic variable to a range of zero to one, the following transformation is applied [98]:

$$\underset{j}{\text{m}_{\text{sn}}} = 1 - \frac{\underset{j}{c}}{o}. \tag{3.70}$$

In the presented version, this method allows the use of only such a pattern that takes the largest values of all variables as coordinates, and in the case of an anti-pattern the smallest. However, you can make such a modification that allows you to use any pattern and anti-pattern. Such a modification is described in the work [98].

III method of the Hellwig's development path was presented in the work [98]. As the weight values in orthogonal projection, the author proposes to adopt the following [98]:

$$w_i = \frac{\underset{\text{w}}{x_i''} - \underset{\text{aw}}{x_i''}}{\text{d}\left(\underset{\text{w}}{X''}, \underset{\text{aw}}{X''}\right)}, \tag{3.71}$$

where:

$\underset{\text{w}}{x_i''}$—$i$-th coordinate of the pattern.

$\underset{\text{aw}}{x_i''}$—$i$-th coordinate of the anti-pattern.

$\text{d}\left(\underset{\text{w}}{X''}, \underset{\text{aw}}{X''}\right)$—Euclidean distance of the pattern from the anti-pattern.

However, the following condition has to be met [98]:

$$\bigwedge_{i=1,2,\ldots,m} \underset{\text{w}}{x_i''} > \underset{\text{aw}}{x_i''}. \tag{3.72}$$

The weights created in this way are a unit vector with positive coordinate values, which ensures that the conditions of formulas (3.67) and (3.68) are met.

After substituting the weights, the formula for the aggregate measure will take the following form:

$$\underset{j}{\mathrm{m_s}} = \frac{\sum_{i=1}^{m} \underset{j}{x_i''} \left(\underset{\mathrm{w}}{x_i''} - \underset{\mathrm{aw}}{x_i''} \right)}{\mathrm{d}\left(\underset{\mathrm{w}}{X''}, \underset{\mathrm{aw}}{X''} \right)}. \tag{3.73}$$

In both the II and III methods of the Hellwig's path, the pattern does not have to be an object with the highest, and the anti-pattern with the lowest measure values. In the II method, they can be any, while in the III method all coordinates of the pattern must be greater than the corresponding coordinates of the anti-pattern. All variables must therefore be stimulants.

3.4 Theoretical Basis of the VMCM Method

VMCM (*Vector Measure Construction Method*) uses the vector calculus to build a vector aggregate measure. It does not require the use of a distance measure; therefore, unlike the Hellwig's method, it can take into account objects that are better than a pattern. The VMCM method uses the projection of a vector onto a vector, which is derived from the definition of a scalar product. The scalar product (A, B) between the two vectors A and B is a binary functional whose arguments are vectors and the result is a scalar. It has to meet the following conditions [27]:

1. Non-negativity:

$$(A, A) \geqslant 0. \tag{3.74}$$

   It means that the scalar product of a vector on itself cannot be a negative value.

2. Only the neutral element of addition in the set of vectors has a scalar product of a vector by itself equal to zero:

$$(A, A) = 0 \Leftrightarrow A \text{ is a zero vector.} \tag{3.75}$$

   The existence of a scalar product of a vector on itself equal to zero means that it is a zero vector (with all coordinates equal to zero).

3. Conjugate symmetry:

$$(A, B) = (B, A)^*, \tag{3.76}$$

   where:

*—is a conjugate number.

4. Separability of a scalar product with respect to addition in the set of vectors:

$$(A + B, C) = (A, C) + (B, C)\,. \tag{3.77}$$

The scalar product of the sum of vectors A and B and vector C is equal to the sum of scalar products of vectors A and C as well as B and C.

5. Excluding the constant before a scalar product:

$$(rA, B) = r\,(A, B)\,. \tag{3.78}$$

If vector A is multiplied by scalar r, then in the case of computing the scalar product of the vector rA by any other vector, the scalar r can be excluded before the scalar product.

A scalar product is defined in a vector space that becomes pre-Hilbert space. There is no distance measure in the pre-Hilbert space. It can be entered on the basis of a scalar product, defining the norm [110]:

$$\|A\| = \sqrt{(A, A)}, \tag{3.79}$$

where:

$\|A\|$—vector norm A.

Thus, pre-Hilbert space becomes unitary. Defining a norm allows you to determine vectors length. You can move a vector so that its two ends are at different points in space. This makes it possible to determine the distance between any two points. Let there be two vectors A and B (Fig. 3.10). Express vector A with B. In other words, say how many vectors B fit in A along the direction of B, which can be noted as follows [18]:

$$A \approx cB. \tag{3.80}$$

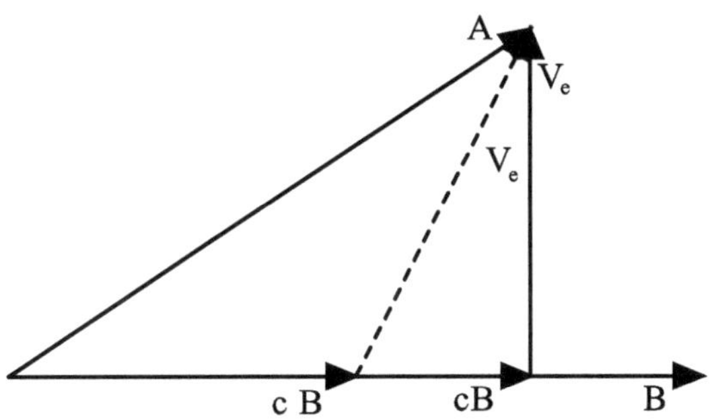

Fig. 3.10 Projection of the vector to vector [18]

The vector cB is an approximation of the vector A along the direction of B. This approximation has an error that can be denoted as V_e. Vector A will then be equal to the sum of its approximation cB and the error vector V_e [18]:

$$A = cB + V_e. \tag{3.81}$$

Due to the fact that vector A is equal to the sum of vectors cB and V_e, the scalar product of A and any other vector X will be equal to the scalar product of the sum of these vectors and the vector X. You can take B as vector X. Then [18]:

$$(A, B) = (cB + V_e, B). \tag{3.82}$$

On the basis of the properties of the scalar product given by the formula (3.77), the following can be noted:

$$(A, B) = (cB, B) + (V_e, B). \tag{3.83}$$

From the property (3.78), the constant can be excluded before the scalar product [18]:

$$(A, B) = c(B, B) + (V_e, B). \tag{3.84}$$

As the value of the scalar product is a scalar, you can take the above formula as the equation with the unknown c and transform it so that c [18]:

$$c = \frac{(A, B) - (V_e, B)}{(B, B)}, \tag{3.85}$$

where:

$(B, B) \neq 0.$

The problem of determining the value of c is the problem of minimizing the vector length V_e. The vector cB will best map A along direction B, if V_e has the shortest length. The length of V_e depends on the angle with the vector B. Figure 3.10 shows that this length will be the shortest when V_e is perpendicular to B, i.e., their scalar product will be equal to zero. Hence [18],

$$c = \frac{(A, B)}{(B, B)}. \tag{3.86}$$

The above formula determines the projection of a vector along the second vector. The condition for determining the projection is choosing B, in such a way that it is not zero. The value of c is the length of vector A along B. However, it is not expressed in the units of the coordinate system in which A and B are given but in the lengths of vector B. If vector A is substituted by the coordinates of objects

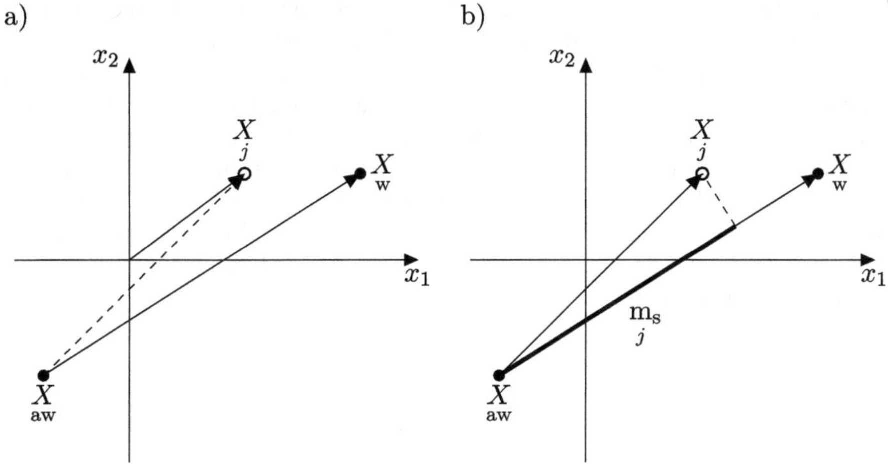

Fig. 3.11 Projection of a vector onto a vector: (**a**) coordinates of the vector representing the object relative to the origin of the coordinate system; (**b**) coordinates of the vector representing the object relative to the anti-pattern

for which the aggregate measure is determined and B by a difference between the coordinates of a pattern and an anti-pattern, then the projection becomes the value of the aggregate measure:

$$\underset{j}{m_s} = \frac{\left(\underset{j}{X''}, \underset{w}{X''} - \underset{aw}{X''}\right)}{\left(\underset{w}{X''} - \underset{aw}{X''}, \underset{w}{X''} - \underset{aw}{X''}\right)}. \tag{3.87}$$

The disadvantage of a measure formulated in this way is that if maximum values of the objects' coordinates are taken as the pattern, and the minimum values as the anti-pattern, the value of the measure will not be normalized in the range from one to zero. This is due to the fact that the coordinates of the object are taken into account as the coordinates of the projected vector, and basically the difference between the coordinates of the point and the point being the origin of the coordinate system. The coordinates of the projected vector are calculated as the difference between the coordinates of a pattern and anti-pattern. The point of attachment of both vectors is therefore different. To make the projection, both vectors must be moved to the same anchor point. It is illustrated in Fig. 3.11a.

Due to different anchor points, even if a vector representing the pattern is projected, its aggregate measure will be equal to at most one. The case when it is equal to one will occur only when the anti-pattern is placed at the origin of the coordinate system. In all other cases, it will be less than one. The smallest possible value for the measure to achieve is minus one. It will occur when the pattern is at the origin of the coordinate system. In fact, the actual measurement range will be different. The lower minimum value will be greater than minus one, and the upper maximum value will be less than one. It will depend on the position of the pattern and anti-pattern in relation to the origin of the coordinate system. Of course, the limitations as to the value of the measure are true only for the pattern having the maximum values of all variables, and the anti-pattern—minimal.

From a practical point of view, the best solution is that the measure value for the pattern to be equal to one, and for the anti-pattern—minus one. This can be achieved by counting the coordinates of the vectors relative to the anti-pattern, not the origin of the coordinate system. It is illustrated in Fig. 3.11b. The formula for the aggregate measure will then take the form of

$$\underset{j}{\mathrm{m_s}} = \frac{\left(\underset{j}{X''} - \underset{\mathrm{aw}}{X''}, \underset{\mathrm{w}}{X''} - \underset{\mathrm{aw}}{X''}\right)}{\left(\underset{\mathrm{w}}{X''} - \underset{\mathrm{aw}}{X''}, \underset{\mathrm{w}}{X''} - \underset{\mathrm{aw}}{X''}\right)}. \tag{3.88}$$

This is a general formula that can be used with any scalar product. For the most common scalar product given by the formula [103]:

$$(A, B) = \sum_{i=1}^{m} a_i b_i, \tag{3.89}$$

where:

a_i, b_i—coordinates of vectors A and B, respectively,

and the formula for the aggregate measure will be as follows:

$$\underset{j}{\mathrm{m_s}} = \frac{\sum_{i=1}^{m} \left(\underset{j}{x_i''} - \underset{\mathrm{aw}}{x_i''}\right)\left(\underset{\mathrm{w}}{x_i''} - \underset{\mathrm{aw}}{x_i''}\right)}{\sum_{i=1}^{m} \left(\underset{\mathrm{w}}{x_i''} - \underset{\mathrm{aw}}{x_i''}\right)^2}. \tag{3.90}$$

For such a constructed measure, all objects better than the anti-pattern and worse than the pattern will have the measure value in the range from zero to one. The pattern will have a measure value of one, and the anti-pattern will be zero. It is also possible to specify measure values for objects that are superior to the pattern. They will have measure values greater than one. Objects worse than the anti-pattern will take a negative measure value. Thanks to this, you can easily determine the position of an object in the ranking in relation to the pattern and anti-pattern.

The value of an aggregate measure based on the projection of a vector onto a vector has all the positive features of the II path measure while maintaining the simplicity of calculation, the III path measure. It has a very simple geometric interpretation; moreover, its application is not limited to the Euclidean space. It can

Table 3.3 Comparison of aggregate measures based on projections

Property	Aggregate measure based on Orthogonal projection (II path)	Orthogonal projection (III path)	VMCM
Determination conditions	Pattern and anti-pattern cannot be the same	The pattern must have all coordinates greater than the anti-pattern, and the arithmetic means of the standardized features must be equal to zero	The scalar product of the difference of the pattern vectors and anti-pattern vectors on each other cannot be equal to zero (in real Euclidean spaces, the pattern and anti-pattern cannot be the same)
Type of a measure distance	Real Euclidean space (possibility of using complex space not specified by the author of the method)	Real Euclidean space (possibility of using complex space not specified by the author of the method)	Is not required
Type of scalar product	Euclidean space	Euclidean space	Any that meets the conditions (3.74)–(3.78)
Type of variables	Stimulant and destimulants	Stimulant	Stimulant and destimulants
Measure value for a pattern	1	Dependent on set of objects	1
Measure value for an anti-pattern	0	Dependent on set of objects	0

be used with any dot product of a pre-Hilbert space, moreover, with any dot product satisfying the conditions (3.74)–(3.78), which is also with a dot product of each Euclidean space (Table 3.3).

When conducting research, it is often carried out on the basis of a pattern calculated from the maximum (or minimum for a destimulant) values of the coordinates of the objects. However, this is not always beneficial due to the extreme elements that often have abnormally high coordinate values. Before the measure value is determined, all variables are normalized. The influence of atypical objects on the variables values depends on the choice of the normalization method. In general, standardization methods are not very "resistant" to the appearance of atypical objects. In the case of standardization, atypical objects achieve a very high value of this variable, for which they have atypical value. As a result, the maximum value for this variable will be much greater than for the others. This will result in "favoring" when determining the value of the measure for atypical objects of this variable compared to others, while for other objects it may make this variable less important than others. The influence of atypical objects on the ranking of all objects will depend on the choice of a normalization method and the measure calculation.

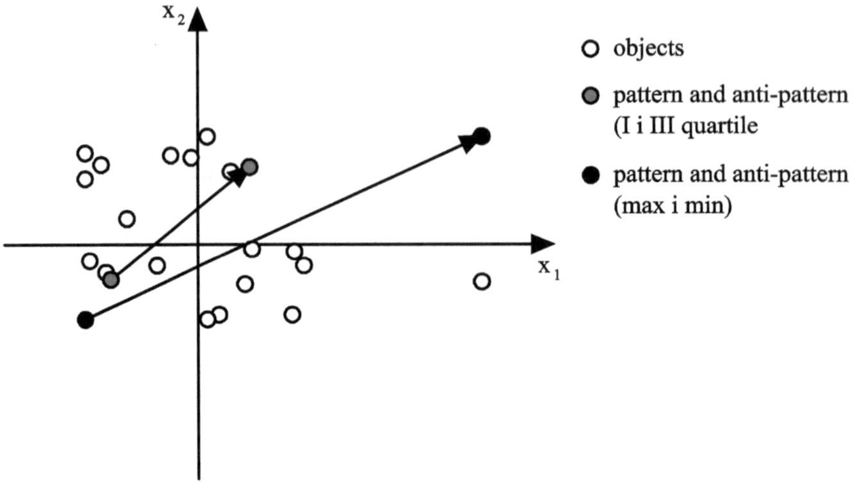

Fig. 3.12 The vector that is projected for the pattern calculated as the maximum values of the coordinates and for the pattern calculated on the basis of quartiles

At the normalization stage, the impact of atypical objects on the coordinate values of other objects should be minimized by selecting an appropriate standardization method. However, reducing the impact on the coordinate values of other objects does not have to cause that the coordinate values of atypical objects will not differ from the other. Therefore, it may be necessary to choose appropriate methods of pattern selection. In the work [98], it was proposed to adopt the values of the third and first quartiles as the pattern and anti-pattern. In the measure calculated based on the projection of a vector onto a vector, the difference in coordinates of these patterns gives the coordinates of a vector onto which the projection is made, while for a stimulant the pattern of the third quartile is subtracted from the pattern of the third quartile, and for the destimulant the order of subtraction is the reverse.

In Fig. 3.12, the I and III quartile patterns are marked in gray. Due to the difference of coordinates, a vector was created and projected onto it. Looking at the direction of the vector on which the projection is made with the I and III quartiles and the vector calculated on the basis of the maximum and minimum values, it can be noticed that thanks to the quartiles the weight of x_1'' and x_2'' variables will be similar, which will have a similar effect on the measure value.

In the aggregate measure calculated from the maximum or minimum coordinate values, the position of a pattern is influenced by highly atypical objects (if any), which is illustrated in Fig. 3.13. Almost all objects except one are within the selected rectangle. The pattern should therefore be placed on one of the corners of this rectangle. However, the object farthest to the right will decide the position of a pattern (if the pattern will be calculated on the basis of the maximum values). As a result, the variable related to the horizontal axis will be more strongly considered in creating the aggregate measure than the variable related to the vertical axis. Objects

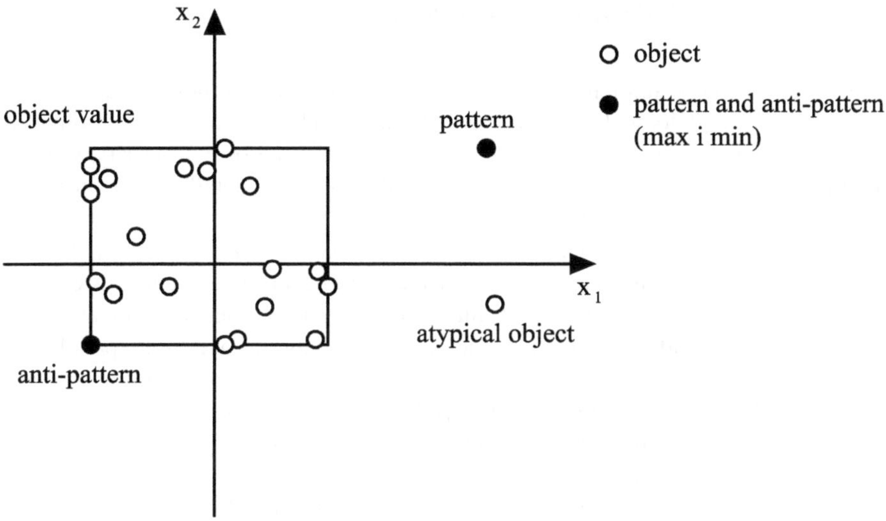

Fig. 3.13 The area of typical values of objects and an atypical object

that stand out from others are rare. Sometimes they can have an unusual value for only one variable. Due to their rarity, their inclusion in the test set is purely random, and the values of the measure take on a random character. The use of quartiles to determine patterns means that atypical objects have very little impact on the aggregate measure value.

3.5 Description of Vector Measure Construction Method (VMCM)

Vector measure construction method is the relatively new method (methodological bases have been developed in 2009 [133]), and thus it will be presented in detail. The method utilizes the vector calculus properties in order to build vector synthetic measure (basing on the definition of the scalar product). Such an approach allows for making raking, classification of objects, and study of change dynamics.

The procedure of VMCM comprises 8 stages:

Stage 1. Selection of variables
Stage 2. Elimination of variables
Stage 3. Defining the diagnostic variables character
Stage 4. Assigning weights to diagnostic variables
Stage 5. Normalization of variables
Stage 6. Determination of the pattern and anti-pattern
Stage 7. Building the synthetic measure
Stage 8. Classification of objects

3.5.1 Stage 1: Selection of Variables

The selection can be implemented in two ways, namely using the approach related to substantive and logical selection and the approach related to the elimination of variables such as those characterized by a high degree of collinearity. Criteria for the selection of diagnostic variables are described in detail in the literature, e.g., [133]. They define the characters of such variables, e.g., they should include the most important properties of considered phenomena, should be precisely defined, logically connected with each other, and they should be measurable (directly or indirectly) and expressed in natural units (in the form of intensity indicators). In addition, they should contain a large load of information, have high spatial variability, should be highly correlated with non-diagnostic variables, and a synthetic variable, and should not be highly correlated, etc. The procedure for the selection of diagnostic variables is related to a variety of statistical analyzes, during which many of different criteria are considered.

On the basis of collected data, the observation matrix $O\,[n \times m]$ where rows represent objects and columns represent variables is created. When making calculations in the vector space, rows in the matrix are considered as vectors (objects) and columns as coordinates for these vectors ($\underset{j}{x_i}$).

The amount $\underset{j}{x_i}$ represents the value of i-th variable for j-th object, n is the number of objects, and m is the number of variables.

3.5.2 Stage 2: Elimination of Variables

Elimination of variables is carried out by using significance coefficient of features [108]:

$$V_{x_i} = \frac{\sigma_i}{\bar{x}_i}, \tag{3.91}$$

where:

x_i—i-th variable
σ_i—standard deviation of the i-th variable
$\bar{x}_i$—mean value of the i-th variable

whereas

$$\bar{x}_i = \frac{\sum_{j=1}^{n} \underset{j}{x_i}}{n}, \tag{3.92}$$

and

$$\sigma_i = \sqrt{\frac{\sum_{j=1}^{n}\left(\underset{j}{x_i} - \bar{x}_i\right)^2}{n-1}}. \tag{3.93}$$

Variables, for which significance coefficient values are within the range ⟨0; 0.1⟩, are quasi-constant, and such variables should be eliminated from the set of variables under consideration [108, 129].

3.5.3 Stage 3: Defining the Diagnostic Variables Character

Definition of the diagnostic variables character refers to assigning diagnostic variables to the one of three groups, namely stimulants, destimulants, and nominants. Stimulants are such variables whose greater values mean the higher level of development of studied phenomena, e.g., considering the quality of life, there will be: the number of GPs, cars, residential area per person, etc. Destimulants are such variables whose smaller values mean the higher level of development, for instance, considering the standard of living there will be: inflation, unemployment, etc., while nominations are such variables whose desired values are within a specific range (e.g., natural growth, lending rate, etc.).

3.5.4 Stage 4: Assigning Weights to Diagnostic Variables

In order to take into account the different impact of diagnostic variables on aggregate measures, weight systems are constructed. Two approaches apply when determining variable weights. The first uses non-statistical information, in which the weights are usually determined by the expert assessment method, and they are the so-called substantive weights. The second approach is related to the use of information from various types of statistical materials. In this case, we are talking about statistical weights. In practice, we often set weights using the second approach, which is based on statistical resources.

Weighing variables can be carried out for example with the use of a relative information value meter [146] (other measures may also be used):

$$w_i = \frac{V_{x_i}}{\sum_{k=1}^{m} V_{x_k}}, \tag{3.94}$$

where w_i means variable's weight.

The variable will have the greater impact on the value of the measure, the higher the w_i value will be, what means the greater variability for the analyzed set of objects the given variable will have. However, it should be remembered that the weights are to be positive and meet the following condition:

$$\sum_{i=1}^{m} w_i = 1. \tag{3.95}$$

Nevertheless, regardless of the system adopted, the weights should be normalized.

3.5.5 Stage 5: Normalization of Variables

The variables used in studies are heterogeneous because they describe the various properties of objects. They can occur in different units of measure, which additionally hinder any arithmetic operations. Therefore, the next stage in the construction of the measure of development that must be carried out consists in *normalizing variables*. This process leads not only to the elimination of units of measurement, but also to equalize the values of variables. Standardization is the most commonly used normalization techniques:

$$x'_{\underset{j}{i}} = \frac{a_i}{\sigma_i}, \tag{3.96}$$

where nominator a_i can be defined in any way, e.g.,

$$a_i = x_{\underset{j}{i}} - \bar{x}_i, \tag{3.97}$$

where $x'_{\underset{j}{i}}$ is the normalized value of the i-th variable for the j-th object.

3.5.6 Stage 6: Determination of Pattern and Anti-pattern

Pattern and anti-pattern can be selected as real-life objects. It is also possible to automatically determine the pattern and anti-pattern based on the first and third quartiles [98], where for stimulants values of the third quartile and for destimulants values of the first quartile are taken as coordinates of the pattern accordingly:

$$\underset{\text{w}}{x'_i} = \begin{cases} \underset{q_{\text{III}}}{x'_i} & \text{for stimulants} \\ \underset{q_{\text{I}}}{x'_i} & \text{for destimulants} \end{cases}, \tag{3.98}$$

where $\underset{\text{w}}{x'_i}$ is the value of the i-th normalized variable for the pattern, $\underset{q_{\text{I}}}{x'_i}$—the value of the i-th normalized variable for the first quartile, and $\underset{q_{\text{III}}}{x'_i}$—the value of the i-th normalized variable for the third quartile.

In case of anti-pattern, the procedure is inversed, values in the first quartile are anti-pattern coordinates for stimulants, and values in the third quartile for destimulants:

$$\underset{\text{aw}}{x'_i} = \begin{cases} \underset{q_{\text{I}}}{x'_i} & \text{for stimulants} \\ \underset{q_{\text{III}}}{x'_i} & \text{for destimulants} \end{cases}, \tag{3.99}$$

where $\underset{\text{aw}}{x'_i}$ means the value of the i-th normalized variable for anti-pattern.

The first quartile is determined following the formulas [6]:

1. For n divided by 4:

$$q_{\text{I}} = \frac{x_{i,\frac{n}{4}} + x_{i,\frac{n}{4}+1}}{2}. \tag{3.100}$$

2. For $n + 1$ divided by 4:

$$q_{\text{I}} = x_{i,\frac{n}{4}}. \tag{3.101}$$

3. For $n + 2$ divided by 4:

$$q_{\text{I}} = x_{i,\frac{n}{4}+0.5}. \tag{3.102}$$

4. For $n + 3$ divided by 4:

$$q_{\text{I}} = \frac{x_{i,\frac{n}{4}-0.5} + x_{i,\frac{n}{4}+0.5}}{2}. \tag{3.103}$$

While the third quartile is determined following the formulas:

1. For n divided by 4:

$$q_{\text{III}} = \frac{x_{i,\frac{3n}{4}} + x_{i,\frac{3n}{4}+1}}{2} \tag{3.104}$$

2. For $n + 1$ divided by 4:

$$q_{\mathrm{III}} = x_{i,\frac{3(n+1)}{4}} \tag{3.105}$$

3. For $n + 2$ divided by 4:

$$q_{\mathrm{III}} = x_{i,\frac{3n}{4}+0.5} \tag{3.106}$$

4. For $n + 3$ divided by 4:

$$q_{\mathrm{III}} = \frac{x_{i,\frac{3(n+1)}{4}-0.5} + x_{i,\frac{3(n+1)}{4}+0.5}}{2} \tag{3.107}$$

where:

q_{I}—the first quartile
q_{III}—the third quartile
n—the number of objects

3.5.7 Stage 7: Construction of the Synthetic Measure

The values of the variables of the examined objects in the vector space are interpreted as vector coordinates. Each object therefore determines a specific direction in space. The pattern and anti-pattern difference is also a vector that determines a certain direction in space. Along this direction, the aggregate measure value for each object is calculated. This difference can be treated as a monodimensional coordinate system, in which the coordinates are calculated based on the formula [128, 129]:

$$c = \frac{\left(\vec{A}, \vec{B}\right)}{\left(\vec{B}, \vec{B}\right)}. \tag{3.108}$$

In turn, $\vec{A}$ and $\vec{B}$ are vectors, and is the scalar product, which can be defined as follows:

$$\left(\vec{A}, \vec{B}\right) = \sum_{k=1}^{n} a_k b_k, \tag{3.109}$$

where: a_k, b_k—coordinates of the appropriate vector $\vec{A}$ and $\vec{B}$.

We consider the $\vec{B}$ vector as the monodimensional coordinates system, and thus it represents a difference between the pattern and anti-pattern. By entering coordinates of the pattern and anti-pattern as well as the object into the formula (3.108), the result is as follows [128, 129]:

$$\underset{j}{m_s} = \frac{\sum_{i=1}^{m} \left(\underset{j}{x_i'} - \underset{\text{aw}}{x_i'} \right) \left(\underset{\text{w}}{x_i'} - \underset{\text{aw}}{x_i'} \right)}{\sum_{i=1}^{m} \left(\underset{\text{w}}{x_i'} - \underset{\text{aw}}{x_i'} \right)^2}. \tag{3.110}$$

For a synthetic measure so constructed, all objects that are better than the anti-pattern and worse than the pattern will have the measure value in the range from zero to one. The pattern will have the value equal to one and anti-pattern equal to zero. It is also possible to specify the value of the objects' measure better than the pattern. They will have values greater than one. Objects that are worse than the anti-pattern will have a negative value of measure. Thanks to this, the position of the object in the ranking in relation to the pattern and anti-pattern will be easy to determinate.

In VMCM method, a measuring vector $\underset{j}{\vec{M}'}$ is a difference between the vector of the pattern $\underset{\text{w}}{\vec{\text{X}}'}$ and the vector of the anti-pattern $\underset{\text{aw}}{\vec{\text{X}}'}$ (Fig. 3.14a). The vector $\underset{j}{\vec{M}'}$ determines a monodimensional coordinates system having the origin in the point determined by the end of the vector of anti-pattern $\underset{\text{aw}}{\vec{\text{X}}'}$. The synthetic measure $\underset{j}{m_s}$ is the component (value of projection) of the vector $\underset{j}{\text{X}_i'} - \underset{\text{aw}}{\text{X}_i'}$ on the vector $\underset{j}{\vec{M}'}$ (Fig. 3.14b).

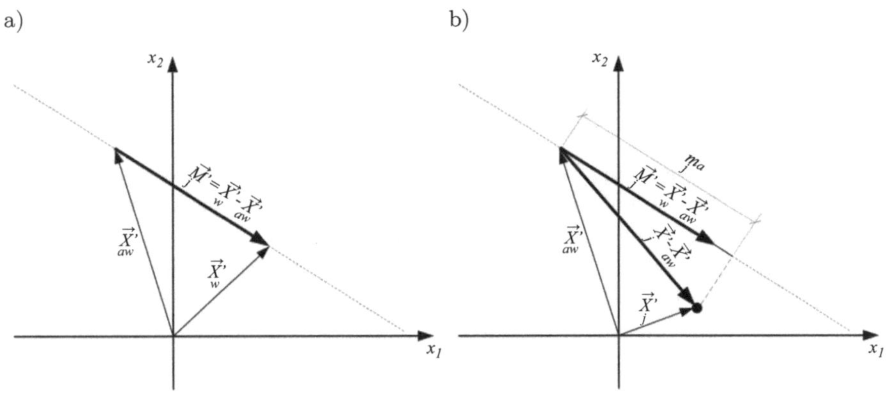

Fig. 3.14 Measure value depending on the object's position: (**a**); (**b**)

3.5.8 Stage 8: Classification of Objects

The values of the aggregate measure allow for ranking objects, and thus it is possible to determine which of them are "better" and which are "worse." They also allow determining which are similar to each other in terms of adopted criteria. In order to better visualize the results of calculations, objects can be divided into classes with similar measurement values. This is particularly important in the case of spatial objects. Such a ranking can be presented in the form of a map, where individual objects are visualized using the colors assigned to individual classes. In the simplest case, objects can be classified based on mean value $\overline{m}_{m_{s0}}$ and standard deviation of the synthetic measure $\sigma_{m_{s0}}$. Objects are classified into four classes [133]:

$$\begin{cases} 1 \text{ for } \underset{j}{m_s} \in \left\langle \overline{m}_{m_{s0}} + \sigma_{m_{s0}}; \infty \right) \\ 2 \text{ for } \underset{j}{m_s} \in \left\langle \overline{m}_{m_{s0}}; \overline{m}_{m_{s0}} + \sigma_{m_{s0}} \right) \\ 3 \text{ for } \underset{j}{m_s} \in \left\langle \overline{m}_{m_{s0}} - \sigma_{m_{s0}}; \overline{m}_{m_{s0}} \right) \\ 4 \text{ for } \underset{j}{m_s} \in \left(-\infty; \overline{m}_{m_{s0}} - \sigma_{m_{s0}} \right) \end{cases}. \tag{3.111}$$

It is also possible to classify objects into any number of classes by using quantiles:

$$\begin{cases} 1 \text{ for } \underset{j}{m_s} \in \left\langle Q_{\frac{0}{n_c}}; Q_{\frac{1}{n_c}} \right) \\ 2 \text{ for } \underset{j}{m_s} \in \left\langle Q_{\frac{1}{n_c}}; Q_{\frac{2}{n_c}} \right) \\ \vdots \\ n_c \text{ for } \underset{j}{m_s} \in \left\langle Q_{\frac{n_c-1}{n_c}}; Q_{\frac{n_c}{n_c}} \right\rangle \end{cases}, \tag{3.112}$$

where: Q_k—quantile of the k-th order, and n_c—the number of classes. After minor modifications, the method to construct vector aggregate measures VMCM can be used as a tool for solving multi-criteria decision problems.

The VMCM method makes it possible to study dynamics—for example—of socio-economic objects development. To do this, you need to calculate the measure values for the same objects in different time units, for example years. It is necessary to ensure the comparability of measure values in individual years, and therefore, it is necessary:

1. To select a year (or another time unit, e.g., month, day) to which measurement values in other years (months, days) will be related, hereinafter referred to as the base year (month, day).
2. Using the formula (2.45) from the values of A_i and B_i, they should be determined for the base year and used in the normalization in all years (Step 5).

3. The pattern is determined only for the base year (Step 6).
4. Base year pattern is used to build the measure in all years (Step 7).

3.6 Grouping Objects Based on the Aggregate Measure Value

The measure values allow you to rank objects, so it is possible to determine which are "better" and which are "worse." They also allow you to determine which are similar in terms of adopted criteria. In order to better visualize the calculation results, objects can be divided into groups with similar measure values. This is particularly important in the case of objects of a spatial nature, such as, for example, poviats or communes. Such a ranking can be presented in the form of a map, where individual objects are visualized using colors assigned to each category. In the simplest case, grouping can be performed based on the mean value $\overline{\mathrm{m}}_{\mathrm{s}0}$ and the standard deviation of the aggregate measure $\sigma_{\mathrm{m}_{\mathrm{s}0}}$, divided into four classes [140]:

$$\begin{cases} 1 \text{ dla } \underset{j}{\mathrm{m}_{\mathrm{s}}} \in \left\langle \overline{\mathrm{m}}_{\mathrm{s}0} + \sigma_{\mathrm{m}_{\mathrm{s}0}}; \infty \right), \\ 2 \text{ dla } \underset{j}{\mathrm{m}_{\mathrm{s}}} \in \left\langle \overline{\mathrm{m}}_{\mathrm{s}0}; \overline{\mathrm{m}}_{\mathrm{s}0} + \sigma_{\mathrm{m}_{\mathrm{s}0}} \right), \\ 3 \text{ dla } \underset{j}{\mathrm{m}_{\mathrm{s}}} \in \left\langle \overline{\mathrm{m}}_{\mathrm{s}0} - \sigma_{\mathrm{m}_{\mathrm{s}0}}; \overline{\mathrm{m}}_{\mathrm{s}0} \right), \\ 4 \text{ dla } \underset{j}{\mathrm{m}_{\mathrm{s}}} \in \left(-\infty; \overline{\mathrm{m}}_{\mathrm{s}0} - \sigma_{\mathrm{m}_{\mathrm{s}0}} \right). \end{cases} \tag{3.113}$$

The width of classes can be adjusted by using its multiplicity instead of the standard deviation. If the multiple of the standard deviation is less than one, it is possible to divide into more than four classes. For example, when the multiplicity is 0.5, the number of classes can be doubled to eight. Another simple method of division into classes is proposed in the paper [140]. For example, the mean value $\overline{\mathrm{m}}_{\mathrm{s}0}$ from all measure values is determined, which is the limit that divides objects into two subsets. Two separate mean values, which constitute the boundary dividing these two subsets into consecutive subsets, are calculated for them. In this way, four subsets are obtained, which can be treated as four classes. This kind of division can be continued, obtaining a number of classes that is a multiple of two (8, 16, 32 itd.).

The disadvantage of the presented methods is the division that does not take into account the characteristics of the set of aggregate measure values. The situation may occur, where a boundary between classes is between two objects that are very close to each other, but far from others. Such a division may lead to misinterpretation of the obtained results. One solution may be to increase the number of classes, but in black and white publications, it may result in poor readability. Moreover, such a solution still does not reflect the characteristics of the set of aggregate measure values. In order to reproduce such characteristics,

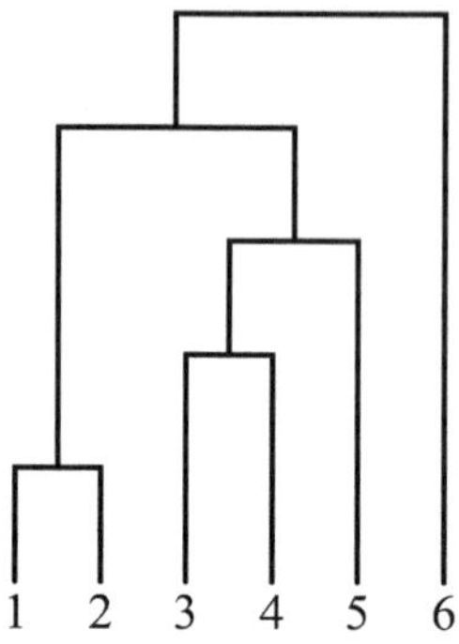

Fig. 3.15 Sample of a dendrogram

classification methods (patternless classification) should be applied. Due to a non-complicated one-dimensional problem, it is possible to use the simplest hierarchical grouping methods. The idea behind hierarchical methods is to create a classification hierarchy. The hierarchy contains n classifications, where n is the number of objects. The two extreme classifications are a classification where all objects belong to one class and one where each object is in a separate class. In between are all the other classifications ranging from 2 to $n - 1$ class.

Taking into account the start of grouping criterion, the following methods can be distinguished [152]:

- Agglomeration
- Division

The difference between these methods is the grouping starting point. In division methods, the starting point is one set, which is divided into smaller and smaller subsets in the next steps. The starting point in agglomeration methods are n sets, where n is equal to the number of objects. In the next steps, these sets are combined and get bigger. In practical applications, agglomeration methods are of great importance thanks to the fact that they are best developed in terms of methodology [56]. Their advantages include [56]:

1. They work according to one procedure.
2. The grouping process consists of a series of steps that form a grouping hierarchy that facilitates determination of the correct number of classes.
3. Grouping results can be presented in the form of a dendrogram showing the relationship between individual classifications.

A dendrogram, otherwise known as a classification tree, illustrates how classes are combined. At the lowest level, all objects are allocated to separate classes. At a higher level, it shows which classes have been combined to reduce their number by one. Moving to each level higher reduces the number of classes by one. A sample dendrogram is shown in Fig. 3.15.

Thanks to the agglomeration methods, a number of consistent classes can be obtained. The starting point for all agglomeration methods is to create a distance matrix based on a selected distance measure. The right choice of this measure is an important element affecting the way agglomeration methods work. A very important group of distance measures are those based on the Minkowski measure given by the formula (3.13). Agglomeration methods use this measure to determine which objects are closer and which are further from each other. In the one-dimensional case, the choice of p affects only distance values but not the ordering of which objects are closer and which are further away. Hence, the simplest urban metric was selected, which can be described by a formula for a one-dimensional case:

$$\mathrm{d}\left(\underset{j}{\mathrm{m_S}}, \underset{k}{\mathrm{m_S}}\right) = \left|\underset{j}{\mathrm{m_S}} - \underset{k}{\mathrm{m_S}}\right|. \tag{3.114}$$

The starting point for calculations in agglomeration methods is the

$$\begin{array}{c} \\ \underset{1}{\mathrm{m_S}} \\ \underset{2}{\mathrm{m_S}} \\ \vdots \\ \underset{n}{\mathrm{m_S}} \end{array} \overset{\begin{array}{cccc} \underset{1}{\mathrm{m_S}} & \underset{2}{\mathrm{m_S}} & \cdots & \underset{n}{\mathrm{m_S}} \end{array}}{\begin{bmatrix} \mathrm{d}\left(\underset{1}{\mathrm{m_S}}, \underset{1}{\mathrm{m_S}}\right) & \mathrm{d}\left(\underset{1}{\mathrm{m_S}}, \underset{2}{\mathrm{m_S}}\right) & \cdots & \mathrm{d}\left(\underset{1}{\mathrm{m_S}}, \underset{n}{\mathrm{m_S}}\right) \\ \mathrm{d}\left(\underset{2}{\mathrm{m_S}}, \underset{1}{\mathrm{m_S}}\right) & \mathrm{d}\left(\underset{2}{\mathrm{m_S}}, \underset{2}{\mathrm{m_S}}\right) & \cdots & \mathrm{d}\left(\underset{2}{\mathrm{m_S}}, \underset{n}{\mathrm{m_S}}\right) \\ \vdots & \vdots & \ddots & \vdots \\ \mathrm{d}\left(\underset{n}{\mathrm{m_S}}, \underset{1}{\mathrm{m_S}}\right) & \mathrm{d}\left(\underset{n}{\mathrm{m_S}}, \underset{2}{\mathrm{m_S}}\right) & \cdots & \mathrm{d}\left(\underset{n}{\mathrm{m_S}}, \underset{n}{\mathrm{m_S}}\right) \end{bmatrix}} \tag{3.115}$$

For most distance measures, there are all zeros on the main diagonal, and the matrix itself is symmetrical. All agglomeration methods have one grouping algorithm in common, called the central agglomeration procedure, using a distance matrix [140]. The steps of this algorithm are as follows:

1. Assigning each object to a separate class.
2. Finding the smallest value in the distance matrix (omitting the elements on the main diagonal). The row and column numbers identify the numbers of j and k sets.
3. Combining sets indexed j and k in one set.
4. Update of the distance matrix (removal of columns and rows j and k, as well as adding a row and a column describing distances from the newly created set).
5. Check if there is only one set left, if not, move to point 2.

The method of determining the distance between sets of more than one element is determined by a specific agglomeration method. For a one-dimensional case, the calculation can be simplified by sorting $\underset{j}{\mathrm{m_S}}$ measures ascending or descending, receiving a series of sorted out $\underset{j}{\mathrm{m'_S}}$ values. Then, instead of a two-dimensional distance matrix, a one-dimensional matrix can be used:

$$D = \left[d\left(m'_{s_1}, m'_{s_2}\right) d\left(m'_{s_2}, m'_{s_3}\right) \cdots d\left(m'_{s_{n-1}}, m'_{s_n}\right) \right]. \tag{3.116}$$

The central agglomeration procedure will change, and the steps will be as follows:

1. Assigning each object to a separate class.
2. Search for the smallest value in a one-dimensional distance matrix. The element number in this matrix determines the number of j sets.
3. Combination of sets indexed j and $j + 1$ in one set.
4. Update of one-dimensional distance matrix (update of elements D_{j-1} and D_{j+1} and elimination of D_j element).
5. Check if there is only one set left, if not, move to point 2.

The agglomeration methods include, among others, the nearest neighbor method, the farthest neighborhood method, the group average method, and the Ward method. They differ in how the distance between sets is calculated. In the nearest neighborhood method, the distance matrix is updated under the formulas:

$$D_{j-1} = D_{j-1}, \tag{3.117}$$

oraz

$$D_{j+1} = D_{j+1}. \tag{3.118}$$

The idea of determining a distance in this method is illustrated in Fig. 3.16a. Distances are measured between the closest objects in two sets. In the case of one-dimensional with sorted measure values, the calculation of the measure values always includes the extreme elements of sets, i.e., those that have the smallest or largest values in a set.

The farthest neighborhood method is very similar to the nearest neighborhood method. The distance matrix in this method is updated based on the formulas:

$$D_{j-1} = D_{j-1} + D_j, \tag{3.119}$$

oraz

$$D_{j+1} = D_{j+1} + D_j. \tag{3.120}$$

The method of determining a distance is shown in Fig. 3.16b. Distances are measured between the farthest objects in two sets. As in the nearest neighborhood method, the extreme elements of sets are always used in the calculation of the measure values.

In the group mean method, the measure values are calculated based on the mean values of the aggregate measure in each class. This is presented in Fig. 3.16c. Use

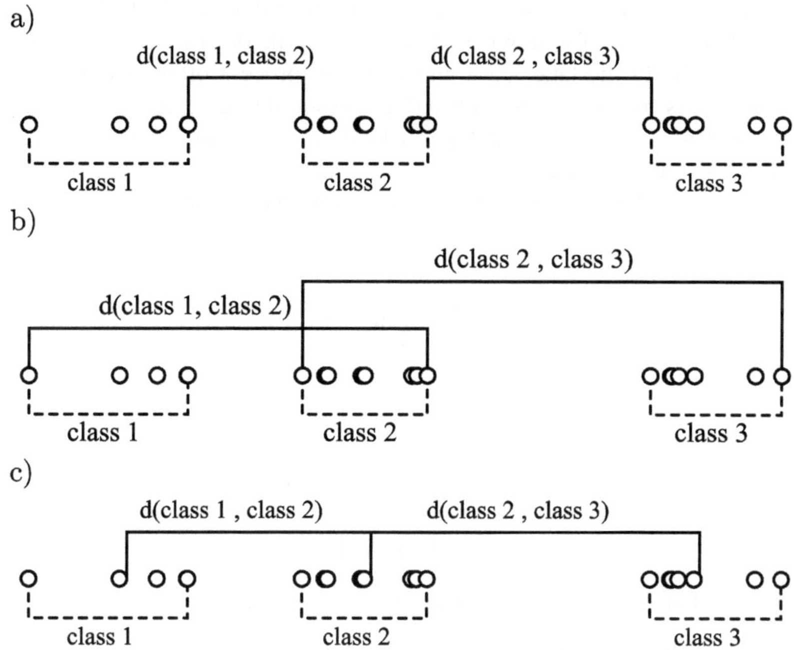

Fig. 3.16 The distance between classes in the method of: (**a**) the nearest neighborhood; (**b**) the farthest neighborhood; (**c**) group mean

the following formulas to update a distance matrix:

$$D_{j-1} = a_p D_{j-1} + a_q D_{j+1} + b D_j, \tag{3.121}$$

where:

a_p, a_q, b—coefficients selected depending on the method,

at the position of $j + 1$ under the formula:

$$D_{j+1} = a_p D_{j+1} + a_q D_{j-1} + b D_j. \tag{3.122}$$

The values of the coefficients will be equal to

$$a_p = \frac{n_j}{n_j + n_{j+1}}, \quad a_q = \frac{n_{j+1}}{n_j + n_{j+1}}, \quad b = 0, \tag{3.123}$$

where:

j—the number of a set
n_j—the number of elements of the j-th set

Agglomeration methods form a set of classifications in which the number of classes is from 1 to n. The number of classes may be determined by a researcher or automatically. In the latter case, the grouping process often lasts until certain conditions for its completion are satisfied. In the simplest case, it is a predetermined number of classes. However, this type of final condition does not guarantee good internal class cohesion. You can use intra- and inter-class variance to determine the number of classes that allow better grouping of objects. The intra-class variance can be noted as

$$\underset{i}{\hat{\sigma}}^2 = \frac{\sum_{\underset{j}{\mathrm{m}'_{\mathrm{s}}} \in \mathrm{K}_i} \left(\underset{j}{\mathrm{m}'_{\mathrm{s}}} - \underset{i}{\overline{\mathrm{m}}'_{\mathrm{s}}} \right)^2}{n_i}, \tag{3.124}$$

where:

n_i—the number of elements of i-th set
$\underset{i}{\overline{\mathrm{m}}'_{\mathrm{s}}}$—average value of the measure in the i-th class
K_i—the set of all values of the aggregate measure in the i-th class

In contrast, the inter-class variance can be noted as [226]

$$\check{\sigma}^2 = \frac{\sum_{i=1}^{n_{\mathrm{K}}} \left(\underset{i}{\overline{\mathrm{m}}'_{\mathrm{s}}} - \overline{\overline{\mathrm{m}}}'_{\mathrm{s}} \right)^2}{n_{\mathrm{K}}}, \tag{3.125}$$

where:

n_{K}—the number of sets
$\overline{\overline{\mathrm{m}}}'_{\mathrm{s}}$—mean value of the $\underset{i}{\overline{\mathrm{m}}'_{\mathrm{s}}}$ measure mean values

Classes containing similar objects, i.e., not significantly different from each other, have a small intra-group variance and a relatively large inter-group variance [86]. The maximum value of the inter-group variance and the minimum intra-group variance occur when the number of classes equals the number of objects. In practice, the optimal one can be the number of classes at which the local slope of the tangent to the plot of inter-class variance increases strongly.

Another method of determining the number of classes is the Hubert–Levine index [56]:

$$G2\left(n_{\mathrm{K}}\right) = \frac{\mathrm{SDW}\left(n_{\mathrm{K}}\right) - r\mathrm{DW}_{\min}}{r\mathrm{DW}_{\max} - r\mathrm{DW}_{\min}}, \tag{3.126}$$

where:

SDW (n_K)—sum of all intra-class distances with the number of classes equal to n_K
DW_{min}—the smallest intra-class distance
DW_{max}—greatest intra-class distance
r—the number of intra-class distances

Value of n_K, for which the smallest value was obtained $G2\,(n_K)$, determines the number of classes for which the optimal division of objects was obtained. The Gamma Baker and Hubert index can also be used to determine its number [56]:

$$G3\,(n_K) = \frac{s\,(+) - s\,(-)}{s\,(+) + s\,(-)}, \tag{3.127}$$

where:

$s\,(+)$—the number of compatible distance pairs
$s\,(-)$—the number of incompatible distance pairs

When calculating the Gamma index, all combinations of pairs of intra-class and inter-class distances are compared with each other. Matching pairs are considered pairs for which the intra-class distance is smaller than the inter-class distance, and pairs for which the intra-class distance is greater than the inter-class distance are considered non-compliant. Cases where they are equal are not taken into account. The maximum value of the Gamma index indicates n_K, for which the optimal division of objects was obtained.

Part II
Multi-criteria Decision Support Methods

Chapter 4
Methods Based on an Outranking Relationship

4.1 The Concept of Preference Relations in Multi-Criteria Methods

Decision-making is directly related to the preferences of a decision-maker. Most often, one can come across two models of aggregating preferences, namely the model based on the utility function (classical decision-making theory) and the one using the outranking relationship [194]. Both approaches have their supporters and critics. The first model assumes the existence of a utility function by means of which the assessment of individual decision variants is made. Variants may be equivalent or prevalence to each other [97]. Such a concept, along with the characteristics of selected methods based on the utility function, is described in Chap. 5.

The second model (approach) is related to the so-called European school of decision support and the assumption is that preferences are aggregated using the outranking relation. In terms of comparing decision variants, four basic preferential situations are distinguished: equivalence, strong preference, low preference, and incomparability [142, 164, 203, 209]:

– Equivalence: variant W_j is equal to variant W_k.
– Strong preference: variant W_j is strongly preferred over W_k, and variant W_k is strongly preferred over variant W_j.
– Low preference: variant W_j is low preferred over W_k, and variant W_k is low preferred over W_j variant.
– Incomparability: variant W_j is incomparable with W_k.

The preferential situation of equivalence and strong preference is understood similarly as in the classical theory of decision-making. The point here is the existence of premises enabling the adoption of equivalence of two decision variants or a strong preference of one variant over the other. We can speak of weak preference when there are grounds for weakening the strong preference of one of the decision variants, but they are not strong enough to speak of the equivalence of both of them

K. Nermend, *Multi-Criteria and Multi-Dimensional Analysis in Decisions*, Vector Optimization, https://doi.org/10.1007/978-3-031-40538-9_4

or the preferences of the other variant. Incomparability of variants is a situation in which there are insufficient reasons to assume that one of the above (basic) preferential situations occurs. These preference situations are linked directly with relationships marked with appropriate symbols [164, 203]:

- Equivalence—relation I
- Strong preference—relation P
- Low preference—relation Q
- Incomparability—relation R

With these relations (I, P, Q, R), it is possible to develop a model of decision-maker's preferences in one of the two ways. The first one is such in which for each pair of different decision variants W_j, W_k from the set of variants W (the completeness condition) one can define one and only one (the condition of mutual exclusion) of the four basic preferential situations. It is therefore a question of accepting as true only one of the following statements [164]:

$$W_j \mathrm{I} W_k,\ W_j \mathrm{P} W_k,\ W_k \mathrm{P} W_j,\ W_j \mathrm{Q} W_k,\ W_k \mathrm{Q} W_j,\ Wj_{\mathrm{R}} W_k. \tag{4.1}$$

The second way is that it is possible to define for each pair of decision variants W_j, W_k, one, two, or three basic preferential situations. Choosing two or three statements does not mean that they are both true at the same time, which can mean that choosing only one true is impossible or pointless for some reason.

Moreover, Roy distinguished five additional preferential situations to these four primary ones [164]:

- No preferences: situations of equivalence and incomparability without the possibility of distinguishing between them
- Preference (in a broad sense): situations of strong and weak preference without the possibility of distinguishing between them
- Preference guess: situations of weak preference and equivalence without being able to distinguish them meaningfully
- K-preference: situations of strong preference and incomparability without being able to distinguish them significantly
- Outranking: situations of preference and presumption of preference without being able to distinguish between situations of strong and weak preference and equivalence

Binary relationships are associated with these preferential situations [164]:

- No preference situation—relation $\sim$:

$$W_j \sim W_k \Leftrightarrow W_j \mathrm{I} W_k \vee W_j \mathrm{R} W_k. \tag{4.2}$$

- Preference situation (in broad sense—relation$\succ$:

$$W_j \succ W_k \Leftrightarrow W_j \mathrm{P} W_k \vee W_j \mathrm{Q} W_k, \tag{4.3}$$

– Presumption of preference situation—relation J:

$$W_j J W_k \Leftrightarrow W_j \mathrm{Q} W_k \vee W_j \mathrm{I} W_k, \tag{4.4}$$

– K-preference situation—relation K:

$$W_j K W_k \Leftrightarrow W_j \mathrm{P} W_k \vee W_j \mathrm{R} W_k, \tag{4.5}$$

– outranking situation—relation S:

$$W_j S W_k \Leftrightarrow W_j \mathrm{P} W_k \vee W_j \mathrm{Q} W_k \vee W_j \mathrm{I} W_k. \tag{4.6}$$

The outranking relation S plays a particularly important role in the so-called European school of decision support. To analyze the decision variants, criterion functions (one or more) are used, by means of which the preferences of a decision-maker can be represented numerically. The function $g\left(W_j\right)$ can be a criterion when it meets the outranking situation, i.e., it is a true condition [142, 203]:

$$g\left(W_k\right) \geqslant g\left(W_j\right) \Rightarrow W_k \mathrm{S}_g W_j, \tag{4.7}$$

where

S_g is the outranking situation related to g condition.

Additionally, the g so-called threshold functions (equivalence threshold, preference threshold) that allow you to distinguish situations of equivalence, strong preference and weak preference.

The q_g equivalence threshold is defined for the following conditions: if the difference between the values of $g\left(W_k\right)$ and $g\left(W_j\right)$ is not higher than the threshold value, then the two decision variants W_j and W_k are equivalent, and in other cases, we are talking about preferences in a broad sense [142]:

$$\bigwedge_{W_j, W_k \in W} 0 \leqslant g\left(W_k\right) - g\left(W_j\right) \leqslant q_g \Rightarrow W_k \mathrm{I}_g W_j, \tag{4.8}$$

and

$$g\left(W_k\right) - g\left(W_j\right) > q_g \Rightarrow W_k \succ W_j. \tag{4.9}$$

On the other hand, p_g preference threshold is defined for the following situation: if a difference between values of $g\left(W_k\right)$ and $g\left(W_j\right)$ is higher than the threshold value, then there is a strong preference for the decision variant W_k over the variant W_j, and in other cases we talk about the preference assumption [142]:

$$\bigwedge_{W_j, W_k \in W} g\left(W_k\right) - g\left(W_j\right) > p_g \Rightarrow W_k \mathrm{P}_g W_j, \tag{4.10}$$

and

$$0 \leqslant g(W_k) - g\left(W_j\right) \leqslant p_g \Rightarrow W_k \mathrm{J}_g W_j. \tag{4.11}$$

From the above entries, it follows that

- $0 \leqslant q_g \leqslant p_g$,
- $\bigwedge_{W_j, W_k \in W} q_g < g(W_k) - g\left(W_j\right) \leqslant p_g \Leftrightarrow W_k \mathrm{Q}_g W_j$.

The q_g equivalence thresholds and the p_g preference thresholds are used to define a pseudo-criterion, i.e., the criterion function g, meeting the implication [142, 203]:

$$g(W_k) \geqslant g\left(W_j\right) \Rightarrow \begin{cases} W_k \mathrm{I}_g W_j \text{ dla } g(W_k) - g\left(W_j\right) \leqslant q_g, \\ W_k \mathrm{Q}_g W_j \text{ dla } q_g < g(W_k) - g\left(W_j\right) \leqslant p_g, \\ W_k \mathrm{P}_g W_j \text{ dla } p_g < g(W_k) - g\left(W_j\right). \end{cases} \tag{4.12}$$

For example, when comparing meals, you can say that their taste is similar, one is tastier than the other, one is much tastier than the other, or their taste is incomparable. In this case, taste is a criterion and the result of comparison—a relation. In connection with the above, we can distinguish the following relationships:

1. *Equivalence*—decision variants are similar to each other.
2. *Weak preference*—one decision variant is better than the other.
3. *Strong preference*—one decision variant is much better than the other.
4. *Incomparability*—it is not possible to compare the decision variants.

Incomparability usually occurs with complex criteria, which are a composition of some more simple criteria, such as taste. The taste results from the composition of ingredients that affect the sensation of sweet, salty, bitter, etc. While it is easy to determine if something is sweeter than something, comparing ice cream with fish in vinegar is a significant problem. It is not always possible to say that ice cream is tastier than fish (or vice versa), but it is also not equivalent. Then, we may only determine that they are incomparable. It should be noted that decomposition of such a criterion into its original components is not always possible. Replacing the taste criterion with the sweet, bitter, spicy, etc. criteria is not possible because the taste is an evaluation of the composition and not a degree of the intensity of these senses.

Pairwise comparison is fundamental to check whether there are indications that a given decision variant has an advantage over others. Table 4.1 shows examples of decision variants considered when purchasing a car by a consumer. It is assumed that the consumer intends to choose between three cars, and hence three variants are defined. The following criteria were assumed as important: *zużycie paliwa na 100 km, pojemność bagażnika* i *cenę*.

For criteria where the lowest possible value is important, all values are multiplied by −1. In the example, the criteria are price and fuel consumption. The values after the change are presented in Table 4.2.

Table 4.1 Decision variants of the consumer's choice of a car

Decision variant	Price [PLN]	Fuel consumption $\left[\frac{1}{100\,\text{km}}\right]$	Trunk capacity [l]
W_1	35,700	6	224
W_2	39,500	6.5	275
W_3	40,715	6	251

Table 4.2 Decision variants of the consumer's choice of a car

Decision variant	Price [PLN]	Fuel consumption $\left[\frac{1}{100\,\text{km}}\right]$	Trunk capacity [l]
W_1	−35,700	−6	224
W_2	−39,500	−6.5	275
W_3	−40,715	−6	251

Table 4.3 Pairwise comparison of decision variants

Pair of decision variants	Price [PLN]	Fuel consumption $\left[\frac{1}{100\,\text{km}}\right]$	Trunk capacity [l]
$W_1 S_i W_1$	1	1	1
$W_1 S_i W_2$	1	1	0
$W_1 S_i W_3$	1	1	0
$W_2 S_i W_1$	0	0	1
$W_2 S_i W_2$	1	1	1
$W_2 S_i W_3$	1	0	1
$W_3 S_i W_1$	0	1	1
$W_3 S_i W_2$	0	1	0
$W_3 S_i W_3$	1	1	1

The comparison is made by combining decision variants into pairs and determining the relationship. Each decision variant is compared with each one, and the relationships are defined separately for each criterion. There are three decision variants in the considered example: W_1, W_2, and W_3. For this set of decision variants, the following pairs can be distinguished: $(W_1; W_1)$, $(W_1; W_2)$, $(W_1; W_3)$, $(W_2; W_1)$, $(W_2; W_2)$, $(W_2; W_3)$, $(W_1; W_3)$, $(W_2; W_3)$, and $(W_3; W_3)$. In ELECTRE methods, each pair is assigned an appropriate relationship. These relations are presented in Table 4.3. The case where the hypothesis of W_j outranking over W_k is true is indicated as number 1, and the case in which it is not true is indicated as number 0. $W_j S_i W_k$ means outranking relation of W_j over W_k in relation to i criterion.

Considering the pair $(W_2; W_1)$ in relation to the criterion of trunk capacity, it can be noted that the value of W_2 is higher than W_1. Therefore it can be concluded that the hypothesis of outranking W_2 over W_1 is true. However it is not true for $W_1 S_k W_2$.

In the case of a greater number of decision variants, the results of the comparisons can be presented in square tables, one for each criterion (this is more clear). Table 4.4 is an example. Rows are related to the first elements of the decision variant pairs

Table 4.4 The comparison result for the price criterion presented in a square table

	W_1	W_2	W_3
W_1	1	1	1
W_2	0	1	1
W_3	0	0	1

and the columns to the second. The value one in the second row and the first column should be interpreted as follows: the hypothesis of outranking W_j over W_k is true.

Methods of comparisons depend on the criteria type, which are divided into four kinds [159]:

1. *True criteria*
2. *Semi-criteria*
3. *Interval criteria*
4. *Pseudo-criteria*

When comparing true criteria, *true criteria* sit is only checked whether the values describing a given variant within criteria are equal or whether one is greater than the other. In this chapter, additional characters of criteria (motivating, demotivating, desirable, and non-desirable) are introduced for the purposes of implementing them in the methods based on the outranking relationship for comparison with the author's PVM method discussed in Chap. 6. They are not part of the ELECTRE methods but can be applied if needed.

The method of determining the *preference relation* depends on the character of criteria, which is explained below:

1. Preference relation for the motivating criterion:[1]

   (a) Preference of variant W_j over variant W_k [159]:

$$g_i\left(W_j\right) > g_i\left(W_k\right), \tag{4.13a}$$

   where

   g_i is a function defining the i-th criterion for a decision variant and W_j is the j-th decision variant.

   (b) Preference of variant W_k over variant W_j:

$$g_i\left(W_k\right) > g_i\left(W_j\right). \tag{4.13b}$$

[1] Motivating criteria mean criteria for which high values are desirable, motivating a decision-maker to make a decision.

2. Preference relation for demotivating criterion:[2]
   (a) Preference of variant W_j over variant W_k:

$$g_i\left(W_j\right) < g_i\left(W_k\right). \tag{4.14a}$$

   (b) Preference of variant W_k over variant W_j:

$$g_i\left(W_k\right) < g_i\left(W_j\right). \tag{4.14b}$$

3. Preference relation to desirable criterion:[3]
   (a) Preference of variant W_j over variant W_k:

$$\left|g_i\left(W_j\right) - \mathrm{p}\right| < \left|g_i\left(W_k\right) - \mathrm{p}\right|, \tag{4.15a}$$

   where
   p—desired value.
   (b) Preference of variant W_k over variant W_j:

$$\left|g_i\left(W_k\right) - \mathrm{p}\right| < \left|g_i\left(W_j\right) - \mathrm{p}\right|. \tag{4.15b}$$

4. Preference relation for non-desirable criterion:[4]
   (a) Preference of variant W_j over variant W_k:

$$\left|g_i\left(W_j\right) - \mathrm{np}\right| > \left|g_i\left(W_k\right) - \mathrm{np}\right|, \tag{4.16a}$$

   where
   np—non-desirable value.
   (b) Preference of variant W_k over variant W_j:

$$\left|g_i\left(W_k\right) - \mathrm{np}\right| > \left|g_i\left(W_j\right) - \mathrm{np}\right|. \tag{4.16b}$$

The equivalence relation for a criterion of a motivating and demotivating character occurs when [159]

$$g_i\left(W_j\right) = g_i\left(W_k\right), \tag{4.17a}$$

---

[2] Demotivating criteria mean criteria for which low values are desirable, and their high values demotivate a decision-maker to make a decision.

[3] Desirable criteria mean criteria for which certain values are desirable, not too high and not too small.

[4] Non-desirable criteria mean criteria for which a particular value is non-desirable.

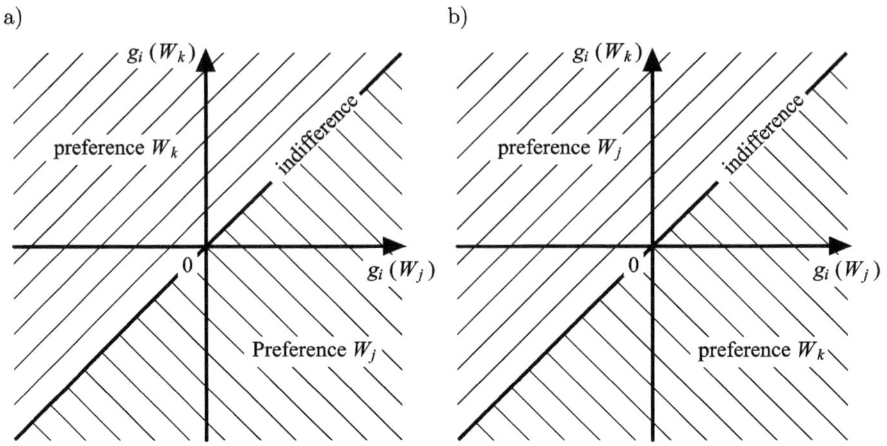

Fig. 4.1 True criterion for a criterion of (**a**) motivating and (**b**) demotivating character

while for a desirable criterion,

$$\left|g_i\left(W_j\right)-\mathrm{p}\right|=\left|g_i\left(W_k\right)-\mathrm{p}\right| \tag{4.17b}$$

and a non-desirable criterion:

$$\left|g_i\left(W_j\right)-\mathrm{np}\right|=\left|g_i\left(W_k\right)-\mathrm{np}\right|. \tag{4.17c}$$

In this case, there is no distinction between slight and strong preference.

True criteria divide decision variants into the equal, better, or worse. This is presented in Fig. 4.1. The values of criteria for the compared variants are presented on the $g_i\left(W_j\right)$ and $g_i\left(W_k\right)$ axes. In the case of the motivating criterion (Fig. 4.1a), the space was divided into three areas: a preference of the first variant $g_i\left(W_k\right)$, a preference of the second variant $g_i\left(W_j\right)$, and the equivalence of the variants. In the latter case, the area covers only the line on which there are points for which $g_i\left(W_k\right)$ is equal to $g_i\left(W_j\right)$. The type of relationship in this case depends on the difference $g_i\left(W_k\right)-g_i\left(W_j\right)$. If the criteria values are the same, i.e., the value difference is zero, the equivalence relation is obtained. A positive sign of difference means a preference for decision variant W_k and a negative sign W_j. For a demotivating criterion, the situation is very similar, and only the preference areas $g_i\left(W_k\right)$ and $g_i\left(W_j\right)$ have been swapped with each other (Fig. 4.1b).

The situation is slightly different in the case of a desirable and non-desirable criteria (Fig. 4.2). The area of the equivalence relation is the two lines that make up the x sign. They intersect at a point with both coordinates equal to the desirable (or non-desirable) value. The first line that creates the equivalence area is the line on which there are points for which $g_i\left(W_k\right)$ is equal to $g_i\left(W_j\right)$. It designates variants that have the same criteria values. The second straight line that delimits this area is

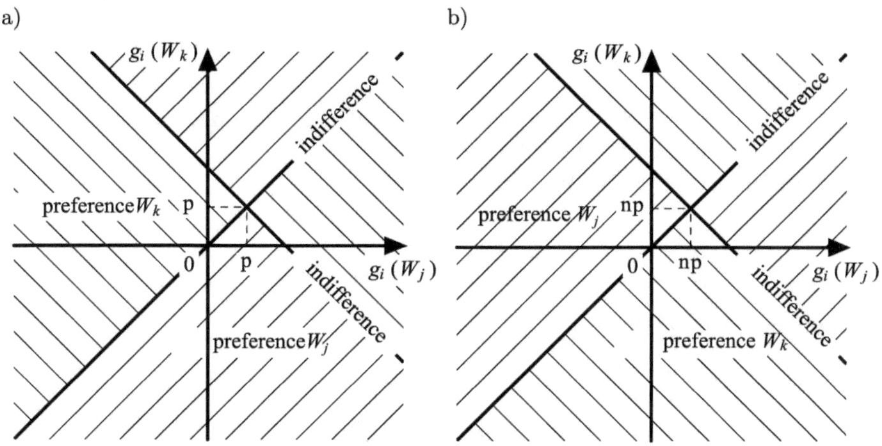

Fig. 4.2 True criterion for a criterion of the following character: (**a**) desirable, with the desired value equal to one and (**b**) non-desirable, with non-desirable value equal

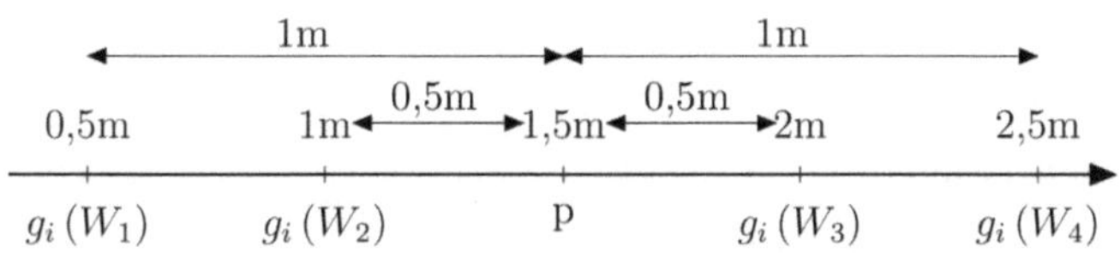

Fig. 4.3 Variants equivalent to a desirable criterion

the line with points for which $g_i(W_k)$ is equal to $-g_i(W_j)$. The decision variants assigned to this area are equivalent only from the point of view of the variant under consideration. In fact, these variants are very different from each other.

Figure 4.3 shows an example of a consumer's preferences who may need to buy a 1.5 m high ladder. The desired point for the consumer is p = 1.5m. Each ladder of a different height does not meet his expectations. Variants W_2 and W_3 are equivalents because they have the same distance from the desired point, although they have completely different altitudes. The situation is analogous for variants W_1 and W_4. As you move away from the point (p), the usefulness of decision variants decreases. In fact, it does not matter in which direction we move away from the desired point because what is important for the decision-maker is a ladder with a height equal to the desired point.

Semi-criteria solve the problem of preferences where slight differences occur. For this purpose, the equivalence and preference relationship has been improved by introducing a parameter that defines the boundary between the equivalence relationship and the preference relationship. The *preference relation* is as follows:

1. For demotivating criterion:

   (a) Preference of variant W_j over variant W_k [159]:

$$g_i\left(W_j\right) > g_i\left(W_k\right) + q_i, \tag{4.18a}$$

where

q_i—the threshold separating the equivalence relation from the preference relation, defined for the i-th criterion.

(b) Preference of variant W_k over variant W_j:

$$g_i\left(W_k\right) > g_i\left(W_j\right) + q_i. \tag{4.18b}$$

2. For demotivating criterion:

(a) Preference of variant W_j over variant W_k:

$$g_i\left(W_j\right) < g_i\left(W_k\right) - q_i. \tag{4.19a}$$

(b) Preference of variant W_k over variant W_j:

$$g_i\left(W_k\right) < g_i\left(W_j\right) - q_i. \tag{4.19b}$$

3. For desirable criterion:

(a) Preference of variant W_j over variant W_k:

$$\left|g_i\left(W_j\right) - \mathrm{p}\right| < \left|g_i\left(W_k\right) - \mathrm{p}\right| - q_i. \tag{4.20a}$$

(b) Preference of variant W_k over variant W_j:

$$\left|g_i\left(W_k\right) - \mathrm{p}\right| < \left|g_i\left(W_j\right) - \mathrm{p}\right| - q_i. \tag{4.20b}$$

4. For a non-desirable criterion:

(a) Preference of variant W_j over variant W_k:

$$\left|g_i\left(W_j\right) - \mathrm{np}\right| > \left|g_i\left(W_k\right) - \mathrm{np}\right| + q_i. \tag{4.21a}$$

(b) Preference of variant W_k over variant W_j:

$$\left|g_i\left(W_k\right) - \mathrm{np}\right| > \left|g_i\left(W_j\right) - \mathrm{np}\right| + q_i. \tag{4.21b}$$

The equivalence relation for a motivating and demotivating criterion can be defined as follows [159]:

$$\left|g_i\left(W_j\right) - g_i\left(W_k\right)\right| \leqslant q_i. \tag{4.22}$$

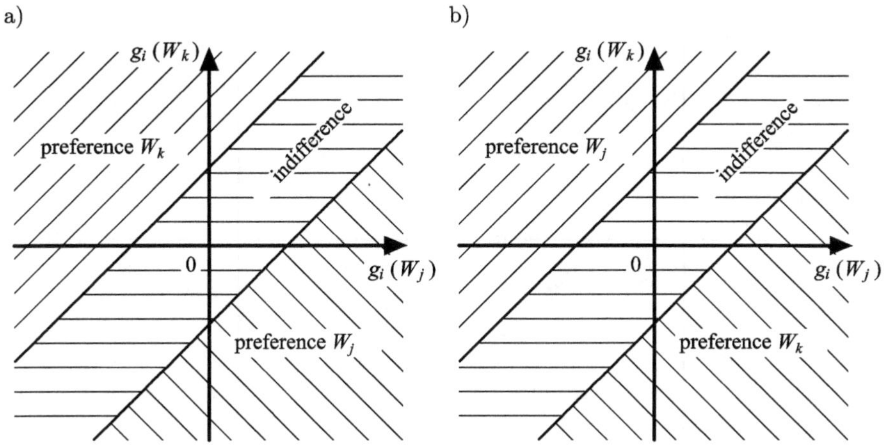

Fig. 4.4 Semi-criterion for a criterion of: (**a**) motivating; (**b**) demotivating character

The q_i parameter is a threshold for the extent to which similar values can be considered equivalent. Thanks to this, with slight differences in values, the relation between decision variants can be considered as an equivalence relation. For example, for the case under consideration, if we assume the *cenę* criterion as a semi-criterion with a threshold of 1000 PLN, then for variants W_2 and W_3 we will get

$$|-39{,}500 - (-40{,}715)| = 675 \leqslant 1000. \tag{4.23}$$

The price difference is below the threshold, which has resulted in considering the relationship between these decision variants as an equivalence relationship.

The semi-criteria also divide the decision variants into the equivalent, better, or worse. The main difference is that the equivalence area is no longer just a line. In the case of criteria of a motivating and demotivating character, it is a stripe whose width is determined by the value of q_i threshold (Fig. 4.4). In the case of desirable and non-desirable criteria, it is an x-shaped area with a certain non-zero arm width (Fig. 4.5).

The threshold approach requires that for each problem considered it is determined independently. The same threshold cannot be used when buying a bicycle as when buying a car. Due to the lower price of bicycles, the threshold for the preference must be lower. The amount of PLN 1,000 when buying a new car is a slight difference, and when buying a bike it is a big difference.

The problem of threshold dependence on a price was solved in the *interval criterion*, in which the *preference relation* was defined as follows:

1. For demotivating criterion:

   (a) Preference of variant W_j over variant W_k [159]:

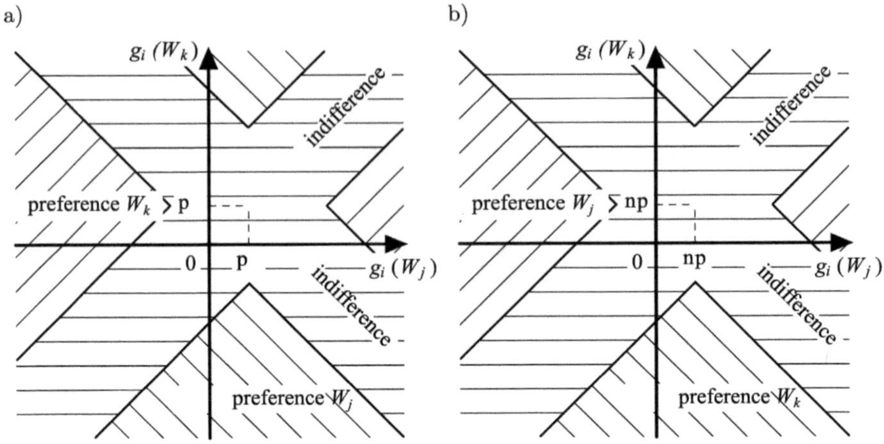

Fig. 4.5 Semi-criteria for (**a**) desirable criterion, with the desired value equal to one and (**b**) non-desirable criterion, with non-desirable value equal to one

$$g_i\left(W_j\right) > g_i\left(W_k\right) + q_i\left(g_i\left(W_k\right)\right), \tag{4.24a}$$

where

q_i ()—function dependent on the value of the i-th criterion.

(b) Preference of variant W_k over variant W_j:

$$g_i\left(W_k\right) > g_i\left(W_j\right) + q_i\left(g_i\left(W_j\right)\right). \tag{4.24b}$$

2. For a demotivating criterion:

(a) Preference of variant W_j over variant W_k:

$$g_i\left(W_j\right) < g_i\left(W_k\right) - q_i\left(g_i\left(W_j\right)\right). \tag{4.25a}$$

(b) Preference of variant W_k over variant W_j:

$$g_i\left(W_k\right) < g_i\left(W_j\right) - q_i\left(g_i\left(W_k\right)\right). \tag{4.25b}$$

3. For a desirable criterion:

(a) Preference of variant W_j over variant W_k:

$$\left|g_i\left(W_j\right) - \mathrm{p}\right| < \left|g_i\left(W_k\right) - \mathrm{p}\right| - q_i\left(\left|g_i\left(W_k\right) - \mathrm{p}\right|\right). \tag{4.26a}$$

(b) Preference of variant W_k over variant W_j:

$$|g_i(W_k) - \mathrm{p}| < |g_i(W_j) - \mathrm{p}| - q_i(|g_i(W_j) - \mathrm{p}|). \tag{4.26b}$$

4. For a non-desirable criterion:
   (a) Preference of variant W_j over variant W_k:

$$|g_i(W_j) - \mathrm{np}| > |g_i(W_k) - \mathrm{np}| + q_i(|g_i(W_j) - \mathrm{np}|). \tag{4.27a}$$

   (b) Preference of variant W_k over variant W_j:

$$|g_i(W_k) - \mathrm{np}| > |g_i(W_j) - \mathrm{np}| + q_i(|g_i(W_k) - \mathrm{np}|). \tag{4.27b}$$

The equivalence relation for the motivating and demotivating criterion can be defined as follows [159]:

$$g_i(W_j) \leqslant g_i(W_k) + q_i(g_i(W_k)) \wedge g_i(W_k) \leqslant g_i(W_j) + q_i(g_i(W_j)). \tag{4.28}$$

Function q_i cannot be any. Its domain must be a set of $g_i(W_j)$ values, and its codomain must be a set of real numbers, and moreover, it must satisfy the following relationship [97]:

$$\bigwedge_{W_j \in \mathbb{W}} \bigwedge_{W_k \in \mathbb{W}} \frac{q_i(g_i(W_j)) - q_i(g_i(W_k))}{g_i(W_j) - g_i(W_k)} \geqslant -1, \tag{4.29a}$$

where
$\mathbb{W}$—a set of decision variants,
and the following relations must follow from $g_i(W_k) \geqslant g_i(W_j)$:

1. Equivalence $g_i(W_k)$ and $g_i(W_j)$ if [159]

$$g_i(W_k) - g_i(W_j) \leqslant q_i(g_i(W_j)). \tag{4.29b}$$

2. Preference $g_i(W_k)$, and [159]

$$q_i(g_i(W_j)) < g_i(W_k) - g_i(W_j). \tag{4.29c}$$

For the interval criterion, the function q_i defines the shape of equivalence area. Figure 4.6 shows the shape of this area with the function q_i defined as $q_i(x) = 2^x$. It can be seen that this area is limited by two functions of q_i, and its use causes that the width of equivalence area depends on the level of criterion value. The higher the value is, the wider the equivalence area. For example, if a bicycle is purchased, the variants differing by PLN 150–200 may be considered equivalent, and by PLN 5,000–10,000 when choosing a car.

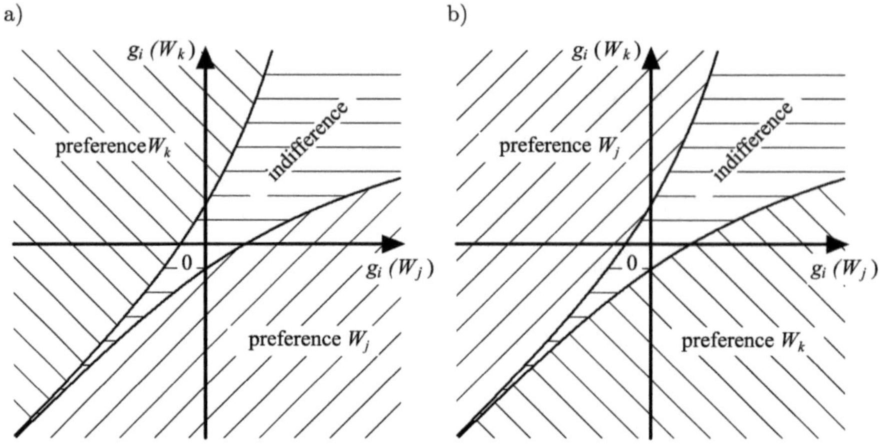

Fig. 4.6 Interval criterion calculated for the function $q_i (x) = 2^x$ for a criterion of the following character: (**a**) motivating; (**b**) demotivating

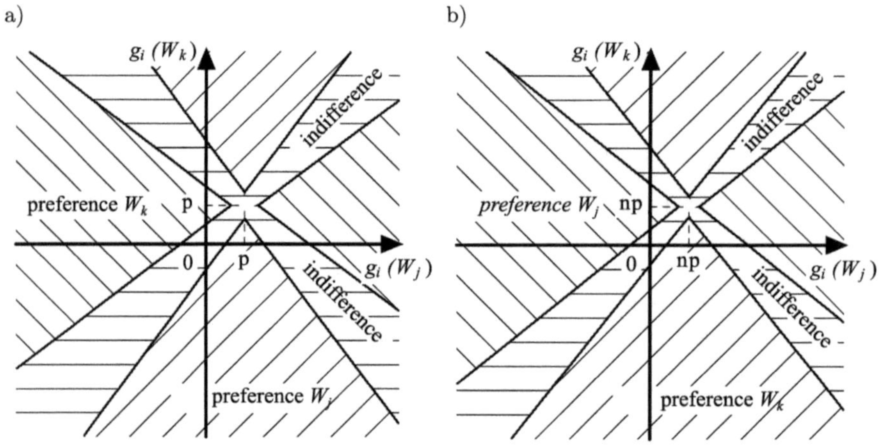

Fig. 4.7 The interval criterion calculated for $q_i (x) = \frac{1}{4}x + \frac{1}{4}$ for a criterion of (**a**) desirable criterion, at desirable value equal to one and (**b**) non-desirable criterion, at non-desirable value equal to one

For desirable and non-desirable criteria, the function $q_i (x) = ax + b$ (Fig. 4.7) has good properties. The coefficient b determines the width of equivalence area and the coefficient a—the slope of lines limiting the area. At a less than one, the equivalence area increases linearly as the criteria values increase.

The above example can be applied to the well-known Weber–Fechner law used in sensory analyses. Human receptors have strong non-linear characteristics. The Weber–Fechner law says "If the sizes of stimuli are compared, our perception is not influenced by the arithmetic difference between them, but by the ratio of the compared quantities" [12]. According to the Weber–Fechner law, the impression of color increase depends on the color level. The feeling of its increase in intensity when the stimulus changes is logarithmic. The same is true for the perception of sound. The logarithmic scale has become a standard in sound processing. The decibel scale that is a logarithmic scale is commonly used here. However, the logarithmic scale is only a rough approximation of the receptor characteristics. Research in the field of sound perception has resulted in a definition of equal loudness curves. These curves clearly indicate deviations from the logarithmic nature of sound perceptions. Therefore, in the criteria where equivalence regions exist, a log function could be used to delimit preference regions.

Formulas (4.24a)–(4.27b) have two important limitations. The first limitation is that you cannot use a logarithmic function as a function of q_i, and the second limitation is that the width of equivalence region can be constant, non-increasing, or non-decreasing. When making an assessment, a human being brings it to the zero level; the greater the value, the greater the tolerance for deviations from it. In the case where the assessed values may take negative values, it is a serious problem.

Defining q_i as a logarithmic function,

$$q_i(x) = c \ln |x + b|, \tag{4.30}$$

where

c—a constant greater than zero that specifies the width of equivalence area,
b—a constant specifying the function displacement,

the preference relation can be defined as follows:

1. For a demotivating criterion:

   (a) Preference of variant W_j over variant W_k:

$$\left|g_i\left(W_j\right) - g_i\left(W_k\right)\right| > q_i\left(\frac{g_i\left(W_j\right) + g_i\left(W_k\right)}{2}\right) \wedge g_i\left(W_j\right) > g_i\left(W_k\right). \tag{4.31a}$$

   Equitation $\left|g_i\left(W_j\right) - g_i\left(W_k\right)\right| = q_i\left(\frac{g_i(W_j)+g_i(W_k)}{2}\right)$ defines boundaries between equivalence area and preference area. Inequality $g_i\left(W_j\right) > g_i\left(W_k\right)$ determines the preference type. In this case, there is a preference W_j, which boundary with the equivalence area is marked with a broken line in Fig. 4.8a.

   (b) Preference of variant W_k over variant W_j:

$$\left|g_i\left(W_j\right) - g_i\left(W_k\right)\right| > q_i\left(\frac{g_i\left(W_j\right) + g_i\left(W_k\right)}{2}\right) \wedge g_i\left(W_k\right) > g_i\left(W_j\right). \tag{4.31b}$$

The inequality $g_i(W_k) > g_i(W_j)$ indicates preference W_k, which boundary with equivalence area is marked with a solid line.

2. For a demotivating criterion:
   (a) Preference of variant W_j over variant W_k:

$$\left|g_i(W_j) - g_i(W_k)\right| > q_i\left(\frac{g_i(W_j) + g_i(W_k)}{2}\right) \wedge g_i(W_j) < g_i(W_k). \tag{4.32a}$$

   (b) Preference of variant W_k over variant W_j:

$$\left|g_i(W_j) - g_i(W_k)\right| > q_i\left(\frac{g_i(W_j) + g_i(W_k)}{2}\right) \wedge g_i(W_k) < g_i(W_j). \tag{4.32b}$$

3. For a desirable criterion:
   (a) Preference of variant W_j over variant W_k:

$$\left|\left|g_i(W_j) - \mathrm{p}\right| - \left|g_i(W_k) - \mathrm{p}\right|\right| > q_i\left(\frac{\left|g_i(W_j) - \mathrm{p}\right| + \left|g_i(W_k) - \mathrm{p}\right|}{2}\right)$$
$$\wedge \left|g_i(W_j) - \mathrm{p}\right| < \left|g_i(W_k) - \mathrm{p}\right|. \tag{4.33a}$$

   (b) Preference of variant W_k over variant W_j:

$$\left|\left|g_i(W_j) - \mathrm{p}\right| - \left|g_i(W_k) - \mathrm{p}\right|\right| > q_i\left(\frac{\left|g_i(W_j) - \mathrm{p}\right| + \left|g_i(W_k) - \mathrm{p}\right|}{2}\right)$$
$$\wedge \left|g_i(W_k) - \mathrm{p}\right| < \left|g_i(W_j) - \mathrm{p}\right|. \tag{4.33b}$$

4. For undesirable criterion:
   (a) Preference of variant W_j over variant W_k:

$$\left|\left|g_i(W_j) - \mathrm{np}\right| - \left|g_i(W_k) - \mathrm{np}\right|\right|$$
$$> q_i\left(\frac{\left|g_i(W_j) - \mathrm{np}\right| + \left|g_i(W_k) - \mathrm{np}\right|}{2}\right)$$
$$\wedge \left|g_i(W_j) - \mathrm{np}\right| > \left|g_i(W_k) - \mathrm{np}\right|. \tag{4.34a}$$

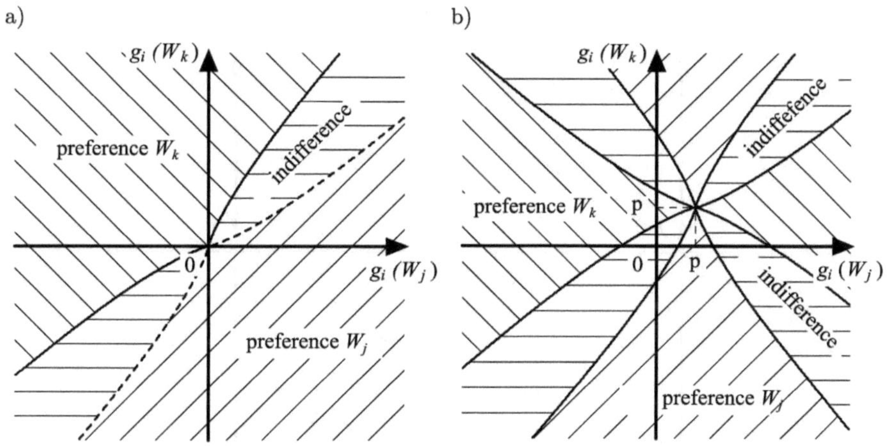

Fig. 4.8 The interval criterion calculated for the function $q_i(x) = \ln|x+1|$ for a criterion of: (**a**) motivating; (**b**) desirable character

(b) Preference of variant W_k over variant W_j:

$$\begin{aligned} &\left|\left|g_i\left(W_j\right)-\mathrm{np}\right|-\left|g_i\left(W_k\right)-\mathrm{np}\right|\right| \\ &\quad > q_i\left(\frac{\left|g_i\left(W_j\right)-\mathrm{np}\right|+\left|g_i\left(W_k\right)-\mathrm{np}\right|}{2}\right) \\ &\quad \wedge \left|g_i\left(W_k\right)-\mathrm{np}\right| > \left|g_i\left(W_j\right)-\mathrm{np}\right|. \end{aligned} \tag{4.34b}$$

The equivalence relation occurs when no preference for W_k over W_j or W_j over W_k exists. Figure 4.8 shows the preference areas and the equivalence areas for the interval criterion. It is visible that the width of equivalence area for the motivating criterion depends on a distance from the origin of the coordinate system. The greater the value of the criterion (in terms of the absolute value), the wider the equivalence area is. However, for a desirable criterion, it depends on a distance from the point determined by the desirable value.

The parameter c of the logarithmic q_i function specifies the width of equivalence area. The greater the parameter is, the greater the equivalence area. Parameter b defines the location of the point where the curves limiting the equivalence area meet. For b equal to zero, these curves connect at the origin of the coordinate system (Fig. 4.8a). For $b > 1$, this point moves away from the origin of the coordinate system in such a way that, to a certain extent, the interval criterion becomes the true criterion (Fig. 4.9a). At $b < 1$, curves limiting the area of equivalence from the first and second quarter of the coordinate system overlap, so that values close to zero become equivalent (Fig. 4.9b).

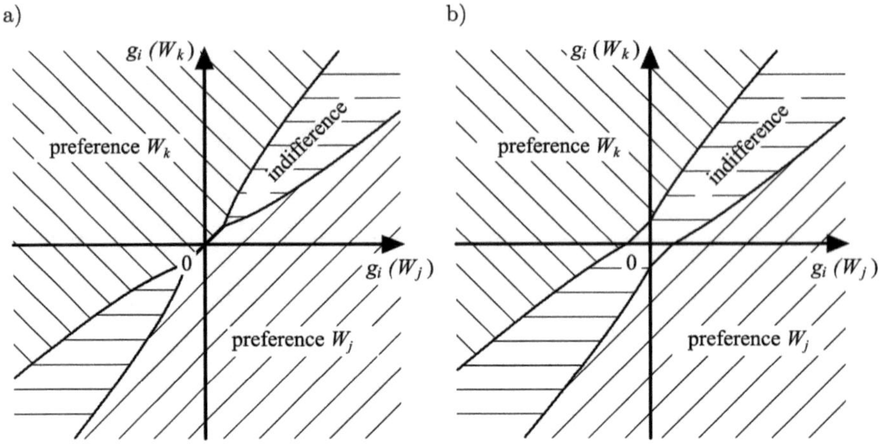

Fig. 4.9 Interval criterion of motivating character at function q_i: (**a**) $q_i(x) = \ln|x + 0.5|$ and (**b**) $q_i(x) = \ln|x - 0.5|$

Pseudo-criteria introduce the possibility of grading preferences. As in the case of a direct comparison, here, a distinction is made between the relationship of slight and strong preference. An additional threshold function $q_i'()$ was introduced in the pseudo-criterion, the value of which depends on the value of a criterion. It allows us to distinguish the relationship of weak preference from the relation of strong preference. In this criterion, a *strong preference relation* can be defined as follows:

1. For a motivation criterion [159, 169]:[5]

   (a) Preference of variant W_j over variant W_k:

$$g_i\left(W_j\right) > g_i\left(W_k\right) + q_i\left(g_i\left(W_k\right)\right), \tag{4.35a}$$

   where

   $q_i()$—a function defined for the i-th criterion.

   The equitation $g_i\left(W_j\right) = g_i\left(W_k\right) + q_i\left(g_i\left(W_k\right)\right)$ is a boundary between the weak and strong preference of W_j decision variant. In Fig. 4.10a, it is marked with the bottom solid line.

   (b) Preference of variant W_k over variant W_j:

$$g_i\left(W_k\right) > g_i\left(W_j\right) + q_i\left(g_i\left(W_j\right)\right). \tag{4.35b}$$

   The equitation $g_i\left(W_k\right) = g_i\left(W_j\right) + q_i\left(g_i\left(W_j\right)\right)$ is a boundary between the weak and strong preference for W_k decision variant. In Fig. 4.10a, it is marked with the top solid line.

[5] Roy and Bouyssou [169] s. 73.

2. For a demotivating criterion:
   (a) Preference of variant W_j over variant W_k:

$$g_i\left(W_j\right) < g_i\left(W_k\right) - q_i\left(g_i\left(W_j\right)\right). \tag{4.36a}$$

   (b) Preference of variant W_k over variant W_j:

$$g_i\left(W_k\right) < g_i\left(W_j\right) - q_i\left(g_i\left(W_k\right)\right). \tag{4.36b}$$

3. For a desirable criterion:
   (a) Preference of variant W_j over variant W_k:

$$\left|g_i\left(W_j\right) - \mathrm{p}\right| < \left|g_i\left(W_k\right) - \mathrm{p}\right| - \left|q_i\left(g_i\left(W_k\right) - \mathrm{p}\right)\right|. \tag{4.37a}$$

   (b) Preference of variant W_k over variant W_j:

$$\left|g_i\left(W_k\right) - \mathrm{p}\right| < \left|g_i\left(W_j\right) - \mathrm{p}\right| - \left|q_i\left(g_i\left(W_j\right) - \mathrm{p}\right)\right|. \tag{4.37b}$$

4. For a non-desirable criterion:
   (a) Preference of variant W_j over variant W_k:

$$\left|g_i\left(W_j\right) - \mathrm{np}\right| > \left|g_i\left(W_k\right) - \mathrm{np}\right| + \left|q_i\left(g_i\left(W_j\right) - \mathrm{np}\right)\right|. \tag{4.38a}$$

   (b) Preference of variant W_k over variant W_j:

$$\left|g_i\left(W_k\right) - \mathrm{np}\right| > \left|g_i\left(W_j\right) - \mathrm{np}\right| + \left|q_i\left(g_i\left(W_k\right) - \mathrm{np}\right)\right|. \tag{4.38b}$$

The weak preference relation can be noted as follows:

1. For a motivating criterion [159]:
   (a) Preference of variant W_j over variant W_k:

$$g_i\left(W_j\right) > g_i\left(W_k\right) + q_i'\left(g_i\left(W_k\right)\right) \wedge g_i\left(W_j\right) \leqslant g_i\left(W_k\right) + q_i\left(g_i\left(W_k\right)\right), \tag{4.39a}$$

   where
   q_i' ()—a function defined for the i-th criterion which separates no preference and weak preference.

   The equitation $g_i\left(W_j\right) = g_i\left(W_k\right) + q_i\left(g_i\left(W_k\right)\right)$ is a boundary between the weak and strong preference (in Fig. 4.10a marked with a bottom solid line), while the equitation $g_i\left(W_j\right) = g_i\left(W_k\right) + q_i'\left(g_i\left(W_k\right)\right)$ is a boundary between a weak preference and equivalence for W_j (marked with a bottom broken line).

(b) Preference of variant W_k over variant W_j:

$$g_i(W_k) > g_i(W_j) + q_i'(g_i(W_j)) \wedge g_i(W_k) \leqslant g_i(W_j) + q_i(g_i(W_j)). \tag{4.39b}$$

The equitation $g_i(W_k) = g_i(W_j) + q_i(g_i(W_j))$ is a boundary between the weak and strong preference (marked with a top solid line), and the equitation $g_i(W_k) = g_i(W_j) + q_i'(g_i(W_j))$ is a boundary between the weak preference and equivalence for W_j decision variant (marked with a top broken line).

2. For a demotivating criterion::

(a) Preference of variant W_j over variant W_k:

$$g_i(W_j) < g_i(W_k) - q_i'(g_i(W_j)) \wedge g_i(W_j) \geqslant g_i(W_k) - q_i(g_i(W_j)). \tag{4.40a}$$

(b) Preference of variant W_k over variant W_j:

$$g_i(W_k) < g_i(W_j) - q_i'(g_i(W_k)) \wedge g_i(W_k) \geqslant g_i(W_j) - q_i(g_i(W_k)). \tag{4.40b}$$

3. For a desirable criterion:

(a) Preference of variant W_j over variant W_k:

$$\begin{aligned} &|g_i(W_j) - \mathrm{p}| < |g_i(W_k) - \mathrm{p}| - |q_i'(g_i(W_k) - \mathrm{p})| \wedge \\ &|g_i(W_j) - \mathrm{p}| \geqslant |g_i(W_k) - \mathrm{p}| - |q_i(g_i(W_k) - \mathrm{p})|. \end{aligned} \tag{4.41a}$$

(b) Preference of variant W_k over variant W_j:

$$\begin{aligned} &|g_i(W_k) - \mathrm{p}| < |g_i(W_j) - \mathrm{p}| - |q_i'(g_i(W_j) - \mathrm{p})| \wedge \\ &|g_i(W_k) - \mathrm{p}| \geqslant |g_i(W_j) - \mathrm{p}| - |q_i(g_i(W_j) - \mathrm{p})|. \end{aligned} \tag{4.41b}$$

4. For a non-desirable criterion:

(a) Preference of variant W_j over variant W_k:

$$\begin{aligned} &|g_i(W_j) - \mathrm{np}| \\ &\quad > |g_i(W_k) - \mathrm{np}| + |q_i'(g_i(W_j) - \mathrm{np})| \wedge \\ &\quad |g_i(W_j) - \mathrm{np}| \leqslant |g_i(W_k) - \mathrm{np}| + |q_i(g_i(W_j) - \mathrm{np})|. \end{aligned} \tag{4.42a}$$

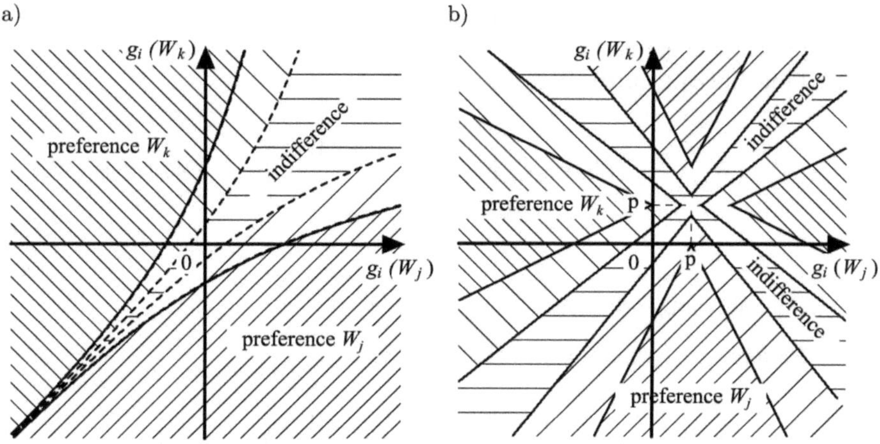

Fig. 4.10 Pseudo-criterion calculated for the threshold function q_i: (**a**) $q_i(x) = 2^{x+1}$ and $q_i'(x) = 2^{x-1}$ for a motivating criteria and (**b**) $q_i(x) = \frac{1}{2}x + \frac{1}{2}$ and $q_i'(x) = \frac{1}{5}x + \frac{1}{5}$ for a desirable criteria and a desired value equal to one

(b) Preference of variant W_k over variant W_j:

$$\begin{aligned} &|g_i(W_k) - \mathrm{np}| \\ &\quad > \left|g_i(W_j) - \mathrm{np}\right| + \left|q_i'(g_i(W_k) - \mathrm{np})\right| \wedge \\ &|g_i(W_k) - \mathrm{np}| \leqslant \left|g_i(W_j) - \mathrm{np}\right| + |q_i(g_i(W_k) - \mathrm{np})|. \end{aligned} \tag{4.42b}$$

The equivalence relation occurs when neither weak nor strong preference W_k over W_j, or W_j over W_k exists. Figure 4.10 shows the areas of weak and strong preference and the areas of equivalence. Preference areas are marked with diagonal lines, more dense show the strong one, less dense—the weak one.

For the logarithmic function given by the formula (4.30), *the strong preference relation* can be defined as follows:

1. For a motivating criterion:

(a) Preference of variant W_j over variant W_k:

$$\left|g_i(W_j) - g_i(W_k)\right| > q_i\left(\frac{g_i(W_j) + g_i(W_k)}{2}\right) \wedge g_i(W_j) > g_i(W_k). \tag{4.43a}$$

Equation $\left|g_i(W_j) - g_i(W_k)\right| = q_i\left(\frac{g_i(W_j)+g_i(W_k)}{2}\right)$ defines the boundaries between the equivalence area and the preference areas. Inequality $g_i(W_j) > g_i(W_k)$ determines a preference type. In this case, there is a preference W_j, which boundary with equivalence area is marked with a broken line in Fig. 4.11a:

(b) Preference of variant W_k over variant W_j:

$$\left|g_i\left(W_j\right)-g_i\left(W_k\right)\right|>q_i\left(\frac{g_i\left(W_j\right)+g_i\left(W_k\right)}{2}\right)\wedge g_i\left(W_k\right)>g_i\left(W_j\right). \tag{4.43b}$$

2. For a demotivating criterion:

(a) Preference of variant W_j over variant W_k:

$$\left|g_i\left(W_j\right)-g_i\left(W_k\right)\right|>q_i\left(\frac{g_i\left(W_j\right)+g_i\left(W_k\right)}{2}\right)\wedge g_i\left(W_j\right)<g_i\left(W_k\right). \tag{4.44a}$$

(b) Preference of variant W_k over variant W_j:

$$\left|g_i\left(W_j\right)-g_i\left(W_k\right)\right|>q_i\left(\frac{g_i\left(W_j\right)+g_i\left(W_k\right)}{2}\right)\wedge g_i\left(W_k\right)<g_i\left(W_j\right). \tag{4.44b}$$

3. For a desirable criterion:

(a) Preference of variant W_j over variant W_k:

$$\left|\left|g_i\left(W_j\right)-\mathrm{p}\right|-\left|g_i\left(W_k\right)-\mathrm{p}\right|\right|>q_i\left(\frac{\left|g_i\left(W_j\right)-\mathrm{p}\right|+\left|g_i\left(W_k\right)-\mathrm{p}\right|}{2}\right)$$
$$\wedge\left|g_i\left(W_j\right)-\mathrm{p}\right|<\left|g_i\left(W_k\right)-\mathrm{p}\right|. \tag{4.45a}$$

(b) Preference of variant W_k over variant W_j:

$$\left|\left|g_i\left(W_j\right)-\mathrm{p}\right|-\left|g_i\left(W_k\right)-\mathrm{p}\right|\right|>q_i\left(\frac{\left|g_i\left(W_j\right)-\mathrm{p}\right|+\left|g_i\left(W_k\right)-\mathrm{p}\right|}{2}\right)$$
$$\wedge\left|g_i\left(W_k\right)-\mathrm{p}\right|<\left|g_i\left(W_j\right)-\mathrm{p}\right|. \tag{4.45b}$$

4. For non-desirable criterion:

(a) Preference of variant W_j over variant W_k:

$$\left|\left|g_i\left(W_j\right)-\mathrm{np}\right|-\left|g_i\left(W_k\right)-\mathrm{np}\right|\right|$$

$$> q_i \left(\frac{\left| g_i \left(W_j \right) - \mathrm{np} \right| + \left| g_i \left(W_k \right) - \mathrm{np} \right|}{2} \right)$$

$$\wedge \left| g_i \left(W_j \right) - \mathrm{np} \right| > \left| g_i \left(W_k \right) - \mathrm{np} \right| . \tag{4.46a}$$

(b) Preference of variant W_k over variant W_j:

$$\left| \left| g_i \left(W_j \right) - \mathrm{np} \right| - \left| g_i \left(W_k \right) - \mathrm{np} \right| \right|$$

$$> q_i \left(\frac{\left| g_i \left(W_j \right) - \mathrm{np} \right| + \left| g_i \left(W_k \right) - \mathrm{np} \right|}{2} \right)$$

$$\wedge \left| g_i \left(W_k \right) - \mathrm{np} \right| > \left| g_i \left(W_j \right) - \mathrm{np} \right| . \tag{4.46b}$$

The weak preference relation can be described as follows:

1. For a motivating criterion:

(a) Preference of variant W_j over variant W_k:

$$\left| g_i \left(W_j \right) - g_i \left(W_k \right) \right| > q_i' \left(\frac{g_i \left(W_j \right) + g_i \left(W_k \right)}{2} \right) \wedge g_i \left(W_j \right) > g_i \left(W_k \right) \wedge$$

$$\left| g_i \left(W_j \right) - g_i \left(W_k \right) \right| \leqslant q_i \left(\frac{g_i \left(W_j \right) + g_i \left(W_k \right)}{2} \right). \tag{4.47a}$$

Equitation $\left| g_i \left(W_j \right) - g_i \left(W_k \right) \right| = q_i \left(\frac{g_i(W_j)+g_i(W_k)}{2} \right)$ is a boundary between the weak and strong preference (in Fig. 4.11a marked with a broken line) and equitation $\left| g_i \left(W_j \right) - g_i \left(W_k \right) \right| = q_i' \left(\frac{g_i(W_j)+g_i(W_k)}{2} \right)$—between the weak preference and the equivalence (a solid line). The equitation $g_i \left(W_j \right) > g_i \left(W_k \right)$ determines a preferred decision variant, in this case W_j.

(b) Preference of variant W_k over variant W_j:

$$\left| g_i \left(W_j \right) - g_i \left(W_k \right) \right| > q_i' \left(\frac{g_i \left(W_j \right) + g_i \left(W_k \right)}{2} \right) \wedge g_i \left(W_k \right) > g_i \left(W_j \right) \wedge$$

$$\left| g_i \left(W_j \right) - g_i \left(W_k \right) \right| \leqslant q_i \left(\frac{g_i \left(W_j \right) + g_i \left(W_k \right)}{2} \right). \tag{4.47b}$$

2. For a demotivating criterion:

(a) Preference of variant W_j over variant W_k:

$$\left|g_i\left(W_j\right)-g_i\left(W_k\right)\right|>q_i'\left(\frac{g_i\left(W_j\right)+g_i\left(W_k\right)}{2}\right)\wedge g_i\left(W_j\right)<g_i\left(W_k\right)\wedge$$

$$\left|g_i\left(W_j\right)-g_i\left(W_k\right)\right|\leqslant q_i\left(\frac{g_i\left(W_j\right)+g_i\left(W_k\right)}{2}\right). \tag{4.48a}$$

(b) Preference of variant W_k over variant W_j:

$$\left|g_i\left(W_j\right)-g_i\left(W_k\right)\right|>q_i'\left(\frac{g_i\left(W_j\right)+g_i\left(W_k\right)}{2}\right)\wedge g_i\left(W_k\right)<g_i\left(W_j\right)\wedge$$

$$\left|g_i\left(W_j\right)-g_i\left(W_k\right)\right|\leqslant q_i\left(\frac{g_i\left(W_j\right)+g_i\left(W_k\right)}{2}\right). \tag{4.48b}$$

3. For a desirable criterion:

(a) Preference of variant W_j over variant W_k:

$$\left|\left|g_i\left(W_j\right)-\mathrm{p}\right|-\left|g_i\left(W_k\right)-\mathrm{p}\right|\right|>q_i'\left(\frac{\left|g_i\left(W_j\right)-\mathrm{p}\right|+\left|g_i\left(W_k\right)-\mathrm{p}\right|}{2}\right)\wedge$$

$$\left|g_i\left(W_j\right)-\mathrm{p}\right|<\left|g_i\left(W_k\right)-\mathrm{p}\right|\wedge$$

$$\left|\left|g_i\left(W_j\right)-\mathrm{p}\right|-\left|g_i\left(W_k\right)-\mathrm{p}\right|\right|\leqslant q_i\left(\frac{\left|g_i\left(W_j\right)-\mathrm{p}\right|+\left|g_i\left(W_k\right)-\mathrm{p}\right|}{2}\right). \tag{4.49a}$$

(b) Preference of variant W_k over variant W_j:

$$\left|\left|g_i\left(W_j\right)-\mathrm{p}\right|-\left|g_i\left(W_k\right)-\mathrm{p}\right|\right|>q_i'\left(\frac{\left|g_i\left(W_j\right)-\mathrm{p}\right|+\left|g_i\left(W_k\right)-\mathrm{p}\right|}{2}\right)\wedge$$

$$\left|g_i\left(W_k\right)-\mathrm{p}\right|<\left|g_i\left(W_j\right)-\mathrm{p}\right|\wedge$$

$$\left|\left|g_i\left(W_j\right)-\mathrm{p}\right|-\left|g_i\left(W_k\right)-\mathrm{p}\right|\right|\leqslant q_i\left(\frac{\left|g_i\left(W_j\right)-\mathrm{p}\right|+\left|g_i\left(W_k\right)-\mathrm{p}\right|}{2}\right). \tag{4.49b}$$

4. For a non-desirable criterion:

(a) Preference of variant W_j over variant W_k:

$$\left|\left|g_i\left(W_j\right)-\mathrm{np}\right|-\left|g_i\left(W_k\right)-\mathrm{np}\right|\right|$$

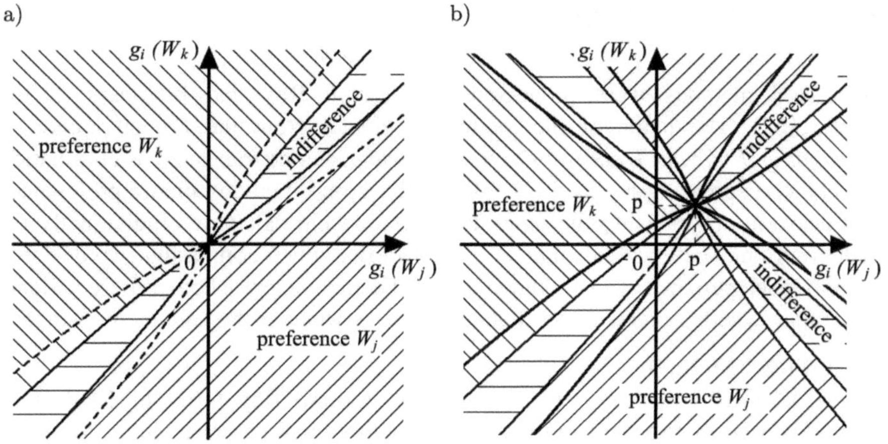

Fig. 4.11 Pseudo-criterion calculated for $q_i(x) = \ln|x+1|$ and $q_i'(x) = 0.5\ln|x+1|$ for (**a**) motivating and (**b**) desirable criterion with a desirable value equal to one

$$> q_i'\left(\frac{|g_i(W_j) - \mathrm{np}| + |g_i(W_k) - \mathrm{np}|}{2}\right) \wedge$$

$$|g_i(W_j) - \mathrm{np}| > |g_i(W_k) - \mathrm{np}| \wedge$$

$$\big||g_i(W_j) - \mathrm{np}| - |g_i(W_k) - \mathrm{np}|\big|$$

$$\leqslant q_i\left(\frac{|g_i(W_j) - \mathrm{np}| + |g_i(W_k) - \mathrm{np}|}{2}\right). \tag{4.50a}$$

(b) Preference of variant W_k over variant W_j:

$$\big||g_i(W_j) - \mathrm{np}| - |g_i(W_k) - \mathrm{np}|\big|$$

$$> q_i'\left(\frac{|g_i(W_j) - \mathrm{np}| + |g_i(W_k) - \mathrm{np}|}{2}\right) \wedge$$

$$|g_i(W_k) - \mathrm{np}| > |g_i(W_j) - \mathrm{np}| \wedge$$

$$\big||g_i(W_j) - \mathrm{np}| - |g_i(W_k) - \mathrm{np}|\big|$$

$$\leqslant q_i\left(\frac{|g_i(W_j) - \mathrm{np}| + |g_i(W_k) - \mathrm{np}|}{2}\right). \tag{4.50b}$$

The equivalence relation occurs when neither weak nor strong preference W_k over W_j or W_j over W_k exists. Figure 4.11 shows the preference areas and the equivalence areas for the pseudo-criteria.

4.2 ELECTRE Methods

ELECTRE methods were pioneered by Bernard Roy and his team in the 1960s [162]. The name of the method originates from the French language: *ELimination Et Choix Traduisant la Realité*, which can be translated as elimination and choice expressing reality [97]. ELECTRE group methods model preferences of a decision-maker using the outranking relationship calculated individually for each criterion. They take advantage of the fact that when comparing two decision variants, each person can easily indicate in a specific context whether these variants are similar, whether one is better than the other, or whether they are incomparable.

ELECTRE I Method

The ELECTRE I method was proposed by Bernard Roy [162] in 1968. This method is used to select the optimal variant without making a ranking of decision variants. It only uses preference relationships without distinguishing between weak and strong preference relationships. Each criterion is assigned a weight depending on preferences of a decision-maker. The ELECTRE I method algorithm can be described in the following steps:

Step 1: Preliminary operations on criteria
Step 2: Computing concordance indices
Step 3: Determining the concordance set
Step 4: Computing the discordance level
Step 5: Determining the discordance set
Step 6: Determining the outranking relation
Step 7: Creating the outranking graph

Step1

In this step, data is prepared (weights selection, determination of criteria character, normalization of criteria) for calculations. In the considered example from Table 4.2, the weights equal to one for the *fuel consumption* and *price,* criteria were assumed and weight equal to 0.5 for the criterion of *trunk capacity*. *Appearance* criterion was skipped. This means that *fuel consumption* and *price* were considered the most important criteria. The *trunk capacity* is less important. The weights are normalized so that their sum amounts to one:

$$w_i' = \frac{w_i}{\sum_{j=1}^{N} w_i}, \tag{4.51}$$

where

w_i—weight value of the i-th criterion before normalization,
w_i'—weight value of the i-th criterion before normalization,
N—the number of criteria.

Table 4.5 Exemplary decision variants

Variant Decision	Price [PLN]	Fuel consumption $[\frac{1}{100\,\text{km}}]$	Trunk capacity [l]
W_1	−30,700	−6	224
W_2	−39,500	−6.5	275
W_3	−40,715	−6	251
W_4	−35,500	−6.1	262
W_5	−32,000	−5.9	243

After normalization, the criteria weights were as follows: *price*—0.4, *fuel consumption*—0.4, and *trunk capacity*—0.2, and then the sign of criteria for which the low value is important is changed.

Table 4.5 shows decision variants from Table 4.2 extended by variants W_4 and W_5. Because the decision-maker is interested in the lowest possible value of *price* and *fuel consumption*, they were multiplied by -1.

Due to the fact that the values of the criteria are expressed with different ranges and measurement units, they will be normalized in order to standardize the measures, using one of the normalization methods specified in Chapter 2. For the presented example, the data were normalized according to the formula:

$$\underset{j}{x'_i} = \frac{\underset{j}{x_i} - \min_j\left(\underset{j}{x_i}\right)}{\max_j\left(\underset{j}{x_i}\right) - \min_j\left(\underset{j}{x_i}\right)}, \tag{4.52}$$

where

$\underset{j}{x'_i}$—value of i-th criterion for the j-th variant after normalization,
$\underset{j}{x_i}$—value of i-th criterion for the j-th variant before normalization.

In the referenced literature [30, 46, 88],

$$\underset{j}{x'_i} = \frac{\underset{j}{x_i}}{\sqrt{\sum_j \underset{j}{x_i^2}}}. \tag{4.53}$$

The disadvantage of this normalization is that it can be used when data has only positive values. The values of the criteria after normalization are presented in Table 4.6.

Step2

Table 4.6 Value of criteria after normalization

Variant decision	Price [PLN]	Fuel consumption $[\frac{1}{100\,\mathrm{km}}]$	Trunk capacity [l]
W_1	1	0.83	0
W_2	0.12	0	1
W_3	0	0.83	0.53
W_4	0.52	0.67	0.75
W_5	0.87	1	0.37

Based on data from Table 4.6 for each pair of variants $g_i\left(W_j, W_k\right)$, the values of concordance indices, which form the concordance indices matrices, were computed. These matrices can be computed for any type of criteria, excluding pseudo-criteria. The rows and columns of these matrices correspond to the successive variants. The example uses a true criterion. On the basis of the outranking relation, the values of the concordance indices are calculated. The outranking relation of W_j decision variant over W_k is equal to one when the outranking relation of W_j over W_k; Otherwise, it is equal to zero. The outranking ratios are counted for each pair of decision variants under each criterion. The values of these ratios form the matrix of comparisons Υ_i, whose rows and columns correspond to the subsequent variants. An exemplary concordance indices matrix for the *fuel consumption* is determined according to the formula:

$$\Upsilon_i\left(W_j, W_k\right) = \begin{cases} 1 \text{ dla } g_i\left(W_j\right) \geqslant g_i\left(W_k\right), \\ 0 \text{ dla } g_i\left(W_j\right) < g_i\left(W_k\right). \end{cases} \tag{4.54}$$

The matrix below shows the values of concordance indices for the *fuel consumption*:

$$\Upsilon_2 = \begin{bmatrix} 1\,1\,1\,1\,0 \\ 0\,1\,0\,0\,0 \\ 1\,1\,1\,1\,0 \\ 0\,1\,0\,1\,0 \\ 1\,1\,1\,1\,1 \end{bmatrix}. \tag{4.55}$$

Then, we multiply all values of concordance indices for the k-th criterion by the weights and sum up to obtain the matrix C *of concordance indices* [97]:

$$C = \sum_{i=1}^{N} w_i' \Upsilon_i, \tag{4.56}$$

where

C—matrix of concordance indices $c_{i,j}$.

For the case under consideration, this matrix will take the following values:

$$C = \begin{bmatrix} 1 & 0.8 & 0.8 & 0.8 & 0.4 \\ 0.2 & 1 & 0.6 & 0.2 & 0.2 \\ 0.6 & 0.4 & 1 & 0.4 & 0.2 \\ 0.2 & 0.8 & 0.6 & 1 & 0.2 \\ 0.6 & 0.8 & 0.8 & 0.8 & 1 \end{bmatrix}. \tag{4.57}$$

Step3
For each pair of variants (W_j, W_k), we determine the concordance set of all pairs of variants, the values of which are greater than the concordance threshold s provided by a decision-maker. A threshold value should be greater than 0.5. Exceeding the concordance level by $c_{j,k}$ means that the variant related to a given row exceeds the variant related to the column. On this basis, the Ω_C, concordance set is determined, which elements are included in the set after concordance indices exceed the threshold s:

$$c_{j,k} \geqslant s \text{ dla } j \neq k, \tag{4.58}$$

przy czym:

$$s \in \langle 0.5; 1 \rangle . \tag{4.59}$$

Assuming the concordance level at 0.6, the values of the concordance index of matrix C in the first row, the second, third, and fourth columns will exceed this value. This means that the W_1 variant outranks the decision variants W_2, W_3, and W_4.

$$\begin{aligned}\Omega_C = \{&(W_1; W_2); (W_1; W_3); (W_1; W_4); (W_2; W_3); (W_3; W_1);\\ &(W_4; W_2); (W_4; W_3); (W_5; W_1); (W_5; W_2); (W_5; W_3); (W_5; W_4)\}.\end{aligned} \tag{4.60}$$

The relationships between decision variants can be illustrated as a graph (Fig. 4.12a). The arrows in the graph are run from the outranking variant to the outranked variant [159].

Step 4
Based on the concordance set Ω_C obtained from the formula (4.60) for each pair of variants (W_j, W_k) belonging to Ω_C, we compute the discordance level following the formula:

$$d_{j,k} = \max_{g_i(W_j) > g_i(W_k)} \left\{ g_i(W_k) - g_i(W_j) \right\}. \tag{4.61}$$

In the presented example, for the first pair (W_1, W_2) from the Ω_C set, we estimate the discordance level under the formula (4.61):

$$d_{1,2} = \max_{g_1(W_2)>g_1(W_1)} \{g_1(W_2) - g_1(W_1)\} =$$
$$\max\{(0.12 - 1); (0 - 0.82); (1 - 0)\} = 1, \qquad (4.62)$$

and for (W_5, W_4)

$$d_{5,4} = \max_{g_1(W_4)>g_1(W_5)} \{g_1(W_4) - g_1(W_5)\} =$$
$$\max\{(0.52 - 0.87); (0.67 - 1); (0.75 - 0.37)\} = 0.38. \qquad (4.63)$$

Similarly, we calculate for all pairs from the Ω_C set and the results of the calculations form the discordance matrix D:

$$D = \begin{bmatrix} * & 1 & 0.53 & 0.75 & * \\ * & * & 0.83 & * & * \\ 1 & * & * & * & * \\ * & 0.25 & 0.16 & * & * \\ 0.13 & 0.63 & 0.16 & 0.38 & * \end{bmatrix}. \qquad (4.64)$$

Step 5

For the calculated discordance indices, a threshold value called the v *discordance level* provided by a decision-maker is taken. Exceeding a discordance level by $d_{j,k}$ means that discordance between the variant related to a given row and the variant related to a column exists. Based on that, the discordance set Ω_D is determined, which elements are included in the set when a v-discordance level threshold is exceeded:

$$d_{j,k} \geqslant v. \qquad (4.65)$$

For the considered example, a discordance set at $v = 0.4$ will be as follows:

$$\Omega_D = \{(W_1; W_2); (W_1; W_3); (W_1; W_4); (W_2; W_3); (W_3; W_1); (W_5; W_2)\}. \qquad (4.66)$$

Step 6

On the basis of the Ω_C and Ω_D sets, the Ω_S set is created, containing ordered pairs, which define the outranking relations:

$$\Omega_S = \Omega_C \backslash \Omega_D. \qquad (4.67)$$

For the example considered, it will contain the following elements:

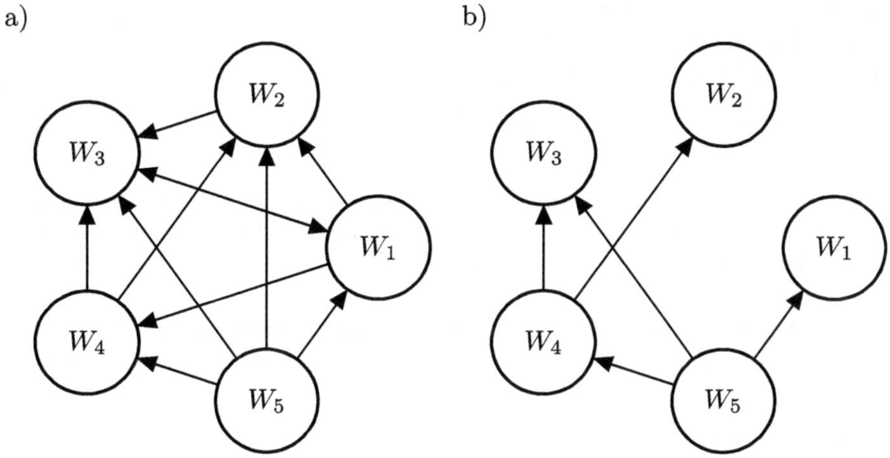

Fig. 4.12 The relationship between decision variants illustrated as a graph created based on matrices: (**a**) C and (**b**) C i D

$$\Omega_S = \{(W_4;\ W_2)\,;\ (W_4;\ W_3)\,;\ (W_5;\ W_1)\,;\ (W_5;\ W_3)\,;\ (W_5;\ W_4)\}\,. \tag{4.68}$$

Step 7
Based on the outranking relation, a graph is created. According to the graph in Fig. 4.12a, W_5 variant turned out to be better than W_1 and W_3 variants. W_5 car variant has the lowest price and the lowest fuel consumption. The trunk has quite a small capacity, but the weight of this criterion was lower than the others.

ELECTRE IV Method
The ELECTRE I method has been refined by many scientists who have eliminated various problems associated with its application. One such problem was the issue of unacceptable differences between decision options under one criterion. For example, when choosing a car, a decision-maker may encounter a situation where one of the cars is significantly better than the others, but its price significantly exceeds the prices of others. The ELECTRE I method would rate such a car very high, but the price may be unacceptable to a consumer. Of course, it is possible to properly determine the weight for a price criterion, but it may cause the dominance of this criterion, which in turn could make a price the most important when choosing a car. However, it is important for a consumer only in case of large price differences. To solve this problem, a veto threshold was introduced into the ELECTRE I method [121]. The ELECTRE I method modified in this way is unofficially called the ELECTRE Iv method [49]. The ELECTRE Iv method algorithm is as follows:

Step 1: Preliminary operations on the criteria
Step 2: Computing the concordance indices
Step 3: Determining the concordance set
Step 4: Computing the discordance level

Step 5: Determining the discordance set
Step 6: Determining the outranking relation
Step 7: Creating the outranking graph

Steps 1–3 are the same like in ELECTRE I method.

Step 4
Veto threshold in the ELECTRE IV method, which determines how much criteria values may differ between the compared decision variants. Exceeding this threshold means that one variant is better than the other, regardless of the value in the concordance matrix.

In the ELECTRE IV method, the matrix of discordance indices is not determined. Instead, it is checked whether the discordance between the two decision variants occurred:

1. Discordance [49]:

$$g_i\left(W_j\right) > g_i\left(W_k\right) + v_i\left(g_i\left(W_k\right)\right), \tag{4.69a}$$

   where
   v_i ()—veto function dependent on the i-th criterion value.
2. Lack discordance:

$$g_i\left(W_j\right) \leqslant g_i\left(W_k\right) + v_i\left(g_i\left(W_k\right)\right). \tag{4.69b}$$

Function v_i () can also be defined as a constant function. Then a decision-maker gives the maximum acceptable differences in value for each criterion. For data from Table 4.6, these differences are presented in Table 4.7. They have to be defined by a decision-maker based on his preferences. They define the maximum difference in criteria values which is still acceptable to him.

The values obtained from a decision-maker must be normalized according to the formula:

$$x'_{\substack{i\\j}} = \frac{x_{\substack{i\\j}}}{\max\limits_j\left(x_{\substack{i\\j}}\right) - \min\limits_j\left(x_{\substack{i\\j}}\right)}, \tag{4.70}$$

where the maximum and minimum values are calculated for the criteria values from Table 4.5. The normalization result is presented in Table 4.8. With normalization applied, a value greater than one for a given criterion means that veto will never occur.

Table 4.7 The maximum differences between the criteria values of decision variants

Price [PLN]	Fuel consumption $[\frac{1}{100\,\text{km}}]$	Trunk capacity [l]
4000	1.5	50

Table 4.8 Normalized maximum differences between the criteria values of decision variants

Price [PLN]	Fuel consumption $[\frac{1}{100\,\text{km}}]$	Trunk capacity [l]
0.4	2.5	0.98

For the presented example from the Ω_C concordance set under the formula (4.60), the results for the pair (W_2, W_3) and (W_3, W_1) will be calculated according to the formulas (4.69) for *price*:

$$(W_2, W_3) : g_1(W_2) + v_1(g_1(W_3)) \geqslant g_1(W_3) \Rightarrow 0.12 + 0.4 \geqslant 0. \tag{4.71}$$

In this case, discordance occurs, and we insert the value of one. For (W_3, W_1) pair, the result is

$$(W_3, W_1) : g_1(W_3) + v_1(g_1(W_1)) < g_1(W_1) \Rightarrow 0 + 0.4 < 1. \tag{4.72}$$

In this case, discordance does not occur, and we insert the value of zero. The results of the calculations will create the matrix of values of discordance indices D_1 for the *price* criterion. An example of a matrix of discordance indices for the *price* criterion is as follows:

$$\mathrm{D}_1 = \begin{bmatrix} * & 0 & 0 & 0 & 0 \\ 1 & * & 0 & 0 & 1 \\ 1 & 0 & * & 1 & 1 \\ 0 & 0 & 0 & * & 0 \\ 0 & 0 & 0 & 0 & * \end{bmatrix}, \tag{4.73}$$

where

D_1—a discordance matrix for the first criterion (*price*).

The one in the second row, in the first column of the matrix, means that the veto occurs between the decision variants W_2 and W_1 in favor of W_1. For convenience, on the basis of all D_i matrices, it is possible to create a collective D' matrix, which in the ELECTRE Iv method is called a discordance matrix. This matrix will have the value of 1 in a given row and column if the value 1 appears in any D_i matrix in the same row and column. In the example under consideration, only in D_2 matrix, there is one for the elements W_1 and W_2, and hence in D' matrix only for these elements an additional one will appear:

$$\mathrm{D}' = \begin{bmatrix} * & 1 & 0 & 0 & 0 \\ 1 & * & 0 & 0 & 1 \\ 1 & 0 & * & 1 & 1 \\ 1 & 0 & 0 & * & 0 \\ 0 & 0 & 0 & 0 & * \end{bmatrix}. \tag{4.74}$$

Step 5
Furthermore, based on the discordance threshold of D′ matrix, the *discordance set* $\Omega_{D'}$ is determined:

$$\Omega_{D'} = \{(W_1;\, W_2)\,;\, (W_2;\, W_1)\,;\, (W_2;\, W_5)\,;\, (W_3;\, W_1)\,; \\ (W_3;\, W_4)\,;\, (W_3;\, W_5)\,;\, (W_4;\, W_1)\}\,. \tag{4.75}$$

The elements of this set are ordered pairs for which at least one criterion has been vetoed. In D′ matrix, these pairs are represented by values of 1. $(W_1;\, W_2)$ notation means that a veto exists in favor of W_2, decision variant, i.e., W_1 decision variant cannot outrank W_2.

Step 6 i 7
Based on Ω_C and $\Omega_{D'}$ set is created Ω_S. includes all decision variants, which are in Ω_S and are not in Ω_C and do not belong to $\Omega_{D'}$. In the considered example, Ω_S set will be as follows:

$$\Omega_S = \{(W_1;\, W_3)\,;\, (W_1;\, W_4)\,;\, (W_2;\, W_3)\,;\, (W_4;\, W_2)\,; \\ (W_4;\, W_3)\,;\, (W_5;\, W_1)\,;\, (W_5;\, W_2)\,;\, (W_5;\, W_3)\,;\, (W_5;\, W_4)\}\,. \tag{4.76}$$

In the ELECTRE Iv method, the graph can be created in the same way as in the ELECTRE I method. The literature also provides a modified method of creating a graph, allowing for the creation of a ranking [97, 202]. Based on Ω_S set, two graphs are created. One is constructed from the best to the worst and the other from the worst to the best. In the first case, the best decision variants are selected first, i.e., those that are not outranked by any other variant. They are the first group of objects that make up a graph. In the considered example, this is W_5 variant. In Fig. 4.13a, it is drawn as a white circle with the largest diameter. Then, decision variants are added to the graph, which are only outranked by the variants already placed in the graph. They form the second group of variants. In the example, it is W_1 variant, marked as a light gray circle with a smaller diameter. The third group of variants consists of variants outranked by elements already added to the graph. In the example, it is the W_4 variant presented as a gray circle with the smallest diameter. The procedure is repeated until all variants are exhausted. Then the graph is completed with arrows.

In the case of a graph compiled from worst to best, the procedure is very similar. The order of the pairs in the Ω_S set is reversed, and thus the $\Omega_{S'}$ set is created. In the considered example, $\Omega_{S'}$ has the following form:

$$\Omega_{S'} = \{(W_1;\, W_5)\,;\, (W_2;\, W_4)\,;\, (W_2;\, W_5)\,;\, (W_3;\, W_1)\,; \\ (W_3;\, W_2)\,;\, (W_3;\, W_4)\,;\, (W_3;\, W_5)\,;\, (W_4;\, W_1)\,;\, (W_4;\, W_5)\}\,. \tag{4.77}$$

Such a change in pairs' order means a change of relations between objects. Now the objects W_1 and W_4 outrank W_5. Then the graph is created according to the

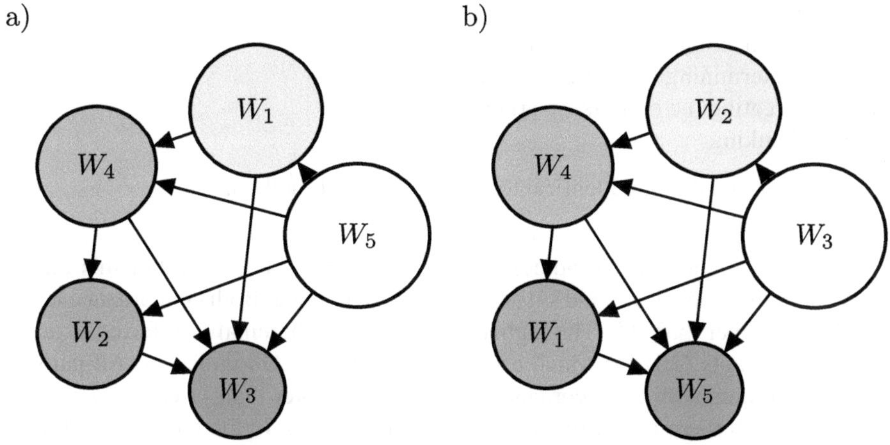

Fig. 4.13 The relationship for the second example between the decision variants illustrated in the form of created graph: (**a**) from the best to the worst variants and (**b**) from the worst to best variants

procedure described earlier. Finally, the direction of arrows must be changed to correspond to real relationships. The result is shown in Fig. 4.13b.

Subsequent groups of variants added to the graph determine the position in the ranking. In the example for the graph in Fig. 4.13a, there are five groups. The first includes the W_5 variant, the second W_1, the third W_4, the fourth W_2, and the fifth W_3, so we may say that W_5 variant belongs to the first class, W_1 variant to the second, etc. The situation is similar in the case of graph in Fig. 4.13b, where the first class includes W_3, object, the second class includes W_2 object, etc. In order to compare the results of both rankings, you can calculate the average position of the first ranking and the reverse of the second one. The average position of W_1 object is 2 W_2 is 4, W_3 is 5, W_4 is 3, and W_5 is 1. This allows objects to be ranked from best to the worst. The decision variant W_5 turned out to be the best. The car associated with this variant had the lowest fuel consumption and low price. It has also the largest trunk, although the weight of this criterion was lower than the others.

ELECTRE II Method

The ELECTRE II method is the first method designed with the concept of ranking. It also introduced two concordance levels and two discordance levels. This makes it possible to produce two types of graphs: the graph of strong and weak outranks. The strong outranking graph shows which decision variants strongly dominate the others and the slight outranking graph—those, which domination is weak. The calculation procedure of the ELECTRE II method is very similar to the ELECTRE I. The algorithm of the ELECTRE II method can be described in the following steps:

Step 1: Preliminary operations on the criteria
Step 2: Computing the concordance indices
Step 3: Determining the concordance set

Step 4: Computing the discordance level
Step 5: Determining the discordance set
Step 6: Determining the outranking relation
Step 7: Creating the outranking graph
Step 8: Ranking

Steps 1–2 and 4–5 are identical to the ELECTRE I method.

Step 3
The matrix of concordance indices is computed in the same way. For this matrix two concordance levels (s_1 and s_2) are determined, not one. Both concordance levels should be greater than 0.5. The higher of these levels, hereinafter referred to as s_2, identifies variants (set) for which a strong outranking relation occurs. All pairs of decision variants with a concordance index value greater than or equal to s_2 form a set for which there is a strong outranking relationship. In the analyzed example, it can be assumed that the concordance level s_2 is 0.8. For the concordance matrix given by the formula (4.57), Ω_{C_S} set will include the following elements:

$$\begin{aligned}\Omega_{C_S} = \{&(W_1;\ W_2)\ ;\ (W_1;\ W_3)\ ;\ (W_1;\ W_4)\ ;\\ &(W_4;\ W_2)\ ;\ (W_5;\ W_2)\ ;\ (W_5;\ W_3)\ ;\ (W_5;\ W_4)\}\,.\end{aligned} \tag{4.78}$$

All pairs of decision variants with a consistency coefficient value greater than or equal to $s_1$and less than s_2 form a set of weak outranking. Assuming that s_1 is 0.5 and s_2 is 0.8 for the concordance matrix given by formula (4.57), the set will be as follows:

$$\Omega_{C_W} = \{(W_2;\ W_3)\ ;\ (W_3;\ W_1)\ (W_4;\ W_3)\ ;\ (W_5;\ W_1)\}\,. \tag{4.79}$$

Step 5
The matrix of discordance indices is calculated in the same way. One discordance level is also determined for this matrix (d). In the analyzed example, it can be assumed that the discordance level is 0.4. For the discordance matrix given by the formula (4.64), the discordance set Ω_D will contain the following elements:

$$\Omega_D = \{(W_1;\ W_2)\ ;\ (W_1;\ W_3)\ ;\ (W_1;\ W_4)\ ;\ (W_2;\ W_3)\ ;\ (W_3;\ W_1)\ ;\ (W_5;\ W_2)\}\,. \tag{4.80}$$

Step 6
Based on Ω_{C_S} and Ω_D sets Ω_{S_S}, set is created, including ordered pairs, defining the strong preference relations:

$$\Omega_{S_S} = \Omega_{C_S} \backslash \Omega_D. \tag{4.81}$$

For the example considered, it will contain the following elements:

$$\Omega_{S_S} = \{(W_4;\ W_2)\ ;\ (W_5;\ W_3)\ ;\ (W_5;\ W_4)\}\,. \tag{4.82}$$

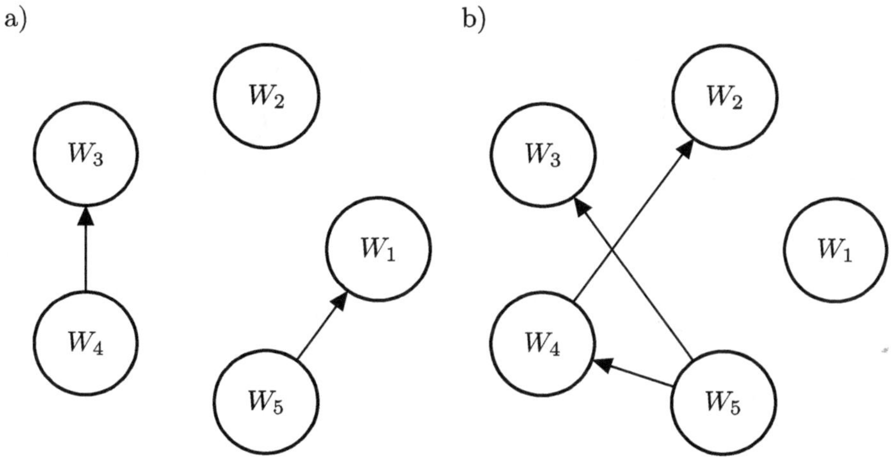

Fig. 4.14 The relationship between the decision variants for the second example is illustrated in a graph form: (**a**) for weak outranking and (**b**) for strong outranking

Ω_{S_S} set includes all elements of Ω_{C_S}, set that do not belong to Ω_D set. Similarly, Ω_{S_W} is created with ordered pairs which define weak preference relations:

$$\Omega_{S_W} = \Omega_{C_W} \backslash \Omega_D. \tag{4.83}$$

For the example considered, it will contain the following elements:

$$\Omega_{S_W} = \{(W_4;\ W_3)\,;\,(W_5;\ W_1)\}\,. \tag{4.84}$$

Step 7
Based on Ω_{S_S} and Ω_{S_W} sets, two graphs are created, weak (Fig. 4.14a) and strong (Fig. 4.14b) outranking, respectively. These graphs are produced identically as in the ELECTRE I and ELECTRE Iv methods.

Based on Ω_{Z_S} and Ω_{Z_W} sets, the ranking is created. In the first stage of ranking, loops are removed from a graph. Figure 4.15a shows an example of a graph containing a loop. Loops represent decision variants W_1, W_2, and W_5. In W_1, W_2, W_5 loop, W_1 variants outrank W_2, W_2—W_5, and W_5—W_1. Therefore it is not possible to determine which variant is the best or the worst. Loop decision variants can be treated as equivalent. For this reason, in the graph of strong outranking, variants included in the same loop are replaced by one. For example, if the graph in Fig. 4.15a were a strong outranking graph, then the objects in the loop would be replaced by the object marked in Fig. 4.15b with the value of one.

Step 8
After the loops are removed, the ranking procedure is performed in the following steps [159]:

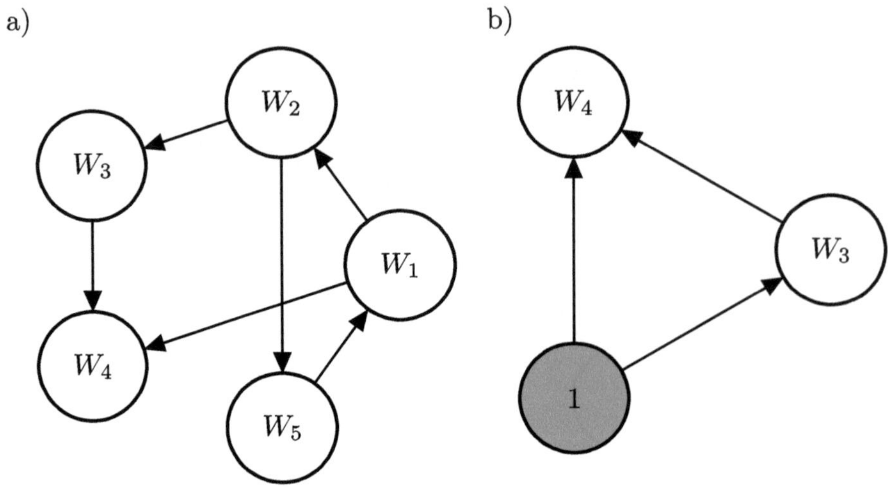

Fig. 4.15 Removing loops: (**a**) graph with a loop W_1, W_2, and W_5 and (**b**) graph after removing the loop

1. At the beginning, the numerator value is set at $l = 1$, what determines the position in ranking.
2. All decision variants that are not strongly outranked by any other variants constitute Ω_N set.
3. All variants that belong to the Ω_N set and participate in slight outranking constitute the Ω_U set.
4. All variants that belong to Ω_U set and are not outranked by any other element in the Ω_U set constitute the Ω_B set.
5. The set $\Omega_W = (\Omega_N \setminus \Omega_U) \cup \Omega_B$ is created.
6. If $\Omega_W = \emptyset$, it is assumed that $\Omega_W = \Omega_N$.
7. All elements from the Ω_W set are assigned a position l in the ranking.
8. The position l in ranking is increased by one.
9. Objects belonging to the Ω_W set are removed from the set of objects participating in the ranking.
10. If the set of not-ranked elements is empty, the ranking procedure is terminated—otherwise, it returns to point 2.

The order created in this way ranks the objects from the best to the worst. Then a ranking of the items from the worst to the best is made. To do this, the directions of the arrows are reversed in the graphs, and then the ranking procedure is repeated. In the created ranking, the order of the items is reversed, which means that the last item is assigned the first place, the penultimate item is the second, etc. To receive the final ranking, each variant is assigned points, one for each object that outranks. Points are allocated for each of the two rankings and the score is then added up. The number of points earned determines the position.

For the considered example, graphs for strong and weak outranks were obtained (Fig. 4.14). There is no loop in the strong outranks graph. Therefore, you can immediately proceed to creating a ranking according to the previously discussed procedure:

1. The value of the nominator is set at $l = 1$.
2. The decision variants W_1 and W_5 are not strongly outranked by any other variants, so the elements of the Ω_N set will be

$$\Omega_N = \{W_1; W_5\}. \tag{4.85a}$$

3. From the set Ω_N, the elements W_1 and W_5 participate in the weak outranking, so the set Ω_U will be as follows:

$$\Omega_U = \{W_1; W_5\}. \tag{4.85b}$$

4. The element W_5 is not subject to weak outranking of any other element in the Ω_U set, and hence the Ω_B set will contain:

$$\Omega_B = \{W_5\}. \tag{4.85c}$$

5. The following set Ω_W is created:

$$\Omega_W = (\{W_1; W_3\} \setminus \{W_1; W_3\}) \cup \{W_1\} = \emptyset \cup \{W_5\} = \{W_5\}. \tag{4.85d}$$

6. The Ω_W set is not empty, so it does not change.
7. Object W_5 gets the first position in the ranking.
8. Numerator l takes the value of two.
9. Only the elements W_1, W_2, W_3, and W_4 participate in the further ranking.

Due to the fact that not all elements have been ranked yet, the procedure is repeated from point 2:

2. The decision variants W_1, W_2, and W_3 are not outranked by any other variants, which means that Ω_N set takes the following elements:

$$\Omega_N = \{W_1; W_3; W_4\}. \tag{4.85e}$$

3. From the set Ω_N, the elements W_3 and W_4 participate in the slight outranking, so the set Ω_U will be as follows:

$$\Omega_U = \{W_3; W_4\}. \tag{4.85f}$$

4. The element W_4 set not subject to slight outranking of any other element in the Ω_U set, and hence the Ω_B set will contain:

$$\Omega_B = \{W_4\}\,. \tag{4.85g}$$

5. Ω_W set is created:

$$\Omega_W = (\{W_1;\, W_3;\, W_4\} \setminus \{W_3;\, W_4\}) \cup \{W_4\} = \{W_1\} \cup \{W_4\} = \{W_1;\, W_4\}\,. \tag{4.85h}$$

6. Ω_W set is not empty, so it shows that it does not change.
7. Object W_1 and W_4 are given a second position in ranking.
8. Numerator l takes the value of three.
9. Only the elements W_2 and W_3 participate in the further ranking.

Due to the fact that not all elements have been ranked yet, the procedure is repeated from point 2:

2. The decision variants W_2 and W_3 are not outranked by any other variants, which means that Ω_N set takes the following elements:

$$\Omega_N = \{W_2;\, W_3\}\,. \tag{4.85i}$$

3. None of the elements from Ω_N set participates in slight outranking, and thus Ω_U set will be empty:

$$\Omega_U = \emptyset. \tag{4.85j}$$

4. Because Ω_U set is empty, Ω_B will also be an empty set:

$$\Omega_B = \emptyset. \tag{4.85k}$$

5. Ω_W set is created:

$$\Omega_W = (\{W_2;\, W_3\} \setminus \emptyset) \cup \emptyset = \{W_2;\, W_3\} \cup \emptyset = \{W_2;\, W_3\}\,. \tag{4.85l}$$

6. Ω_W set is not empty, so it shows that it does not change.
7. Objects W_2 and W_3 receive the third position in ranking.
8. Numinator l takes the value of four.
9. No element is involved in the further ranking.

Because all the items have been ordered, the ranking procedure is now complete. The first position in ranking is taken by W_5 object and the second by W_1 and W_4 objects, and the third by W_2 and W_3. Then the strong and weak graphs are inverted (Fig. 4.16), and the entire ranking procedure is repeated. As a result, for the example under consideration, the first position was given to the objects W_1, W_2, and W_3, the second to W_4, and the third to W_5. The ranking order is inverted, so the first position is given to W_5, the second to W_4, and the third to W_1, W_2 and W_3. Each decision variant is assigned points for its position in the ranking. The W_5 variant

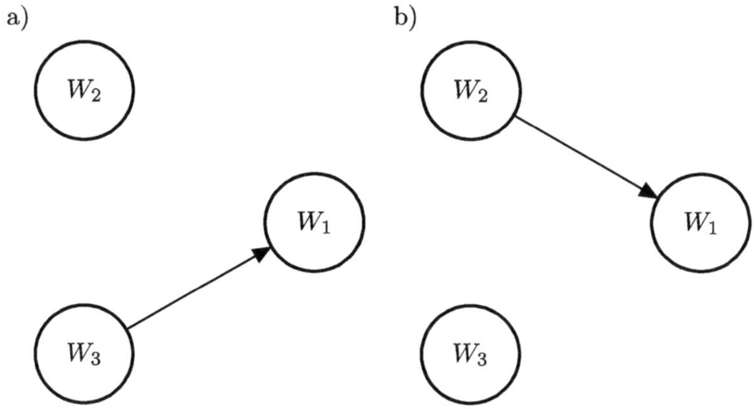

Fig. 4.16 The relationship between decision variants is illustrated in the form of an inverted graph constructed for: (**a**) weak outranking and (**b**) strong outranking

in the first ranking is better than all objects. For each of these objects, the variant receives one point, i.e., four points. In the second ranking, it is also better than all objects, and hence it gets another four points, making a total of eight. The W_1 variant in the first ranking is better than the W_2 and W_3 objects, and in the second ranking it is not better than any object. Therefore it receives two points for the first ranking and three for the second, which is a total of two points. Finally, the ranking is as follows: W_5 variant received eight points and took the first place, the decision variant W_4 received five points and took the second place, W_1 variant received two points and took the third place, and W_2 and W_3 variants received zero points and took the last place.

ELECTRE III Method

The ELECTRE III method introduces two-level preferences. It is assumed that the decision options within the criteria may slightly or strongly outrank each other. In the ELECTRE methods presented earlier, the comparison could only determine whether one object was better than the other or whether it was similar. For example, when comparing prices, if it is assumed that the equivalence threshold is PLN 10, then each greater difference results in the same relation of preferences. Price differences greater than the equivalence threshold (PLN 11, PLN 100, PLN 1000, etc.) are indistinguishable by the ELECTRE I , ELECTRE Iv, and ELECTRE II methods, but it may be important for a decision-maker whether prices differ by PLN 1 or PLN 100. Therefore, in ELECTRE III, the concept of strong and weak preference was introduced to distinguish between situations in which the decision variants differ slightly and very much from each other. The ELECTRE III method algorithm can be described in the following steps:

Step 1: Preliminary operations on criteria
Step 2: Computing the concordance indices
Step 3: Computing the credibility indices

Step 4: Determining the order of decision variants using descending and ascending distillation

Step 5: Final ranking determination

Step 1 is identical as in the ELECTRE I.

Step 2

In the ELECTRE III method, similarly, the values of the concordance indices $\upsilon_{i,j,k}$ are calculated. However, matrices Υ_i are computed differently:

1. For $g_i(W_k) + q_i'(g_i(W_k)) \geqslant g_i(W_j)$ value $\upsilon_{i,j,k}$ is 1.
2. For $g_i(W_j) > g_i(W_k) + q_i(g_i(W_k))$ value $\upsilon_{i,j,k}$ equals 0.
3. In other cases,

$$\upsilon_{i,j,k} = \frac{g_i(W_k) + q(g_i(W_k)) - g_i(W_j)}{q(g_i(W_k)) - q'(g_i(W_k))}. \tag{4.86}$$

$q_i(g_i(W_k))$ is the preference threshold, for the k-th variant with respect to the i criterion. The preference threshold determines what the minimum difference in the values of criteria between variants must be for one variant to be clearly better than the other according to a given criterion. $q_i'(g_i(W_k))$ is the equivalence threshold, for the k-variant with respect to the criterion i. The equivalence threshold determines what the maximum difference in the values of the criteria between variants must be for the variants to be comparable according to the given criterion. Most often q_i and q_i' are not functions but constant numbers for a given criterion. Values q_i and q_i' are obtained from a decision-maker and must be normalized according to the formula:

$$\underset{j}{x_i'} = \frac{\underset{j}{x_i}}{\max\limits_j\left(\underset{j}{x_i}\right) - \min\limits_j\left(\underset{j}{x_i}\right)}. \tag{4.87}$$

Then, like in ELECTRE I method, the concordance indices values are calculated:

$$C = \sum_{i=1}^{N} w_i' \Upsilon_i. \tag{4.88}$$

Calculations were made for the example in Table 4.5. The values from this table have been normalized (Table 4.6). Preference thresholds were adopted for the purposes of the calculations: 2500 for the *price* criterion, 0.5 for the *fuel consumption* criterion, and 25 for the *trunk capacity* criterion. Values were normalized. The difference between the highest and the lowest value for the *price* was 10,015, and therefore the value of the normalized preference threshold is 0.25. The value of the normalized preference threshold for the *fuel consumption* was 0.83, and for the *trunk capacity* was 0.49. The following values were assumed as the equivalence thresholds: 1000 for the *price*, 0.1 for the *fuel consumption* , and 10 for the *trunk capacity*. After normalization, these values were as follows: 0.1 for the *price* , 0.17 for the *fuel consumption* , and 0.19 for the *trunk capacity*.

Then $\upsilon_{i,j,k}$. values were determined. For the decision variants W_1 and W_2 for the *price* criterion, the value of $\upsilon_{1,1,2}$ will be calculated as follows:

$$g_1\left(W_1\right) + q_1'\left(g_1\left(W_1\right)\right) \geqslant g_1\left(W_2\right) \Rightarrow 1 + 0.1 \geqslant 0.12. \tag{4.89}$$

The condition is met, so the first case occurs. Value of $\upsilon_{1,1,2}$ is equal to one.

For the decision variants W_3 and W_2 for the *price* criterion, the value of $\upsilon_{1,3,2}$ will be calculated as

$$g_1\left(W_3\right) + q_1'\left(g_1\left(W_3\right)\right) \geqslant g_1\left(W_2\right) \Rightarrow 0 + 0.1 < 0.12. \tag{4.90}$$

The condition is not met, and the second case should be checked:

$$g_1\left(W_2\right) > g_1\left(W_3\right) + q_1\left(g_1\left(W_3\right)\right) \Rightarrow 0.12 \leqslant 0 + 0.25. \tag{4.91}$$

The condition is not met, and thus the third case occurs:

$$\upsilon_{1,3,2} = \frac{g_1\left(W_3\right) + q_1\left(g_1\left(W_3\right)\right) - g_1\left(W_2\right)}{q_1\left(g_1\left(W_3\right)\right) - q_1'\left(g_1\left(W_3\right)\right)}, \tag{4.92}$$

hence

$$\upsilon_{1,3,2} = \frac{0 + 0.25 - 0.12}{0.25 - 0.1} = 0.86. \tag{4.93}$$

Entire Υ_1 matrix will be as follows:

$$\Upsilon_1 = \begin{bmatrix} 1 & 1 & 1 & 1 & 1 \\ 0 & 1 & 1 & 0 & 0 \\ 0 & 0.86 & 1 & 0 & 0 \\ 0 & 1 & 1 & 1 & 0 \\ 0.8 & 1 & 1 & 1 & 1 \end{bmatrix}. \tag{4.94}$$

Matrix Υ_2 for *fuel consumption*:

$$\Upsilon_2 = \begin{bmatrix} 1 & 1 & 1 & 1 & 1 \\ 0 & 1 & 0 & 0.25 & 0 \\ 1 & 1 & 1 & 1 & 1 \\ 1 & 1 & 1 & 1 & 0.75 \\ 1 & 1 & 1 & 1 & 1 \end{bmatrix}. \tag{4.95}$$

Matrix Υ_3 fortrunk capacity:

$$\Upsilon_3 = \begin{bmatrix} 1 & 0 & 0 & 0 & 0.4 \\ 1 & 1 & 1 & 1 & 1 \\ 1 & 0.07 & 1 & 0.93 & 1 \\ 1 & 0.8 & 1 & 1 & 1 \\ 1 & 0 & 1 & 0.4 & 1 \end{bmatrix}. \tag{4.96}$$

The assumed weights were similar as in the previous examples. After normalization, they were as follows: *price*—0.4, *fuel consumption*—0.4, and *trunk capacity*—0.2. The value of the concordance index for variants W_1, W_2 was

$$c_{1,2} = w'_1 \upsilon_{1,1,2} + w'_2 \upsilon_{2,1,2} + w'_3 \upsilon_{3,1,2} = 0.4 \cdot 1 + 0.4 \cdot 1 + 0.2 \cdot 0 = 0.8. \tag{4.97}$$

The entire concordance indices matrix will be as follows:

$$C = \begin{bmatrix} 1 & 0.8 & 0.8 & 0.8 & 0.88 \\ 0.2 & 1 & 0.6 & 0.3 & 0.2 \\ 0.6 & 0.76 & 1 & 0.59 & 0.6 \\ 0.6 & 0.96 & 1 & 1 & 0.5 \\ 0.92 & 0.8 & 1 & 0.88 & 1 \end{bmatrix}. \tag{4.98}$$

Step 3

In this step, the values of reliability coefficients are calculated. For this purpose, matrices of discordance indices $d_{i,j,k}$ for individual criteria are calculated:

1. For $g_i\left(W_j\right) > g_i\left(W_k\right) + v_i\left(g_i\left(W_k\right)\right)$ value $d_{i,j,k}$ is 1.
2. For $g_i\left(W_j\right) \leqslant g_i\left(W_k\right) + q_i\left(g_i\left(W_k\right)\right)$ the value of $d_{i,j,k}$ is 0.
3. In other cases,

$$d_{i,j,k} = \frac{g_i\left(W_j\right) - g_i\left(W_k\right) - q_i\left(g_i\left(W_k\right)\right)}{v_i\left(g_i\left(W_k\right)\right) - q_i\left(g_i\left(W_k\right)\right)}. \tag{4.99}$$

$v_i\left(g_i\left(W_k\right)\right)$ is the discordance threshold, for k-th variant in relation to i criterion. The discordance threshold determines the minimum difference in the values of criteria between the variants for one variant to be clearly discordant to the other according to a given criterion. Most often v_i is not a function but a number, constant for a given criterion. Values v are obtained from a decision-maker and have to be normalized according to the formula (4.87).

Based on the concordance indices matrix and the discordance matrix, elements of the credibility matrix are calculated *credibility matrix* [49]:

$$\sigma_{j,k} = \begin{cases} c_{j,k} & \text{dla } \max_i \left(d_{i,j,k}\right) \leqslant c_{j,k}, \\ c_{j,k} \prod\limits_{d_{i,j,k} > c_{j,k}} \dfrac{1 - d_{i,j,k}}{1 - c_{j,k}} & \text{dla } \max_i \left(d_{i,j,k}\right) > c_{j,k}. \end{cases} \tag{4.100}$$

For the purposes of the calculations, the following values of discordance thresholds were taken: 4,000 for *price*, 1.5 for *fuel consumption* and 50 for *trunk capacity*. After normalization, these values were as follows: 0.4 for *price*, 2.5 for *fuel consumption*, and 0.98 for *trunk capacity*.

The values of $d_{i,j,k}$ were determined. For example, for the decision variants W_5 and W_2 for the *trunk capacity* criterion, the value $d_{3,5,2}$ will be calculated as follows:

$$g_3\left(W_2\right) > g_3\left(W_5\right) + v_3\left(g_3\left(W_5\right)\right) \Rightarrow 1 > 0.37 + 0.98. \tag{4.101}$$

The condition is not met, and the second case should be checked:

$$g_3\left(W_2\right) \leqslant g_3\left(W_5\right) + q_3\left(g_3\left(W_5\right)\right) \Rightarrow 1 \leqslant 0.37 + 0.49. \tag{4.102}$$

The condition is not met, and hence the third case occurs:

$$d_{3,5,2} = \frac{g_3\left(W_2\right) - g_3\left(W_5\right) - q_3\left(g_3\left(W_5\right)\right)}{v_3\left(g_3\left(W_5\right)\right) - q_3\left(g_3\left(W_5\right)\right)}, \tag{4.103}$$

hence

$$d_{3,5,2} = \frac{1 - 0.37 - 0.49}{0.98 - 0.49} = 0.28. \tag{4.104}$$

Entire D_3 matrix will be as follows:

$$D_3 = \begin{bmatrix} 0 & 1 & 0.08 & 0.52 & 0 \\ 0 & 0 & 0 & 0 & 0 \\ 0 & 0 & 0 & 0 & 0 \\ 0 & 0 & 0 & 0 & 0 \\ 0 & 0.28 & 0 & 0 & 0 \end{bmatrix}. \tag{4.105}$$

Matrix D_1 for *price* criterion::

$$D_1 = \begin{bmatrix} 0 & 0 & 0 & 0 & 0 \\ 1 & 0 & 0 & 1 & 1 \\ 1 & 0 & 0 & 1 & 1 \\ 1 & 0 & 0 & 0 & 0.67 \\ 0 & 0 & 0 & 0 & 0 \end{bmatrix}. \tag{4.106}$$

Matrix D_2 for *fuel consumption* criterion:

Table 4.9 Values of Table D_c

D_c	W_1	W_2	W_3	W_4	W_5
W_1	Ø	{3}	Ø	Ø	Ø
W_2	{1}	Ø	Ø	{1}	{1}
W_3	{1}	Ø	Ø	{1}	{1}
W_4	{1}	Ø	Ø	Ø	{1}
W_5	Ø	Ø	Ø	Ø	Ø

$$D_2 = \begin{bmatrix} 0\,0\,0\,0 & 0 \\ 0\,0\,0\,0 & 0.1 \\ 0\,0\,0\,0 & 0 \\ 0\,0\,0\,0 & 0 \\ 0\,0\,0\,0 & 0 \end{bmatrix}. \tag{4.107}$$

Based on the matrices D_1, D_2, and D_3, the table D_c is determined using the formula:

$$D_c\left(W_k, W_j\right) = \left\{i : d_{i,k,j} > c_{k,j}\right\}. \tag{4.108}$$

If the condition $d_{i,k,j} > c_{k,j}$ is not met, then an element of the table $D_c\left(W_k, W_j\right)$ is an empty set.

For pairs (W_2, W_1), the value $c_{2,1}$ equals 0.2. Values $d_{i,k,j}$ are equal to $d_{1,2,1} = 1$, $d_{2,2,1} = 0$, $d_{3,2,1} = 0$. Only $d_{1,2,1}$ has the value greater than 0.2, so an element of the table $D_c\left(W_k, W_j\right)$ is the one-element set of criteria numbers {1}. The value of one means the *price*criterion. All sets included in D_c are presented in Table 4.9.

In case where $D_c\left(W_k, W_j\right)$ is the set, empty with regard to credibility index, it is assigned the corresponding value of the concordance index. The other elements of the credibility matrix are computed based on the formula (4.100).

For example, the value of $\sigma_{1,4}$ will be computed for the decision variants W_1 and W_4. The element of $D_c\,(W_1, W_4)$ table is an empty set. For this reason, is entered into the credibility index $\sigma_{1,4}$ the value of 0.8 from the matrix of concordance indices $c_{1,4}$.

The value of $\sigma_{4,5}$ has been calculated for decision variants W_4 and W_5. The element of $D_c\,(W_4, W_5)$ table is the one-element set pointing at $d_{1,4,5} = 0.67$. The value of $\sigma_{4,5}$ should be calculated following the formula:

$$\sigma_{4,5} = c_{4,5} \prod_{d_{i,4,5} > c_{4,5}} \frac{1 - d_{i,4,5}}{1 - c_{4,5}}. \tag{4.109}$$

$d_{i,4,5}$ is greater than $c_{4,5}$ only for *price* ($i = 1$), and thus

$$\sigma_{4,5} = c_{4,5}\frac{1 - d_{1,4,5}}{1 - c_{4,5}} = 0.5\frac{1 - 0.67}{1 - 0.5} = 0.33. \tag{4.110}$$

The entire matrix Σ will be as follows:

$$\Sigma = \begin{bmatrix} * & 0 & 0.8 & 0.8 & 0.88 \\ 0 & * & 0.6 & 0 & 0 \\ 0 & 0.76 & * & 0 & 0 \\ 0 & 0.96 & 1 & * & 0.33 \\ 0.92 & 0.8 & 1 & 0.88 & * \end{bmatrix}. \tag{4.111}$$

Step 4

Based on the Σ matrix, a ranking is constructed using the *descending* and *ascending distillation* procedure. Ascending distillation orders variants from the best to the worst and descending distillation from the worst to the best. The ordering procedure for ranking in the ELECTRE III method is performed using the descending and ascending distillation procedure. To carry out this procedure, the value of λ and the discrimination threshold $s(\lambda)$ are needed [203]:

- λ—cut level belonging to the range $\langle 0; 1\rangle$,
- $s(\lambda)$—discrimination threshold for the credibility index is given in the literature as follows [159]:

$$s(\lambda) = \alpha\lambda + \beta. \tag{4.112}$$

Values α and β are assumed to be at the level of −0.15 and 0.3, respectively, [159].

In ELECTRE III, it is checked whether between two variants $\left(W_k, W_j\right)$ λ_l-preference relation ($\overset{\lambda_l}{\succ}$) for each level of cut λ_l:

$$W_k \overset{\lambda_l}{\succ} W_j \Leftrightarrow \sigma_{k,j} - s\left(\sigma_{k,j}\right) > \sigma_{j,k} \wedge \sigma_{k,j} > \lambda_l. \tag{4.113}$$

Based on the results, at each level of calculation, the matrix Σ′ is created. In this matrix, the value of 1 is placed, when λ_l-preference relation occurs for the pair $\left(W_k, W_j\right)$, and when such relation does not exist—the value of zero. Based on Σ′ matrix, the set of variants $\Omega_{D_0)}$ is determined, which is the subset of Ω_{A_n}, where Ω_{A_n} is the set of all variants. Elements of Σ′ matrix are computed under the following formula:

$$q^{\lambda_l}_{\Omega_{D_l}}\left(W_k\right) = p^{\lambda_l}_{\Omega_{D_l}}\left(W_k\right) - f^{\lambda_l}_{\Omega_{D_l}}\left(W_k\right), \tag{4.114}$$

where:

- $p^{\lambda_l}_{\Omega_{D_l}}\left(W_k\right)$ is the number of variants in Ω_{D_l}, set compared to which W_k is preferred for λ_l level,
- $f^{\lambda_l}_{\Omega_{D_l}}\left(W_k\right)$ is the number of variants in Ω_{D_l}, set, which are preferred compared to W_k for λ_l level.

Distillation procedure is presented in the flowchart in Fig. 4.17. The initial value of λ_0 is calculated under the formula:

$$\lambda_0 = \max_{i \neq j} \sigma_{i,j}. \tag{4.115}$$

In the next iterations, the value of λ_{l+1} is determined as follows:

$$\lambda_{l+1} = \begin{cases} 0 & \text{where} \quad \bigwedge\limits_{W_j, W_k \in \Omega_{\bar{\mathrm{D}}_k}} \sigma_{j,k} > \lambda_l - f_s(\lambda_l), \\ \max\limits_{W_j, W_k \in \Omega_{\bar{\mathrm{D}}_k} \wedge i \neq j} \sigma_{i,j} & \text{otherwise.} \end{cases} \tag{4.116}$$

In addition, for descending distillation, the following is calculated:

$$\overline{q}_{\Omega D_l} = \max_{W_k \in \Omega_{D_l}} q_{\Omega D_l}^{\lambda_{l+1}}(W_k), \tag{4.117}$$

and for ascending distillation, the following is calculated:

$$\overline{q}_{\Omega D_l} = \min_{W_k \in \Omega_{D_l}} q_{\Omega D_l}^{\lambda_{l+1}}(W_k). \tag{4.118}$$

The top and bottom distillation algorithm is shown as a flowchart in Fig. 4.17.

The exemplary procedure of ascending distillation for the matrix Σ given with the formula (4.111) will be as follows:

Iteration 1

1. Let assume $n = 0$, $\Omega_{\bar{\mathrm{A}}_0} = \{W_1, W_2, W_3, W_4, W_5\}$.
2. We set the initial values of $\lambda_0 = \max_{k \neq j} \sigma_{k,j}$, where $W_k, W_j \in \Omega_{\bar{\mathrm{A}}_0}$. The matrix given by the formula (4.111) shows that the maximum value is equal to 1, i.e., $\lambda_0 = 1$.
3. Let us assume $l = 0$, $\Omega_{D_0} = \Omega_{\bar{\mathrm{A}}_0} = \{W_1, W_2, W_3, W_4, W_5\}$.
4. Let us calculate λ_1 (λ_{l+1}):

$$\lambda_0 - s(\lambda_0) = 1 - (-0.15 \cdot 1 + 0.3) = 0.85. \tag{4.119a}$$

Check if such pairs $(W_k, W_j) \in \Omega_{D_0}$, where $\sigma_{k,j} < \lambda_0 - s(\lambda_0)$, exist. Such pairs exist, and they are (W_1, W_2), (W_1, W_3), (W_1, W_4), (W_2, W_1), (W_2, W_3), (W_2, W_4), (W_2, W_5), etc. We are looking for the highest value of the credibility index for the presented pairs:

$$\lambda_1 = \min\{0; 0.8; 0.8; 0; 0.6; 0; 0; \ldots\} = 0.8. \tag{4.119b}$$

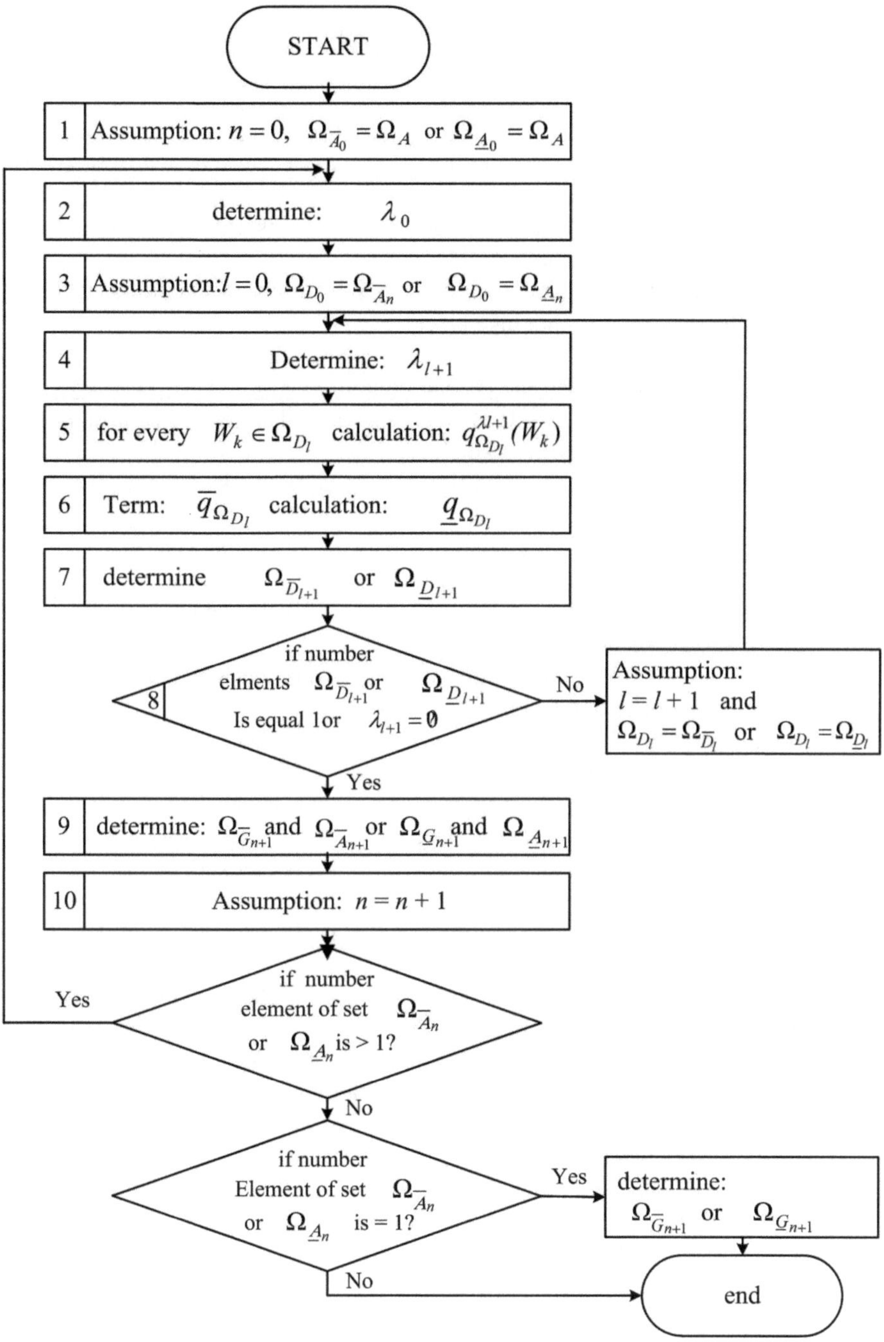

Fig. 4.17 Flowchart of the distillation procedure (based on [203])

5. We calculate $q^{\lambda_1}_{\Omega_{D_0}}(W_k)$ for each decision variant in Ω_{D_0}set. For this purpose, we check if λ-preference ($\overset{\lambda_1}{\succ}$) relation for decision variants in Ω_{D_0} set takes place.

   - For the pair (W_1, W_2), the condition $\sigma_{1,2} > \lambda_1$ is checked, that is, $0 \leqslant 0.8$—the relation does not take place.
   - For the pair (W_1, W_3), the condition $\sigma_{1,3} > \lambda_1$ is checked, that is, $0.8 \leqslant 0.8$—the relation does not take place.
   - For the pair (W_1, W_4), the condition $\sigma_{1,4} > \lambda_1$, is checked, that is, $0.8 \leqslant 0.8$—the relation does not take place.
   - For the pair (W_1, W_5), the condition $\sigma_{1,5} > \lambda_1$, is checked, that is, $0.88 > 0.8$. It is met. We check the second condition: $\sigma_{1,5} - s\left(\sigma_{1,5}\right) > \sigma_{5,1}$, that is, $0.88 - (-0.15 \cdot 0.88 + 0.3) = 0.71 \leqslant 0.92$. The second condition is not met—the relation does not take place.
   - For the pair (W_2, W_1), the condition $\sigma_{2,1} > \lambda_1$, is checked, that is, $0 \leqslant 0.8$—the relation does not take place.
   - For the pair (W_2, W_3), the condition $\sigma_{2,3} > \lambda_1$, is checked, that is, $0.6 \leqslant 0.8$—the relation does not take place.
   - For the pair (W_2, W_4), the condition $\sigma_{2,4} > \lambda_1$, is checked, that is, $0 \leqslant 0.8$—the relation does not take place.
   - For the pair (W_2, W_5), the condition $\sigma_{2,5} > \lambda_1$, is checked, that is, $0 \leqslant 0.8$—the relation does not take place.
   - For the pair (W_3, W_1), the condition $\sigma_{3,1} > \lambda_1$, is checked, that is, $0 \leqslant 0.8$—the relation does not take place.
   - For the pair (W_3, W_2), the condition $\sigma_{3,2} > \lambda_1$, is checked, that is, $0.76 \leqslant 0.8$—the relation does not take place.
   - For the pair (W_3, W_4), the condition $\sigma_{3,4} > \lambda_1$, is checked, that is, $0 \leqslant 0.8$—the relation does not take place.
   - For the pair (W_3, W_5), the condition $\sigma_{3,5} > \lambda_1$, is checked, that is, $0 \leqslant 0.8$—the relation does not take place.
   - For the pair (W_4, W_1), the condition $\sigma_{4,1} > \lambda_1$, is checked, that is, $0 \leqslant 0.8$—the relation does not take place.
   - For the pair (W_4, W_2), the condition $\sigma_{4,2} > \lambda_1$ is checked, that is, $0.96 > 0.8$. It is met. We check the second condition: $\sigma_{4,2} - s\left(\sigma_{4,2}\right) > \sigma_{2,4}$, that is, $0.96 - (-0.15 \cdot 0.96 + 0.3) = 0.8 > 0$. The second condition is met—the relation takes place.
   - For the pair (W_4, W_3), the condition $\sigma_{4,3} > \lambda_1$, is checked, that is, $1 > 0.8$. It is met. We check the second condition: $\sigma_{4,3} - s\left(\sigma_{4,3}\right) > \sigma_{3,4}$, that is, $1-(-0.15 \cdot 1 + 0.3) = 0.85 > 0$. The second condition is met—the relation takes place.
   - For the pair (W_4, W_5), the condition $\sigma_{4,5} > \lambda_1$ is checked, that is, $0.33 \leqslant 0.8$—the relation does not take place.
   - For the pair (W_5, W_1), the condition $\sigma_{5,1} > \lambda_1$ is checked, that is, $0.92 > 0.8$. It is met. We check the second condition: $\sigma_{5,1} - s\left(\sigma_{5,1}\right) > \sigma_{1,5}$, that

is, $0.92 - (-0.15 \cdot 0.92 + 0.3) = 0.76 \leqslant 0.88$. The second condition is not met—the relation does not take place.

- For the pair (W_5, W_2), the condition $\sigma_{5,2} > \lambda_1$ is checked, that is, $0.8 \leqslant 0.8$—the relation does not take place.
- For the pair (W_5, W_3), the condition $\sigma_{5,3} > \lambda_1$ is checked, that is, $1 > 0.8$. It is met. We check the second condition: $\sigma_{5,3} - s\left(\sigma_{5,3}\right) > \sigma_{3,5}$, that is, $1-(-0.15 \cdot 1 + 0.3) = 0.85 > 0$. The second condition is met—the relation takes place.
- For the pair (W_5, W_4), the condition $\sigma_{5,4} > \lambda_1$ is checked, that is, $0.88 > 0.8$. It is met. We check the second condition: $\sigma_{5,4} - s\left(\sigma_{5,4}\right) > \sigma_{4,5}$, that is, $0.88 - (-0.15 \cdot 0.88 + 0.3) = 0.7 > 0.34$. The second condition is met—the relation takes place.

The results are presented in Σ' matrix:

$$\Sigma' = \begin{bmatrix} * & 0 & 0 & 0 & 0 \\ 0 & * & 0 & 0 & 0 \\ 0 & 0 & * & 0 & 0 \\ 0 & 1 & 1 & * & 0 \\ 0 & 0 & 1 & 1 & * \end{bmatrix}. \tag{4.119c}$$

In this matrix, the value one means that for the pair $\left(W_j, W_k\right)$ the relation of λ-preference at $\lambda_1 = 0.8$ takes place and zero when the relation does not take place.

The values of $p^{\lambda_1}_{\Omega_{D_0}}(W_k)$ are determined, which are a number of variants in Ω_{D_0} set, for which variant W_k is preferred for level λ_l. To determine $p^{\lambda_1}_{\Omega_{D_0}}(W_1)$, the number of value one in the first row is counted. It is zero, and hence $p^{\lambda_1}_{\Omega_{D_0}}(W_1) = 0$. In order to determine $p^{\lambda_1}_{\Omega_{D_0}}(W_2)$, the number of value one in the second row is counted. It is zero, then $p^{\lambda_1}_{\Omega_{D_0}}(W_2) = 0$. The other values are $p^{\lambda_1}_{\Omega_{D_0}}(W_3) = 0$ and $p^{\lambda_1}_{\Omega_{D_0}}(W_4) = 2$ i $p^{\lambda_1}_{\Omega_{D_0}}(W_5) = 2$.

The values of $f^{\lambda_1}_{\Omega_{D_0}}(W_k)$ which are the number of variants in Ω_{D_0} set, preferred in relation to W_k at λ_1, are determined. In order to determine $f^{\lambda_1}_{\Omega_{D_0}}(W_1)$, the number of value one in the first column is counted. It is zero, and then $f^{\lambda_1}_{\Omega_{D_0}}(W_1) = 0$. In order to calculate $f^{\lambda_1}_{\Omega_{D_0}}(W_2)$, the number of value one in the second column is counted. It is one, and then $f^{\lambda_1}_{\Omega_{D_0}}(W_2) = 1$. The other values are $f^{\lambda_1}_{\Omega_{D_0}}(W_3) = 2$, $f^{\lambda_1}_{\Omega_{D_0}}(W_4) = 1$, and $f^{\lambda_1}_{\Omega_{D_0}}(W_5) = 0$.

The values of $q^{\lambda_1}_{\Omega_{D_0}}(W_k)$ are calculated under the formula (4.114). The value of $q^{\lambda_1}_{\Omega_{D_0}}(W_1)$ is

$$q_{\Omega D_0}^{\lambda_1}(W_1) = p_{\Omega D_0}^{\lambda_1}(W_1) - q_{\Omega D_0}^{\lambda_1}(W_1) = 0 - 0 = 0. \quad (4.119d)$$

The value of $q_{\Omega D_0}^{\lambda_1}(W_2)$ is:

$$q_{\Omega D_0}^{\lambda_1}(W_2) = p_{\Omega D_0}^{\lambda_1}(W_2) - q_{\Omega D_0}^{\lambda_1}(W_2) = 0 - 1 = -1. \quad (4.119e)$$

The other values are $q_{\Omega D_0}^{\lambda_1}(W_3) = -2$, $q_{\Omega D_0}^{\lambda_1}(W_4) = 1$, and $q_{\Omega D_0}^{\lambda_1}(W_5) = 2$.

6. We calculate $\overline{q}_{\Omega D_0}$:

$$\overline{q}_{\Omega D_0} = \max_{W_k \in \Omega D_0} q_{\Omega D_0}^{\lambda_1}(W_k) = \max\{0; -1; -2; 1; 2\} = 2. \quad (4.119f)$$

7. We determine the $\Omega_{\overline{D}_1}$ set of all decision variants for which $q_{\Omega D_0}^{\lambda_1}(W_k)$ equals $\overline{q}_{\Omega D_0} = 2$:

$$\Omega_{\overline{D}_1} = \left\{ W_k \in \Omega_{\overline{D}_0} : q_{\Omega D_0}^{\lambda_1}(W_k) = \overline{q}_{\Omega D_0} \right\} = \{W_5\}. \quad (4.119g)$$

8. Because $\Omega_{\overline{D}_1}$ set is not empty, we move forward to point 9.
9. We determine

$$\Omega_{\overline{G}_1} = \Omega_{\overline{D}_1} = \{W_5\}. \quad (4.119h)$$

and

$$\Omega_{\overline{A}_1} = \Omega_{\overline{A}_0} \setminus \Omega_{\overline{G}_1} = \{W_1, W_2, W_3, W_4\}. \quad (4.119i)$$

10. We take $n = 1$, and because the number of elements in $\Omega_{\overline{A}_1}$ set is greater than 1, we move forward to point 2.

Iteration 2

2. We set $\lambda_0 = \max_{k \neq j} \sigma_{k,j}$, where $W_k, W_j \in \Omega_{\bar{\mathrm{A}}_1}$. From the matrix given by the formula (4.111), it follows that the maximum value is equal to 1, that is, $\lambda_0 = 1$.
3. Let us assume $l = 0$, $\Omega_{\bar{D}_1} = \Omega_{\bar{\mathrm{A}}_1} = \{W_1, W_2, W_3, W_4\}$.
4. We calculate the coefficient λ_1 (λ_{l+1}):

$$\lambda_0 - s(\lambda_0) = 1 - (-0.15 \cdot 1 + 0.3) = 0.85. \quad (4.120a)$$

Check if such pairs $(W_k, W_j) \in \Omega_{\bar{D}_1}$, where $\sigma_{k,j} < \lambda_0 - s(\lambda_0)$, exist. Such pairs exist. We are looking for the greatest value of the credibility coefficient:

$$\lambda_1 = 0.8. \quad (4.120b)$$

5. We calculate the rating $q^{\lambda_1}_{\Omega_{\bar{D}_1}}(W_k)$ for each decision variant in $\Omega_{\bar{D}_1}$ set. For this reason, we check if λ-preference relation ($\overset{\lambda_1}{\succ}$) for decision variants in $\Omega_{\bar{D}_1}$ set occurs.

   - For the pair (W_1, W_2), the condition $\sigma_{1,2} > \lambda_1$ is checked, that is, $0 \leqslant 0.8$—the relation does not take place.
   - For the pair (W_1, W_3), the condition $\sigma_{1,3} > \lambda_1$ is checked, that is, $0.8 \leqslant 0.8$—the relation does not take place.
   - For the pair (W_1, W_4), the condition $\sigma_{1,4} > \lambda_1$ is checked, that is, $0.8 \leqslant 0.8$—the relation does not take place.
   - For the pair (W_2, W_1), the condition $\sigma_{2,1} > \lambda_1$ is checked, that is, $0 \leqslant 0.8$—the relation does not take place.
   - For the pair (W_2, W_3), the condition $\sigma_{2,3} > \lambda_1$ is checked, that is, $0.6 \leqslant 0.8$—the relation does not take place.
   - For the pair (W_2, W_4), the condition $\sigma_{2,4} > \lambda_1$ is checked, that is, $0 \leqslant 0.8$—the relation does not take place.
   - For the pair (W_3, W_1), the condition $\sigma_{3,1} > \lambda_1$ is checked, that is, $0 \leqslant 0.8$—the relation does not take place.
   - For the pair (W_3, W_2), the condition $\sigma_{3,2} > \lambda_1$ is checked, that is, $0.76 \leqslant 0.8$—the relation does not take place.
   - For the pair (W_3, W_4), the condition $\sigma_{3,4} > \lambda_1$ is checked, that is, $0 \leqslant 0.8$—the relation does not take place.
   - For the pair (W_4, W_1), the condition $\sigma_{4,1} > \lambda_1$ is checked, that is, $0 \leqslant 0.8$—the relation does not take place.
   - For the pair (W_4, W_2), the condition $\sigma_{4,2} > \lambda_1$ is checked, that is, $0.96 > 0.8$. It is met. Check the second condition: $\sigma_{4,2} - s\left(\sigma_{4,2}\right) > \sigma_{2,4}$, that is, $0.96 - (-0.15 \cdot 0.96 + 0.3) = 0.8 > 0$. The second condition is met—the relation takes place.
   - For the pair (W_4, W_3), the condition $\sigma_{4,3} > \lambda_1$ is checked, that is, $1 > 0.8$. It is met. We check the second condition: $\sigma_{4,3} - s\left(\sigma_{4,3}\right) > \sigma_{3,4}$, that is, $1-(-0.15 \cdot 1 + 0.3) = 0.85 > 0$. The second condition is met—the relation takes place.

   The calculation results are presented in matrix Σ':

$$\Sigma' = \begin{bmatrix} * & 0 & 0 & 0 \\ 0 & * & 0 & 0 \\ 0 & 0 & * & 0 \\ 0 & 1 & 1 & * \end{bmatrix}. \tag{4.120c}$$

Calculated values for $p^{\lambda_1}_{\Omega_{\bar{D}_1}}(W_k)$ are $p^{\lambda_1}_{\Omega_{\bar{D}_1}}(W_1) = 0$, $p^{\lambda_1}_{\Omega_{\bar{D}_1}}(W_2) = 0$, $p^{\lambda_1}_{\Omega_{\bar{D}_1}}(W_3) = 0$ i $p^{\lambda_1}_{\Omega_{\bar{D}_1}}(W_4) = 2$.

Calculated values for $f^{\lambda_1}_{\Omega_{\bar{D}_1}}(W_k)$ are $f^{\lambda_1}_{\Omega_{\bar{D}_1}}(W_1) = 0$, $f^{\lambda_1}_{\Omega_{\bar{D}_1}}(W_2) = 1$, $f^{\lambda_1}_{\Omega_{\bar{D}_1}}(W_3) = 1$ i $f^{\lambda_1}_{\Omega_{\bar{D}_1}}(W_4) = 0$.

The values of $q^{\lambda_1}_{\Omega_{\bar{D}_1}}(W_k)$ are as follows: $q^{\lambda_1}_{\Omega_{\bar{D}_1}}(W_1) = 0$, $q^{\lambda_1}_{\Omega_{\bar{D}_1}}(W_2) = -1$, $q^{\lambda_1}_{\Omega_{\bar{D}_1}}(W_3) = -1$, $q^{\lambda_1}_{\Omega_{\bar{D}_1}}(W_4) = 2$.

6. We calculate$\overline{q}_{\Omega_{\bar{D}_1}}$:

$$\overline{q}_{\Omega_{\bar{D}_1}} = \max_{W_k \in \Omega_{\bar{D}_1}} q^{\lambda_1}_{\Omega_{\bar{D}_1}}(W_k) = \max\{0; -1; -1; 2\} = 2. \tag{4.120d}$$

7. We determine $\Omega_{\overline{D}_2}$ set of all decision variants for which values of $q^{\lambda_1}_{\Omega_{\bar{D}_1}}(W_k)$ are equal to $\overline{q}_{\Omega_{\bar{D}_1}} = 2$:

$$\Omega_{\overline{D}_2} = \left\{ W_k \in \Omega_{\overline{D}_1} : q^{\lambda_1}_{\Omega_{\bar{D}_1}}(W_k) = \overline{q}_{\Omega_{\bar{D}_1}} \right\} = \{W_4\}. \tag{4.120e}$$

8. Because $\Omega_{\overline{D}_1}$ set is not empty, we move forward to point 9.
9. We determine

$$\Omega_{\overline{G}_2} = \Omega_{\overline{D}_2} = \{W_4\}. \tag{4.120f}$$

and

$$\Omega_{\overline{A}_2} = \Omega_{\overline{A}_1} \setminus \Omega_{\overline{G}_2} = \{W_1, W_2, W_3\}. \tag{4.120g}$$

10. We assume $n = 2$, and because the number of $\Omega_{\overline{A}_2}$ elements is greater than 1, we move forward to point 2.

Iteration 3

2. We calculate $\lambda_0 = \max_{k \neq j} \sigma_{k,j}$, where $W_k, W_j \in \Omega_{\bar{A}_2}$. From the matrix given by the formula (4.111), it follows that the maximum value is equal to 1, that is, $\lambda_0 = 0.8$.
3. We assume that $l = 0$, $\Omega_{\bar{D}_2} = \Omega_{\bar{A}_2} = \{W_1, W_2, W_3\}$.
4. Let us calculate λ_1 (λ_{l+1}) coefficient:

$$\lambda_0 - s(\lambda_0) = 0.8 - (-0.15 \cdot 0.8 + 0.3) = 0.62. \tag{4.121a}$$

Check if such pairs $\left(W_k, W_j\right) \in \Omega_{\bar{D}_2}$, where $\sigma_{k,j} < \lambda_0 - s(\lambda_0)$ exist. Such pairs exist. We look for the greatest value of the credibility coefficient for such pairs:

$$\lambda_1 = 0.6. \tag{4.121b}$$

5. We calculate the rating $q_{\Omega_{\bar{D}_2}}^{\lambda_1}(W_k)$ for each decision variant in $\Omega_{\bar{D}_2}$ set. For this reason, we check if λ-preference relation $(\overset{\lambda_1}{\succ})$ for decision variants included in $\Omega_{\bar{D}_2}$ set takes place.
   - For the pair (W_1, W_2), the condition $\sigma_{1,2} > \lambda_1$ is checked, that is, $0 \leqslant 0.6$—the relation does not take place.
   - For the pair (W_1, W_3), the condition $\sigma_{1,3} > \lambda_1$ is checked, that is, $0.8 > 0.6$. It is met. We check the second condition: $\sigma_{1,3} - s\left(\sigma_{1,3}\right) > \sigma_{3,1}$, s checked, that is, $0.8 - (-0.15 \cdot 0.8 + 0.3) = 0.62 > 0$. The second condition is met—the relation takes place.
   - For the pair (W_2, W_1), the condition $\sigma_{2,1} > \lambda_1$ is checked, that is, $0 \leqslant 0.6$—the relation does not take place.
   - For the pair (W_2, W_3), the condition $\sigma_{2,3} > \lambda_1$ is checked, that is, $0.6 \leqslant 0.6$—the relation does not take place.
   - For the pair (W_3, W_1), the condition $\sigma_{3,1} > \lambda_1$ is checked, that is, $0 \leqslant 0.6$—the relation does not take place.
   - For the pair (W_3, W_2), the condition $\sigma_{3,2} > \lambda_1$ is checked, that is, $0.76 > 0.6$. It is met. We check the second condition:$\sigma_{3,2} - s\left(\sigma_{3,2}\right) > \sigma_{2,3}$, that is, $0.76 - (-0.15 \cdot 0.76 + 0.3) = 0.57 \leqslant 0.6$. The second condition is not met—the relation does not take place.

   The calculation results are presented in matrix Σ':

$$\Sigma' = \begin{bmatrix} * & 0 & 1 \\ 0 & * & 0 \\ 0 & 0 & * \end{bmatrix}. \tag{4.121c}$$

   Calculated values for $p_{\Omega_{\bar{D}_2}}^{\lambda_1}(W_k)$ are $p_{\Omega_{\bar{D}_2}}^{\lambda_1}(W_1) = 1$, $p_{\Omega_{\bar{D}_2}}^{\lambda_1}(W_2) = 0$ i $p_{\Omega_{\bar{D}_2}}^{\lambda_1}(W_3) = 0$.

   Calculated values for $f_{\Omega_{\bar{D}_2}}^{\lambda_1}(W_k)$ are $f_{\Omega_{\bar{D}_2}}^{\lambda_1}(W_1) = 0$, $f_{\Omega_{\bar{D}_2}}^{\lambda_1}(W_2) = 0$ i $f_{\Omega_{\bar{D}_2}}^{\lambda_1}(W_3) = 1$.

   The values of $q_{\Omega_{\bar{D}_2}}^{\lambda_1}(W_k)$ are as follows: $q_{\Omega_{\bar{D}_2}}^{\lambda_1}(W_1) = 1$, $q_{\Omega_{\bar{D}_2}}^{\lambda_1}(W_2) = 0$ and $q_{\Omega_{\bar{D}_2}}^{\lambda_1}(W_3) = -1$.
6. Let us calculate $\overline{q}_{\Omega_{\bar{D}_2}}$:

$$\overline{q}_{\Omega_{\bar{D}_2}} = \max_{W_k \in \Omega_{\bar{D}_2}} q_{\Omega_{\bar{D}_2}}^{\lambda_1}(W_k) = \max\{1; 0; -1\} = 1. \tag{4.121d}$$

7. We determine $\Omega_{\overline{D}_3}$ set of all decision variants, for which values of $q_{\Omega_{\bar{D}_2}}^{\lambda_1}(W_k)$ are equal to $\overline{q}_{\Omega_{\bar{D}_2}} = 1$:

$$\Omega_{\overline{D}_3} = \left\{ W_k \in \Omega_{\overline{D}_2} : q^{\lambda_1}_{\Omega_{\bar{D}_2}} (W_k) = \overline{q}_{\Omega_{\bar{D}_2}} \right\} = \{W_1\}. \tag{4.121e}$$

8. Because $\Omega_{\overline{D}_2}$ set is not empty, we move forward to point 9.
9. We determine

$$\Omega_{\overline{G}_3} = \Omega_{\overline{D}_2} = \{W_1\}. \tag{4.121f}$$

and

$$\Omega_{\overline{A}_3} = \Omega_{\overline{A}_2} \setminus \Omega_{\overline{C}_3} = \{W_2, W_3\}. \tag{4.121g}$$

10. Let us assume that $n = 2$, and because the number of elements in $\Omega_{\overline{A}_3}$ set is greater than 1, we move forward to point 2.

Iteration 4

2. Let us determine the value $\lambda_0 = \max_{k \neq j} \sigma_{k,j}$, were $W_k, W_j \in \Omega_{\bar{A}_3}$. From the matrix given by the formula (4.111), it follows that the maximum value equals 1, that is, $\lambda_0 = 0.76$.
3. Let us assume that $l = 0$, $\Omega_{\bar{D}_3} = \Omega_{\bar{A}_3} = \{W_2, W_3\}$.
4. Let us calculate the value of λ_1 (λ_{l+1}) coefficient:

$$\lambda_0 - s(\lambda_0) = 0.76 - (-0.15 \cdot 0.76 + 0.3) = 0.57. \tag{4.122a}$$

Check if such pairs $(W_k, W_j) \in \Omega_{\bar{D}_3}$, where $\sigma_{k,j} < \lambda_0 - s(\lambda_0)$, exist. Such pairs do not exist:

$$\lambda_1 = 0. \tag{4.122b}$$

5. We calculate the rating $q^{\lambda_1}_{\Omega_{\bar{D}_3}} (W_k)$ for each decision variant in $\Omega_{\bar{D}_3}$ set. For this reason, we check if λ-preference relation $(\overset{\lambda_1}{\succ})$ for decision variants in $\Omega_{\bar{D}_3}$ takes place.

   - For the pair (W_2, W_3), the condition $\sigma_{2,3} > \lambda_1$ is checked, that is, $0.6 > 0.57$. It is met. We check the second condition: $\sigma_{2,3} - s(\sigma_{2,3}) > \sigma_{3,2}$, that is, $0.6 - (-0.15 \cdot 0.6 + 0.3) = 0.39 \leqslant 0.76$. The second condition is not met—the relation does not take place.
   - For the pair (W_3, W_2), the condition $\sigma_{3,2} > \lambda_1$ is checked, that is, $0.76 > 0.57$. It is met. We check the second condition: $\sigma_{3,2} - s(\sigma_{3,2}) > \sigma_{2,3}$, that is, $0.76 - (-0.15 \cdot 0.76 + 0.3) = 0.57 \leqslant 0.6$. The second condition is not met—the relations does not take place.

   The calculation results are presented in matrix Σ':

$$\Sigma' = \begin{bmatrix} * & 0 \\ 0 & * \end{bmatrix}. \tag{4.122c}$$

Calculated values for $p^{\lambda_1}_{\Omega_{\bar{D}_3}}(W_k)$ are $p^{\lambda_1}_{\Omega_{\bar{D}_3}}(W_2) = 0$ and $p^{\lambda_1}_{\Omega_{\bar{D}_3}}(W_3) = 0$.
Calculated values for $f^{\lambda_1}_{\Omega_{\bar{D}_3}}(W_k)$ are $f^{\lambda_1}_{\Omega_{\bar{D}_3}}(W_2) = 0$ and $f^{\lambda_1}_{\Omega_{\bar{D}_3}}(W_3) = 0$.
The values of $q^{\lambda_1}_{\Omega_{\bar{D}_3}}(W_k)$ are as follows: $q^{\lambda_1}_{\Omega_{\bar{D}_3}}(W_2) = 0$ and $q^{\lambda_1}_{\Omega_{\bar{D}_3}}(W_3) = 0$.

6. We calculate $\overline{q}_{\Omega_{\bar{D}_3}}$:

$$\overline{q}_{\Omega_{\bar{D}_3}} = \max_{W_k \in \Omega_{\bar{D}_3}} q^{\lambda_1}_{\Omega_{\bar{D}_3}}(W_k) = \max\{0; 0\} = 0. \tag{4.122d}$$

7. We determine the $\Omega_{\overline{D}_4}$ set of all decision variants, for which $q^{\lambda_1}_{\Omega_{\bar{D}_3}}(W_k)$ values are equal to $\overline{q}_{\Omega_{\bar{D}_3}} = 0$:

$$\Omega_{\overline{D}_4} = \left\{ W_k \in \Omega_{\overline{D}_3} : q^{\lambda_1}_{\Omega_{\bar{D}_3}}(W_k) = \overline{q}_{\Omega_{\bar{D}_3}} \right\} = \{W_2, W_3\}. \tag{4.122e}$$

8. Because $\Omega_{\overline{D}_3}$ set is not empty, we move forward to point 9.
9. We determine:

$$\Omega_{\overline{G}_4} = \Omega_{\overline{D}_3} = \{W_2, W_3\}. \tag{4.122f}$$

and

$$\Omega_{\overline{A}_4} = \Omega_{\overline{A}_3} \setminus \Omega_{\overline{C}_4} = \emptyset. \tag{4.122g}$$

10. Let us assume that $n = 4$, and because $\Omega_{\overline{A}_3}$ is empty, the descending distillation is finished.

Four classes have been obtained as the result of descending distillation. Class one includes $\Omega_{\overline{G}_1} \in \{W_5\}$, class two—$\Omega_{\overline{G}_2} \in \{W_4\}$, class three—$\Omega_{\overline{G}_3} \in \{W_1\}$, and class four—$\Omega_{\overline{G}_4} \in \{W_3, W_4\}$.

The exemplary descending distillation procedure for the credibility matrix Σ given by the formula (4.111) will be conducted as follows:

Iteration 1

1. We assume that $n = 0$, $\Omega_{\underline{A}_0} = \{W_1, W_2, W_3, W_4, W_5\}$.
2. We calculate the initial values of $\lambda_0 = \max_{k \neq j} \sigma_{k,j}$, where $W_k, W_j \in \Omega_{\underline{A}_0}$. From the matrix given by the formula (4.111), it follows that the maximum value is equal to 1, that is, $\lambda_0 = 1$.
3. We assume that $l = 0$, $\Omega_{D_0} = \Omega_{\underline{A}_0} = \{W_1, W_2, W_3, W_4, W_5\}$.
4. We calculate λ_1 (λ_{l+1}):

$$\lambda_0 - s(\lambda_0) = 1 - (-0.15 \cdot 1 + 0.3) = 0.85. \tag{4.123a}$$

Check if such pairs $\left(W_k, W_j\right) \in \Omega_{D_0}$, where $\sigma_{k,j} < \lambda_0 - s(\lambda_0)$, exist. Such pairs exist, and these are (W_1, W_2), (W_1, W_3), (W_1, W_4), (W_2, W_1), (W_2, W_3), (W_2, W_4), (W_2, W_5), etc. We look for the greatest value of the credibility coefficient for the following pairs:

$$\lambda_1 = \max\{0; 0.8; 0.8; 0; 0.6; 0; 0; \ldots\} = 0.8. \tag{4.123b}$$

5. We calculate the rating $q^{\lambda_1}_{\Omega_{D_0}}(W_k)$ for each decision variant in Ω_{D_0} set. For this reason, we check if λ-preference relation ($\overset{\lambda_1}{\succ}$) for decision variants in Ω_{D_0} set takes place.

   The calculation results are presented in matrix Σ':

$$\Sigma' = \begin{bmatrix} * & 0 & 0 & 0 & 0 \\ 0 & * & 0 & 0 & 0 \\ 0 & 0 & * & 0 & 0 \\ 0 & 1 & 1 & * & 0 \\ 0 & 0 & 1 & 1 & * \end{bmatrix}. \tag{4.123c}$$

   Calculated values for $p^{\lambda_1}_{\Omega_{D_0}}(W_k)$ are as follows: $p^{\lambda_1}_{\Omega_{D_0}}(W_1) = 0$, $p^{\lambda_1}_{\Omega_{D_1}}(W_2) = 0$, $p^{\lambda_1}_{\Omega_{D_2}}(W_3) = 0$, $p^{\lambda_1}_{\Omega_{D_0}}(W_4) = 2$ and $p^{\lambda_1}_{\Omega_{D_0}}(W_5) = 2$.

   Calculated values for $f^{\lambda_1}_{\Omega_{D_0}}(W_k)$ are as follows: $f^{\lambda_1}_{\Omega_{D_0}}(W_1) = 1$, $f^{\lambda_1}_{\Omega_{D_0}}(W_2) = 1$, $f^{\lambda_1}_{\Omega_{D_0}}(W_3) = 2$, $f^{\lambda_1}_{\Omega_{D_0}}(W_4) = 1$ and $f^{\lambda_1}_{\Omega_{D_0}}(W_5) = 0$.

   Calculated values for $q^{\lambda_1}_{\Omega_{D_0}}(W_k)$ are as follows: $q^{\lambda_1}_{\Omega_{D_0}}(W_1) = 0$, $q^{\lambda_1}_{\Omega_{D_0}}(W_2) = -1$, $q^{\lambda_1}_{\Omega_{D_0}}(W_3) = -2$, $q^{\lambda_1}_{\Omega_{D_0}}(W_4) = 1$, $q^{\lambda_1}_{\Omega_{D_0}}(W_5) = 2$.
6. We calculate $\overline{q}_{\Omega_{D_0}}$:

$$\overline{q}_{\Omega_{D_0}} = \min_{W_k \in \Omega_{D_0}} q^{\lambda_1}_{\Omega_{D_0}}(W_k) = \min\{0; -1; -2; 1; 2\} = -2. \tag{4.123d}$$

7. We determine $\Omega_{\underline{D}_1}$ set of all decision variants for which values $q^{\lambda_1}_{\Omega_{D_0}}(W_k)$ are equal to $\underline{q}_{\Omega_{D_0}} = -2$:

$$\Omega_{\underline{D}_1} = \left\{ W_k \in \Omega_{\underline{D}_0} : q^{\lambda_1}_{\Omega_{D_0}}(W_k) = \underline{q}_{\Omega_{D_0}} \right\} = \{W_3\}. \tag{4.123e}$$

8. Because $\Omega_{\underline{D}_1}$ set is not empty, we move forward to point 9.
9. We determine

$$\Omega_{\underline{G}_1} = \Omega_{\underline{D}_1} = \{W_3\}. \tag{4.123f}$$

and

$$\Omega_{\underline{A}_1} = \Omega_{\underline{A}_0} \setminus \Omega_{\underline{G}_1} = \{W_1, W_2, W_4, W_5\}. \tag{4.123g}$$

10. We assume that $n = 1$, and because the number of elements in $\Omega_{\underline{A}_1}$ set is greater than 1, we move forward to point 2.

Iteration 2

2. We determine the value $\lambda_0 = \max_{k \neq j} \sigma_{k,j}$, where $W_k, W_j \in \Omega_{\underline{A}_1}$. From the matrix given by the formula (4.111), it follows that the maximum value is equal to 1, that is, $\lambda_0 = 0.92$.
3. We assume that $l = 0$, $\Omega_{\underline{D}_1} = \Omega_{\underline{A}_1} = \{W_1, W_2, W_4, W_5\}$.
4. We calculate the values of λ_1 (λ_{l+1}) coefficient:

$$\lambda_0 - s(\lambda_0) = 0.92 - (-0.15 \cdot 0.92 + 0.3) = 0.76. \tag{4.124a}$$

Check if such pairs $(W_k, W_j) \in \Omega_{\underline{D}_1}$, where $\sigma_{k,j} < \lambda_0 - s(\lambda_0)$, exist. Such pairs exist. We look for the greatest value of the credibility matrix for such pairs:

$$\lambda_1 = 0.34. \tag{4.124b}$$

5. We calculate the rating $q^{\lambda_1}_{\Omega_{\underline{D}_1}}(W_k)$ for each decision variant in $\Omega_{\underline{D}_1}$ set. For this reason, we check if λ-preference relation ($\overset{\lambda_1}{\succ}$) for decision variants in $\Omega_{\underline{D}_1}$ set takes place.

The results of calculation are presented in matrix Σ':

$$\Sigma' = \begin{bmatrix} * & 0 & 1 & 0 \\ 0 & * & 0 & 0 \\ 0 & 1 & * & 0 \\ 0 & 0 & 1 & * \end{bmatrix}. \tag{4.124c}$$

Calculated values for $p^{\lambda_1}_{\Omega_{\underline{D}_1}}(W_k)$: $p^{\lambda_1}_{\Omega_{\underline{D}_1}}(W_1) = 1$, $p^{\lambda_1}_{\Omega_{\underline{D}_1}}(W_2) = 0$, $p^{\lambda_1}_{\Omega_{\underline{D}_1}}(W_4) = 1$ and $p^{\lambda_1}_{\Omega_{\underline{D}_1}}(W_5) = 1$.

Calculated values for $f^{\lambda_1}_{\Omega_{\underline{D}_1}}(W_k)$: $f^{\lambda_1}_{\Omega_{\underline{D}_1}}(W_1) = 0$, $f^{\lambda_1}_{\Omega_{\underline{D}_1}}(W_2) = 1$, $f^{\lambda_1}_{\Omega_{\underline{D}_1}}(W_4) = 2$ and $f^{\lambda_1}_{\Omega_{\underline{D}_1}}(W_5) = 0$.

Values for $q^{\lambda_1}_{\Omega_{\underline{D}_1}}(W_k)$ are as follows: $q^{\lambda_1}_{\Omega_{\underline{D}_1}}(W_1) = 1$, $q^{\lambda_1}_{\Omega_{\underline{D}_1}}(W_2) = -1$, $q^{\lambda_1}_{\Omega_{\underline{D}_1}}(W_4) = -1$ i $q^{\lambda_1}_{\Omega_{\underline{D}_1}}(W_5) = 1$.

6. We calculate $\overline{q}_{\Omega_{\bar{D}_1}}$:

$$\underline{q}_{\Omega_{\underline{D}_1}} = \min_{W_k \in \Omega_{\underline{D}_1}} q^{\lambda_1}_{\Omega_{\underline{D}_1}}(W_k) = \min\{1; -1; -1; 1\} = -1. \tag{4.124d}$$

7. We calculate $\Omega_{\underline{D}_2}$ set of all decision variants for which $q^{\lambda_1}_{\Omega_{\underline{D}_1}}(W_k)$ is equal to $\underline{q}_{\Omega_{\underline{D}_1}} = -1$:

$$\Omega_{\underline{D}_2} = \left\{ W_k \in \Omega_{\underline{D}_1} : q^{\lambda_1}_{\Omega_{\underline{D}_1}}(W_k) = \underline{q}_{\Omega_{\underline{D}_1}} \right\} = \{W_2, W_4\}. \tag{4.124e}$$

8. Because $\Omega_{\underline{D}_1}$ set is not empty, we move forward to point 9.
9. We calculate:

$$\Omega_{\underline{G}_2} = \Omega_{\underline{D}_2} = \{W_2, W_4\}. \tag{4.124f}$$

and

$$\Omega_{\underline{A}_2} = \Omega_{\underline{A}_1} \setminus \Omega_{\underline{G}_2} = \{W_1, W_5\}. \tag{4.124g}$$

10. We assume that $n = 2$, and because the number of elements in $\Omega_{\underline{A}_2}$ is greater than 1, we move forward to point 2.

Iteration 3

2. We determine values of $\lambda_0 = \max_{k \neq j} \sigma_{k,j}$, where $W_k, W_j \in \Omega_{\underline{A}_2}$. From the matrix given by the formula (4.111), it follows that the maximum value is equal to 0.92, that is, $\lambda_0 = 0.92$.
3. We assume that $l = 0$, $\Omega_{\underline{D}_2} = \Omega_{\underline{A}_2} = \{W_1, W_5\}$.
4. Let us calculate the value of λ_1 (λ_{l+1})coefficient:

$$\lambda_0 - s(\lambda_0) = 0.92 - (-0.15 \cdot 0.92 + 0.3) = 0.76. \tag{4.125a}$$

Check if such pairs $(W_k, W_j) \in \Omega_{\underline{D}_3}$, where $\sigma_{k,j} < \lambda_0 - s(\lambda_0)$. Such pairs do not exist:

$$\lambda_1 = 0. \tag{4.125b}$$

5. We calculate the rating $q^{\lambda_1}_{\Omega_{\underline{D}3}}(W_k)$ for each decision variant in $\Omega_{\underline{D}_3}$ set. For this reason, we check if λ-preference relation $(\overset{\lambda_1}{\succ})$ for decision variants in $\Omega_{\underline{D}_3}$ set takes place.

   The results of calculation are presented in the matrix Σ':

$$\Sigma' = \begin{bmatrix} * & 0 \\ 0 & * \end{bmatrix}. \tag{4.125c}$$

Calculated values for $p^{\lambda_1}_{\Omega_{\underline{D}_3}}(W_k)$ are $p^{\lambda_1}_{\Omega_{\underline{D}_3}}(W_1) = 0$ and $p^{\lambda_1}_{\Omega_{\underline{D}_3}}(W_5) = 0$.

Calculated values for $f^{\lambda_1}_{\Omega_{\underline{D}_3}}(W_k)$ are $f^{\lambda_1}_{\Omega_{\underline{D}_3}}(W_1) = 0$ and $f^{\lambda_1}_{\Omega_{\underline{D}_3}}(W_5) = 0$.

Values for $q^{\lambda_1}_{\Omega_{\underline{D}_3}}(W_k)$ are as follows: $q^{\lambda_1}_{\Omega_{\underline{D}_3}}(W_1) = 0$ and $q^{\lambda_1}_{\Omega_{\underline{D}_3}}(W_5) = 0$.

6. We calculate $\overline{q}_{\Omega_{\underline{D}_3}}$:

$$\overline{q}_{\Omega_{\underline{D}_3}} = \min_{W_k \in \Omega_{\underline{D}_3}} q^{\lambda_1}_{\Omega_{\underline{D}_3}}(W_k) = \min\{0; 0\} = 0. \tag{4.125d}$$

7. We determine $\Omega_{\underline{D}_4}$ set of all decision variants for which values $q^{\lambda_1}_{\Omega_{\underline{D}_3}}(W_k)$ are equal to $\overline{q}_{\Omega_{\underline{D}_3}} = 0$:

$$\Omega_{\underline{D}_4} = \left\{ W_k \in \Omega_{\overline{D}_3} : q^{\lambda_1}_{\Omega_{\underline{D}_3}}(W_k) = \underline{q}_{\Omega_{\underline{D}_3}} \right\} = \{W_1, W_5\}. \tag{4.125e}$$

8. Because $\Omega_{\underline{D}_3}$ set is not empty, we move forward to point 9.
9. We determine

$$\Omega_{\underline{G}_4} = \Omega_{\overline{D}_3} = \{W_1, W_5\}. \tag{4.125f}$$

and

$$\Omega_{\underline{A}_4} = \Omega_{\underline{A}_3} \setminus \Omega_{\underline{C}_4} = \emptyset. \tag{4.125g}$$

10. We assume that $n = 4$, and because $\Omega_{\underline{A}_3}$ set is empty, we end descending distillation.

Four classes have been obtained as the result of descending distillation. Class one includes variant $\Omega_{\underline{G}_1} \in \{W_3\}$, class two—$\Omega_{\underline{G}_2} \in \{W_4, W_3\}$, and class three—$\Omega_{\underline{G}_3} \in \{W_1, W_5\}$.

Step 5

Two decision variants are considered equivalent when in the prescribed order by ascending and descending distillation are in the same class. In the considered example, such example does not take place.

Two decision variants W_k and W_j are incomparable to each other, where in one ranking W_k is ranked higher than W_j, and in the second one W_j is ranked higher than W_k. This case takes place for (W_1, W_4) and (W_4, W_1).

The decision variant W_k is considered better than W_j when:

1. Variant W_k in one ranking is classified higher than W_j, And in the second one, both are in the same class. Such case occurs for the pairs (W_5, W_2), (W_5, W_3), (W_5, W_4), (W_4, W_3), (W_1, W_2), and (W_1, W_3).

Table 4.10 Outranking relations

	W_1	W_2	W_3	W_4	W_5
W_1	I	P	P	R	P^-
W_2	P^-	I	P	P^-	P^-
W_3	P^-	P^-	I	P^-	P^-
W_4	R	P	P	I	P^-
W_5	P	P	P	P	I

Table 4.11 Decision variants ranking

Ascending distillation		Descending distillation		Ranking	
class	variant	class	variant	class	variant
1	W_5	3	W_1, W_5	1	W_5
2	W_4	2	W_2, W_4	2	W_1, W_4
3	W_1	1	W_3	3	W_2
4	W_2, W_3			4	W_3

2. Variant W_k in one order is placed higher than variant W_j and in the other both are in the same class. This case occurs for pairs of variants (W_5, W_1), (W_4, W_2) i (W_2, W_3).

The relationship between the variants is presented in Table 4.10.

The building of the final ranking begins with placing on the highest position variants in relation to which no better variants exist. The second position includes variants compared to which only variants in the first position are better. The third position includes variants compared to which only the first and second positions variants are better, etc. As a result of this procedure, a ranking was created, which results are presented in Table 4.11. The best result was obtained by the decision variant W_5. The car associated with this variant has a low price, the lowest fuel consumption, and a relatively small trunk. However, *Trunk capacity* was a criterion of the lowest weight compared to others.

4.3 PROMETHEE Method

PROMETHEE is an abbreviation of Preference *Ranking Organization METHOD for Enrichment of Evaluations*. PROMETHEE methods are based on the same methodology as those of the ELECTRE. group. These methods were initiated by Brans, who in the publication [24] presented a description of the PROMETHEE I and PROMETHEE II. methods. These methods are primarily focused on creating rankings [97]. Preferences are modeled on the basis of the difference in the values of the criteria. This difference, depending on the criteria character, is computed diversly:

1. For a motivating criterion [25],

$$d_i\left(W_j, W_k\right) = g_i\left(W_j\right) - g_i\left(W_k\right). \tag{4.126}$$

2. For a demotivating criterion,

$$d_i\left(W_j, W_k\right) = g_i\left(W_k\right) - g_i\left(W_j\right). \tag{4.127}$$

3. For a desirable criterion,

$$d_i\left(W_j, W_k\right) = \left|g_i\left(W_k\right) - \mathrm{p}\right| - \left|g_i\left(W_j\right) - \mathrm{p}\right|. \tag{4.128}$$

4. For a non-desirable criterion,

$$d_i\left(W_j, W_k\right) = \left|g_i\left(W_j\right) - \mathrm{p}\right| - \left|g_i\left(W_k\right) - \mathrm{p}\right|. \tag{4.129}$$

The value of $d_i\left(W_j, W_k\right)$ is calculated for all the combinations of decision variants in a given criterion. This value is transformed to the range $\langle 0; 1\rangle$ with the use of preference function $F_i\left(\right)$ [25]:

$$G_i\left(W_j, W_k\right) = F_i\left(d_i\left(W_j, W_k\right)\right). \tag{4.130}$$

$G_i\left(W_j, W_k\right)$ is called the *generalized criterion* related to i criterion [202].

The following three criteria types are applied in practice: level, with linear preference and indifference area *ordinary*, *quasi-criterion*, *with linear preference*, *level*, *with linear preference and indifference area*, and *Gaussian*.

For the ordinary criterion, the preference function takes the following quantities [202]:

$$F_i\left(d_i\left(W_j, W_k\right)\right) = \begin{cases} 0 \text{ dla } d_i\left(W_j, W_k\right) \leqslant 0, \\ 1 \text{ dla } d_i\left(W_j, W_k\right) > 0. \end{cases} \tag{4.131a}$$

Only two possible situation may occur here: preference of variant W_j over W_k and no preference. The preference occurs even with a very small predominance of the variant W_j.

In the case of quasi-criterion, the following relationship must be met [202]:

$$F_i\left(d_i\left(W_j, W_k\right)\right) = \begin{cases} 0 \text{ dla } d_i\left(W_j, W_k\right) \leqslant q_i', \\ 1 \text{ dla } d_i\left(W_j, W_k\right) > q_i'. \end{cases} \tag{4.131b}$$

Only two possible situations may occur here: preference of variant W_j over W_k and no preference. Preference occurs only when the difference between the values of the criteria of both variants exceeds the threshold q_i'.

For the criterion with the linear preference, the following dependence must be met [202]:

$$F_i\left(d_i\left(W_j, W_k\right)\right) = \begin{cases} 0 & \text{dla } d_i\left(W_j, W_k\right) \leqslant 0, \\ \frac{d_i(W_j, W_k)}{q_i} & \text{dla } 0 < d_i\left(W_j, W_k\right) \leqslant q_i, \\ 1 & \text{dla } d_i\left(W_j, W_k\right) > q_i. \end{cases} \tag{4.131c}$$

Here, the preference threshold q_i determines a preference limit . If the difference between the criteria values is less than this threshold and greater than zero, then the value of the F function increases linearly with the increase of this difference.

In the case of a level criterion, the preferences function can take the following values [202]:

$$F_i\left(d_i\left(W_j, W_k\right)\right) = \begin{cases} 0 \text{ dla } d_i\left(W_j, W_k\right) \leqslant q_i', \\ \frac{1}{2} \text{ dla } q_i' < d_i\left(W_j, W_k\right) \leqslant q_i, \\ 1 \text{ dla } d_i\left(W_j, W_k\right) > q_i. \end{cases} \tag{4.131d}$$

There are three possible situations here: preference of the W_j variant over W_k, weak preference of the W_j variant over W_k, and the lack of this preference. A preference occurs when the difference between the values of the criteria of both variants exceeds the threshold q_i, while weak preference exists when a difference between the criteria values of both variants exceeds q_i' threshold and does not exceed q_i.

For a criterion with a linear preference and an area of indifference [97]:

$$F_i\left(d_i\left(W_j, W_k\right)\right) = \begin{cases} 0 & \text{dla } d_i\left(W_j, W_k\right) \leqslant q_i', \\ \frac{d_i(W_j, W_k) - q_i'}{q - q_i'} & \text{dla } q_i' < d_i\left(W_j, W_k\right) \leqslant q_i, \\ 1 & \text{dla } d_i\left(W_j, W_k\right) > q_i, \end{cases} \tag{4.131e}$$

preference threshold q_i determines a preference limit and q_i' an equivalence limit. Between these thresholds F function increases linearly with an increase in the difference of criteria values.

In turn, for the Gaussian criterion [202]:

$$F_i\left(d_i\left(W_j, W_k\right)\right) = \begin{cases} 0 & \text{dla } d_i\left(W_j, W_k\right) \leqslant 0, \\ 1 - e^{\left(-\frac{d_i^2(W_j, W_k)}{2s_i^2}\right)} & \text{dla } d_i\left(W_j, W_k\right) > 0, \end{cases} \tag{4.131f}$$

the value of preference function F_i changes non-linearly. s_i value must be greater than q_i' and smaller than q_i.

Figure 4.18 presents the graphs of $F_i\left(d_i\left(W_j, W_k\right)\right)$ function for individual criteria.

The PROMETHEE I method is used to create a partial ranking [202]. The partial ranking should be understood as the preference relation graph. The position of an object is not determined in relation to other objects, as it is the case with ordinary ranking, but only which objects are better than others. In this method, each criterion is assigned a weight according to preferences of a decision-maker. Weights are

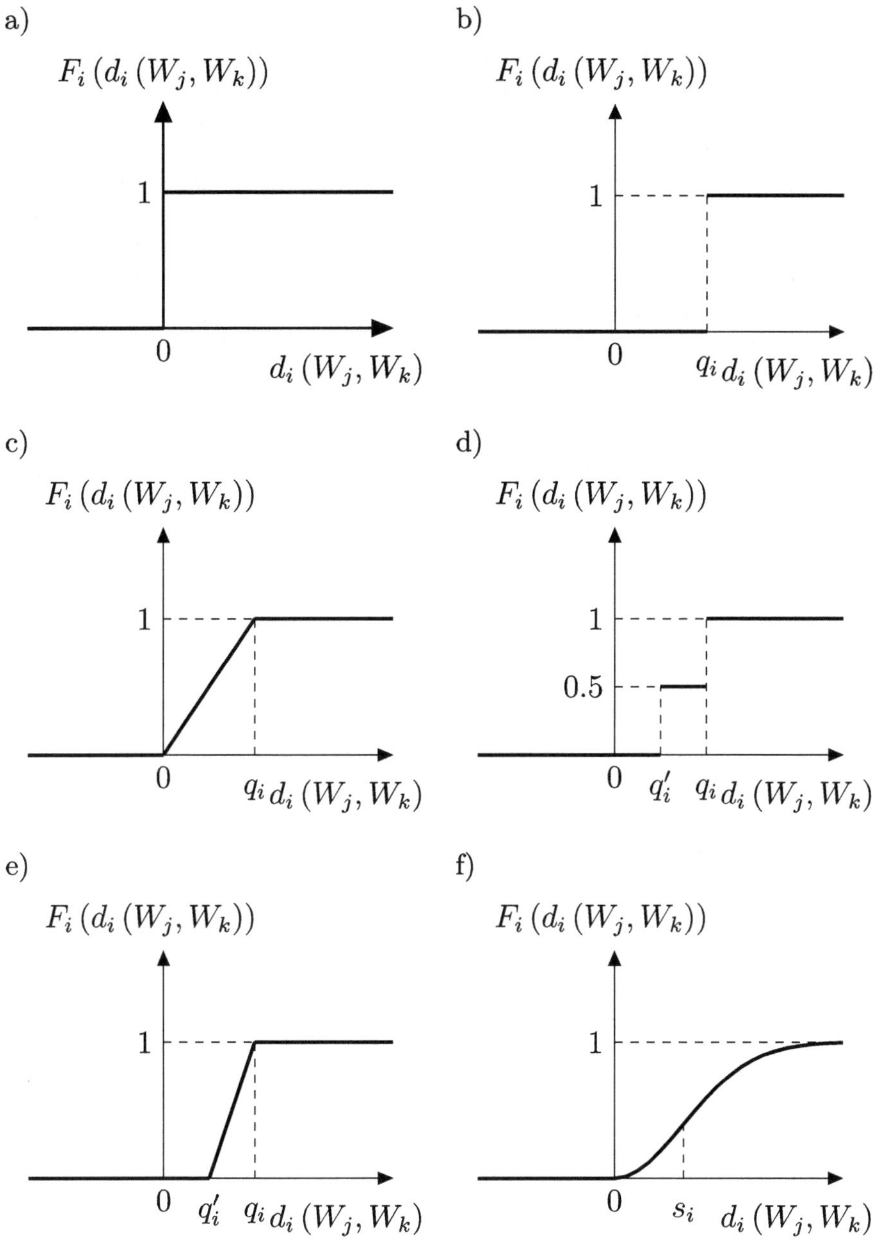

Fig. 4.18 Types of criteria [97]: (**a**) true (ordinary) criterion, (**b**) quasi-criterion (u-shaped criterion), (**c**) criterion with linear preference (v-shaped criterion), (**d**) a level criterion, (**e**) pseudo-criterion (v-shaped criterion with the area of indifference), and (**f**) Gaussian criterion

normalized according to the formula (4.51). Based on the pairwise comparisons, square matrices of comparisons C_i are created, as in the ELECTRE methods. The difference, however, is that the values of this matrix can be numbers in a range $\langle 0; 1\rangle$. The value of one means outranking, and value of zero—no outranking. Intermediate values can be defined as a partial outranking. In practice, degrees of outranking are often expressed with numerical values. For example, you can take values from zero to three, specifying zero as no outranking, one as slight outranking, two as strong, and three as a very strong outranking. After making comparisons by a decision-maker, their results must be normalized to a range of $\langle 0; 1\rangle$ by dividing all the values obtained by the maximum value (in the example above it is three).

Let us consider data from Table 4.1 as an example. Here, the weight of one has been assigned for *price*, *fuel consumption*, and *appearance* and 0.5 for *trunk capacity* criterion. After normalization, these weights were 0.2857 and 0.1429, respectively. When determining preferences, acceptable values have been established: 0, 1, and 2 for the criteria *price*, *trunk capacity*, and *appearance* and values 0 and 1 for *fuel consumption*. Following the comparison of *price*, *trunk capacity*, and *appearance* criteria, values were normalized by dividing them by two. The values for the *fuel consumption* criterion were left unchanged as they are within the range $\langle 0; 1\rangle$. After normalization, the following matrices of comparisons were obtained for each individual criterion:

1. *Price*:

$$C_1 = \begin{bmatrix} 0 & 0.5 & 1 \\ 0 & 0 & 0 \\ 0 & 0 & 0 \end{bmatrix}. \tag{4.132a}$$

2. *Fuel consumption*:

$$C_2 = \begin{bmatrix} 0 & 0 & 0 \\ 1 & 0 & 1 \\ 0 & 0 & 0 \end{bmatrix}. \tag{4.132b}$$

3. *Trunk capacity*:

$$C_3 = \begin{bmatrix} 0 & 0 & 0 \\ 1 & 0 & 0.5 \\ 0 & 0 & 0 \end{bmatrix}. \tag{4.132c}$$

4. *Appearance*:

$$C_4 = \begin{bmatrix} 0 & 0.5 & 1 \\ 0 & 0 & 0 \\ 0 & 0 & 0 \end{bmatrix}. \tag{4.132d}$$

Based on C_i matrix, the following *aggregated preference indexes* are calculated[202]:

$$\pi\left(W_j, W_k\right) = \sum_{i=1}^{N} w'_i \mathrm{mp}_{i,j,k}, \tag{4.133}$$

where

$\mathrm{mp}_{i,j,k}$—element j, k of the matrix C_i.

For example, the aggregate preference index $\pi\left(W_1, W_2\right)$ is determined as follows:

$$\pi\left(W_1, W_2\right) = w'_1 \mathrm{mp}_{1,1,2} + w'_2 \mathrm{mp}_{2,1,2} + w'_3 \mathrm{mp}_{3,1,2} + w'_4 \mathrm{mp}_{4,1,2} =$$
$$0.2857 \cdot 0.5 + 0.2857 \cdot 1 + 0.1429 \cdot 0 + 0.5 \cdot 0.5 + 0.2857 \cdot 0.5 = 0.5714. \tag{4.134}$$

For the example under consideration, the matrix of aggregated preference indexes Π takes the following form:

$$\Pi = \begin{bmatrix} 0 & 0.5714 & 0.5714 \\ 0.1429 & 0 & 0.0714 \\ 0 & 0.2857 & 0 \end{bmatrix}. \tag{4.135}$$

The next step in the PROMETHEE I calculation procedure is the determination of the *positive outranking flow* [202]:

$$\varphi^{+}\left(W_j\right) \frac{1}{M-1} \sum_{k=1}^{M} \pi\left(W_j, W_k\right). \tag{4.136}$$

And the *negative outranking flow* [202] is

$$\varphi^{-}\left(W_j\right) \frac{1}{M-1} \sum_{k=1}^{M} \pi\left(W_k, W_j\right). \tag{4.137}$$

So for e.g. W_2 decision variant the positive outranking flows $\varphi^{+}\left(W_2\right)$ is calculated as follows:

$$\varphi^{+}\left(W_2\right) \frac{1}{M-1} \left(\pi\left(W_2, W_1\right) + \pi\left(W_2, W_2\right) + \pi\left(W_2, W_3\right)\right) =$$
$$= \frac{1}{3-1} (0.1429 + 0 + 0.0714) = 0.1071, \tag{4.138}$$

while negative in a way presented below:

$$\varphi^{-}(W_2)\frac{1}{M-1}(\pi(W_1, W_2)+\pi(W_2, W_2)+\pi(W_3, W_2)) = \\ =\frac{1}{3-1}(0.5714+0+0.2857)=0.4286. \tag{4.139}$$

The matrix of positive outranking flows Φ^{+} will then take the form:

$$\Phi^{+}=\begin{bmatrix}0.5714\\0.1071\\0.1429\end{bmatrix}, \tag{4.140}$$

while the matrix of negative outranking flows Φ^{-} will take the following form:

$$\Phi^{-}=\begin{bmatrix}0.0714\\0.4286\\0.3214\end{bmatrix}. \tag{4.141}$$

Based on the positive and negative outranking flow, a set of preferences Ω_Z is created. Similarly to the ELECTRE group methods, it is a set of ordered pairs between which there is a preference relation. An ordered pair (W_j, W_k) belongs to this set if one of the following conditions is met [202]:

$$\varphi^{+}(W_j)>\varphi^{+}(W_k)\wedge\varphi^{-}(W_j)<\varphi^{-}(W_k), \tag{4.142a}$$

$$\varphi^{+}(W_j)=\varphi^{+}(W_k)\wedge\varphi^{-}(W_j)<\varphi^{-}(W_k), \tag{4.142b}$$

$$\varphi^{+}(W_j)>\varphi^{+}(W_k)\wedge\varphi^{-}(W_j)=\varphi^{-}(W_k). \tag{4.142c}$$

Similarly, a set of ordered pairs (W_j, W_k) can be defined, between which an equivalence relation takes place [202]:

$$\varphi^{+}(W_j)=\varphi^{+}(W_k)\wedge\varphi^{-}(W_j)=\varphi^{-}(W_k), \tag{4.143}$$

as well as a set of ordered pairs (W_j, W_k), between which there is a relation of incomparability. One of the below conditions must be met [202]:

$$\varphi^{+}(W_j)>\varphi^{+}(W_k)\wedge\varphi^{-}(W_j)>\varphi^{-}(W_k), \tag{4.144a}$$

$$\varphi^{+}(W_j)<\varphi^{+}(W_k)\wedge\varphi^{-}(W_j)<\varphi^{-}(W_k). \tag{4.144b}$$

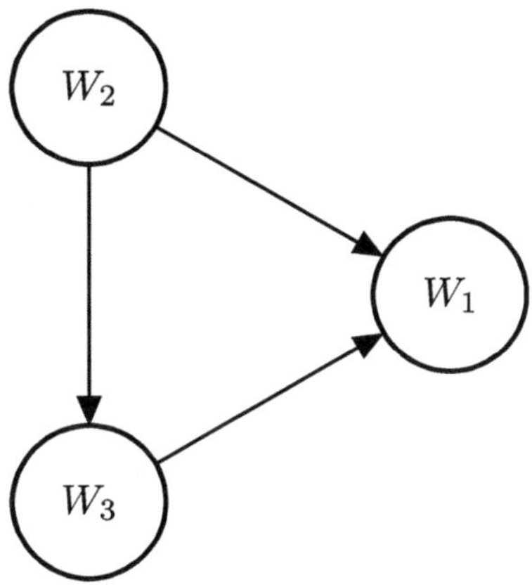

Fig. 4.19 The relation between the decision variants is illustrated in the form of a graph

For example, in the considered example for the pair (W_1, W_2), the relation given by the formula (4.142a) will be as follows:

$$\varphi^+ (W_1) > \varphi^+ (W_2) \wedge \varphi^- (W_1) < \varphi^- (W_2)\,, \tag{4.145a}$$

hence

$$0.5714 > 0.1071 \wedge 0.0714 < 0.4286. \tag{4.145b}$$

The first condition is met, so checking of other conditions is not needed. The pair (W_1, W_2) belongs to the set Ω_Z. In the considered example, Ω_Z set will be as follows:

$$\Omega_Z = \{(W_1, W_2)\,; (W_1, W_3)\,; (W_3, W_2)\}\,. \tag{4.146}$$

Based on Ω_Z set, a graph is created, in which arrows are drawn from the outranking to the outranked element. In the presented example, they are drawn from the decision variant W_2 to W_1, from W_3 to W_1, and from W_2 to W_3 (Fig. 4.19).

In the PROMETHEE method, when decision variants are described with numbers, criteria should be used to compute the C_i matrix . Further steps are analogues to the above presented.

Further calculations will be performed for the data from Table 4.5. For the *price* and *fuel consumption* criteria weights equal to 0.4 were assumed and for the criterion of *trunk capacity* , a weight equal to 0.2 is adopted. The criterion with linear preference was used to determine the comparison matrix. The value of q_i was 2,500 for kryterium *price*, 0.5 for *fuel consumption* , and 25 for *trunk capacity* criteria. The first step is to determine the pairwise comparison matrix. For example, in case of the *price* criterion, the value of $C_{1,2,3}$ will be calculated for the pair of decision variants (W_2, W_3). The *price* criterion is demotivating, and therefore the difference in the values of criteria for variants W_2 and W_3 will be calculated as follows:

$$d_1(W_2, W_3) = g_1(W_3) - g_1(W_2) = 40{,}715 - 39{,}500 = 1215. \tag{4.147}$$

$d_1(W_2, W_3)$ is within the range $\langle 0;\ p_1\rangle$, that is, $\langle 0;\ 2500\rangle$, and hence $F_1(d_1(W_2, W_3))$ should be calculated as follows:

$$F_1(d_1(W_2, W_3)) = \frac{d_1(W_2, W_3)}{p_1} = \frac{1215}{2500} = 0.486. \tag{4.148}$$

As a result of calculations, the following comparison matrices for criteria were obtained:

1. *Price*:

$$C_1 = \begin{bmatrix} 0 & 1 & 1 & 1 & 0.52 \\ 0 & 0 & 0.486 & 0 & 0 \\ 0 & 0 & 0 & 0 & 0 \\ 0 & 1 & 1 & 0 & 0 \\ 0 & 1 & 1 & 1 & 0 \end{bmatrix}. \tag{4.149a}$$

2. *Fuel consumption*:

$$C_2 = \begin{bmatrix} 0 & 1 & 0 & 0.2 & 0 \\ 0 & 0 & 0 & 0 & 0 \\ 0 & 1 & 0 & 0.2 & 0 \\ 0 & 0.8 & 0 & 0 & 0 \\ 0.2 & 1 & 0.2 & 0.4 & 0 \end{bmatrix}. \tag{4.149b}$$

3. *Trunk capacity*:

$$C_3 = \begin{bmatrix} 0 & 0 & 0 & 0 & 0 \\ 1 & 0 & 0.96 & 0.52 & 1 \\ 1 & 0 & 0 & 0 & 0.32 \\ 1 & 0 & 0.44 & 0 & 0.76 \\ 0.76 & 0 & 0 & 0 & 0 \end{bmatrix}. \tag{4.149c}$$

The matrix of aggregated preference indexes takes the following form:

$$\Pi = \begin{bmatrix} 0 & 0.8 & 0.4 & 0.48 & 0.208 \\ 0.2 & 0 & 0.3864 & 0.104 & 0.2 \\ 0.2 & 0.4 & 0 & 0.08 & 0.064 \\ 0.2 & 0.72 & 0.488 & 0 & 0.152 \\ 0.232 & 0.8 & 0.48 & 0.56 & 0 \end{bmatrix}. \tag{4.150}$$

Matrix of positive outranking flows:

$$\Phi^{+} = \begin{bmatrix} 0.4720 \\ 0.2226 \\ 0.1860 \\ 0.3900 \\ 0.5180 \end{bmatrix}. \tag{4.151}$$

Matrix of negative outranking flows:

$$\Phi^{-} = \begin{bmatrix} 0.2080 \\ 0.6800 \\ 0.4386 \\ 0.3060 \\ 0.1560 \end{bmatrix}. \tag{4.152}$$

The set Ω_Z is

$$\Omega_Z = \{(W_1, W_2); (W_1, W_3); (W_1, W_4); (W_4, W_2); (W_4, W_3); (W_5, W_1); \\ (W_5, W_2) (W_5, W_3); (W_5, W_4)\}. \tag{4.153}$$

Based on the Ω_Z set, the graph presented in Fig. 4.20 is created. The best decision variant turned out to be the W_5 variant, which outranks all other decision variants.

The PROMETHEE II method is very similar to the PROMETHEE I method. The most important difference is the possibility of making a ranking, which is created on the basis of net outranking flows: *net outranking flows*:

$$\varphi\left(W_j\right) = \varphi^{+}\left(W_j\right) - \varphi^{-}\left(W_j\right). \tag{4.154}$$

For example, for the matrices of positive and negative data flows given by the formulas (4.151) and (4.152), the matrix of net outranking flows will be as follows:

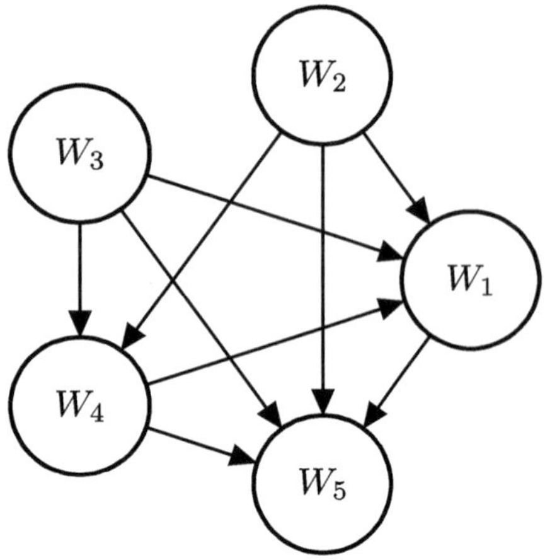

Fig. 4.20 The relationship between the decision variants is illustrated as a graph

$$\Phi = \begin{bmatrix} 0.4720 \\ 0.2226 \\ 0.1860 \\ 0.3900 \\ 0.5180 \end{bmatrix} - \begin{bmatrix} 0.2080 \\ 0.6800 \\ 0.4386 \\ 0.3060 \\ 0.1560 \end{bmatrix} = \begin{bmatrix} 0.2640 \\ -0.4574 \\ -0.2526 \\ 0.0840 \\ 0.3620 \end{bmatrix}. \tag{4.155}$$

The net outranking flow determines the position of a decision variant in the ranking. It is a measure of the position of this variant in the ranking. Following the above flow of net difference, W_5 ($\varphi_5 = 0.362$) object turned out to be the best one. The next positions in the rankings took successively: W_1, W_4, W_3, and W_2.

Chapter 5
Methods Based on Utility Function

5.1 Analytical Hierarchy Process AHP

Analytical hierarchy process called the AHP method was developed by Thomas Saaty. It uses pairwise comparison of objects within the given criteria, as well as the criteria themselves, and the groups of criteria. In this method, criteria or groups of criteria are assigned to each decision variant, criteria subgroups can be assigned to groups, criteria subgroups can be assigned to subgroups, etc. This creates a hierarchy tree, at the top of which is the goal of a decision, and at the bottom criteria to which appropriate weight is assigned.

The generalized hierarchical structure of the problem expressed in terms of the hierarchy tree is presented in Fig. 5.1. At the highest level, the goal of the decision is visible, which may be, for example, the *purchase of a car*. The lower level includes general criteria related to the decision problem, such as, e.g., *costs*, *reliability*, etc. These criteria are detailed at the lower level, where, for example, the *costs* can be broken down into *purchasing* and *operating*. These, in turn, can be further detailed on lower levels, where there are detailed criteria for which comparison matrices are determined.

In the simplest case, when the number of criteria is small, they can be assigned directly to the decision problem without dividing into groups and subgroups. In this situation, the first stage of the AHP method is to build a pairwise comparison matrix of decision variants within individual criteria. Comparisons are made using the nine-point scale proposed by Saaty [173, 202] (Fig. 5.2).

Values 2, 4, 6, 8 represent intermediate situations, applied when a decision-maker hesitates between 1, and 3, 3, and 5, etc. The results of the comparison are placed in a pairwise comparison matrix. For objects that are dominant, the numerical value from the scale is entered, for objects that are dominated—the inverse of this value. Theoretically, for each criterion, this should result in a proportional matrix satisfying the condition [202]:

K. Nermend, *Multi-Criteria and Multi-Dimensional Analysis in Decisions*, Vector Optimization, https://doi.org/10.1007/978-3-031-40538-9_5

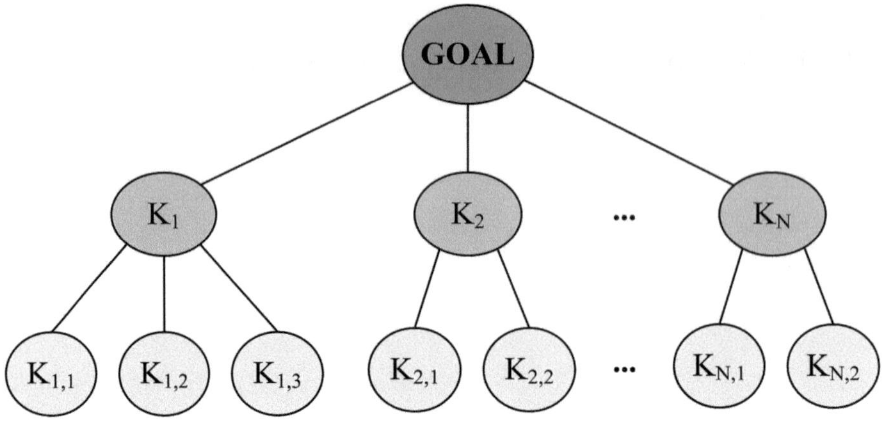

Fig. 5.1 The hierarchical structure of the problem expressed in terms of a hierarchy tree

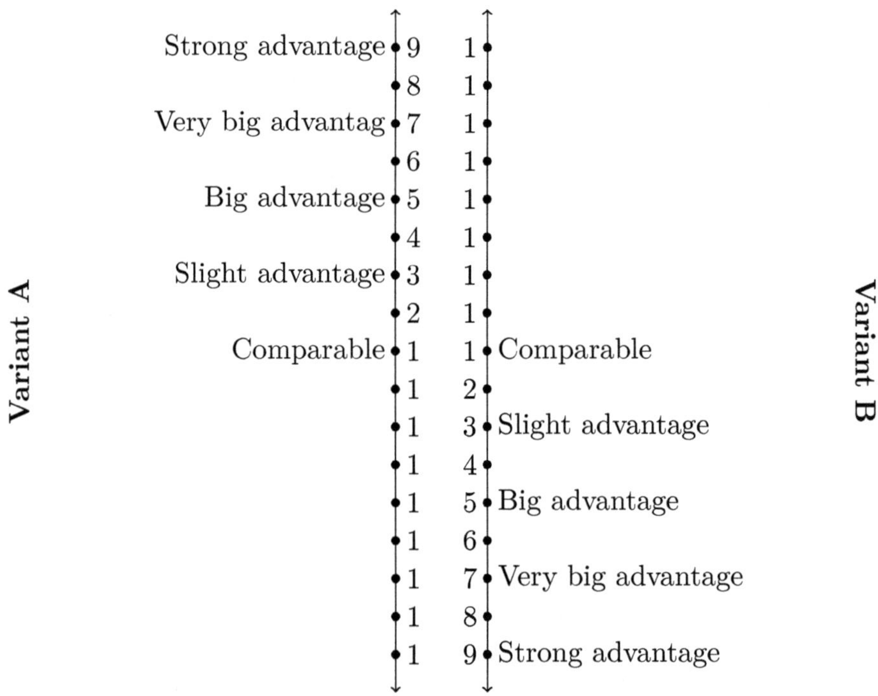

Fig. 5.2 Nine-point Saaty scale

$$\bigwedge_{j,k,l} c_{i,j,k} = \frac{1}{c_{i,k,j}}, \tag{5.1}$$

that is,

$$C_i = \begin{bmatrix} 1 & c_{i,1,2} & c_{i,1,3} & \cdots & c_{i,1,M} \\ \frac{1}{c_{i,1,2}} & 1 & c_{i,2,3} & \cdots & c_{i,2,M} \\ \frac{1}{c_{i,1,3}} & \frac{1}{c_{i,2,3}} & 1 & \cdots & c_{i,3,M} \\ \vdots & \vdots & \vdots & \ddots & \vdots \\ \frac{1}{c_{i,1,M}} & \frac{1}{c_{i,2,M}} & \frac{1}{c_{i,3,M}} & \cdots & 1 \end{bmatrix} \tag{5.2}$$

and consistent [202]:

$$\bigwedge_{j,k,l} c_{i,j,k} c_{i,k,l} = c_{i,j,l}. \tag{5.3}$$

When the consistency condition is satisfied, it automatically satisfies the proportionality condition. When creating the C_i matrix, it is assumed that if a decision-maker compared the decision variants W_j and W_k in terms of a given criterion and found that W_j is b times better than W_k, then comparing W_k with W_j, he finds that W_k is b times worse than W_j. This is due to the condition of proportionality and consistency. The consistency condition additionally shows that if W_1 is a times better than W_2, W_2 is b times better than W_3, then W_1 is $a \cdot b$ better than W_3. In practice, this does not have to be the case; therefore, some deviations from the theoretical value of the matrix C_i are allowed. The degree of this deviation is examined using CI (*consistency index*) [155, 178]:

$$\mathrm{CI} = \frac{\lambda_{\max} - M}{M - 1}, \tag{5.4}$$

where:

$\lambda_{\max}$—the greatest real eigenvalue of the matrix C_i

and CR (*consistency ratio*) [155, 178]:

$$\mathrm{CR} = \frac{\mathrm{CI}}{\mathrm{R}}. \tag{5.5}$$

The $\lambda_{\max}$ is obtained in the process of determining weights or preferences from a pairwise comparison matrix, which will be described further. R is a constant, depending on the dimension of the matrix C_i, the values of which are presented in Table 5.1. The ideal value of CR ratio is zero, and it means that the matrix is consistent. In practice, slight deviations from this value are allowed at the level of 0.1, and in some cases even 0.15 [97].

Table 5.1 Properties of R coefficient [175]

M	1	2	3	4	5	6	7	8	9	10	11	12
R	0	0	0.52	0.89	1.11	1.25	1.35	1.40	1.45	1.49	1.52	1.54
M	13	14	15									
R	1.56	1.58	1.59									

The example of C_3 matrix for the *trunk capacity* based on data from Table 4.1 will be as follows:

$$C_3 = \begin{bmatrix} 1 & \frac{1}{9} & \frac{1}{3} \\ 9 & 1 & 5 \\ 3 & \frac{1}{5} & 1 \end{bmatrix}. \tag{5.6}$$

If the decision variant from a given row is better than the decision variant from a given column, a value greater than one is entered in the appropriate place of the matrix C_i and if this variant is worse—less than one. In the presented example, the decision variant W_3 has big advantage over W_1, and thus $c_{3,3,1}$ element of C_3 matrix has the value greater than one. In turn, the decision variant W_2 has a great advantage over it; therefore, the element $c_{3,3,2}$ has the value less than one.

Based on the comparison matrix, weights or preferences are determined. There are many methods of their determination, and below are some examples:

1. The method of simple column sums and normalized column sums (Saaty's method) [82, 204]
2. Right eigenvector and normalized right eigenvector methods [31, 181]
3. Left eigenvector method [119]
4. Least squares method [23, 177]
5. Weighted least absolute error method [115, 125]
6. Weighted least worst absolute error method [15, 184]

Two of them will be presented in more detail: the Saaty method and the right eigenvector method.

According to *Saaty method*, a comparison matrix C_i is normalized in relation to individual columns, following the formula [82]:

$$\mathrm{cu}_{i,j,k} = \frac{c_{i,j,k}}{\sum_{l=1}^{M} c_{i,l,k}}. \tag{5.7}$$

Then, the elements $c'_{i,j,k}$ of the preference matrix C'_i are determined [204]:

$$c'_{i,j} = \frac{\sum_{k=1}^{M} \mathrm{cu}_{i,j,k}}{\sum_{l=1}^{M} \sum_{k=1}^{M} \mathrm{cu}_{i,l,k}} = \frac{\sum_{k=1}^{M} \mathrm{cu}_{i,j,k}}{M}. \tag{5.8}$$

In this method, eigenvectors are not calculated, so λ_{max} can be approximated using the formula [97]:

$$\lambda_{maxi} \approx \sum_{j=1}^{M} \left(c'_{i,j} \sum_{k=1}^{M} c_{i,j,k} \right), \tag{5.9}$$

where:

$\lambda_{\max i}$—value of $\lambda_{\max}$ for the i-th criterion.

For example, for the matrix C_i given by the formula (5.6), element $cu_{3,2,1}$ will be calculated as follows:

$$cu_{3,2,1} = \frac{c_{3,2,1}}{c_{3,1,1} + c_{3,2,1} + c_{3,3,1}} = \frac{9}{1+9+3} = 0.6923. \tag{5.10}$$

The entire matrix CU_3 will take the following form:

$$CU_3 = \begin{bmatrix} 0.0769 & 0.0847 & 0.0526 \\ 0.6923 & 0.7627 & 0.7895 \\ 0.2308 & 0.1525 & 0.1579 \end{bmatrix}. \tag{5.11}$$

Element $c'_{3,2}$ can be determined with the following formula:

$$c'_{3,2} = \frac{cu_{3,2,1} + cu_{3,2,2} + cu_{3,2,3}}{\sum_{l=1}^{M} \sum_{k=1}^{M} cu_{3,l,k}}. \tag{5.12a}$$

The denominator in this case takes the following value:

$$cu_{3,1,1}+cu_{3,1,2}+cu_{3,1,3}+cu_{3,2,1}+cu_{3,2,2}+cu_{3,2,3}+cu_{3,3,1}+cu_{3,3,2}+cu_{3,3,3} = 0.0769 + 0.0847 + 0.0526 + 0.6923 + 0.7627 + 0.7895 + 0.2308 + 0.1525 + 0.1579 = 3; \tag{5.12b}$$

hence,

$$c'_{3,2} = \frac{0.6923 + 0.7627 + 0.7895}{3} = 0.7482. \tag{5.12c}$$

Eventually, the entire matrix C'_3 will take the following form:

$$C'_3 = \begin{bmatrix} 0.0714 \\ 0.7482 \\ 0.1804 \end{bmatrix}. \tag{5.13}$$

In turn, λ_{max3} will be calculated as follows:

$$\lambda_{max3} \approx c'_{3,1}\left(c_{3,1,1}+c_{3,2,1}+c_{3,3,1}\right)+c'_{3,2}\left(c_{3,1,2}+c_{3,2,2}+c_{3,3,2}\right)+ c'_{3,3}\left(c_{3,1,3}+c_{3,2,3}+c_{3,3,3}\right). \tag{5.14a}$$

Substituting specific numbers, we get

$$\lambda_{max3} \approx 0.0714\,(1+9+3)+0.7482\left(\frac{1}{9}+1+\frac{1}{5}\right)+0.1804\left(\frac{1}{3}+5+1\right)= 3.0521. \tag{5.14b}$$

Based on the calculated λ_{max3} index and then CI, ratio can be determined: CR:

$$\mathrm{CI}=\frac{\lambda_{\max i}-M}{M-1}=\frac{3.0521-3}{3-1}=0.0261, \tag{5.15}$$

$$\mathrm{CR}=\frac{\mathrm{CI}}{\mathrm{R}}=\frac{0.0261}{0.52}=0.0501. \tag{5.16}$$

The CR value is below the maximum recommended value; therefore, the matrix C_3 can be assumed to be consistent.

In the *right eigenvector method,* based on the comparison matrix C_i, the eigenvectors WW and the eigenvalues λ of the matrix C_i are determined[181]:

$$C_i\mathrm{WW}=\lambda\mathrm{WW}. \tag{5.17}$$

In order to obtain the C_i' preference matrix, the eigenvector with the highest value of λ is selected, while vectors and eigenvalues with complex values are ignored. The values of the WW_i vector should be normalized using the formula:

$$c'_{i,j}=\frac{\mathrm{ww}_{i,j}}{\sum_{k=1}^{M}\mathrm{ww}_{i,k}}. \tag{5.18}$$

Calculating eigenvectors is quite a complicated procedure, so the most common are ready-made functions (or modules) for their calculation.

For the matrix C_3 given by the formula (5.6), the following eigenvectors:

$$WW_1 = \begin{bmatrix} 0.0908 \\ 0.9690 \\ 0.2298 \end{bmatrix}, \; WW_2 = \begin{bmatrix} -0.0454 - i0.0786 \\ 0.9690 \\ -0.1149 + i0.1990 \end{bmatrix}, \quad WW_3 = \begin{bmatrix} -0.0454 + i0.0786 \\ 0.9690 \\ -0.1149 - i0.1990 \end{bmatrix}, \tag{5.19a}$$

and eigenvalues were obtained:

$$\lambda_1 = 3.0291, \; \lambda_2 = -0.0145 + i0.2964, \; \lambda_3 = -0.0145 - i0.2964. \tag{5.19b}$$

The values λ_2 and λ_3 are complex so only the value of λ_1 can be considered. The value of $\lambda_{\max 3}$ should be taken as λ_1:

$$\lambda_{\max 3} = \lambda_1 = 3.0291, \tag{5.20}$$

and for the preference matrix, the eigenvector normalized according to the formula (5.18) corresponding to the eigenvalue λ_1, that is, WW_1:

$$c'_{3,1} = \frac{ww_{1,1}}{ww_{1,1} + ww_{1,2} + ww_{1,2}} = \frac{0.0908}{0.0908 + 0.9690 + 0.2298} = 0.0714. \tag{5.21}$$

The complete C'_3 matrix takes the following form:

$$C'_3 = \begin{bmatrix} 0.0714 \\ 0.7482 \\ 0.1804 \end{bmatrix}. \tag{5.22}$$

Further, based on $\lambda_{\max 3}$ CI index:

$$CI = \frac{\lambda_{\max 3} - M}{M - 1} = \frac{3.0291 - 3}{3 - 1} = 0.0145, \tag{5.23}$$

and CR ratio:

$$CR = \frac{CI}{R} = \frac{0.0146}{0.52} = 0.0279 are determined. \tag{5.24}$$

are determined. The value of CR is below the maximum, recommended value, so it can be assumed that the matrix C_3 is consistent.

Preference matrices are determined for all criteria. Next, applying the Saaty's method for the data from Table 4.1, the values of the matrix C'_i were determined:

$$C'_1 = \begin{bmatrix} 0.7651 \\ 0.1288 \\ 0.1062 \end{bmatrix}, \; C'_2 = \begin{bmatrix} 0.4737 \\ 0.0526 \\ 0.4737 \end{bmatrix}, \; C'_3 = \begin{bmatrix} 0.0714 \\ 0.7482 \\ 0.1804 \end{bmatrix}. \tag{5.25}$$

While the values $\lambda_{\max i}$ were:

$$\lambda_{\max 1} = 3.0723, \; \lambda_{\max 2} = 3, \; \lambda_{\max 3} = 3.0521, \tag{5.26}$$

so CR will be equal to: 0.0696, 0, and 0.0501, respectively. Thus, all matrixes C_i were consistent.

The next step in the AHP method is to establish criteria weights. These weights are determined based on the pairs comparison matrix of CK criteria. Such a matrix is determined for each group and subgroup of criteria. Only one group, i.e., one CK. Matrix is in the considered example. When creating it, the decision-maker determines how much a given criterion is more important (less important) than the others. The same creation rules apply for creation of this matrix as for C_i. An example of the CK matrix for the criteria in Table 4.1 is as follows:

$$C\text{K} = \begin{bmatrix} 1 & 5 & 3 \\ \frac{1}{5} & 1 & 2 \\ \frac{1}{3} & \frac{1}{2} & 1 \end{bmatrix}. \tag{5.27}$$

Further, for the CK matrix, the $C\text{K}'$ criteria preference matrix, and the CR, ratio are determined, analogously as it was in the case of C'_i matrix. The $C\text{K}'$ criteria preference matrix calculated with the Saaty method for the CK matrix given by the formula (5.27) will be as follows:

$$C\text{K}' = \begin{bmatrix} 0.640 \\ 0.206 \\ 0.154 \end{bmatrix}. \tag{5.28}$$

CR ratio for the matrix (5.27) is 0.144. So this matrix is consistent.

On the basis of the C'_i and $C\text{K}'$ matrices, a measure that defines the compatibility of a variant with the preferences of a decision-maker is calculated. If there is no hierarchy of criteria, it can be determined under the formula:

$$\text{mz}_j = \sum_{i=1}^{N} c'_{i,j}\text{ck}'_i. \tag{5.29}$$

For the case under consideration, the value of mz_1 for the first decision variant:

$$\text{mz}_1 = c'_{1,1}\text{ck}'_1 + c'_{2,1}\text{ck}'_2 + c'_{3,1}\text{ck}'_3 =$$

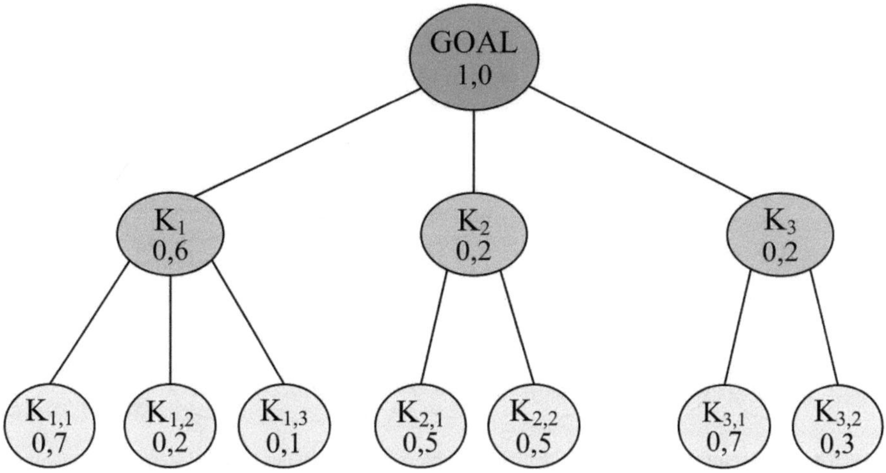

Fig. 5.3 Weights assigned to individual criteria presented in the hierarchy tree

$$0.7651 \cdot 0.640 + 0.4737 \cdot 0.206 + 0.0714 \cdot 0.154 = 0.765. \tag{5.30}$$

Value of mz_2 for the second variant is equal to 0.2084, and for mz_3 0.1933. In this example, the best decision variant turned out to be W_1, and the worst W_3.

In more complex decision problems, a criteria hierarchy tree is built. Each criterion is assigned a weight. The sum of the weights within each branch of the tree must be one. An example of a decision tree with marked weights is presented in Fig. 5.3. At the top of this tree is the goal of a decision problem, which is assigned a weight of one. At the lower level, the main categories of criteria (K_1, K_2, and K_3) are placed, and they are assigned weights, the sum of which should be equal to one. Each main criterion is assigned sub-criteria, creating groups related to the main criteria. The sub-criteria are assigned weights so that their sum within a group is equal to one. For example, for the subgroup of criterion K_3, the weights for the criteria are 0.7 and 0.3, which gives the total value of one. You can also associate sub-criteria with the next sub-criteria, creating a criteria hierarchy tree with any number of levels. Criteria weights can be assigned either directly or using a pairwise comparison matrix.

For example, the decision problem of choosing an IT system for managing a small- and medium-sized enterprise can be considered. The goal is to select the system; therefore, the selection of the IT system is placed at the top of the decision tree (Fig. 5.4). The decision-maker has determined that three criteria for decision-making will be important to him during the purchase: *compliance of the system functionality with the company's needs* (K_1), *system quality* (K_2), and *costs associated with the purchase of a system and its development* (K_3). All these criteria are quite general, so by creating sub-criteria they can be more specific. For the criterion of *compliance of the system functionality with the company's needs*, the

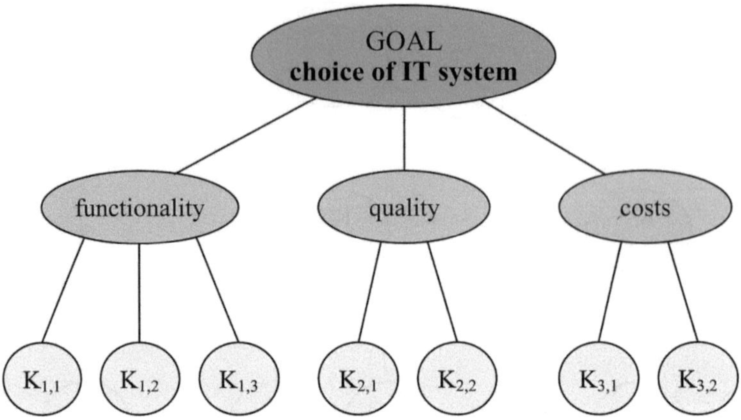

Fig. 5.4 Hierarchy of criteria for a decision problem of purchasing an IT system for managing a small- and medium-sized enterprise

sub-criteria will be: *accounting and finance capabilities* ($K_{1,1}$), *human resources management* ($K_{1,2}$), and *control, supervision, and reporting mechanisms* ($K_{1,3}$). For the criterion *system quality* sub-criteria are *reliability* ($K_{2,1}$) and *user-friendly program interface* ($K_{2,2}$), and for the *costs associated with the purchase of a system and its development—purchase costs of a system* ($K_{3,1}$) and the *costs of system development* ($K_{3,2}$).

It is necessary to determine weights for the defined main criteria. They will be specified on the basis of the comparison matrix. It was assumed that the decision-maker made pairwise comparison, and as a result, the following comparison matrix of CK criteria was obtained:

$$CK = \begin{bmatrix} 1 & 3 & 5 \\ \frac{1}{3} & 1 & 3 \\ \frac{1}{5} & \frac{1}{3} & 1 \end{bmatrix}. \tag{5.31}$$

Using the right eigenvector method, the following eigenvalues were obtained:

$$\lambda_1 = 3.0385,\ \lambda_2 = -0.0193 + \mathrm{i}0.3415,\ \lambda_3 = -0.0193 - \mathrm{i}0.3415. \tag{5.32}$$

In this case only λ_1, it is not a complex value. Further, it was assumed that $\lambda_{\max} = \lambda_1$, and the eigenvector corresponding to this value takes the following form:

$$WW_1 = \begin{bmatrix} 0.9161 \\ 0.3715 \\ 0.1506 \end{bmatrix}. \tag{5.33}$$

The value of $\lambda_{\max}$ determined under CI was

$$\mathrm{CI} = \frac{\lambda_{\max} - M}{M - 1} = \frac{3.0385 - 3}{3 - 1} = 0.0192, \tag{5.34}$$

and CR:

$$\mathrm{CR} = \frac{\mathrm{CI}}{\mathrm{R}} = \frac{0.0192}{0.52} = 0.0369. \tag{5.35}$$

This value is less than the limit value, so the $C\mathrm{K}$ matrix is consistent. By normalizing the eigenvector WW_1, the $C\mathrm{K}'$ criteria preference matrix is obtained:

$$C\mathrm{K}' = \begin{bmatrix} 0.6370 \\ 0.2583 \\ 0.1047 \end{bmatrix}. \tag{5.36}$$

Three sub-criteria were defined for the criterion K_1 for which the following comparison matrix for $C\mathrm{K}_1$ criterion was obtained:

$$C\mathrm{K}_1 = \begin{bmatrix} 1 & 1 & 3 \\ 1 & 1 & 3 \\ \frac{1}{3} & \frac{1}{3} & 1 \end{bmatrix}. \tag{5.37}$$

Eigenvalues for this matrix are equal to

$$\lambda_1 = 0,\ \lambda_2 = 3,\ \lambda_3 = 0. \tag{5.38}$$

This time, three real values were obtained, out of which the greatest is λ_2, consequently $\lambda_{\max 1} = \lambda_2$. CI index and CR ratio are zero; hence, the $C\mathrm{K}_i$ matrix is consistent. The eigenvector corresponding to λ_2 is as follows:

$$\mathrm{WW}_2 = \begin{bmatrix} 0.6882 \\ 0.6882 \\ 0.2294 \end{bmatrix}. \tag{5.39}$$

Then, after normalization, the $C\mathrm{K}_1'$ matrix was obtained:

$$C\mathrm{K}_1' = \begin{bmatrix} 0.4286 \\ 0.4286 \\ 0.1429 \end{bmatrix}. \tag{5.40}$$

For the K_2 criterion, two sub-criteria were defined, for which the following comparison matrix for $C\mathrm{K}_2$ criteria was obtained:

$$CK_2 = \begin{bmatrix} 1 & 3 \\ \frac{1}{3} & 1 \end{bmatrix}. \tag{5.41}$$

$\lambda_{\max 2}$ was 2, and CI and CR zero, so CK_2 matrix is consistent. Thus, the following CK_2' matrix was obtained:

$$CK_2' = \begin{bmatrix} 0.75 \\ 0.25 \end{bmatrix}. \tag{5.42}$$

For the K_3 criterion, two sub-criteria were defined, for which the following comparison matrix for CK_3 criterion was equal to

$$CK_3 = \begin{bmatrix} 1 & 1 \\ 1 & 1 \end{bmatrix}. \tag{5.43}$$

$\lambda_{\max 3}$ was 2, and CI and CR were zero; hence, CK_3 matrix is consistent. The obtained CK_3' matrix takes the following form:

$$CK_3' = \begin{bmatrix} 0.5 \\ 0.5 \end{bmatrix}. \tag{5.44}$$

The decision-maker considered choosing one of the three IT systems. Therefore, there are three decision variants: W_1, W_2, and W_3. The decision variants under all sub-criteria were compared. For the sub-criterion $K_{1,1}$, the following comparison matrix $C_{1,1}$ was obtained:

$$C_{1,1} = \begin{bmatrix} 1 & 6 & 3 \\ \frac{1}{6} & 1 & \frac{1}{3} \\ \frac{1}{3} & 3 & 1 \end{bmatrix}. \tag{5.45}$$

Using the right eigenvector method, the following eigenvalues were obtained:

$$\lambda_1 = 3.0183,\ \lambda_2 = -0.0091 + i0.2348,\ \lambda_3 = -0.0091 - i0.2348. \tag{5.46}$$

Only the eigenvalue λ_1 is not a complex value. Hence, it was assumed that $\lambda_{\max} = \lambda_1$. The eigenvector corresponding to this eigenvalue took the following form:

$$WW_1 = \begin{bmatrix} 0.9258 \\ 0.1348 \\ 0.3532 \end{bmatrix}. \tag{5.47}$$

The value of $\lambda_{\max}$ determined under CI was

$$\text{CI} = \frac{\lambda_{\max} - M}{M - 1} = \frac{3.0183 - 3}{3 - 1} = 0.0091, \tag{5.48}$$

and CR:

$$\text{CR} = \frac{\text{CI}}{\text{R}} = \frac{0.0091}{0.52} = 0.0175. \tag{5.49}$$

This value is less than the limit value, so the matrix $C_{1,1}$ is consistent. By normalizing the eigenvector WW_1, the preference matrix of criteria $C'_{1,1}$ is obtained:

$$C'_{1,1} = \begin{bmatrix} 0.6548 \\ 0.0953 \\ 0.2499 \end{bmatrix}. \tag{5.50}$$

For the remaining decision variants, the following comparison matrices were obtained:

$$\begin{gathered} C_{1,2} = \begin{bmatrix} 1 & 4 & 1 \\ \frac{1}{4} & 1 & \frac{1}{4} \\ 1 & 4 & 1 \end{bmatrix}, \quad C_{1,3} = \begin{bmatrix} 1 & 8 & 9 \\ \frac{1}{8} & 1 & \frac{1}{2} \\ \frac{1}{9} & 2 & 1 \end{bmatrix}, \quad C_{2,1} = \begin{bmatrix} 1 & \frac{1}{7} & \frac{1}{4} \\ 7 & 1 & 2 \\ 4 & \frac{1}{2} & 1 \end{bmatrix}, \\ C_{2,2} = \begin{bmatrix} 1 & 3 & \frac{1}{7} \\ \frac{1}{3} & 1 & \frac{1}{9} \\ 7 & 9 & 1 \end{bmatrix}, \quad C_{3,1} = \begin{bmatrix} 1 & 3 & 2 \\ \frac{1}{3} & 1 & \frac{1}{2} \\ \frac{1}{2} & 2 & 1 \end{bmatrix}, \quad C_{3,2} = \begin{bmatrix} 1 & \frac{1}{4} & 2 \\ 4 & 1 & 8 \\ \frac{1}{2} & \frac{1}{8} & 1 \end{bmatrix}. \end{gathered} \tag{5.51}$$

On their basis, the eigenvalues were calculated:

$$\begin{gathered} \lambda_{\max 1,2} = 3, \quad \lambda_{\max 1,3} = 3.0735, \quad \lambda_{\max 2,1} = 3.0020, \\ \lambda_{\max 2,2} = 3.0803, \quad \lambda_{\max 3,1} = 3.0092, \quad \lambda_{\max 3,2} = 3. \end{gathered} \tag{5.52}$$

All CR ratios were below the limit value; therefore, all comparison matrices are consistent.

Matrices C' took the following forms:

$$\begin{gathered} C'_{1,2} = \begin{bmatrix} 0.4444 \\ 0.1111 \\ 0.4444 \end{bmatrix}, \quad C'_{1,3} = \begin{bmatrix} 0.8058 \\ 0.0769 \\ 0.1173 \end{bmatrix}, \quad C'_{2,1} = \begin{bmatrix} 0.0823 \\ 0.6026 \\ 0.3150 \end{bmatrix}, \\ C'_{2,2} = \begin{bmatrix} 0.1488 \\ 0.0658 \\ 0.7854 \end{bmatrix}, \quad C'_{3,1} = \begin{bmatrix} 0.5396 \\ 0.1634 \\ 0.2970 \end{bmatrix}, \quad C'_{3,2} = \begin{bmatrix} 0.1818 \\ 0.7273 \\ 0.0909 \end{bmatrix}. \end{gathered} \tag{5.53}$$

Next, the $\text{mz}_{j\cdot}$ measures should be determined. In order to define them for a given decision variant, first the mz_i components for individual sub-criteria at the bottom

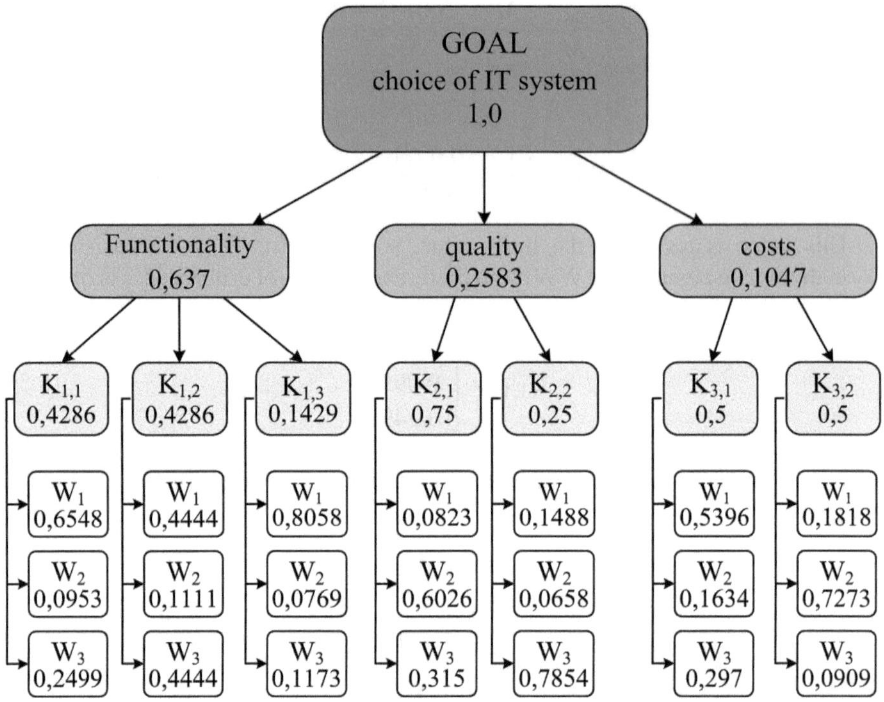

Fig. 5.5 Weights defined for the decision problem: selection of the IT system

of the tree should be determined. These components will be indicated as $\text{mzs}_{j,i}$. In order to determine the component, go from the bottom of the tree, starting from the i-th criterion of the j-th decision variant to its vertex, and multiply all encountered weights by each other. For the W_1, variant, and K_1 criterion, at the lowest level of the tree 0.6548 weight is located (Fig. 5.5), moving up the tree we spot the weight of 0.4286, and then 0.637 and at the end the goal weight equal to 1, consequently $\text{mzs}_{1,1}$ is

$$\text{mzs}_{1,1} = 0.6548 \cdot 0.4286 \cdot 0.637 \cdot 1 = 0.1788. \tag{5.54}$$

For the W_1 variant and the K_2 criterion, the weight of 0.4444 is at the lowest level of the tree, while moving up the tree the weights are 0.4286, 0.637, and finally, the target weight equal to 1:

$$\text{mzs}_{1,2} = 0.4444 \cdot 0.4286 \cdot 0.637 \cdot 1 = 0.1213. \tag{5.55}$$

The other values are

$$\mathrm{mzs}_{1,3} = 0.0733, \quad \mathrm{mzs}_{1,4} = 0.0159, \quad \mathrm{mzs}_{1,5} = 0.0096,$$
$$\mathrm{mzs}_{1,6} = 0.029, \quad \mathrm{mzs}_{1,7} = 0.0098. \tag{5.56}$$

Eventually, mz_1 is

$$\mathrm{mz}_1 = \mathrm{mzs}_{1,1} + \mathrm{mzs}_{1,2} + \mathrm{mzs}_{1,3} + \mathrm{mzs}_{1,4} + \mathrm{mzs}_{1,5} + \mathrm{mzs}_{1,6} + \mathrm{mzs}_{1,7} =$$
$$0.1788 + 0.1213 + 0.0733 + 0.0159 + 0.0096 + 0.029 + 0.0098 = 0.4378. \tag{5.57}$$

For the decision variant W_2 mz_2 is 0.2322, and for the decision variant W_3 $\mathrm{mz}_3 = 0.3328$. Variant W_1 turned out to be the best one, and this is because it achieved the best $c'_{i,j,k}$ values for the principal criterion *functionalityć*, which had the highest weight.

5.2 The Analytical Network Process ANP

The Analytical Network Process method was created by Professor Thomas L. Saaty in 1975 as the expansion of the AHP method. The first book: (*Decision Making with Dependence and Feedback. The Analytic Network Process*) was developed only in 2001. It is distinguished from AHP by the possibility of reducing dependence between any elements of the hierarchy tree. These dependencies can be multidirectional (and not only from the top to the bottom of a decision tree); therefore, they are marked with arrows in the figures (Fig. 5.6). The ANP method makes it possible to define any dependencies between the graph elements, regardless of the position of interacting elements in the graph. It is also possible to influence a goal as well as an element itself.

Relationships between objects can create a very complex network; therefore, the graph can be broken down into components. Ingredients of components are called elements. Usually, one component is made up of decision variants (W in Fig. 5.7), one goal (Goal), and decision criteria are distributed among various components. The graph in Fig. 5.6 can be simplified by combining the sub-criteria $K_{1,1}$, $K_{1,2}$, $K_{1,3}$, and K_1 into one aggregate. In Fig. 5.7, this component is marked as K_1, and K_2 criterion was unchanged and remained as a component. All relationships between the elements of the components and other components are transferred to the components. The graph of components facilitates the analysis of general relationships. In more complicated cases, this graph can be created at the beginning of the analysis.

ANP Method Algorithm

Step 1 The first step in the ANP method is to build dependency and component graphs.

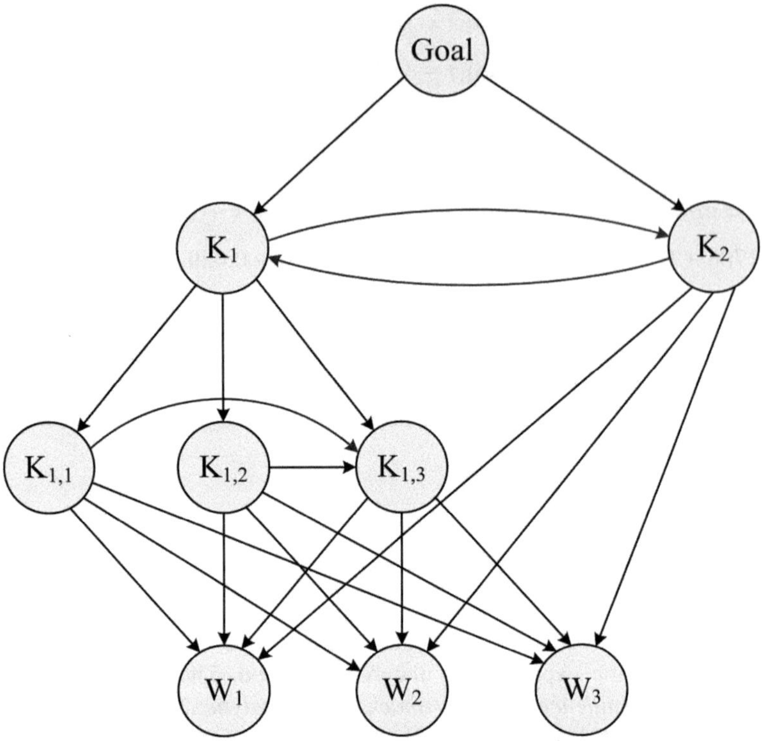

Fig. 5.6 Example of the ANP relationship graph

Fig. 5.7 Sample ANP component graph

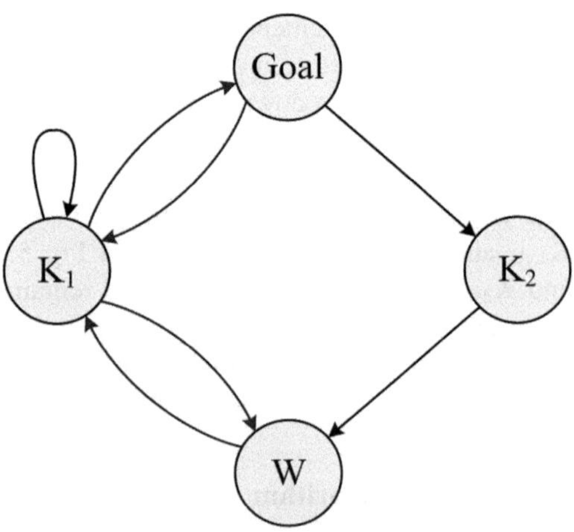

Step 2 Based on the dependency graph, the supermatrix is divided into seven blocks, marked as (Bl and a number of a given block) according to the relationship graph from Fig. (5.6) is presented below:

$$
\begin{array}{c|c|ccccc|ccc|}
 & \text{Cel} & \text{K}_1 & \text{K}_2 & \text{K}_{1,1} & \text{K}_{1,2} & \text{K}_{1,3} & \text{W}_1 & \text{W}_2 & \text{W}_3 \\
\text{Cel} & \multicolumn{9}{c|}{\text{Bl.1}} \\
\text{K}_1 & & & & & & & & & \\
\text{K}_2 & & & & & & & & & \\
\text{K}_{1,1} & \text{Bl. 2} & & & \text{Bl. 3} & & & & \text{Bl. 4} & \\
\text{K}_{1,2} & & & & & & & & & \\
\text{K}_{1,3} & & & & & & & & & \\
\text{W}_1 & & & & & & & & & \\
\text{W}_2 & \text{Bl. 5} & & & \text{Bl. 6} & & & & \text{Bl. 7} & \\
\text{W}_3 & & & & & & & & &
\end{array} \quad (5.58)
$$

On the other hand, the below supermatrix illustrates the relationship between the goal, criteria, sub-criteria, and variants. They are marked with x:

$$
\begin{array}{c|c|ccccc|ccc|}
 & \text{Cel} & \text{K}_1 & \text{K}_2 & \text{K}_{1,1} & \text{K}_{1,2} & \text{K}_{1,3} & \text{W}_1 & \text{W}_2 & \text{W}_3 \\
\text{Cel} & & \text{x} & & & & & & & \\
\text{K}_1 & \text{x} & & \text{x} & & \text{x} & & & & \\
\text{K}_2 & \text{x} & \text{x} & & & & & & & \\
\text{K}_{1,1} & & \text{x} & & \text{x} & & & & & \\
\text{K}_{1,2} & & \text{x} & & \text{x} & & & \text{x} & & \\
\text{K}_{1,3} & & \text{x} & & \text{x} & & & & & \\
\text{W}_1 & & & \text{x} & \text{x} & \text{x} & \text{x} & & & \\
\text{W}_2 & & & \text{x} & \text{x} & \text{x} & \text{x} & & & \\
\text{W}_3 & & & \text{x} & \text{x} & \text{x} & \text{x} & \text{x} & &
\end{array} \quad (5.59)
$$

The Interpretation of the Marked Areas of the Supermatrix Is as Follows:

1. The first block describes what criteria, sub-criteria, and variants affect the goal. The x sign in the first row of the second column (5.59) means that the goal is influenced by the K_1 criterion.
2. The second block illustrates which criteria are directly affected by the goal.
3. The third block defines the relationship between the criteria.
4. The fourth block defines which decision variants affect the criteria.
5. The fifth block shows which decision variants are affected by the goal.
6. The sixth block describes which criteria directly influence the decision variants.
7. The seventh block shows the interaction of decision variants.

Step 3 In the supermatrix, x signs are replaced by numerical values. They are determined with a pairwise comparison matrix. These matrices are created for each column with x marks and separately for each block.

Procedure for Determining Numerical Values

1. Determination of eigenvalues and eigenvectors
2. Eigenvector selection based on eigenvalues
3. Checking the consistency of the pairwise comparison matrix
4. Normalization of the selected eigenvector
5. Entering the obtained values into the appropriate block of the supermatrix

For example, the matrix given by the formula (5.59), in the first column (Goal) and the second block, includes x signs for K_1 and K_2 criteria. This means that the pairwise comparison matrix for the criteria K_1 and K_2 with respect to the goal should be created. This is done in the same way as in the AHP method. The obtained result is entered into the supermatrix in the place marked with x. In the second column (K_1) in the first block, there is one x for the goal. Since there are no alternatives for the goal, the value of one is entered in place of x. In the second column in the third block, there are four x signes for K_2, $K_{1,1}$, $K_{1,2}$, and $K_{1,3}$ criteria. For these criteria, the pairwise comparison matrix should be created, and the result entered in the place of x.

Step 4 After filling in the columns with values, the supermatrix is divided by the sums of their sum. This creates a normalized supermatrix whose columns sum up to one.

Step 5 The normalized supermatrix is raised to the k-th power in a matrix, where k is an odd number. However, if calculations are performed using ANP for AHP, it is enough to raise the normalized supermatrix to the 3rd power. In general, it is raised to a power in which the successive odd powers do not differ much or at all from each other. It may happen that the successive calculated values will change cyclically. The average values over the cycle are then taken as the result. In practice, for example, the value of 35 can be taken as the power of a normalized supermatrix. The result will be in the fifth block (in the example: the column Goal, the rows W_1, W_2, and W_3).

5.2.1 *Calculating AHP Using ANP*

ANP method is an expansion of AHP method. Therefore, all calculations that are performed in the AHP method can be executed in the ANP method. The example of AHP for a typical problem being solved with AHP method is as follows:

$$
\begin{array}{c}
 \\
\text{Cel} \\ \text{K}_1 \\ \text{K}_2 \\ \text{K}_{1,1} \\ \text{K}_{1,2} \\ \text{K}_{2,1} \\ \text{K}_{2,2} \\ \text{W}_1 \\ \text{W}_2 \\ \text{W}_3
\end{array}
\begin{array}{c}
\begin{array}{cccccccccc}
\text{Cel} & \text{K}_1 & \text{K}_2 & \text{K}_{1,1} & \text{K}_{1,2} & \text{K}_{2,1} & \text{K}_{2,2} & \text{W}_1 & \text{W}_2 & \text{W}_3
\end{array} \\
\left[
\begin{array}{cccccccccc}
 & & & & & & & & & \\
\text{x} & & & & & & & & & \\
\text{x} & & & & & & & & & \\
 & \text{x} & & & & & & & & \\
 & \text{x} & & & & & & & & \\
 & & \text{x} & & & & & & & \\
 & & \text{x} & & & & & & & \\
 & & & \text{x} & \text{x} & \text{x} & \text{x} & 1 & & \\
 & & & \text{x} & \text{x} & \text{x} & \text{x} & & 1 & \\
 & & & \text{x} & \text{x} & \text{x} & \text{x} & & & 1
\end{array}
\right].
\end{array}
\tag{5.60}
$$

K_1 and K_2 are main criteria that are affected only by the goal. The x signs are entered in the first column. K_1 criterion affects $K_{1,1}$ and $K_{1,2}$ sub-criteria. Therefore, the x signs have been entered in the K_1 column. K_2 criterion affects $K_{2,1}$ and $K_{2,2}$ criteria x signs are placed in the column K_2. $K_{1,1}$, $K_{1,2}$, $K_{2,1}$, and $K_{2,2}$ sub-criteria affect all decision variants. So x signs have been placed in columns $K_{1,1}$, $K_{1,2}$, $K_{2,1}$, and $K_{2,2}$. In addition, in the case of the AHP method, one values are always entered on the diagonal of a supermatrix in the last (seventh) block of a matrix. Columns W_1, W_2, ... cannot include only zero values. In such a case, one value on the diagonal of a supermatrix for columns with all zeros should be entered.

5.2.2 An Example of Using the ANP Method to Select an IT System

As an example, a decision problem of choosing an IT system, as it was in the AHP method, was selected. However, the problem has been simplified by reducing the number of criteria. Two criteria were set to be important during the selection process:*compliance of the system functionality with the company's needs* (K_1) and *costs related to purchase of the system* (K_2). For *compliance of the system functionality with the company's needs*, sub-criteria will be as follows: *accounting and finance capabilities* ($K_{1,1}$), *human resources management* ($K_{1,2}$), and *control, supervision, and reporting mechanisms* ($K_{1,3}$). The criterion *purchase costs* was not divided into sub-criteria.

Step 1 Therefore, in the graph, the arrows leave the goal and follow toward the criteria K_1 and K_2 and leave K_1 and follow toward $K_{1,1}$, $K_{1,2}$, and $K_{1,3}$ criteria (Fig. 5.8).

It was agreed that a decision problem applies to selection of the one out of three IT systems. Thus, there are three decision variants W_1, W_2, and W_3. In the graph, arrows follow toward sub-criteria $K_{1,1}$, $K_{1,2}$, $K_{1,3}$, and K_1 criterion toward all decision variants. Additionally, it was found that costs are closely related to the

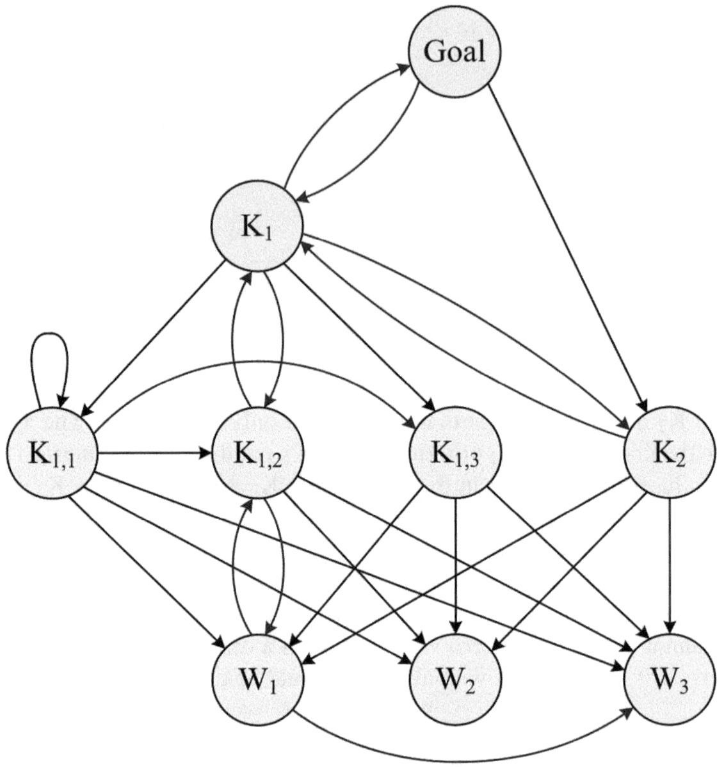

Fig. 5.8 ANP relationship graph to select an IT system

functionality of the system. Each of the systems can be extended with additional modules increasing its functionality, which increases costs. On the other hand, increasing costs allows for increasing the functionality of the system, and the relationship is therefore two way. The arrows go in both directions from K_1 to K_2 and from K_2 to K_1. There is also a relationship between reporting modules of the IT systems in question, and accounting, finance, and human resource management modules. The more complex these two modules are, the more extensive the reporting module is. For this reason, arrows leave $K_{1,1}$ and $K_{1,2}$ and follow toward $K_{1,3}$. Based on the graph, a supermatrix was built.

Step 2 Columns W_1, W_2, and W_3 of the supermonly zero values were included; therefore, one values were entered in the appropriate places of main diagonal:

$$
\begin{array}{c} \\ \text{Cel} \\ \text{K}_1 \\ \text{K}_2 \\ \text{K}_{1,1} \\ \text{K}_{1,2} \\ \text{K}_{1,3} \\ \text{W}_1 \\ \text{W}_2 \\ \text{W}_3 \end{array}
\begin{array}{c}
\begin{array}{ccccccccc} \text{Cel} & \text{K}_1 & \text{K}_2 & \text{K}_{1,1} & \text{K}_{1,2} & \text{K}_{1,3} & \text{W}_1 & \text{W}_2 & \text{W}_3 \end{array} \\
\left[\begin{array}{ccccccccc}
 & & & & & & & & \\
\text{x} & & \text{x} & & & & & & \\
\text{x} & \text{x} & & & & & & & \\
 & \text{x} & & & & \text{x} & & & \\
 & \text{x} & & & & \text{x} & & & \\
 & \text{x} & & & & & & & \\
 & & \text{x} & \text{x} & \text{x} & \text{x} & 1 & & \\
 & & \text{x} & \text{x} & \text{x} & \text{x} & & 1 & \\
 & & \text{x} & \text{x} & \text{x} & \text{x} & & & 1
\end{array}\right]
\end{array}. \tag{5.61}
$$

Step 3. Determining Numerical Values
Block 2. There are two x signs in the second block (column Goal). Therefore, the criteria of K_1 and K_2 should be compared in relation to the goal. The comparison is made similarly to the AHP method, applying the $C\text{K}$ criteria comparison matrix. It was assumed that the decision-maker made a pairwise comparison, considering both criteria equally important, in result the following criteria comparison matrix $C\text{K}$ was obtained:

$$
C\text{K} = \begin{bmatrix} 1 & 1 \\ 1 & 1 \end{bmatrix}. \tag{5.62}
$$

Determining numerical values for the criteria K_1 and K_2 in relation to the goal:

1. **Determining eigenvalues and eigenvectors**
   Using the right-hand eigenvector method, the following eigenvalues were calculated:

$$
\lambda_1 = 0,\ \lambda_2 = 2. \tag{5.63}
$$

2. **Choosing eigenvector based on eigenvalues**
   The greatest eigenvalue, in terms of the absolute value, is λ_2. It was assumed that $\lambda_{\max} = \lambda_2$. The eigenvector corresponding to this eigenvalue is as follows:

$$
\text{WW}_2 = \begin{bmatrix} 0.7071 \\ 0.7071 \end{bmatrix}. \tag{5.64}
$$

3. **Checking the consistency of the pairwise comparison matrix**
   $\lambda_{\max}$ is equal to the number of compared criteria, which means that comparisons of K_1 with K_2 and K_2 with K_1 are fully compliant. There is no need to calculate CI and CR $C\text{K}$ matrix is consistent.
4. **Normalization of the selected eigenvector**

During normalization of the eigenvector WW_1, a criteria preference matrix CK' is obtained:

$$CK' = \begin{bmatrix} 0.5 \\ 0.5 \end{bmatrix}. \tag{5.65}$$

5. **Entering the obtained values into the appropriate area of the supermatrix**
   Enter the obtained values in the column Goal, replacing x:

$$\begin{array}{c} \\ \text{Cel} \\ \text{K}_1 \\ \text{K}_2 \\ \text{K}_{1,1} \\ \text{K}_{1,2} \\ \text{K}_{1,3} \\ \text{W}_1 \\ \text{W}_2 \\ \text{W}_3 \end{array}
\begin{array}{c} \begin{array}{ccccccccc} \text{Cel} & \text{K}_1 & \text{K}_2 & \text{K}_{1,1} & \text{K}_{1,2} & \text{K}_{1,3} & \text{W}_1 & \text{W}_2 & \text{W}_3 \end{array} \\
\begin{bmatrix} & & & & & & & & \\ 0{,}5 & & x & & & & & & \\ 0{,}5 & x & & & & & & & \\ & x & & & & x & & & \\ & x & & & & x & & & \\ & x & & & & & & & \\ & & x & x & x & x & 1 & & \\ & & x & x & x & x & & 1 & \\ & & x & x & x & x & & & 1 \end{bmatrix} \end{array}. \tag{5.66}$$

Block 3, section 1. In the third block (column K_1), three x are entered. Therefore, K_2 criteria and $\text{K}_{1,2}$, $\text{K}_{1,3}$, $\text{K}_{1,4}$ sub-criteria should be compared in relation to K_1 criterion. It was assumed that a decision-maker made a pairwise comparison, and as a result, the following $C\text{K}$ matrix of criteria comparisons was obtained:

$$C\text{K} = \begin{bmatrix} 1 & 3 & 7 & 9 \\ \frac{1}{3} & 1 & 3 & 8 \\ \frac{1}{7} & \frac{1}{3} & 1 & 6 \\ \frac{1}{9} & \frac{1}{8} & \frac{1}{6} & 1 \end{bmatrix}. \tag{5.67}$$

Determining numerical values for the K_2 criterion and the $\text{K}_{1,2}$, $\text{K}_{1,3}$, $\text{K}_{1,4}$ criteria in relation to the K_1 criterion:

1. **Determining eigenvalues and eigenvectors**
   Using the right-hand eigenvector method, the following eigenvalues were obtained:

$$\lambda_1 = 4.2623, \; \lambda_2 = -0.0925 + \text{i}1.0466,$$
$$\lambda_3 = -0.0925 - \text{i}1.0466, \; \lambda_4 = -0.0773. \tag{5.68}$$

2. **Eigenvector selection based on eigenvalues**

Eigenvalues λ_2 and λ_3 are complex. λ_1 is the greatest eigenvalue in terms of absolute value out of the remaining values. It was assumed that $\lambda_{max} = \lambda_1$. The eigenvector corresponding to this eigenvalue is as follows:

$$\mathrm{WW}_1 = \begin{bmatrix} -0.9001 \\ -0.3927 \\ -0.1806 \\ -0.0549 \end{bmatrix}. \tag{5.69}$$

3. **Checking the consistency of the pairwise comparison matrix**
   The value of λ_{max} determined under CI was

$$\mathrm{CI} = \frac{\lambda_{max} - M}{M - 1} = \frac{4.2623 - 4}{4 - 1} = 0.0874, \tag{5.70}$$

and CR:

$$\mathrm{CR} = \frac{\mathrm{CI}}{\mathrm{R}} = \frac{0.0874}{0.89} = 0.0982. \tag{5.71}$$

   This value is less than the limit value, so the $C\mathrm{K}$ matrix is consistent.
4. **Normalization of the selected eigenvector**
   During normalization of the eigenvector WW_1, a criteria preference matrix $C\mathrm{K}'$ is obtained:

$$C\mathrm{K}' = \begin{bmatrix} 0.5890 \\ 0.2570 \\ 0.1181 \\ 0.0359 \end{bmatrix}. \tag{5.72}$$

5. **Entering the obtained values into the appropriate area of the supermatrix**
   Enter the obtained values in the third block, column K_1:

	Cel	K_1	K_2	$K_{1,1}$	$K_{1,2}$	$K_{1,3}$	W_1	W_2	W_3
Cel									
K_1	0,5		x						
K_2	0,5	0,5890							
$K_{1,1}$		0,2570				x			
$K_{1,2}$		0,1181				x			
$K_{1,3}$		0,0359							
W_1			x	x	x	x	1		
W_2			x	x	x	x		1	
W_3			x	x	x	x			1

(5.73)

Block 3, section. 2. In the third block (column K_2), one x is placed. In this case, one value should be placed instead of this sign:

	Cel	K_1	K_2	$K_{1,1}$	$K_{1,2}$	$K_{1,3}$	W_1	W_2	W_3
Cel									
K_1	0,5		1						
K_2	0,5	0,5890							
$K_{1,1}$		0,2570				x			
$K_{1,2}$		0,1181				x			
$K_{1,3}$		0,0359							
W_1			x	x	x	x	1		
W_2			x	x	x	x		1	
W_3			x	x	x	x			1

(5.74)

In the third block (column $K_{1,3}$), two x signs are entered. Therefore, $K_{1,1}$ criteria and $K_{1,2}$ sub-criteria should be compared with the $K_{1,3}$ criterion. It was assumed that the decision-maker made a pairwise comparison, and in result, the following comparison matrix of CK criteria was obtained:

$$CK = \begin{bmatrix} 1 & 6 \\ \frac{1}{6} & 1 \end{bmatrix}. \tag{5.75}$$

Determining numerical values for $K_{1,1}$ criteria and $K_{1,2}$, sub-criteria, in relation to the $K_{1,3}$ criterion:

1. **Determination of eigenvalues and eigenvectors**
   Using the right eigenvector method, the following eigenvalues were obtained:

$$\lambda_1 = 2, \ \lambda_2 = 0. \tag{5.76}$$

2. **Selection of eigenvector based on eigenvalues**
   is the greatest eigenvalue in terms of the absolute value. It was assumed that λ_1.
   $\lambda_{max} = \lambda_1$. The eigenvector corresponding to this eigenvalue is as follows:

$$WW_1 = \begin{bmatrix} 0.9864 \\ 0.1644 \end{bmatrix}. \tag{5.77}$$

3. **Checking the consistency of the pairwise comparison matrix**
   λ_{max} is equal to the number of compared criteria, which means that calculation of CI and CRis not necessary. CK matrix is consistent.
4. **Normalization of the selected eigenvector**
   During normalization of the eigenvector WW_1, a criteria preference matrix CK' is obtained:

$$CK' = \begin{bmatrix} 0.8571 \\ 0.1429 \end{bmatrix}. \tag{5.78}$$

5. **Entering the obtained values into the appropriate area of the supermatrix**
   Enter the obtained values in the third section in the column $K_{1,3}$:

	Cel	K_1	K_2	$K_{1,1}$	$K_{1,2}$	$K_{1,3}$	W_1	W_2	W_3
Cel									
K_1	0,5		1						
K_2	0,5	0,5890							
$K_{1,1}$		0,2570				0,8571			
$K_{1,2}$		0,1181				0,1429			
$K_{1,3}$		0,0359							
W_1			x	x	x	x	1		
W_2			x	x	x	x		1	
W_3			x	x	x	x			1

(5.79)

Block 6, section 1. In the sixth block (column K_2), three x signs are entered. Therefore, W_1, W_2 variants and K_3 criterion should be compared in relation to K_2 criterion. It was assumed that the decision-maker made pairwise comparison, and as a result, the following matrix of comparisons of CK criteria was obtained:

$$CK = \begin{bmatrix} 1 & 2 & 5 \\ \frac{1}{2} & 1 & 3 \\ \frac{1}{5} & \frac{1}{3} & 1 \end{bmatrix}. \tag{5.80}$$

Determining numerical values for variants W_1, W_2 and K_3 criterion in relation to the K_2 criterion:

1. **Determination of eigenvalues and eigenvectors**
   Using the right eigenvector method, the following eigenvalues were obtained:

$$\lambda_1 = 3.0037,\ \lambda_2 = -0.0018 + i0.1053,\ \lambda_3 = -0.0018 - i0.1053. \tag{5.81}$$

2. **Eigenvector selection based on eigenvalues**
   Only the eigenvalue λ_1 is not a complex value. It was assumed that $\lambda_{max} = \lambda_1$. The eigenvector corresponding to this eigenvalue is as follows:

$$WW_1 = \begin{bmatrix} -0.8711 \\ -0.4629 \\ -0.1640 \end{bmatrix}. \tag{5.82}$$

3. **Checking the consistency of the pairwise comparison matrix**

The value of $\lambda_{\max}$ determined under CI was

$$\mathrm{CI} = \frac{\lambda_{\max} - M}{M - 1} = \frac{3.0037 - 3}{3 - 1} = 0.0012, \tag{5.83}$$

oraz CR:

$$\mathrm{CR} = \frac{\mathrm{CI}}{\mathrm{R}} = \frac{0.0012}{0.52} = 0.0024. \tag{5.84}$$

This value is less than the limit value; therefore, the $C\mathrm{K}$ matrix is consistent.

4. **Normalization of the selected eigenvector**
During normalization of the eigenvector WW_1, the $C\mathrm{K}'$ criteria preference matrix is obtained:

$$C\mathrm{K}' = \begin{bmatrix} 0.5816 \\ 0.3090 \\ 0.1095 \end{bmatrix}. \tag{5.85}$$

5. **Entering the obtained values into the appropriate area of the supermatrix**
Enter the obtained values in the third block in column K_2:

	Cel	K_1	K_2	$K_{1,1}$	$K_{1,2}$	$K_{1,3}$	W_1	W_2	W_3
Cel									
K_1	0,5		1						
K_2	0,5	0,5890							
$K_{1,1}$		0,2570				0,8571			
$K_{1,2}$		0,1181				0,1429			
$K_{1,3}$		0,0359							
W_1			0,5816	x	x	x	1		
W_2			0,3090	x	x	x		1	
W_3			0,1095	x	x	x			1

(5.86)

Block 6, section. 2. In the sixth block, column $\mathrm{K}_{1,1}$, three x signs are entered. Therefore, the variants W_1, W_2, and K_3 criterion should be compared in relation to $\mathrm{K}_{1,1}$ criterion. It was assumed that the decision-maker made pairwise comparison, and in result, the following matrix of comparisons of $C\mathrm{K}$ criteria was obtained:

$$C\mathrm{K} = \begin{bmatrix} 1 & 2 & \frac{1}{3} \\ \frac{1}{2} & 1 & \frac{1}{5} \\ 3 & 5 & 1 \end{bmatrix}. \tag{5.87}$$

Determining numerical values for variants W_1, W_2 and K_3 **criterion in relation to the** $\mathrm{K}_{1,1}$ **criterion:**

1. **Determination of eigenvalues and eigenvectors**
   Using the right eigenvector method, the following eigenvalues were obtained:

$$\lambda_1 = 3.0037,\ \lambda_2 = -0.0018 + i0.1053,\ \lambda_3 = -0.0018 - i0.1053. \tag{5.88}$$

2. **Eigenvector selection based on eigenvalues**
   Only the eigenvalue λ_1 is not a complex value. It was assumed that $\lambda_{max} = \lambda_1$ eigenvector corresponding to this eigenvalue is as follows:

$$\mathrm{WW}_1 = \begin{bmatrix} -0.3288 \\ -0.1747 \\ -0.9281 \end{bmatrix}. \tag{5.89}$$

3. **Checking the consistency of the pairwise comparison matrix**
   The value of λ_{max} determined under CI was

$$\mathrm{CI} = \frac{\lambda_{max} - M}{M - 1} = \frac{3.0037 - 3}{3 - 1} = 0.0012, \tag{5.90}$$

   and CR:

$$\mathrm{CR} = \frac{\mathrm{CI}}{\mathrm{R}} = \frac{0.0012}{0.52} = 0.0024. \tag{5.91}$$

   This value is less than the limit value, so the $C\mathrm{K}$ matrix is consistent.
4. **Normalization of the selected eigenvector**
   During normalization of the eigenvector WW_1, the $C\mathrm{K}'$ criteria preference matrix is obtained:

$$C\mathrm{K}' = \begin{bmatrix} 0.2297 \\ 0.1220 \\ 0.6483 \end{bmatrix}. \tag{5.92}$$

5. **Entering the obtained values into the appropriate area of the supermatrix**
   Enter the obtained values in the third section in the column $\mathrm{K}_{1,1}$:

	Cel	K_1	K_2	$K_{1,1}$	$K_{1,2}$	$K_{1,3}$	W_1	W_2	W_3
Cel									
K_1	0,5		1						
K_2	0,5	0,5890							
$K_{1,1}$		0,2570				0,8571			
$K_{1,2}$		0,1181				0,1429			
$K_{1,3}$		0,0359							
W_1			0,5816	0,2297	x	x	1		
W_2			0,3090	0,1220	x	x		1	
W_3			0,1095	0,6483	x	x			1

(5.93)

Block 6, section 3. In the sixth section, column $K_{1,2}$, three x signs are entered. Therefore, the variants W_1, W_2 and K_3 criterion should be compared in relation to the $K_{1,2}$ criterion. It was assumed that the decision-maker made a pairwise comparison of variants, and in result, the following comparison matrix of CK criteria was obtained:

$$CK = \begin{bmatrix} 1 & \frac{1}{2} & 4 \\ 2 & 1 & 6 \\ \frac{1}{4} & \frac{1}{6} & 1 \end{bmatrix}. \tag{5.94}$$

Determining numerical values for variants W_1, W_2 and K_3 criterion in relation to the $K_{1,2}$ criterion:

1. **Determination of eigenvalues and eigenvectors**

   Using the right eigenvector method, the following eigenvalues were obtained:

$$\lambda_1 = 3.0092,\ \lambda_2 = -0.0046 + i0.1663,\ \lambda_3 = -0.0046 - i0.1663. \tag{5.95}$$

2. **Eigenvector selection based on eigenvalues**

   Only the eigenvalue λ_1 is not a complex value. It was assumed that $\lambda_{max} = \lambda_1$. The eigenvector corresponding to this eigenvalue is as follows:

$$WW_1 = \begin{bmatrix} -0.4779 \\ -0.8685 \\ -0.1315 \end{bmatrix}. \tag{5.96}$$

3. **Checking the consistency of the pairwise comparison matrix**

   The value of λ_{max} determined under CI was

$$CI = \frac{\lambda_{max} - M}{M - 1} = \frac{3.0092 - 3}{3 - 1} = 0.0031, \tag{5.97}$$

   and CR:

$$\mathrm{CR} = \frac{\mathrm{CI}}{\mathrm{R}} = \frac{0.0031}{0.52} = 0.0059. \tag{5.98}$$

This value is smaller than the limit value, so the $C\mathrm{K}$ matrix is consistent.

4. **Normalization of the selected eigenvector**
   During normalization of the eigenvector WW_1, the $C\mathrm{K}'$ criteria preference matrix is obtained:

$$C\mathrm{K}' = \begin{bmatrix} 0.3234 \\ 0.5876 \\ 0.0890 \end{bmatrix}. \tag{5.99}$$

5. **Entering the obtained values into the appropriate area of the supermatrix**
   Enter the obtained values in the third block, column $\mathrm{K}_{1,2}$:

	Cel	K_1	K_2	$K_{1,1}$	$K_{1,2}$	$K_{1,3}$	W_1	W_2	W_3
Cel									
K_1	0,5		1						
K_2	0,5	0,5890							
$K_{1,1}$		0,2570				0,8571			
$K_{1,2}$		0,1181				0,1429			
$K_{1,3}$		0,0359							
W_1			0,5816	0,2297	0,3234	x	1		
W_2			0,3090	0,1220	0,5876	x		1	
W_3			0,1095	0,6483	0,0890	x			1

(5.100)

Block 6, section 4. In the sixth section, column $\mathrm{K}_{1,3}$, three x signs are entered. Therefore, the variants W_1, W_2 and K_3 criterion should be compared in relation to $\mathrm{K}_{1,3}$. It was assumed that the decision-maker made a pairwise comparison of variants, and in result, the following comparison matrix of $C\mathrm{K}$ criteria was obtained:

$$C\mathrm{K} = \begin{bmatrix} 1 & \frac{1}{2} & \frac{1}{4} \\ 2 & 1 & \frac{1}{3} \\ 4 & 3 & 1 \end{bmatrix}. \tag{5.101}$$

Determining numerical values for variants W_1, W_2 and K_3 criterion in relation to $\mathrm{K}_{1,3}$ criterion:

1. **Determination of eigenvalues and eigenvectors**
   Using the right eigenvector method, the following eigenvalues were obtained:

$$\lambda_1 = 3.0183,\ \lambda_2 = -0.0091 + \mathrm{i}0.2348,\ \lambda_3 = -0.0091 - \mathrm{i}0.2348. \tag{5.102}$$

2. **Eigenvector selection based on eigenvalues**

   Only the eigenvalue λ_1 is not a complex value. It was assumed that $\lambda_{\max} = \lambda_1$. The eigenvector corresponding to this eigenvalue is as follows:

$$\mathrm{WW}_1 = \begin{bmatrix} -0.1999 \\ -0.3493 \\ -0.9154 \end{bmatrix}. \tag{5.103}$$

3. **Checking the consistency of the pairwise comparison matrix**

   The value of $\lambda_{\max}$ determined under CI was

$$\mathrm{CI} = \frac{\lambda_{\max} - M}{M - 1} = \frac{3.0183 - 3}{3 - 1} = 0.0061, \tag{5.104}$$

   and CR:

$$\mathrm{CR} = \frac{\mathrm{CI}}{\mathrm{R}} = \frac{0.0061}{0.52} = 0.0117. \tag{5.105}$$

   This value is smaller than the limit value, so the $C\mathrm{K}$ matrix is consistent.

4. **Normalization of the selected eigenvector**

   During normalization of the eigenvector WW_1, the $C\mathrm{K}'$ criteria preference matrix is obtained:

$$C\mathrm{K}' = \begin{bmatrix} 0.1365 \\ 0.2385 \\ 0.6250 \end{bmatrix}. \tag{5.106}$$

5. **Entering the obtained values into the appropriate area of the supermatrix**

   Enter the obtained values in the third block in column $\mathrm{K}_{1,3}$:

	Cel	K_1	K_2	$K_{1,1}$	$K_{1,2}$	$K_{1,3}$	W_1	W_2	W_3
Cel									
K_1	0,5		1						
K_2	0,5	0,5890							
$K_{1,1}$		0,2570				0,8571			
$K_{1,2}$		0,1181				0,1429			
$K_{1,3}$		0,0359							
W_1			0,5816	0,2297	0,3234	0,1365	1		
W_2			0,3090	0,1220	0,5876	0,2385		1	
W_3			0,1095	0,6483	0,0890	0,6250			1

(5.107)

Step 4 The supermatrix obtained in this way is normalized by dividing its columns by their sums. Sums of the first column are $0.5 + 0.5 = 1$. Sums of other columns are, respectively: 1, 2, 1, 1, 2, 1, 1, 1. The normalized supermatrix will take the following form:

	Cel	K_1	K_2	$K_{1,1}$	$K_{1,2}$	$K_{1,3}$	W_1	W_2	W_3
Cel									
K_1	0,5		0,5						
K_2	0,5	0,5890							
$K_{1,1}$		0,2570				0,4285			
$K_{1,2}$		0,1181				0,0714			
$K_{1,3}$		0,0359							
W_1			0,2908	0,2297	0,3234	0,0683	1		
W_2			0,1545	0,1220	0,5876	0,1192		1	
W_3			0,0547	0,6483	0,0890	0,3125			1

(5.108)

Step 5 The normalized supermatrix was matrix-raised to the 35-th power:

	Cel	K_1	K_2	$K_{1,1}$	$K_{1,2}$	$K_{1,3}$	W_1	W_2	W_3
Cel									
K_1									
K_2									
$K_{1,1}$									
$K_{1,2}$									
$K_{1,3}$									
W_1	0,4381	0,3902	0,4859	0,2297	0,3234	0,1898	1		
W_2	0,2892	0,2826	0,2958	0,1220	0,5876	0,2135		1	
W_3	0,2727	0,3271	0,2183	0,6483	0,0890	0,5967			1

(5.109)

For the normalized one, raised to the 33 and 37 power, the result was the same. This means that the obtained values can be taken as the result. Read the value of decision variants W_1, W_2, and W_3, from the first column (Goal). These values define the compliance of decision variants with the preference of the decision-maker. Variant W_1 has obtained the highest value (0.4859). Its advantage over the other variants is significant. The decision variants W_2 and W_3 can be considered equivalent because the values obtained for them are very similar.

5.3 REMBRANDT Method

REMBRANDT method (*Ratio Estimation in Magnitudes or deci-Bells to Rate Alternatives that are Non-DominaTed*) was developed in the Netherlands by a team of scientists led by Lootsm. The hierarchical structure of the REMBRANDT method has only three levels. The goal is on the highest level, the criteria on the middle, and the decision variants on the lowest level. This method does not have the hierarchical structure of criteria themselves. It introduces a nine-point logarithmic scale modeled on the AHP method [202]:

−8. Strong advantage of variant B over A
−7. Intermediate situation
−6. Very big advantage of variant B over A
−5. Intermediate situation
−4. Big advantage of variant B over A
−3. Intermediate situation
−2. Slight advantage of variant B over A
−1. Intermediate situation
0. Comparability (equivalence)
1. Intermediate situation
2. Slight advantage of variant A over B
3. Intermediate situation
4. Big advantage of variant A over B
5. Intermediate situation
6. Very big advantage of variant A over B
7. Intermediate situation
8. Strong advantage of variant A over B

Values 1, 3, 5, 7 describe intermediate situation when a decision-maker hesitates between 0 and 2, 2 and 4, etc.

The REMBRANDT Method Algorithm

Step 1 Construction of the comparison matrix.

The results of the comparison of criteria and decision variants are entered in the pairwise comparison matrix. For objects that are dominant, a positive value is entered, and for objects that are dominated—a negative value.

Step 2 Converting the value of a pairwise comparison matrix into a geometric scale according to the formula [202]:

$$r_{i,j,k} = \exp\left(\gamma c_{i,j,k}\right), \tag{5.110}$$

where:

γ—a constant equal to $\ln 2$ during decision variants comparison and $\ln\sqrt{2}$ while criteria comparison.

The amount of $r_{i,j,k}$ k is an approximation of the preference relations estimation of individual decision variants. Values of $r_{i,j,k}$ form R_i matrix.

For example, if we take into account one evaluation criterion for three decision variants, then a pairwise comparison matrix may take the following form:

$$C_1 = \begin{bmatrix} 0 & 8 & 0 \\ -8 & 0 & -8 \\ 0 & 8 & 0 \end{bmatrix}. \tag{5.111}$$

The value of $r_{1,1,1}$ as the element of R_1 matrix will be as follows:

$$r_{1,1,1} = \exp\left(\gamma c_{1,1,1}\right) = \exp\left(\ln\sqrt{2}\cdot 0\right) = 1. \tag{5.112}$$

While the entire R_1 matrix will take the following values:

$$R_1 = \begin{bmatrix} 1 & 256 & 1 \\ 0.0039 & 1 & 0.0039 \\ 1 & 256 & 1 \end{bmatrix}. \tag{5.113}$$

Step 3 On the basis of the approximate values of the preference ratios $r_{i,j,k}$, the approximate values of the V_i preference matrix are determined (for the i-th criterion). This is achieved by minimizing the value of the expression below [202]:

$$\sum_{j=1}^{n}\sum_{k=j+1}^{n}\left(\ln r_{i,j,k} - \left(\ln v_{i,j} - \ln v_{i,k}\right)\right)^2. \tag{5.114}$$

Taking the assumption that [202]:

$$\prod_{j=1}^{n} v_{i,j} = 1, \tag{5.115}$$

we will receive the following solution [202]:

$$v_{i,j} = \exp\left(\frac{1}{n}\gamma\sum_{k=1}^{n} c_{i,j,k}\right) = \prod_{k=1}^{n} r_{i,j,k}^{\frac{1}{n}}. \tag{5.116}$$

In the example under consideration, $v_{1,1}$ takes the following value:

$$v_{1,1} = r_{1,1,1}^{\frac{1}{3}}\cdot r_{1,1,2}^{\frac{1}{3}}\cdot r_{1,1,3}^{\frac{1}{3}} = 1^{\frac{1}{3}}\cdot 256^{\frac{1}{3}}\cdot 1^{\frac{1}{3}} = 1\cdot 6.3496\cdot 1 = 6.3496, \tag{5.117}$$

while the entire V_1 matrix will have the following form:

$$V_1 = \begin{bmatrix} 6.3496 \\ 0.0248 \\ 6.3496 \end{bmatrix}. \tag{5.118}$$

Step 4 Normalization of the V_i, vector using the following formula:

$$V_i' = \frac{V_i}{\sum_{j=1}^{n} v_{i,j}}. \tag{5.119}$$

To continue, element $v_{1,1}$ of V_1 matrix after normalization will be equal to:

$$v_{1,1}' = \frac{v_{1,1}}{v_{1,1} + v_{1,2} + v_{1,3}} = \frac{6.3496}{6.3496 + 0.0248 + 6.3496} = 0.4990. \tag{5.120}$$

Complete V_1' matrix will take the following values:

$$V_1' = \begin{bmatrix} 0.4990 \\ 0.0019 \\ 0.4990 \end{bmatrix}. \tag{5.121}$$

Assuming that comparison matrices for the remaining criteria (K_1, K_2, K_3) will take the following values:

$$C_2 = \begin{bmatrix} 0 & -8 & -2 \\ 8 & 0 & 4 \\ 1 & -4 & 0 \end{bmatrix}, \ C_3 = \begin{bmatrix} 0 & 4 & 8 \\ -4 & 0 & 0 \\ -8 & 0 & 0 \end{bmatrix}, \ C_4 = \begin{bmatrix} 0 & 4 & 8 \\ -4 & 0 & 0 \\ -8 & 0 & 0 \end{bmatrix}, \tag{5.122}$$

the following matrices V_i', will be obtained:

$$V_2' = \begin{bmatrix} 0.0059 \\ 0.9564 \\ 0.0377 \end{bmatrix}, \ V_3' = \begin{bmatrix} 0.9665 \\ 0.0240 \\ 0.0095 \end{bmatrix}, \ V_4' = \begin{bmatrix} 0.9665 \\ 0.0240 \\ 0.0095 \end{bmatrix}. \tag{5.123}$$

Step 5 After calculation of V_i' matrices for the decision variants, $C\text{K}$, matrix is determined, which describes the importance of individual criteria.

For the presented example, the criteria pairwise comparison matrix can be as follows:

$$C\text{K} = \begin{bmatrix} 0 & 1 & 0 & 0 \\ -1 & 0 & -1 & -1 \\ 0 & 1 & 0 & 0 \\ 0 & 1 & 0 & 0 \end{bmatrix}. \tag{5.124}$$

Then elements of $R\text{K}$ matrix are determined according to the formula:

$$r\mathrm{K}_{j,k} = \exp\left(\gamma c\mathrm{k}_{j,k}\right) = \exp\left(\ln\sqrt{2}c\mathrm{k}_{j,k}\right). \tag{5.125}$$

For example, $r\mathrm{K}_{1,1}$ values as the elements of $R\mathrm{K}$ matrix will be as follows:

$$r\mathrm{K}_{1,1} = \exp\left(\gamma c\mathrm{k}_{1,1}\right) = \exp\left(\ln\sqrt{2}\cdot 0\right) = 1. \tag{5.126}$$

The entire $R\mathrm{K}$ matrix will take the following form:

$$R\mathrm{K} = \begin{bmatrix} 1 & 1.4142 & 1 & 1 \\ 0.7071 & 1 & 0.7071 & 0.7071 \\ 1 & 1.4142 & 1 & 1 \\ 1 & 1.4142 & 1 & 1 \end{bmatrix}. \tag{5.127}$$

Next, based on the formulas:

$$v\mathrm{K}_i = \prod_{j=1}^{m} r\mathrm{K}_{i,j}^{\frac{1}{m}}, \tag{5.128}$$

and:

$$C\mathrm{K} = \frac{V\mathrm{K}}{\sum_{i=1}^{m} v\mathrm{K}_i}, \tag{5.129}$$

the matrix $C\mathrm{K}$, describing weights of individual criteria, is determined. For the example considered, this matrix will be as follows:

$$C\mathrm{K} = \begin{bmatrix} 0.2698 \\ 0.1907 \\ 0.2698 \\ 0.2698 \end{bmatrix}. \tag{5.130}$$

Step 6 Final values of priorities for decision variants are calculated according to the formula:

$$c\mathrm{p}_i = \prod_{j=1}^{m} \left(v'_{j,i}\right)^{c\mathrm{K}_j}. \tag{5.131}$$

These values make it possible to rank the variants where the best one has the highest $c\mathrm{p}_i$ value.

For the considered example, the priority value for the first variant is

$$cp_1 = \left(v'_{1,1}\right)^{cK_1} + \left(v'_{2,1}\right)^{cK_2} + \left(v'_{3,1}\right)^{cK_3} + \left(v'_{4,1}\right)^{cK_4} =$$

$$0.4990^{0.2698} \cdot 0.0059^{0.1907} \cdot 0.9665^{0.2698} \cdot 0.9665^{0.2698} = 0.3061. \qquad (5.132)$$

The final form of CP matrix is as follows:

$$CP = \begin{bmatrix} 0.3061 \\ 0.0246 \\ 0.0360 \end{bmatrix}. \qquad (5.133)$$

The first variant turned out to be the best decision-making variant here. Taking into account the value of its priority, it has a significant advantage over the other two decision variants.

5.4 DEMATEL Method

DEMATEL method (*Decision-MAking Trial and Evaluation Laboratory*) was proposed in the 70's by Gabus and Fontela [55]. It was developed with the idea of studying cause and effect relationships. The starting point for the calculations is the cause and effect graph. An example of such a graph is presented in Fig. 5.9. Arrows show the relationship between factors or events (Z_1, Z_2, Z_3, Z_4). The direction of an arrow determines the impact (influence) of a factor. The value above the arrow is the strength of the impact. Various scales can be used to determine this power. An example scale may take the following elements [97]:

0. No dependency
1. Slight impact
2. Big impact
3. Strong impact

Algorithm of DEMANTEL Method

Step 1 Develop a cause and effect graph.

Step 2 Based on the graph, a direct impact matrix B

is built. The matrix B created for the graph in Fig. 5.9 will be as follows:

$$B = \begin{bmatrix} 0 & 2 & 3 & 0 \\ 1 & 0 & 1 & 0 \\ 0 & 0 & 0 & 2 \\ 1 & 0 & 0 & 0 \end{bmatrix}. \qquad (5.134)$$

Fig. 5.9 The example of the cause and effect graph

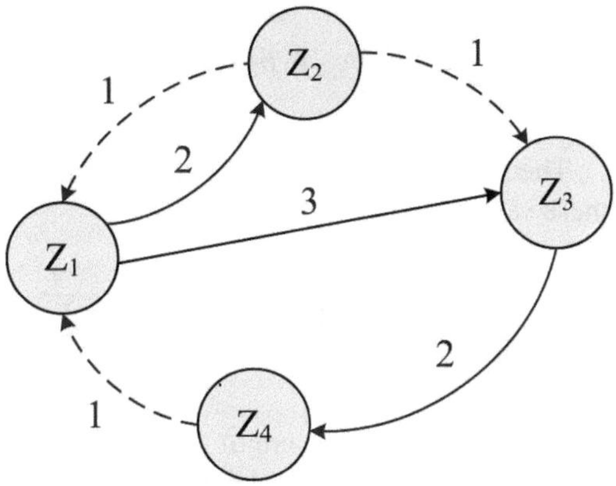

All values on the main diagonal of this matrix are always zero. They represent the impact of a given factor on each other. The other values are determined from the graph. For example, in the graph in Fig. 5.9, Z_1 has big impact on Z_2. Therefore, in a row defined by a number of the first incident (1) and a column defined by a number of the second incident (2), a value corresponding to the high impact (2) should be entered. The dependence is two way. Z_2 has little impact on Z_1, so in row two and column one, enter a value that corresponds to slight impact (1). If a dependence is one way, as between the factors Z_3 and Z_4, then the value zero is entered where there is no feedback dependence. Factor Z_4 does not have impact on Z_3; therefore, in the fourth row and third column, the zero value is entered. For factors that have no relation to each other, zeros are entered into the matrix B. For example, there is no relations between Z_2 and Z_4 factors, so in the second row and fourth column zero is entered, alike in the fourth row and second column.

Step 3 Normalization of B matrix following the formula [57]:

$$BN = \frac{1}{\lambda} B, \tag{5.135}$$

where [57]

$$\lambda = \max\left\{\max_j \sum_{i=1}^{n} b_{i,j}; \max_i \sum_{j=1}^{n} b_{i,j}\right\}. \tag{5.136}$$

To calculate λ first, the sum of columns should be determined.

In the considered example, the sum of the first column will be as follows:

$$\sum_{i=1}^{4} b_{i,1} = b_{1,1} + b_{2,1} + b_{3,1} + b_{4,1} = 0 + 1 + 0 + 1 = 2. \tag{5.137}$$

The sums of other columns are 2, 4 and 2, Z. The maximum is calculated from these values:

$$\max_j \sum_{i=1}^{4} b_{i,j} = \max\left\{\sum_{i=1}^{4} b_{i,1};\ \sum_{i=1}^{4} b_{i,2};\ \sum_{i=1}^{4} b_{i,3};\ \sum_{i=1}^{4} b_{i,4}\right\} = \max\{2;\ 2;\ 4;\ 2\} = 4. \tag{5.138}$$

To calculate λ also the sum of rows should be determined.

For the analyzed example, the sum of the first row will be

$$\sum_{j=1}^{4} b_{1,j} = b_{1,1} + b_{1,2} + b_{1,3} + b_{1,4} = 0 + 2 + 3 + 0 = 5, \tag{5.139}$$

while sums of other rows: 2, 2, and 1.

Next, the maximum is determined from these values:

$$\max_j \sum_{i=1}^{4} b_{i,j} = \max\left\{\sum_{j=1}^{4} b_{1,j};\ \sum_{j=1}^{4} b_{2,j};\ \sum_{j=1}^{4} b_{3,j};\ \sum_{j=1}^{4} b_{4,j}\right\} = \max\{5;\ 2;\ 2;\ 1\} = 5. \tag{5.140}$$

Finally, the value of λ will be

$$\lambda = \max\left\{\max_j \sum_{i=1}^{4} b_{i,j};\ \max_i \sum_{j=1}^{4} b_{i,j}\right\} = \max\{4;\ 5\} = 5. \tag{5.141}$$

Having λ, determined, matrix B can be normalized.

For example, the normalized value of $b_{i,j}$ for the first row and the second column of the matrix B is determined as follows:

$$b\mathrm{N}_{1,2} = \frac{1}{\lambda} b_{1,2} = \frac{1}{5} 2 = 0.4. \tag{5.142}$$

After repeating the calculations for all elements, the complete $B\mathrm{N}$ matrix is calculated:

$$B\mathrm{N} = \begin{bmatrix} 0 & 0.4 & 0.6 & 0 \\ 0.2 & 0 & 0.2 & 0 \\ 0 & 0 & 0 & 0.4 \\ 0.2 & 0 & 0 & 0 \end{bmatrix}. \tag{5.143}$$

The impact matrix BN is the matrix that determines only a direct impact. However, there may also be indirect influences between the factors. For example, Z_3 does not directly affect Z_1. However, it directly influence Z_4, which in turn directly affects Z_1. It follows that there is an indirect influence of Z_3 on Z_1. Matrix BNdoes not include the information about such impact, while it is included in the total impact matrix T, which is the sum of matrix BN and the indirect impact matrix $\widehat{B}$.

Step 4 The total impact matrix T is built according to the formula [97]:

$$T = B\mathrm{N} + \widehat{B}. \tag{5.144}$$

The indirect impact matrix $\widehat{B}$ is derived from the direct impact matrix BN in the matrix multiplication process. Matrix multiplication $B\mathrm{N}\cdot B\mathrm{N}$ determines the indirect influence through one factor. An example would be the influence of Z_3 on Z_1, which takes place through Z_4. Matrix multiplications $B\mathrm{N} \cdot B\mathrm{N} \cdot B\mathrm{N}$ determine indirect impact by two factors. Z_3 indirectly influences Z_2 by two factors Z_4 and Z_1.

To determine $\widehat{B}$, all the partial matrices of the intermediate impact should be summed up [57]:

$$\widehat{B} = B\mathrm{N}^2 + B\mathrm{N}^3 + \ldots = \sum_{i=2}^{\infty} B\mathrm{N}^i. \tag{5.145}$$

If we enter $\widehat{B}$ to the formula (5.144):

$$T = B\mathrm{N} + B\mathrm{N}^2 + B\mathrm{N}^3 + \ldots = \sum_{i=1}^{\infty} B\mathrm{N}^i, \tag{5.146}$$

which equals to [57]:

$$T = B\mathrm{N}\,(I - B\mathrm{N})^{-1}. \tag{5.147}$$

The indirect impact can be calculated with the formula [97]:

$$\widehat{B} = B\mathrm{N}^2\,(I - B\mathrm{N})^{-1}. \tag{5.148}$$

To determine T first $(I - B\mathrm{N})$ should be calculated.

In the considered example, it will be as follows:

$$(I - B\mathrm{N}) = \begin{bmatrix} 1 & 0 & 0 & 0 \\ 0 & 1 & 0 & 0 \\ 0 & 0 & 1 & 0 \\ 0 & 0 & 0 & 1 \end{bmatrix} - \begin{bmatrix} 0 & 0.4 & 0.6 & 0 \\ 0.2 & 0 & 0.2 & 0 \\ 0 & 0 & 0 & 0.4 \\ 0.2 & 0 & 0 & 0 \end{bmatrix} =$$

$$\begin{bmatrix} 1 & -0.4 & -0.6 & 0 \\ 0.2 & 1 & -0.2 & 0 \\ 0 & 0 & 1 & -0.4 \\ -0.2 & 0 & 0 & 1 \end{bmatrix}. \tag{5.149}$$

For the obtained matrix $(I - B\mathrm{N})$, the inverse matrix $(I - B\mathrm{N})^{-1}$ is then determined:

$$(I - B\mathrm{N})^{-1} = \begin{bmatrix} 1.1553 & 0.4621 & 0.7856 & 0.3142 \\ 0.2495 & 1.0998 & 0.3697 & 0.1479 \\ 0.0924 & 0.0370 & 1.0628 & 0.4251 \\ 0.2311 & 0.0924 & 0.1571 & 1.0628 \end{bmatrix}. \tag{5.150}$$

Next, the total impact matrix should be determined:

$$T = B\mathrm{N}\,(I - B\mathrm{N})^{-1} =$$

$$\begin{bmatrix} 0 & 0.4 & 0.6 & 0 \\ 0.2 & 0 & 0.2 & 0 \\ 0 & 0 & 0 & 0.4 \\ 0.2 & 0 & 0 & 0 \end{bmatrix} \begin{bmatrix} 1.1553 & 0.4621 & 0.7856 & 0.3142 \\ 0.2495 & 1.0998 & 0.3697 & 0.1479 \\ 0.0924 & 0.0370 & 1.0628 & 0.4251 \\ 0.2311 & 0.0924 & 0.1571 & 1.0628 \end{bmatrix} =$$

$$\begin{bmatrix} 0.1553 & 0.4621 & 0.7856 & 0.3142 \\ 0.2495 & 0.0998 & 0.3697 & 0.1479 \\ 0.0924 & 0.0370 & 0.0628 & 0.4251 \\ 0.2311 & 0.0924 & 0.1571 & 0.0628 \end{bmatrix}. \tag{5.151}$$

The values of the T matrix indicate the degree of influence of factors on each other. At the same time, it takes into account both direct and indirect impacts. Hence, one can see that all the impact values have increased. Some even to a considerable extent. For example, the influence of Z_1 on Z_4 increased from zero to 0.3142. This is because Z_1 has strong impact on Z_3 (at the level of 0.7856), and Z_3 has big impact on Z_4 (at the level of 0.4251), what consequently translates into big indirect impact of Z_1 on Z_4.

Determination of the $\widehat{B}$ matrix makes it possible to determine only indirect impacts. In the discussed example, this matrix will be as follows:

$$\widehat{B} = B\mathrm{N}^2\,(I - B\mathrm{N})^{-1} =$$

$$\begin{bmatrix} 0 & 0.4 & 0.6 & 0 \\ 0.2 & 0 & 0.2 & 0 \\ 0 & 0 & 0 & 0.4 \\ 0.2 & 0 & 0 & 0 \end{bmatrix}^2 \begin{bmatrix} 1.1553 & 0.4621 & 0.7856 & 0.3142 \\ 0.2495 & 1.0998 & 0.3697 & 0.1479 \\ 0.0924 & 0.0370 & 1.0628 & 0.4251 \\ 0.2311 & 0.0924 & 0.1571 & 1.0628 \end{bmatrix} =$$

$$\begin{bmatrix} 0.1553 & 0.0621 & 0.1856 & 0.3142 \\ 0.0495 & 0.0998 & 0.1697 & 0.1479 \\ 0.0924 & 0.0370 & 0.0628 & 0.0251 \\ 0.0311 & 0.0924 & 0.1571 & 0.0628 \end{bmatrix}. \tag{5.152}$$

Matrix $\widehat{B}$ defines indirect impacts only; therefore, values in matrix T and $\widehat{B}$ are the same wherever zero is present in BN matrix. If the collective analysis of all impacts is required, *prominence indicators* are determined for each factor.

Step 5 Calculation of prominence and relation indicators.

Prominence indicators are derived from the formula [97]:

$$t_i^+ = \sum_{j=1}^{n} t_{i,j} + \sum_{j=1}^{n} t_{j,i}, \tag{5.153}$$

while the *relation indicator* from the formula [97]:

$$t_i^- = \sum_{j=1}^{n} t_{i,j} - \sum_{j=1}^{n} t_{j,i}. \tag{5.154}$$

The prominence indicator determines the overall share of an object in the influence network. The greater it is, the more the factor influences other factors and/or the other factors influence it. The relationship indicator determines whether a factor influences the others more, or whether these factors affect it more. When it is close to zero, it means that a factor affects the others equally and the others affect it. The greater it is, the degree of its impact on others is greater, and the degree of impact of other factors on it is smaller. Conversely, the smaller it is, the degree of its influence on other factors is smaller and the degree of influence of others on this factor is greater. For the considered example, the value of the prominence indicator for the first object will be as follows:

$$t_1^+ = t_{1,1} + t_{1,2} + t_{1,3} + t_{1,4} + t_{1,1} + t_{2,1} + t_{3,1} + t_{4,1} =$$
$$0.1553+0.4621+0.7856+0.3142+0.1553+0.2495+0.0924+0.2311 = 2.4455. \tag{5.155}$$

Values of t_i^+ for other factors are $t_2^+ = 1.5582$, $t_3^+ = 1.9926$, and $t_4^+ = 1.4935$. You can see that the first factor has the greatest value of t_i^+. Therefore, it has the greatest share in creating a network of influence. It does not mean, however, that its influence is the greatest or that the influence of other factors on this factor is very strong. To determine this, the relation indicator should be defined:

$$t_1^- = t_{1,1} + t_{1,2} + t_{1,3} + t_{1,4} - t_{1,1} - t_{2,1} - t_{3,1} - t_{4,1} =$$

$$0.1553+0.4621+0.7856+0.3142-0.1553-0.2495-0.0924-0.2311 = 0.9889. \quad (5.156)$$

Values of t_i^- for other factors are $t_2^- = 0.1756$, $t_3^- = -0.7579$, and $t_4^- = -0.4067$. The first and second factors have a positive value of the relation indicator. This means that their influence on other factors is stronger than that on others. The first factor has a very high value of the prominence and relationship indicator. It follows that it has a large share in the creation of the influence network (prominence indicator) and that this share mainly consists of influencing other factors (high positive value of the relation indicator). The dependences between the prominence and relation indicators are presented on the prominence–relation graph (Fig. 5.10). They are depicted in a coordinate system where the values of prominence indicator are on the OX axis and the values of the relation indicator are on the OY axis. These factors can be found on the graph:

1. In the upper right part, they strongly influence other factors.
2. In the middle right part, they strongly influence the other factors, and other factors strongly affect them.
3. In the lower right part, other factors strongly influence them.
4. In the upper left part, they slightly influence other factors.
5. In the middle left part, they slightly influence other factors, and other factors slightly affect them.
6. In the lower left part, other factors affect them slightly.

For example, in Fig. 5.10, the first factor is located in the upper right part of the graph. This should be interpreted as having a strong impact on all other factors.

Application of the DEMATEL Method to Study the Cause and Effect Relations of Factors Influencing Investments

Using the DEMATEL method, the cause and effect relationships between macroeconomic factors influencing investments were investigated (Z_1). The following factors were analyzed:

Z_1—*Investments* (the value of investment expenditure or their share in the GDP value).

Z_2—*Economic stability*. It determines the degree of risk in the economy, including investments. It is expressed as the GDP growth rate, showing the level of economic growth. Its fluctuations testify to the instability of management conditions affecting investment processes. The investments made and the previous level of economic growth and its fluctuations are important in assessing the current economic growth. It is also influenced by the openness of the economy, which indicates the links between the economy and its external environment.

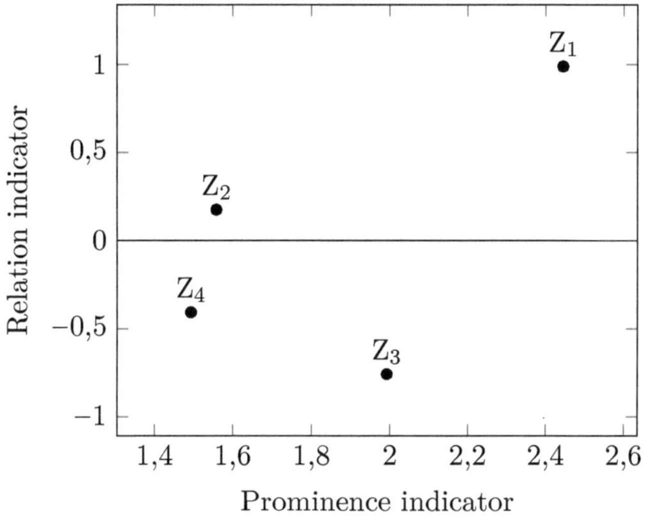

Fig. 5.10 Graph of the prominence of relations in the DEMATEL method

Z_3—*Budget policy*. It can influence investment by directly deciding on the scale of public investments. It also has an indirect impact by determining the fiscal rate. This rate shows to what extent the public sector revenues from taxes affect GDP and thus indirectly shows the tax burden on entities. Fiscal policy also influences the level of the interest rate by determining budget expenditure and the rate of redistribution of GDP, which may have the effect of crowding out private investment.

Z_4—*Monetary policy*. It primarily affects the inflation rate. The main goal of the monetary policy is to achieve and maintain the inflation rate at a certain level. This is important for investors who are guided by the inflation rate when planning long-term investments. This rate also indirectly influences investments through an increase in the interest rate (along with the increase in inflation) and the exchange rate (along with the increase in the interest rate). For open economies, the exchange rate will have a significant impact on investments.

Z_5—*Financial market development*. It can be defined by the degree of: financial intermediation, stock market capitalization, and diversification of investment financing sources. The share of corporate claims toward the banking sector in relation to GDP shows the extent to which the banking system intermediates in financing private entities. The share of stock exchange turnover in the GDP describes the development of capital market. It can be treated on one hand as the indicator of the possibility of investing free funds in financial investments, which are an alternative to real investments (e.g., treasury securities), and on the other—as the indicator showing the possibility (ease) of obtaining funds on the capital market. This may ensure an increase in the degree of diversification of investment financing sources.

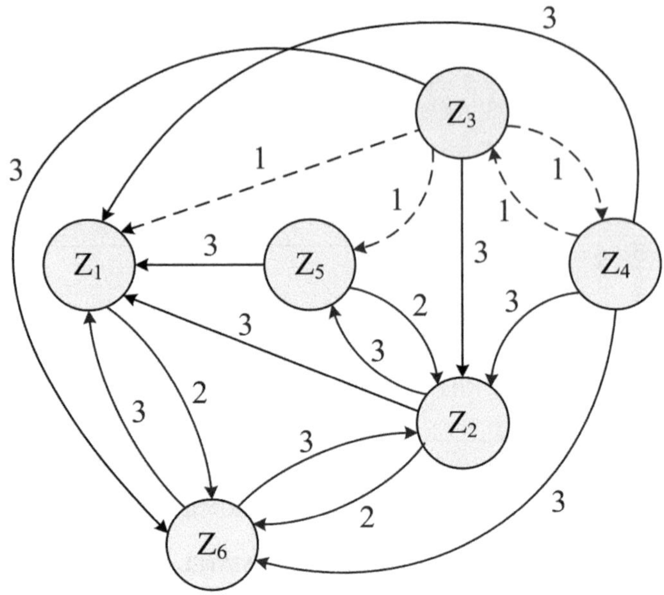

Fig. 5.11 Cause and effect graph of the impact of macroeconomic factors on investments

Z_6—*Macroeconomic situation*. Determined by the value of GDP. The value of the gross domestic product (GDP) is the indicator describing the scale of economic activity based on the result of activity of all entities in the economy. It illustrates the current state of the economy on which investment decisions depend. It is one of the factors that investors are guided by when choosing a place to invest.

Eight experts took part in the study. Each of them defined the power of factors in the scale from 0 to 3 (0 meant no direct impact, and 3—strong direct impact). On this basis, 8 partial, direct impact matrices (one for each expert) were created. From these matrices, the direct impact matrix was determined by counting the dominants:

$$B = \begin{bmatrix} 0\,0\,0\,0\,0\,2 \\ 3\,0\,0\,0\,3\,2 \\ 1\,3\,0\,1\,1\,3 \\ 3\,3\,1\,0\,0\,3 \\ 3\,2\,0\,0\,0\,0 \\ 3\,3\,0\,0\,0\,0 \end{bmatrix}. \tag{5.157}$$

Figure 5.11 shows the cause and effect graph, derived from the direct impact matrix.

Next, the direct impact matrix was subject to normalization:

$$BN = \begin{bmatrix} 0 & 0 & 0 & 0 & 0 & 0.15 \\ 0.23 & 0 & 0 & 0 & 0.23 & 0.15 \\ 0.08 & 0.23 & 0 & 0.08 & 0.08 & 0.23 \\ 0.23 & 0.23 & 0.08 & 0 & 0 & 0.23 \\ 0.23 & 0.15 & 0 & 0 & 0 & 0 \\ 0.23 & 0.23 & 0 & 0 & 0 & 0 \end{bmatrix}. \tag{5.158}$$

The normalized direct impact matrix was used to calculate the indirect impact matrix:

$$\widehat{B} = \begin{bmatrix} 0.05 & 0.04 & 0 & 0 & 0.01 & 0.01 \\ 0.13 & 0.09 & 0 & 0 & 0.02 & 0.07 \\ 0.22 & 0.12 & 0.01 & 0 & 0.08 & 0.12 \\ 0.19 & 0.12 & 0 & 0.01 & 0.09 & 0.14 \\ 0.07 & 0.02 & 0 & 0 & 0.04 & 0.07 \\ 0.09 & 0.03 & 0 & 0 & 0.06 & 0.09 \end{bmatrix}, \tag{5.159}$$

and full impact matrix:

$$T = \begin{bmatrix} 0.05 & 0.04 & 0 & 0 & 0.01 & 0.17 \\ 0.36 & 0.09 & 0 & 0 & 0.25 & 0.22 \\ 0.29 & 0.36 & 0.01 & 0.08 & 0.16 & 0.35 \\ 0.42 & 0.35 & 0.08 & 0.01 & 0.09 & 0.37 \\ 0.30 & 0.18 & 0 & 0 & 0.04 & 0.07 \\ 0.33 & 0.26 & 0 & 0 & 0.06 & 0.09 \end{bmatrix}. \tag{5.160}$$

Based on the above matrices, the cause–effect graph of the total impact was determined (Fig. 5.12). It was obtained by multiplying the total impact matrix by the normalizing factor of the direct influence matrix ($\lambda = 13$) and by creating connections between the factors in a similar way to creating the direct impact matrix from the cause–effect graph.

This graph shows that the largest impact on investments (Z_1) has monetary policy (Z_4). It is the result of the overlapping of both direct and indirect effects. The indirect impact matrix shows that budget policy has the strongest indirect impact (Z_3), with a very low direct impact at the same time.

The prominence and relation indicators were also determined:

$$T^+ = \begin{bmatrix} 2.02 \\ 2.20 \\ 1.33 \\ 1.39 \\ 1.20 \\ 2.01 \end{bmatrix}, \quad T^- = \begin{bmatrix} -1.49 \\ -0.35 \\ 1.16 \\ 1.23 \\ -0.02 \\ -0.54 \end{bmatrix}. \tag{5.161}$$

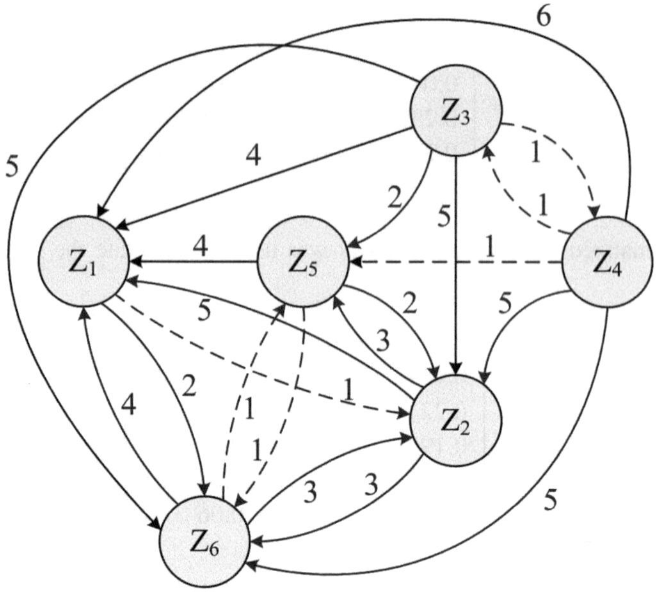

Fig. 5.12 Cause and effect graph of total impact on investment

It can be concluded from the research that there is a strong interaction between investment and other factors. The t_1^+ value of -1.49 indicates that it is mainly the other factors considered that affect investment. High t_i^+ values for the *monetary policy* (Z_4) and *budget policy* (Z_3) show that these two factors influence more other factors than such factors influence them. *Economic stability* (Z_2) and *macroeconomic situation* (Z_6) have high values of t_i^-, which means that their relation with other factors is very strong. At the same time, because they lie under the OX axis, it can be concluded that other factors affect them more than they affect other.

The investments presented in Fig. 5.13 are in the lower right corner, which means that they are strongly related to other factors and that other factors affect investments more than investments affect those factors. If investments were moved along the axis of the predominance indicator to the lower left corner of the chart, it would mean that the interaction of investments with other factors would decrease, but still other factors would have a greater impact on investments than investments on them. If, on the other hand, they were moved up the graph without changing the value of the predominance indicator, it would mean that the strength of mutual interaction between investments and other factors would not change, and other factors would have less impact on investments than investments on them.

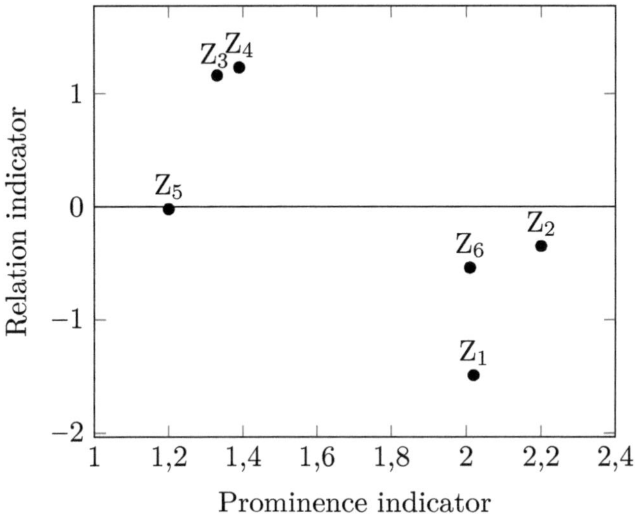

Fig. 5.13 The prominence-impact graph of the studied variables—final results of the analysis

Chapter 6
Multi-criteria Methods Using the Reference Points Approach

6.1 TOPSIS Multi-criteria Method

The TOPSIS (*Technique for Order Preference by Similarity to Ideal Solution*) method is a modification of the distance reference method developed by Hwang and Yoon [80]. It differs from the classical distance method by introducing an anti-pattern called the anti-ideal reference solution. The pattern is called the ideal reference solution. Between each decision variant and the ideal and anti-ideal solution, the distances are calculated, on the basis of which the value of the measure is determined.

The first step of the method is to normalize the variables. The authors propose various normalization methods, out of which the recommended one is such where $A_i = 0$, and B_i is given by the formula (2.77) [202]:

$$x''_{\substack{i\\j}} = \frac{x'_{\substack{i\\j}}}{\sqrt{\sum_{k=1}^{n} x'^{2}_{\substack{i\\k}}}}. \tag{6.1}$$

Then the normalized values are multiplied by the weights [202]:

$$v_{\substack{i\\j}} = x''_{\substack{i\\j}} \mathrm{w}_i. \tag{6.2}$$

The values obtained in this way are used to determine the ideal reference solution [202]:

$$v_i^+ = \begin{cases} \max\limits_{j} v_{\substack{i\\j}} & \text{for stimulants,} \\ \min\limits_{j} v_{\substack{i\\j}} & \text{for destimulants} \end{cases} \tag{6.3}$$

K. Nermend, *Multi-Criteria and Multi-Dimensional Analysis in Decisions*, Vector Optimization, https://doi.org/10.1007/978-3-031-40538-9_6

and the anti-ideal reference solution [202]:

$$v_i^- = \begin{cases} \min_j v_{i_j} & \text{for stimulants,} \\ \max_j v_{i_j} & \text{for destimulants.} \end{cases} \tag{6.4}$$

Like in the classic distance method, the distance from the reference object, i.e., the ideal reference solution, is determined [202]:

$$d_j^+ = \sqrt[p]{\sum_{i=1}^{m} \left| v_{i_j} - v_i^+ \right|^p}, \tag{6.5}$$

where

p—a constant specifying the type of metric.

Additionally, the distance from the anti-ideal reference solution is calculated [202]:

$$d_j^- = \sqrt[p]{\sum_{i=1}^{m} \left| v_{i_j} - v_i^- \right|^p}. \tag{6.6}$$

Ultimately, the value of the measure is calculated from the formula [202]:

$$S_j = \frac{d_j^-}{d_j^+ + d_j^-}. \tag{6.7}$$

The value of S_j is a number within the range from zero to one. One means the best object, while zero—the worst.

6.2 VIKOR Multi-criteria Method

The VIKOR method (an abbreviation from the Serbian language: *VIsekrzterijumska Optimizacija i Kompromisno Resenje*) [144, 145]. The great advantage of this method is the possibility of determining not only the best solution but also compromise solutions, if they exist. For this purpose, a second measure is determined that allows finding compromise solutions.

The first step of this method is normalization:

$$r_{\substack{i\\j}} = \frac{x_i'^{+} - x'_{\substack{i\\j}}}{x_i'^{+} - x_i'^{-}}. \tag{6.8}$$

Values of x'_{Li} and x'_{Pi} are taken depending on criteria. For stimulants x'_{Li} and x'_{Pi}, values are as follows [202]:

$$x_i'^{-} = \min_j \left(x'_{\substack{i\\j}} \right), \; x_i'^{+} = \max_j \left(x'_{\substack{i\\j}} \right), \tag{6.9}$$

while for destimulants [97] values are

$$x_i'^{-} = \max_j \left(x'_{\substack{i\\j}} \right), \; x_i'^{+} = \min_j \left(x'_{\substack{i\\j}} \right). \tag{6.10}$$

After normalization, the average value of the S_j measure is determined [203]:

$$S_j = \sum_{i=1}^{m} \mathrm{w}_i r_{\substack{i\\j}}, \tag{6.11}$$

and the maximum value of the measure is

$$R_j = \max_i \left(\mathrm{w}_i r_{\substack{i\\j}} \right). \tag{6.12}$$

On their basis, the comprehensive index Q_j [145, 203] is calculated:

$$Q_j = q \frac{S_j - \min_k S_k}{\max_k S_k - \min_k S_k} + (1-q) \frac{R_j - \min_k R_k}{\max_k R_k - \min_k R_k}, \tag{6.13}$$

where $q \in [0, 1]$ is a weight reflecting the validity of the majority criteria strategy, while the difference $1 - q$ determines the veto power. The following q values are assumed:

1. $q > 0.5$—if majority choice is preferred.
2. $q \approx 0.5$—if consensus preference is preferred.
3. $q < 0.5$—in case of veto choice.

The option is more favorable, the smaller the value from the Q_j metric (minimum).

The comprehensive index Q_j is the mean value of $q \in \langle 0; 1 \rangle$, values normalized to the range S_j and R_j weighted by $\langle 0; 1 \rangle$ parameter. Parameter q allows defining S_j and R_j share in the result. However, the value of this parameter cannot be too close to zero. This is because R_j differentiates objects in relation to the maximum values of their criteria. This means that the object with criteria values equal to 0, 0, 0, 10 will always be better than the object with criteria values 9, 9, 9, 9. In the ranking based on R_j, an object that meets very well only one criterion and does not meet others at all wins. Instead, the losers are those who meet all the criteria at a good level, but none at a very good level. If R_j were to be used to assess students, students would have to answer very well only one question to get a very good grade. As you can see, the spontaneous use of R_j has little practical significance. By counting the weighted average of S_j and R_j, you can raise the ranking of those objects that are outstandingly good in terms of some criterion. The lower the q value, the stronger the promotion of such features.

In the next step, the objects are ordered in relation to Q_j, S_j, and R_j. Three rankings are created this way: Q, S, and R. Then we choose the best object in the ranking Q_j (further denoted as a_1) and the following object (a_2). An acceptable advantage condition is checked for these objects [202]:

$$Q(a_2) - Q(a_1) \geq DQ, \tag{6.14}$$

where [202]

$$DQ = \frac{1}{n-1}, \tag{6.15}$$

where

n—m is the number of variants

and the condition of acceptable decision stability. The condition of the acceptable decision stability is met if the object a_1 also took the best place in the S or/and R rankings.

Three cases may occur:

1. The condition of the acceptable advantage and the condition of the acceptable decision stability are met. Variant a_1 is the best and there is no alternative.
2. The condition of the acceptable decision stability is met, but the condition of the acceptable advantage is not. Variant a_1 is the best, but variant a_2 is the alternative.
3. The condition of the acceptable advantage is not met. The condition for variants a_k from the Q ranking [202]:

$$Q(a_k) - Q(a_1) < DQ, \tag{6.16}$$

for all k in the range from 2 to n, Is checked. The first variant that satisfies the above condition is the last alternative. For example, if a_4 was the first to satisfy this condition, then the alternatives would be a_2, a_3, and a_4.

The resulting compromise solution can be accepted by the decision-maker because it provides maximum group utility (represented by min S) and minimum opposition from opponents (represented by min R).

6.3 Examples of Calculating Aggregate Measures

In the literature, the TOPSIS and VIKOR methods are classified as multi-criteria methods using reference points. However, their features are more similar to methods based on aggregate measures of multidimensional comparative analysis. The example below shows that the calculation procedure and the obtained results are very similar to the VMCM and Hellwig's methods described in Chap. 3.

Using the aggregate measures presented before, calculations were made to determine the ranking of regions in terms of the best place to live for a young person. Accordingly, the following indicators were taken into account:

x_{1j}—*university graduates under 27 years of age (the number of people per 1000 inhabitants),*

x_{2j}—*the average monthly wages and salary in relation to the average domestic (Poland = 100),*

x_{3j}—*food and non-alcoholic beverages price index.*

The index values are presented in Table 6.1. The data referred to 2013 and were available from the Central Statistical Office of Poland, from the local data bank. It was assumed that the most important index was the *average monthly wages and salary*, and hence it was assigned the highest weight. The aim is to maximize this index, so it was assigned with the character of stimulant. For other indexes, efforts are made to minimize them, which is why they obtained the character of destimulant. For the purpose of the calculation example, no variables were eliminated, and therefore $x'_{ij} = x_{ij}$.

Table 6.1 Indexes and decision variants used to select a region for a young person to live in (source: the Central Statistical Office)

Decision variant	x_{1j}	x_{2j}	x_{3j}
Central region	0.6238	116.5	102.0
South region	0.7734	99.2	102.4
East region	1.2976	87.3	101.8
North–West region	0.6175	90.0	102.1
South–West region	0.5998	97.8	102.2
North region	0.6689	91.1	101.9
Weights	0.25	0.5	0.25
Type of criterion	Destimulant	Stimulant	Destimulant

Table 6.2 Index values after normalization for data from Table 6.1

Decision variant	x_{1j}	x_{2j}	x_{3j}
Central region	0.3175	0.4880	0.4080
South region	0.3937	0.4155	0.4096
East region	0.6605	0.3657	0.4072
North–West region	0.3143	0.3770	0.4084
South–West region	0.3053	0.4096	0.4088
North region	0.3405	0.3816	0.4076

Table 6.3 Index values after normalization and multiplication by weights for data from Table 6.1

Decision variant	x_{1j}	x_{2j}	x_{3j}
Central region	0.0794	0.2440	0.1020
South region	0.0984	0.2078	0.1024
East region	0.1651	0.1828	0.1018
North–West region	0.0786	0.1885	0.1021
South–West region	0.0763	0.2048	0.1022
North region	0.0851	0.1908	0.1019

Example 1 The first method by which the ranking was created is the TOPSIS method. First, the indexes were normalized. For example, for the first object and the first index, it will be calculated as follows:

$$x''_{1_1} = \frac{x'_{1_1}}{\sqrt{x'^2_{1_1} + x'^2_{1_2} + x'^2_{1_3} + x'^2_{1_4} + x'^2_{1_5} + x'^2_{1_6}}} = \frac{0,6238}{\sqrt{0.6238^2 + 0.7734^2 + 1.2976^2 + 0.6175^2 + 0.5998^2 + 0.6689^2}} = 0.3175. \tag{6.17}$$

All values after normalization are presented in Table 6.2.

In the next step, the normalized index values are multiplied by weights:

$$v_{1_1} = x''_{1_1} w_1 = 0.3175 \cdot 0.25 = 0.0794. \tag{6.18}$$

The results of this multiplication are presented in Table 6.3.

Then the ideal reference solution is determined. The first index is a destimulant. Thus, v_1^+ is the minimum out of all the index values, while v_1^- is the maximum value:

$$v_1^+ = \min_j v_{1_j} = 0.0763,\ v_1^- = \max_j v_{1_j} = 0.1651. \tag{6.19}$$

The second index is a stimulant. Thus v_2^+ is the maximum value of all index values, while v_2^- is the minimum:

$$v_2^+ = \max_j v_{2j} = 0.2440,\ v_2^- = \min_j v_{3j} = 0.1828. \tag{6.20}$$

Values of v_3^+ and v_3^- are the following:

$$v_3^+ = \min_j v_{3j} = 0.1018,\ v_3^- = \max_j v_{3j} = 0.1024. \tag{6.21}$$

In the next step, distances from the ideal reference solution are determined. For the first object, at $p = 2$, it will be

$$d_1^+ = \sqrt{\left(v_{1\,1} - v_1^+\right)^2 + \left(v_{2\,1} - v_2^+\right)^2 + \left(v_{3\,1} - v_3^+\right)^2} =$$
$$\sqrt{(0.0794 - 0.0763)^2 + (0.2440 - 0.2440)^2 + (0.1020 - 0.1018)^2} = 0.0031. \tag{6.22}$$

The other d_j^+ values are

$$d_2^+ = 0.0424,\ d_3^+ = 0.1078,\ d_4^+ = 0.0555,\ d_5^+ = 0.0392,\ d_6^+ = 0.0539. \tag{6.23}$$

Then the distances from the anti-ideal reference solution are determined. For the first object, at $p = 2$, it will be

$$d_1^- = \sqrt{\left(v_{1\,1} - v_1^-\right)^2 + \left(v_{2\,1} - v_2^-\right)^2 + \left(v_{3\,1} - v_3^-\right)^2} =$$
$$\sqrt{(0.0794 - 0.1651)^2 + (0.2440 - 0.1828)^2 + (0.1020 - 0.1024)^2} = 0.1053. \tag{6.24}$$

Succeeding d_j^- values are $d_2^- = 0.0712$, $d_3^- = 0.0006$, $d_4^- = 0.0867$, $d_5^- = 0.0915$, and $d_6^- = 0.0804$. At the end, S_j value is calculated:

$$S_1 = \frac{d_1^-}{d_1^+ + d_1^-} = \frac{0.1053}{0.0031 + 0.1053} = 0.9718. \tag{6.25}$$

Table 6.4 Calculated $\underset{j}{r_i}$ values for data from Table 6.1

Decision variant	$\underset{j}{x_1}$	$\underset{j}{x_2}$	$\underset{j}{x_3}$
Central region	0.0343	0	0.3333
South region	0.2487	0.5925	1
East region	1	1	0
North–West region	0.0253	0.9075	0.5
South–West region	0	0.6404	0.6667
North region	0.0989	0.8699	0.1667

S_j values for the rest of objects are as follows: $S_2 = 0.6266$, $S_3 = 0.0055$, $S_4 = 0.6096$, $S_5 = 0.7002$, and $S_6 = 0.5986$. The first object, i.e., the central region, turned out to be the best object.

Example 2 The second method by which the aggregate measure was calculated is VIKOR. First, the value of $\underset{1}{r_1}$ was determined:

$$\underset{1}{r_1} = \frac{x_1^{\prime +} - \underset{1}{x_1^{\prime}}}{x_1^{\prime +} - x_1^{\prime -}}. \tag{6.26}$$

$\underset{1}{X}$ index is a destimulant, and then

$$x_1^{\prime -} = \max_j \left(\underset{j}{x_1^{\prime}} \right) = 1.2976, \quad x_1^{\prime +} = \min_j \left(\underset{j}{x_1^{\prime}} \right) = 0.5998. \tag{6.27}$$

Hence, $\underset{1}{r_1}$ is

$$\underset{1}{r_1} = \frac{0.5998 - 0.6238}{0.5998 - 1.2976} = \frac{-0.0240}{-0.6978} = 0.0343. \tag{6.28}$$

All determined $\underset{i}{r_j}$ values are presented in Table 6.4.

The mean value of the measure for the first object is equal to

$$S_1 = w_1 \underset{1}{r_1} + w_2 \underset{1}{r_2} + w_3 \underset{1}{r_3} = 0.25 \cdot 0.0343 + 0.5 \cdot 0 + 0.25 \cdot 0.3333 = 0.0919. \tag{6.29}$$

For the rest of the objects, S_j values will be $S_2 = 0.6084$, $S_3 = 0.75$, $S_4 = 0.5851$, $S_5 = 0.4869$, and $S_6 = 0.5013$.

The maximum value of the measure for the first object is as follows:

$$R_1 = \max\left(\mathrm{w}_1 r_1^1; \mathrm{w}_2 r_2^1; \mathrm{w}_3 r_3^1\right) =$$

$$\max(0.25 \cdot 0.0343; 0.5 \cdot 0; 0.25 \cdot 0.3333) = 0.0833. \quad (6.30)$$

R_j values for the rest of objects are equal to $R_2 = 0.2962$, $R_3 = 0.5$, $R_4 = 0.4538$, $R_5 = 0.3202$, and $R_6 = 0.4349$.

Comprehensive indexes of the minimum and maximum S_j and R_j values for the first object are

$$\min_k(S_k) = 0.0919,\ \max_k(S_k) = 0.75,\ \min_k(R_k) = 0.0833,\ \max_k(R_k) = 0.5. \quad (6.31)$$

The comprehensive index at $q = 0.6$ will be equal to

$$Q_1 = 0.6 \frac{S_1 - \min_k S_k}{\max_k S_k - \min_k S_k} + (1 - 0.6) \frac{R_1 - \min_k R_k}{\max_k R_k - \min_k R_k} =$$

$$0.6 \frac{0.0919 - 0.0919}{0.75 - 0.0919} + 0.4 \frac{0.0833 - 0.0833}{0.5 - 0.0833} = 0. \quad (6.32)$$

For other objects, Q_j values will be as follows: $Q_2 = 0.6753$, $Q_3 = 1$, $Q_4 = 0.8053$, $Q_5 = 0.5875$, and $Q_6 = 0.7108$.

In this example, the first option, the central region, turned out to be the best decision-making variant. Then it is checked whether there is an acceptable alternative to this variant, i.e., the condition of an acceptable advantage between it and the next variant in the ranking. In this case, it is the fifth option, i.e., the South-West region. Furthermore, DQ parameter is calculated:

$$DQ = \frac{1}{n-1} = \frac{1}{6-1} = 0.2. \quad (6.33)$$

The condition for an acceptable advantage will be as follows:

$$0.5875 - 0 \geq 0.2. \quad (6.34)$$

It is met, and therefore there is no alternative for the first variant.

Example 3 The third method by which the ranking was created is the Hellwig method. The normalization was performed with A_i being the mean value (2.79) and B_i—the standard deviation (2.49). A_i for the first indicator is equal to

$$A_1 = \bar{x}_1' = \frac{x_{1_1}' + x_{1_2}' + x_{1_3}' + x_{1_4}' + x_{1_5}' + x_{1_6}'}{6} =$$

Table 6.5 Index values after normalization for data from Table 6.1

Decision variant	$x_{1\,j}$	$x_{2\,j}$	$x_{3\,j}$
Central region	−0.5193	1.8382	−0.3086
South region	0.0367	0.2088	1.5430
East region	1.9852	−0.9120	−1.2344
North–West region	−0.5426	−0.6577	0.1543
South–West region	−0.6083	0.0769	0.6172
North region	−0.3517	−0.5541	−0.7715

$$\frac{0.6238 + 0.7734 + 1.2976 + 0.6175 + 0.5998 + 0.6689}{6} = 0.7635. \quad (6.35)$$

B_i for the first indicator is equal to

$$B_1 = \sqrt{\frac{\left(\underset{1}{x'_1} - \bar{x}'_1\right)^2 + \left(\underset{1}{x'_2} - \bar{x}'_2\right)^2 + \ldots + \left(\underset{1}{x'_6} - \bar{x}'_6\right)^2}{5}} =$$

$$\sqrt{\frac{(0.6238 - 0.7635)^2 + (0.7734 - 0.7635)^2 + \ldots + (0.6689 - 0.7635)^2}{5}} =$$

$$0.2691. \quad (6.36)$$

Normalization of the first index of the first object will be as follows:

$$\underset{1}{x''_1} = \frac{\underset{1}{x''_1} - A_1}{B_1} = \frac{0.6238 - 0.7635}{0.2691} = -0.5193. \quad (6.37)$$

All values after normalization are presented in Table 6.5.

In the next step, the values of the normalized indexes are multiplied by weights:

$$\underset{1}{x'''_1} = \underset{1}{x''_1} w_1 = -0.5193 \cdot 0.25 = -0.1298. \quad (6.38)$$

The results of this operation are presented in Table 6.6.

The next step is to determine a pattern. The first index is a destimulant. Thus $\underset{w}{x'''_1}$ is the minimum of the all index values:

$$\underset{w}{x'''_1} = \min_j \underset{j}{x'''_1} = -0.1521. \quad (6.39)$$

The second index is a stimulant. Therefore, $\underset{w}{x'''_2}$ is the maximum value:

Table 6.6 Index values after normalization and multiplication by weights for data from Table 6.1

Decision variant	x_{1j}	x_{2j}	x_{3j}
Central region	−0.1298	0.9191	−0.0772
South region	0.0092	0.1044	0.3858
East region	0.4963	−0.4560	−0.3086
North–West region	−0.1357	−0.3289	0.0386
South–West region	−0.1521	0.0385	0.1543
North region	−0.0879	−0.2771	−0.1929

$$x'''_{2\mathrm{w}} = \max_j x'''_{2j} = 0.9191. \tag{6.40}$$

The value of $x'''_{3\mathrm{w}}$ is

$$x'''_{3\mathrm{w}} = \min_j x'''_{3j} = -0.3086. \tag{6.41}$$

The Euclidean metric was used as a distance measure (3.15). The measure value for the first object is

$$\mathrm{m_s}_1 = \sqrt{\left(x'''_{11} - x'''_{1\mathrm{w}}\right)^2 + \left(x'''_{21} - x'''_{2\mathrm{w}}\right)^2 + \left(x'''_{31} - x'''_{3\mathrm{w}}\right)^2} =$$
$$\sqrt{(-0.1298 + 0.1521)^2 + (0.9191 - 0.9191)^2 + (-0.0772 + 0.3086)^2} = 0.2325. \tag{6.42}$$

Values of $\mathrm{m_s}_j$ for the other objects are $\mathrm{m_s}_2 = 1.0825$, $\mathrm{m_s}_3 = 1.5203$, $\mathrm{m_s}_4 = 1.2955$, $\mathrm{m_s}_5 = 0.9949$, and $\mathrm{m_s}_6 = 1.2035$.

Then the mean value of $\mathrm{m_s}_j$ is determined:

$$\overline{\mathrm{m}}_{\mathrm{s}0} = \frac{\mathrm{m_s}_1 + \mathrm{m_s}_2 + \mathrm{m_s}_3 + \mathrm{m_s}_4 + \mathrm{m_s}_5 + \mathrm{m_s}_6}{6} =$$
$$\frac{0.2325 + 1.0825 + 1.5203 + 1.2955 + 0.9949 + 1.2035}{6} = 1.0549 \tag{6.43}$$

and its standard deviation $\mathrm{m_s}_j$:

$$\sigma_{m_{s0}} = \sqrt{\frac{\left(\underset{1}{m_s} - \overline{m}_{s0}\right)^2 + \left(\underset{2}{m_s} - \overline{m}_{s0}\right)^2 + \ldots + \left(\underset{6}{m_s} - \overline{m}_{s0}\right)^2}{5}} =$$

$$\sqrt{\frac{(0.2325 - 1.0549)^2 + (1.0825 - 1.0549)^2 + \ldots + (1.2035 - 1.0549)^2}{5}} =$$

$$0.4421. \tag{6.44}$$

Next, the m_{s0} value is calculated:

$$m_{s0} = \overline{m}_{s0} + 2\sigma_{m_{s0}} = 1.0549 + 2 \cdot 0.4421 = 1.9390. \tag{6.45}$$

Eventually, the measure value for the first object will be

$$\underset{1}{m_{sn}} = 1 - \frac{\underset{1}{m_s}}{m_{s0}} = 1 - \frac{0.2325}{1.9390} = 0.8801. \tag{6.46}$$

The measure values for the remaining objects are as follows: $\underset{2}{m_{sn}} = 0.4417$, $\underset{3}{m_{sn}} = 0.2160$, $\underset{4}{m_{sn}} = 0.3319$, $\underset{5}{m_{sn}} = 0.4869$, and $\underset{6}{m_{sn}} = 0.3794$. Again, the first object, i.e., the central region, was found to be the best one.

The last method used for ranking was the VMCM method. Data describing one decision variant are treated here as vector coordinates. Thus, the first variant (central region) is represented by the vector $\underset{1}{X}$, the second by the vector $\underset{2}{X}$, etc. The criteria normalization and their weighting were carried out identically as in Hellwig's method. As a result of the normalization and weighting of variables, a set of vectors was created $\underset{j}{X'''}$ (Table 6.6).

In the next step, vectors representing pattern and antipattern are selected. The first and the third quartiles of indexes were adopted as the coordinates of the pattern and anti-pattern. The first index is a destimulant. The first coordinate of the pattern is thus the value of the first quartile. In general, we may say that the *first quartile* (*the first quartile value*) is the value of a number that divides the set of numbers so that 1/4 of the numbers are greater and 3/4 are smaller. Similarly, the *third quartile* (*the third quartile value*) is the value of a number that divides the set of numbers so that 3/4 of the numbers are smaller and 1/4 are greater than this quartile [224]. In computer technology, for practical reasons, quartiles are calculated on the basis of quantiles. This is because quartile counting software packages also counts quantiles, and the calculation of quartiles and quantiles is very similar. According to the programming best practices, in order not to duplicate the program code, it is recommended in this case that the functions counting quartiles use functions that count the quantiles. A p-th *quantile* is the value of a number that divides the set of numbers in such a way that $p \cdot 100\%$ of numbers have greater values and

$(1-p) \cdot 100\%$ smaller values than such number. The quartiles can be defined from the quantiles as follows: the first quartile is the 0.25, quantile, and the third quartile is the 0.75 quantile.

Despite such an unambiguous definition of quartiles, there are many ways to calculate them [111]. Hence, by using different software packages, you can get different results. In Excel, the position of the p-quantile is calculated as follows [111]:

$$\text{pozKw}_p = (n-1)\,p + 1. \tag{6.47}$$

If pozKw_p is an integer, it points directly to the position of an element p-th quantile in a set of sorted values. If it is non-integer, then the p-th quantile is computed as the weighted average of two adjacent numbers. Non-integer part of pozKw_p is used as a weight here.

In the considered example, to find the first quartile for the first index, all values are sorted and will have the following order: −0.1521, −0.1357, −0.1298, −0.0879, 0.0092, 0.4963. For the first quartile, the quantile order is, 0.25, so its position is the following:

$$\text{pozKw}_{0.25} = (6-1) \cdot 0.25 + 1 = 2.25. \tag{6.48}$$

The value 2.25 is not an integer, so the first quartile is derived from items 2 and 3. The weight for the first item, i.e., number two, is $1-0.25$, and for the item number three it is 0.25. The value of $\underset{\mathrm{w}}{x_1'''}$, as the first quartile, is

$$\underset{\mathrm{w}}{x_1'''} = -0.1357 \cdot (1-0.25) + (-0.1298)\,0.25 = -0.1342. \tag{6.49}$$

The Mathematica and Matlab programs utilized to compute quantiles use the method proposed by Hazen [72]. The position of the p-th quantile in this method is determined as follows [111]:

$$\text{pozKw}_p = np + 0.5. \tag{6.50}$$

Further procedure is the same as in the previously described method. In the considered example, for the first quartile, the order of the quantile is 0.25, so the position of the first quartile is as follows:

$$\text{pozKw}_{0.25} = 6 \cdot 0.25 + 0.5 = 2. \tag{6.51}$$

The value of 2 is the integer, so $\underset{\mathrm{w}}{x_1'''}$, as the first quartile, is equal to

$$\underset{\mathrm{w}}{x_1'''} = -0.1357. \tag{6.52}$$

If $\text{pozKw}_{0.25}$ was not an integer, the procedure is analogous to the method of calculating quartiles presented earlier.

The second index is a stimulant. The second coordinate of a pattern is therefore the value of the third quartile. Index value after sorting will be as follows: −0.4560, −0.3289, −0.2771, 0.03854, 0.1044, 0.9191. The position of the third quartile is

$$\text{pozKw}_{0.75} = 6 \cdot 0.75 + 0.5 = 5. \tag{6.53}$$

The value of 5 is the integer, so the value of $\underset{\text{w}}{x_2'''}$ being the third quartile is

$$\underset{\text{w}}{x_2'''} = -0.1044. \tag{6.54}$$

The third coordinate of a pattern is $\underset{\text{w}}{x_3'''} = -0.1929$.

When coordinates of a pattern are defined, coordinates of an anti-pattern are determined. For stimulants, the coordinates of an anti-pattern are the first quartile and for destimulants the third quartile:

$$\underset{\text{aw}}{x_1'''} = 0.0092,\ \underset{\text{aw}}{x_2'''} = -0.3289,\ \underset{\text{aw}}{x_3'''} = 0.1543. \tag{6.55}$$

After the pattern and anti-pattern are established, the value of the measure is calculated. For the first object, it will be

$$\underset{1}{\text{m}_\text{s}} = \frac{\left(\underset{1}{x_1'''} - \underset{\text{aw}}{x_1'''}\right)\left(\underset{\text{w}}{x_1'''} - \underset{\text{aw}}{x_1'''}\right) + \ldots + \left(\underset{1}{x_3'''} - \underset{\text{aw}}{x_3'''}\right)\left(\underset{\text{w}}{x_3'''} - \underset{\text{aw}}{x_3'''}\right)}{\left(\underset{\text{w}}{x_1'''} - \underset{\text{aw}}{x_1'''}\right)^2 + \left(\underset{\text{w}}{x_2'''} - \underset{\text{aw}}{x_2'''}\right)^2 + \left(\underset{\text{w}}{x_3'''} - \underset{\text{aw}}{x_3'''}\right)^2}, \tag{6.56}$$

hence

$$\underset{1}{\text{m}_\text{s}} = \frac{(-0.1298 - 0.0092)\,(-0.1357 - 0.0092) + \ldots}{(-0.1357 - 0.0092)^2 + (-0.1044 + 0.3289)^2 + (-0.1929 - 0.1543)^2} = 1.9476. \tag{6.57}$$

The measure values for the rest of decision variants are as follows: $\underset{2}{\text{m}_\text{s}} = 0.3261$, $\underset{3}{\text{m}_\text{s}} = 0.1065$, $\underset{4}{\text{m}_\text{s}} = 0.1858$, $\underset{5}{\text{m}_\text{s}} = 0.5543$, and $\underset{6}{\text{m}_\text{s}} = 0.4770$.

As in the other methods, the first variant turned out to be the best decision-making option. Figure 6.1 shows the results in the form of a map with the measurement

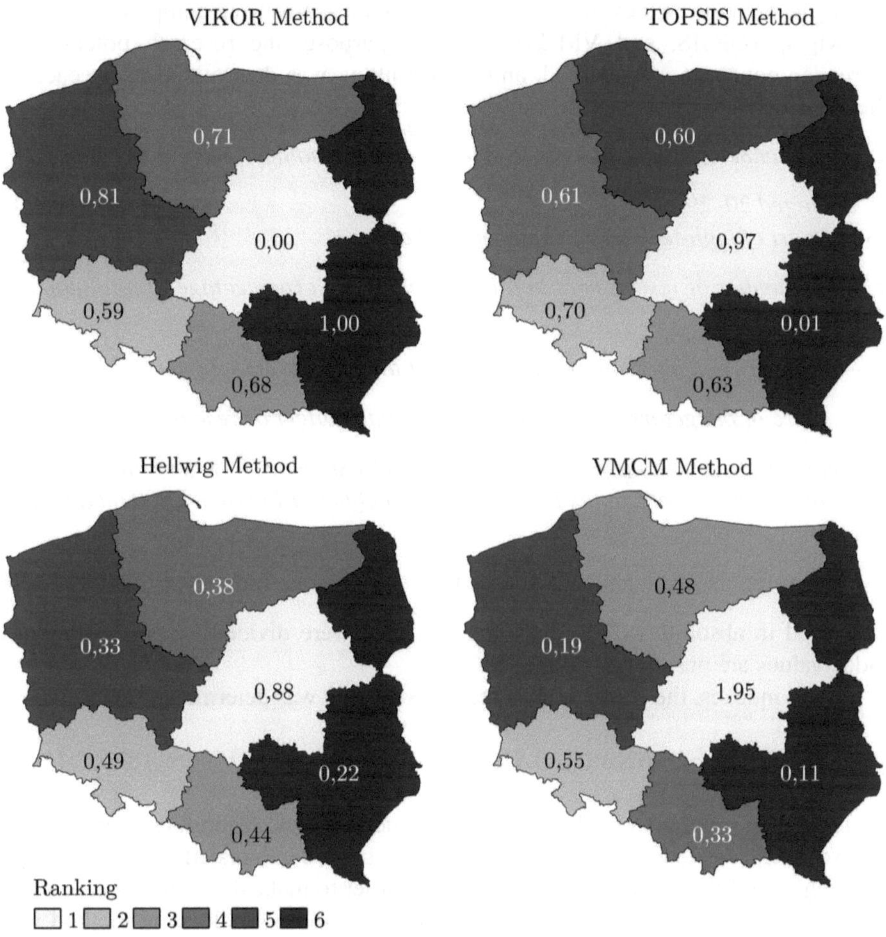

Fig. 6.1 Ranking results for VIKOR, TOPSIS, Hellwig's, and VMCM's methods

values for individual objects. The position in the ranking is distinguished by colors. The best variant is highlighted by the brightest color and the worst by the darkest. You can see that the results are very similar. In all rankings, the worst and the best decision variants are the same. This is due to the fact that the index values differ significantly from the others. The best region—i.e., central one—includes the capital, where the headquarters and centers of many companies aimed at Poland and Central Europe are located, which makes the job offer for young people much better than in other regions. The worst region is the eastern region. It is a poorly industrialized region with a strong agricultural character, which means that the cost of living here is the lowest. The labor market is also very specific, giving young people the chance to work only in a small number of professions.

Example 4 In the next example, four aggregate measures were compared: VIKOR, Hellwig's, TOPSIS, and VMCM. For this purpose, the research potential of European countries was studied, and their ranking was determined using each of these methods. Six indicators were selected for the study:

x_j^1—*the number of PhD students in science and technology (percentage of population aged 20–29),*
x_j^2—*export of high-tech (percentage of total export),*
x_j^3—*the number of researchers in full time equivalent (percentage of total population),*
x_j^4—*turnover from innovation (percentage of total turnover),*
x_j^5— *share of budgetary resources, from the state budget or research and development costs(percentage of total expenditures by state or local governments),*
x_j^6—*patent applications to the European Patent Office (EPO) per 1,000 inhabitants.*

Data refer to 2012 and are sourced from Eurostat. Indexes x_j^2 and x_j^6 were expressed in absolute values, and therefore they were divided by population. All index values are presented in Table 6.7.

For all indexes, the coefficient of feature variation was determined (2.1):

$$V_1 = 0.67,\ V_2 = 0.62,\ V_3 = 0.51,\ V_4 = 0.35,\ V_5 = 0.38,\ V_6 = 1.18. \qquad (6.58)$$

They take values well above the recommended 0.1. Therefore, none of the indexes was rejected. Then, the measure values were calculated for the VIKOR, Hellwig's, TOPSIS, and VMCM methods. In order to make the results independent of the choice of the standardization method, the same normalization method was adopted for Hellwig's, TOPSIS, and VMCM methods. It was assumed that A_i is the mean value (2.79) and B_i standard deviation (2.49). Only the VIKOR method, due to its character, had the normalization method proposed by its author. In the VIKOR method, the parameter q was assumed to be 0.6. In VMCM, the pattern and anti-pattern were determined based on quartiles. The calculation results are presented in Table 6.8.

The results obtained are quite similar to each other. In Table 6.8, the three countries obtaining the best measure values are marked in gray. These countries more or less repeat one another. The largest deviations were shown by the Vikor metoa and the Hellwig method. In the Vikor method, the top three countries did not include Sweden, which ranked only sixth. Of the four methods considered, this is the lowest place achieved. In the Hellwig method, the worst-performing Germany ranked as high as tenth. This is a rather unexpected result, due to the fact that in the other methods they were at the top by taking mostly first and second places. Looking at Figs. 6.2 and 6.3, one can see that the general trends for all methods are

Table 6.7 Index values used to study the scientific and research potential of European countries (source of Eurostat data)

Decision variant	x_{1j}	x_{2j}	x_{3j}	x_{4j}	x_{5j}	x_{6j}
Belgium	0.4	8.6	0.39	11.2	1.17	0.13564
Bulgaria	0.2	3.8	0.15	4.2	0.70	0.00463
Czech Republic	0.9	16.1	0.32	13.4	1.47	0.02206
Denmark	0.5	9.4	0.73	13.9	1.71	0.23574
Germany	1.0	14.2	0.44	13.0	1.98	0.27267
Estonia	0.7	14.1	0.35	7.8	2.08	0.01790
Greece	0.6	3.2	0.22	11.8	0.70	0.00919
Spain	0.2	5.0	0.27	14.3	1.24	0.03245
France	0.4	20.0	0.40	13.5	1.28	0.14000
Croatia	0.2	7.2	0.16	10.0	1.54	0.00453
Italy	0.2	6.4	0.19	11.0	1.08	0.07278
Cyprus	0.2	11.7	0.10	11.4	0.86	0.00289
Latvia	0.3	6.4	0.19	5.0	0.40	0.01333
Lithuania	0.3	5.8	0.27	5.5	0.99	0.01089
Luxembourg	0.3	27.1	0.47	7.9	1.48	0.12696
Hungary	0.2	17.3	0.24	9.7	0.70	0.02094
Malta	0.0	29.6	0.20	10.2	0.66	0.01309
The Netherlands	0.2	18.8	0.43	11.8	1.54	0.20229
Austria	0.7	12.8	0.47	9.8	1.52	0.22099
Poland	0.2	6.0	0.18	6.3	0.83	0.01269
Portugal	0.6	3.3	0.40	12.4	1.89	0.01066
Romania	0.2	6.3	0.09	5.4	0.59	0.00357
Slovenia	0.7	5.2	0.43	10.5	1.10	0.06159
Slovakia	0.6	8.2	0.28	19.6	1.02	0.00823
Finland	1.3	7.3	0.75	11.1	1.84	0.30252
Sweden	0.7	12.8	0.52	6.1	1.61	0.32414
Great Britain	0.4	17.4	0.40	14.1	1.17	0.08459

preserved. One can see a division of Europe into Western Europe (excluding Spain and Portugal) and Northern Europe with high scientific potential and Eastern and Southern Europe with medium or low potential, with Eastern Europe in particular having low potential. The Hellwig method recorded the most outliers. This is mainly due to the lack of sites belonging to the fourth class.

6.4 Multi-criteria Preference Vector Method (PVM)

The PVM method can be classified as the one of the group of methods (e.g., TOPSIS, VIKOR, and TMAI) which have common features of methods in the field of multidimensional comparative analysis and multi-criteria decision analysis. They are characterized by the fact that the participation of a decision-maker is limited

Table 6.8 Measure values based on data from Table 6.7

Method	VIKOR	Hellwig's	TOPSIS	VMCM
Belgium	0,52	0,52	0,39	0,58
Bulgaria	1,00	0,21	0,06	-0,23
Czech Republic	0,58	0,32	0,28	0,91
Denmark	0,28	0,73	0,63	1,21
Germany	0,05	0,38	0,76	1,38
Estonia	0,62	0,29	0,24	0,79
Greece	0,86	0,25	0,17	0,24
Spain	0,74	0,30	0,14	0,38
France	0,32	0,55	0,43	0,88
Croatia	0,84	0,24	0,10	0,25
Italy	0,73	0,37	0,21	0,23
Cyprus	0,84	0,23	0,11	0,14
Latvia	0,98	0,23	0,10	-0,16
Lithuania	0,88	0,24	0,11	0,06
Luxembourg	0,39	0,51	0,42	0,86
Hungary	0,79	0,28	0,17	0,25
Malta	0,80	0,26	0,24	0,33
The Netherlands	0,46	0,65	0,54	0,88
Austria	0,23	0,69	0,62	0,97
Poland	0,91	0,24	0,08	-0,06
Portugal	0,70	0,28	0,20	0,70
Romania	1,00	0,21	0,07	-0,22
Slovenia	0,67	0,37	0,27	0,57
Slovakia	0,64	0,27	0,19	0,70
Finland	0,25	0,81	0,78	1,54
Sweden	0,43	0,76	0,76	1,00
Great Britain	0,42	0,43	0,31	0,78

to the necessary minimum, and thus, a decision-making process can be largely automated. The possibility of operating on qualitative data has been added to the PVM method, applying for this purpose the pairwise comparison matrices used in the AHP method.

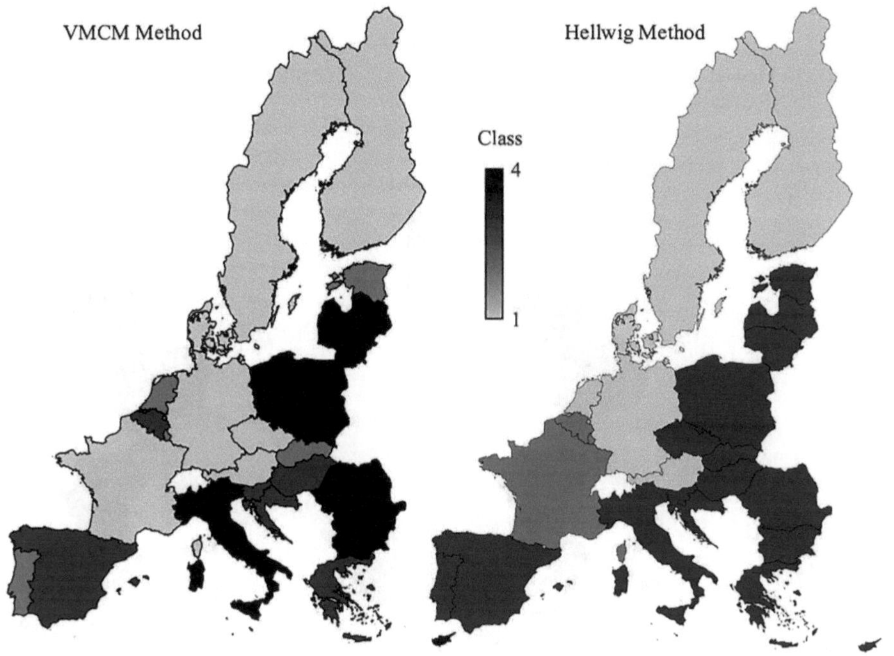

Fig. 6.2 Ranking results for Hellwig's and the VMCM method

6.4.1 Description of the Preference Vector Method (PVM)

The author's PVM (*Preference Vector Method*) method was first described in the Indian Journal of Fundamental and Applied Life Sciences in, Indian Journal of Fundamental and Applied Life Sciences" in 2014. [137]. A detailed mathematical description of the method was presented in the "Statistical Review" in 2015 [136]. The Preference Vector Method constitutes development of the Vector Measure Construction Method and is a tool for solving multi-criteria decision-making problems. When solving decision-making problems by means of the PVM, the decision-maker can express own preferences in a variety of ways. Figure 6.4 shows the examples of alternative ways to solve decision-making problems:

- Variant A. The decision-maker specifies own preferences by defining criteria, attributes them with characters (whether they are motivating, demotivating, desirable, non-desirable), and defines weights, provides criteria's values in the form of two vectors (motivating and demotivating preference vector), based on which the preference vector compliant to decision-maker's preferences is calculated.
- Variant B. The decision-maker specifies own preferences by defining criteria and attributes them with a character (whether they are motivating, demotivating, desirable, non-desirable). For motivating and demotivating criteria (on the basis

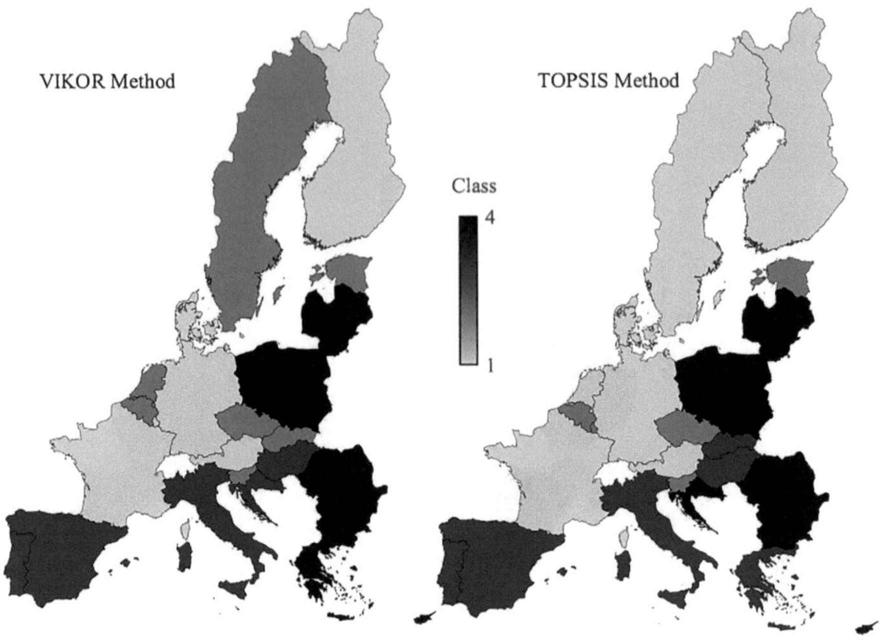

Fig. 6.3 Ranking results for the VIKOR and TOPSIS methods

of I and II quartiles), motivating and demotivating preference vector is calculated. Under these vectors, weight attributed to criteria is determined automatically and artificial preference vector is calculated.

In case of desirable and non-desirable criteria the decision-maker should specify own preferences, providing preference vector values.

In the majority of variants, the PVM research procedure is run in ten stages (Fig. 6.5): formulating a decision problem, defining decision variants, setting evaluation criteria for decision variants, defining the criterion's character, assigning weight to criteria, standardizing the criterion values, determining the preferences vector, making the ranking (based on importance factor), selection a decision variant (solution), and assessment of effects of decision variant implementation.

6.4.2 Stages I and II: Formulation of Decision Problem and Defining Decision Variants

These stages of the calculating procedure in PVM are the same as in the majority of multi-criteria methods of decision-making. These stages have been described in Sect. 1.1 in Fig. 1.2 when discussing the first level of the procedure (formulation of decision problem).

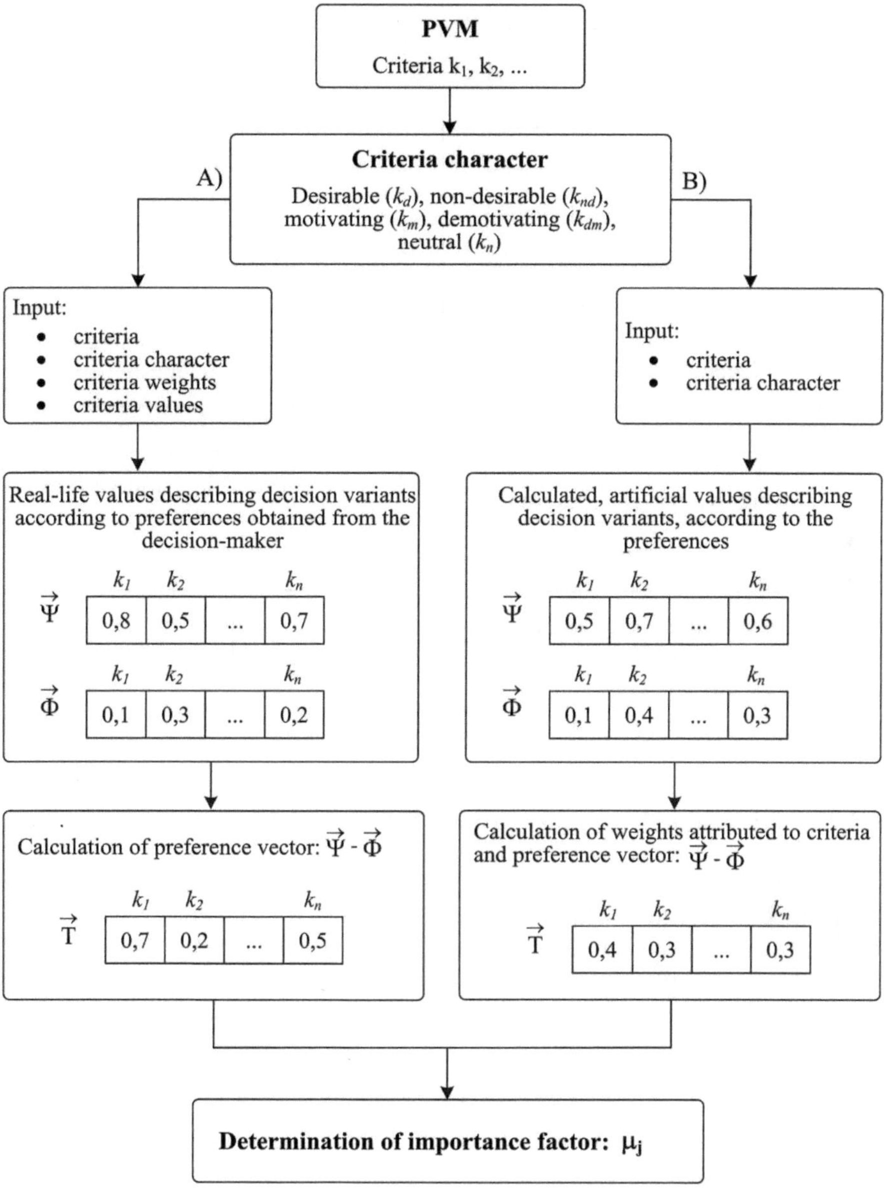

Fig. 6.4 Selected possible PVM variants designated for solving decision-making problems (k_i—the i-th criterion, $\vec{\Psi}$—the motivating preference vector, and $\vec{\Phi}$—the demotivating preference vector). Source: own elaboration

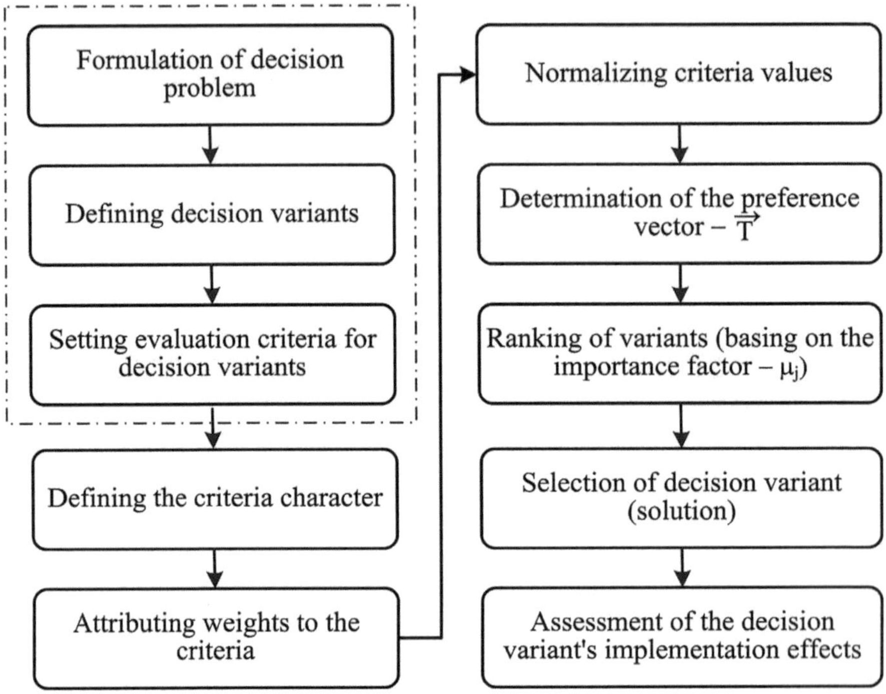

Fig. 6.5 Procedure for calculating PVM. Source: own elaboration

6.4.2.1 III. Setting Evaluation Criteria for Decision Variants

The selection of criteria is determined by decision-maker's preferences and depends on the type of decision-making situation. For many such situations, we are able to define a permanent set of criteria which can be used in similar cases. The criteria will further be denoted by k_i (the subscript index represents the number of a criterion), decision variant as $\underset{j}{\vec{X}'}$, where j represents the number of a variant. For instance, for the decision-maker, criteria describing cars may be as follows: fuel consumptions, engine power, etc. These criteria are expressed in the $\underset{j}{x_i}$ values (the value of the i-th criterion of the j-th decision variant). Based on the defined criteria, a set of criterion values for considered decision variants is created. However, not always numerical values can be assigned to all criteria. The qualitative (subjective) criteria can be an example. The procedure for dealing with such criteria will be described in the last stage of PVM.

6.4.2.2 IV. Defining the Criteria Character

Typically, the decision-makers are not able to quantify their preferences, but they can indicate which decision variants are acceptable or unacceptable for them. Therefore, the proposed criterion character should correspond to their intuition. The classification of criteria is as follows: desirable, non-desirable, motivating, demotivating, and neutral. They form the criteria sets [137]:

- Desirable ($k_i \in \kappa_{\mathrm{d}}$)—whose required values are neither too big nor too small,
- Non-desirable ($k_i \in \kappa_{\mathrm{nd}}$)—whose specified value is not desirable
- Motivating ($k_i \in \kappa_{\mathrm{m}}$—whose required values are big, and they motivate a decision-maker to make a decision
- Demotivating ($k_i \in \kappa_{\mathrm{dm}}$)—whose required values are small, and their big value makes a decision-maker discouraged to make a decision
- Neutral ($k_i \in \kappa_{\mathrm{n}}$)—criteria, which are not important in the specific decision problem, and their values should not have any impact on decision made

At this stage, specific characteristics should be assigned to every criterion. Each of criteria can be attributed with the one of the abovementioned characters. These definitions could be replaced by terms applied in the multidimensional comparative analysis, i.e., stimulant, destimulant, etc., but in the author's opinion they are less comprehensible for a decision-maker.

6.4.2.3 Stage V. Attributing Weights to the Criteria

In the process of decision support, the importance of criteria comes from the subjective assessment of the situation by a decision-maker. For example, one criterion may be much more important than the others. There are different systems for determining weights for criteria, and their selection depends on the decision-maker and the purpose and scope of the study. An example can be a price as it is often the principal selection criterion. Therefore, we have to attribute to this criterion a higher weight value. By default, we can, for example, assume that the weights of criteria wi are equal to 1. In a situation when it is necessary to add the importance of certain criteria, we can increase or reduce the weights. For example, if we assign the weight of 2 to a given criterion, it will become twice as important as the remaining ones, and if the assigned weight is 0.5, the criterion will be twice less important than the remaining ones. The weights may also adopt values ranging from 0 to 100% or 0 to 1, assuming that their total is 100% or 1, respectively. In this way, weights determine the importance of the criterion at which they occur. At the same time, they become the measure of the criterion importance. Once we have determined the weights, they should be normalized in order to eliminate the scales of values in which they have been expressed:

$$w_i' = \frac{w_i}{\sum_{k=1}^{m} w_k}, \tag{6.59}$$

where w_k is the weight value for the k-th criterion, w_i'—the value of a normalized weight for the i-th criterion, and m—the number of criteria.

Another better and more preferred method of determining weights is to determine them based on pairwise comparisons used in the AHP method.

6.4.2.4 Stage VI. Normalizing the Criteria

By principle, the criteria that describe decision variants are usually heterogeneous because they define different parameters of variants, which are expressed in different measurement units and have different scales of value. Consequently, the data that are recorded in this way are incomparable. Therefore, we have to bring them to a form in which they can be compared. Hence the next stage of the PVM is the normalization of the criteria by which the measurement units are eliminated and the scales of the criterion values in studies are brought roughly to the same level.

In the situation where a decision-maker provides only the values of the motivating preference vector and is not able to determine own demotivating criteria in the form of a demotivating preference vector, it is recommended to normalize the decision variants by means of a standard. Figure (Fig. 6.6) shows the case when inappropriate method of normalization was applied. For comparison, Fig. 6.7 presents the result of normalization for the same points using standardization. Subtracting the average value during standardization may change the nature of the preference criteria for motivating and demotivating criteria. This situation occurs when the vector $\vec{\mathrm{T}}'_{\mathrm{V}}$ changes its direction and sense.

$$x'_{\substack{i\\j}} = \frac{x_{\substack{i\\j}}}{\left\|\vec{\mathrm{X}}_j\right\|}, \tag{6.60}$$

where

$$\left\|\vec{\mathrm{X}}_j\right\| = \sqrt{\sum_{i=1}^{m} x_i^2}. \tag{6.61}$$

The normalized values will be further denoted by $'$ (prim).

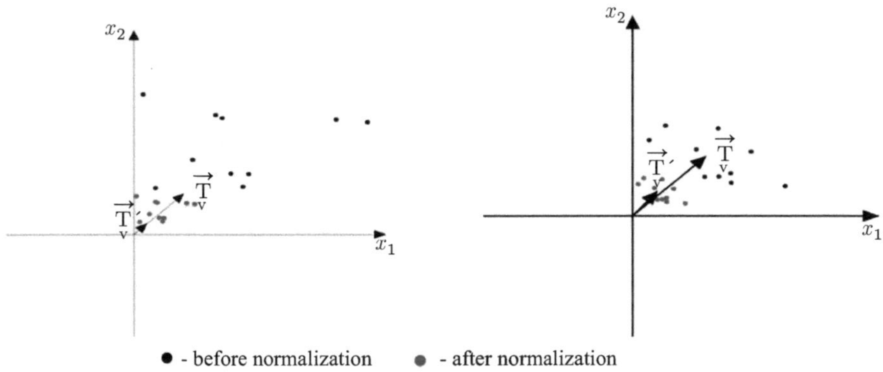

Fig. 6.6 Normalization of criteria values with the formula (6.60) ($\underset{v}{\vec{T}'} = \underset{v}{\vec{\Psi}'}$). Source: own elaboration

$$\underset{j}{x'_i} = \frac{\underset{j}{x_i} - \bar{x}_i}{\sigma_i}, \tag{6.62}$$

where

x_i—i-th variable,
σ_i—standard deviation of the i-th variable,
$\bar{x}_i$—mean value of the i-th variable,

whereas

$$\bar{x}_i = \frac{\sum_{j=1}^{n} \underset{j}{x_i}}{n}, \tag{6.63}$$

and

$$\sigma_i = \sqrt{\frac{\sum_{j=1}^{n} \left(\underset{j}{x_i} - \bar{x}_i \right)^2}{n-1}}. \tag{6.64}$$

The appearance of non-standard variants after normalization may result in less distinguishability of variants along one of the criteria. In Fig. 6.8, this is the criterion x_1 (variants in gray). This means that the differences between the values of criterion x_1 for typical variants have very little influence on the choice of the decision-making option. The very appearance of a non-typical variant may fundamentally change the

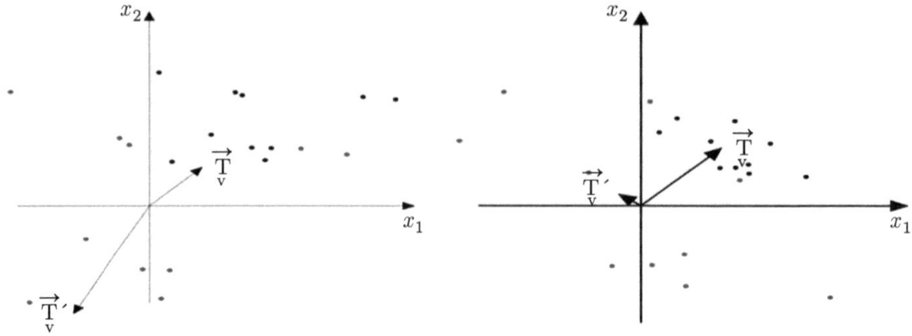

Fig. 6.7 Normalization of criteria values with the formula (6.62) ($\underset{v}{\vec{T}'} = \underset{v}{\vec{\Psi}'}$). Source: own elaboration

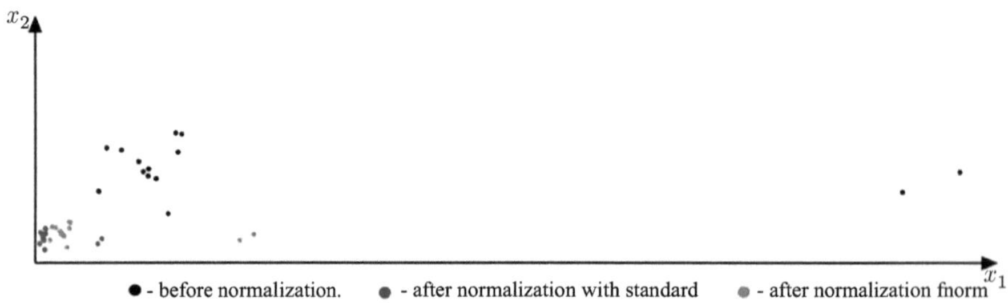

Fig. 6.8 Normalization of criteria values with the formula (6.65) and formula (6.66). Source: own elaboration

recommended decision variant, even if it does not concern a variant with unusually high (or low) values of criteria.

In order to reduce the impact of non-typical variations on the distinguishability of variants, in case where in the set of decision variants there are variants with the criteria values significantly different from the others, it is possible to use the formula:

$$\underset{j}{x'_i} = \frac{\underset{j}{x_i}}{f_{\text{norm}}\left(\underset{j}{\vec{X}'}\right)}, \tag{6.65}$$

where

$$f_{\text{norm}}\left(\underset{j}{\vec{X}'}\right) = \sqrt{\sum_{i=1}^{m} \begin{cases} x_i^2 \text{ dla } \underset{j}{x_i} \in \left\langle \bar{x}_i - S_{x_i}; \bar{x}_i + S_{x_i} \right\rangle \\ 0 \text{ dla } \underset{j}{x_i} \notin \left\langle \bar{x}_i - S_{x_i}; \bar{x}_i + S_{x_i} \right\rangle, \end{cases}} \tag{6.66}$$

whereas $\bar{x}_i$ is the mean value, and S_{x_i} is the standard deviation of the i-th criterion.

Indicators created on the basis of pairwise comparisons should be normalized according to the same formula. In Fig. 6.8, it can be seen that the distinction of objects along the x_1 criterion increased. See more on normalizing in [108, 134, 135, 137].

6.4.2.5 Stage VII. Determining the Preference Vector

The preference vector represents the decision-maker's requirements with regard to the analyzed decision variants. It is a vector whose coordinates are made of values of the criteria calculated on the criterion's character. The criterion values of motivating or demotivating character. For criteria of motivating or demotivating character, the coordinates of this vector are the criteria values calculated on the basis of the difference between motivating $\vec{\Psi}$ and demotivating $\vec{\Phi}$ vector of preferences. The criteria values for the vector $\vec{\Psi}$ are given by the decision-maker and usually meet his expectations. The vector $\vec{\Phi}$ represents the values of the criteria that the decision-maker found undesirable. How to interpret and determine the preference vectors depends on which variant to calculate PVM we have chosen. For the desirable and undesirable criteria, the coordinates of this vector are determined explicitly. In the calculation process, the preference vector is treated (with respect to the character of the criteria and the way of their normalizing) in the same way as any other vector which represents the decision variant. In a situation where the values of the motivating and demotivating preference vector and the part of the preference vector associated with desired and undesired criteria are given by the decision-maker from outside the test sample, the preference vector should be normalized using the same parameters as were used to normalize the criteria:

$$\tau_i' = \frac{\tau_i}{\left\| \underset{j}{\vec{\mathrm{X}}} \right\|}, \tag{6.67}$$

where τ_i is the value of the i-th coordinate of the vector $\vec{\mathrm{T}}$, and τ_i' is the value of the i-th coordinate of the vector $\vec{\mathrm{T}}'$ after normalization or

$$\tau_i' = \frac{\tau_i - \bar{x}_i}{\left\| \underset{j}{\vec{\mathrm{X}}} \right\|}. \tag{6.68}$$

To build the preference vector, we need first to separate criteria. Neutral criteria are rejected and the remaining ones are divided into three groups:

1. Motivating and demotivating criteria
2. Desirable criteria
3. Non-desirable criteria

Table 6.9 Calculation of vectors $\underset{v}{\vec{\Psi}'}$ and $\underset{v}{\vec{\Phi}'}$ depending on the criterion character

	Criterion	
Vector	Motivating	Demotivating
$\underset{v}{\vec{\Psi}'}$	III quartile	I quartile
$\underset{v}{\vec{\Phi}'}$	I quartile	III quartile

Table 6.10 Calculation of $\vec{\mathrm{T}}'$ vector for desirable and non-desirable criteria

	Criterion	
Vector	Desirable	Non-desirable
$\vec{\mathrm{T}}'$	Max	Min

The technique to calculate the motivating and demotivating preference vector depends on the criterion character. For motivating and demotivating criteria, they are calculated based on I and III quartiles (Table 6.9).

For the motivating and demotivating criteria, the preference vector $\vec{\mathrm{T}}'$ is calculated by determining the maximum and minimum (Table 6.10). Neutral criteria are of no importance for the measurement value.

For the case (B) in Fig. 6.4, a decision-maker specifies criteria and their character. The values of the vector $\underset{v}{\vec{\Psi}'}$ and $\underset{v}{\vec{\Phi}'}$ are calculated based on data. The procedure depends on criteria character. For the case (A) in Fig. 6.4, a decision-maker specifies criteria and the character of the motivating $\underset{v}{\vec{\Psi}'}$ and demotivating $\underset{v}{\vec{\Phi}'}$ preference vector in a form of two decision variants coming from or outside of the test sample: the first one which he likes and the second one which he does not like.

For the motivating and demotivating criteria, the preference vector is calculated by determining the length of the projection of the vector representing the j-th decision variant on the preference vector $\underset{v}{\vec{\mathrm{T}}'}$, which is calculated, as the difference between the vectors $\underset{v}{\vec{\Psi}'}$ and $\underset{v}{\vec{\Phi}'}$:

$$\underset{v}{\vec{\mathrm{T}}'} = \underset{v}{\vec{\Psi}'} - \underset{v}{\vec{\Phi}'}. \tag{6.69}$$

Motivating and demotivating criteria form the coordinates of vector $\underset{v}{\vec{\Psi}'}$ and $\underset{v}{\vec{\Phi}'}$. Figure 6.9a represents the monodirectional coordinates system based on the vector $\underset{v}{\vec{\mathrm{T}}'}$. The origin of the coordinates system is determined by the vector $\underset{v}{\vec{\Phi}'}$, and the measurement unit is length $\underset{v}{\vec{\mathrm{T}}'}$.

The sign of the vector $\underset{v}{\vec{\mathrm{T}}'}$ depends on the character of the criteria. The positive sign indicates a motivating criterion, while the negative one indicates a demotivating criterion. It is not always consistent with the criterion character defined in Stage I because sometimes the decision-makers ignore the transitivity of their preferences and assign higher values to demotivating criteria than to the motivating ones. Therefore, we have to make adjustments to the criterion in question by changing its sign in vector $\underset{v}{\vec{\mathrm{T}}'}$ coordinates. The coordinates associated with a motivating criterion

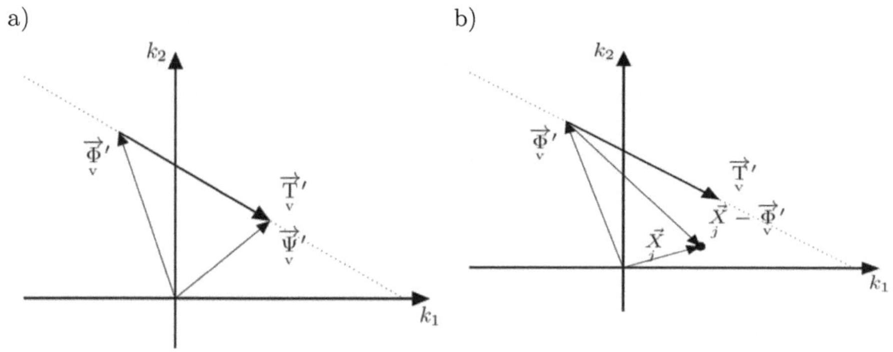

Fig. 6.9 The preference vector $\underset{v}{\vec{T}}'$: (**a**) position in the coordinate system of the criteria (k_1—criterion 1, k_2—criterion 2) and (**b**) determining the position of the object against the origin $\underset{v}{\vec{T}}'$

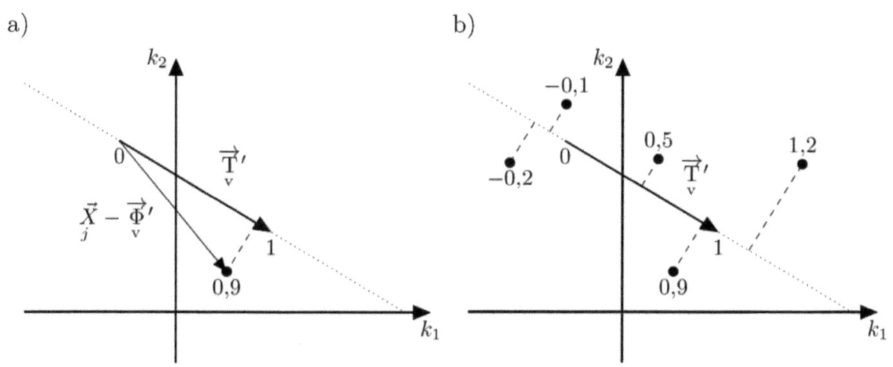

Fig. 6.10 Coordinates of decision variants in the coordinates system $\underset{v}{\vec{T}}'$: (**a**) determination of the variant's coordinate $\underset{j}{\vec{X}}'$ and (**b**) position of the variants and their coordinates

are given a positive sign, whereas the demotivating ones are considered negative. For each decision variant $\underset{j}{\vec{X}}'$, we should determine its position against the origin of the coordinates system. For this purpose, we calculate the difference between this variant and the vector $\underset{v}{\vec{T}}'$ (Fig. 6.9b). Based on this difference, we determine the coordinate of the decision variant $\underset{j}{\vec{X}}'$ in the coordinates system $\underset{v}{\vec{T}}'$ (Fig. 6.10a). The length of the vector $\underset{v}{\vec{T}}'$ is a unit of measure in this coordinate system. The value of the decision variant coordinate $\underset{j}{\vec{X}}'$ depends on its position against the coordinates system $\underset{v}{\vec{T}}'$. This is shown in (Fig. 6.10b).

The fact that the coordinates system $\underset{\mathrm{v}}{\vec{\mathrm{T}}'}$ has different measurement unit than the coordinate system of the criteria k_1, k_2 becomes a problem, when we have to confront these coordinates with the values of the distance measure calculated in k_1, k_2. Hence, the vector $\underset{\mathrm{v}}{\vec{\mathrm{T}}'}$ is brought to the form of a unit vector:

$$\underset{\mathrm{v}}{\vec{\mathrm{T}}''} = \frac{\underset{\mathrm{v}}{\vec{\mathrm{T}}'}}{\left\| \underset{\mathrm{v}}{\vec{\mathrm{T}}'} \right\|}, \tag{6.70}$$

whereas in the PVM we assume that

$$\left\| \underset{\mathrm{v}}{\vec{\mathrm{T}}'} \right\| = \sqrt{\sum_{i=1}^{m_{\mathrm{v}}} \underset{\mathrm{v}}{\tau'^2_i}}, \tag{6.71}$$

where m_v is the number of motivating and demotivating criteria, and $\underset{\mathrm{v}}{\tau'_i}$ is the i-th coordinate of the vector $\underset{\mathrm{v}}{\vec{\mathrm{T}}'}$.

The coordinate of the j-th decision variant in the coordinates system $\underset{\mathrm{v}}{\vec{\mathrm{T}}''}$ may be calculated by formula:

$$\underset{\mathrm{v}}{\mu_j} = \sum_{i=1}^{m_{\mathrm{v}}} \left(\underset{j}{x'_i} - \underset{\mathrm{v}}{\phi'_i} \right) \underset{\mathrm{v}}{\tau''_i} w'_i, \tag{6.72}$$

where $\underset{\mathrm{v}}{\phi'_i}$ is the i-th coordinate of the vector $\underset{\mathrm{v}}{\Phi'}$, and $\underset{\mathrm{v}}{\tau''_i}$ is the i-th coordinate of the vector $\underset{\mathrm{v}}{\vec{\mathrm{T}}''}$.

The bigger the value of $\underset{\mathrm{v}}{\mu_j}$, the higher the rank of the j-th decision variant. In the case of desirable criteria, we include in the calculation the vector $\underset{\mathrm{d}}{\vec{\mathrm{T}}'}$, whose coordinates are the desirable criteria of the vector $\vec{\mathrm{T}}'$. The value $\underset{\mathrm{d}}{\mu_j}$ is calculated as the distance between points (Fig. 6.11) [137]:

$$\underset{\mathrm{d}}{\mu_j} = \sqrt{\sum_{i=1}^{m_{\mathrm{d}}} w'^2_i \left(\underset{j}{x'_i} - \underset{\mathrm{d}}{\tau'_i} \right)^2}, \tag{6.73}$$

where $\underset{\mathrm{d}}{\mu_j}$ is the number of desirable criteria, and $\underset{\mathrm{d}}{\tau'_i}$ is the i-th coordinate of the vector $\underset{\mathrm{d}}{\vec{\mathrm{T}}'}$.

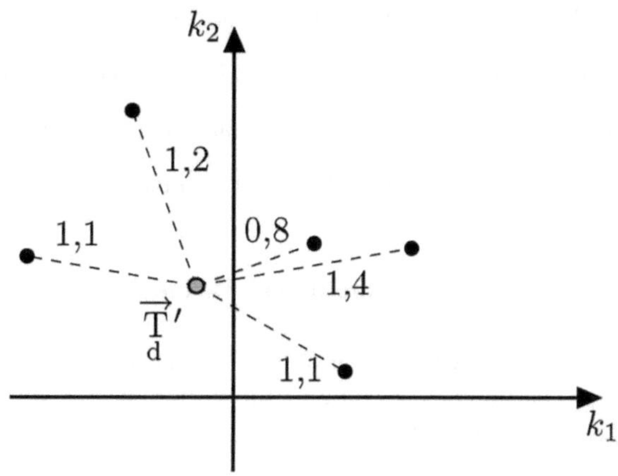

Fig. 6.11 Distance of the decision variants of the preference vectors for desirable criteria. Source: own elaboration

The smaller the value of $\underset{\mathrm{d}}{\mu_j}$, the better the decision variant's position in the ranking. The factor measure value for the best decision variants is equal to zero.

In case of the non-desirable criteria, we include in the calculation the vector $\underset{\mathrm{nd}}{\vec{\mathrm{T}}'}$ whose coordinates are non-desirable criteria of the vector $\vec{\mathrm{T}}'$. Just like above, the measure value is calculated as the distance between points [137]:

$$\underset{\mathrm{nd}}{\mu_j} = \sqrt{\sum_{i=1}^{m_{\mathrm{nd}}} w_i'^2 \left(\underset{j}{x_i'} - \underset{\mathrm{nd}}{\tau_i'} \right)^2}, \tag{6.74}$$

where m_{nd} is the number of non-desirable criteria, and $\underset{\mathrm{nd}}{\tau_i'}$ is the i-th coordinate of the vector $\underset{\mathrm{nd}}{\vec{\mathrm{T}}'}$.

The bigger the value of $\underset{\mathrm{nd}}{\mu_j}$, the higher the position in the ranking. The worst decision variants have an index value equal to zero.

6.4.2.6 Stage VIII. Determination of Importance Factor

The final value of the importance factor measure μ_j is determined by calculating the weighted average value of the factors $\underset{\mathrm{v}}{\mu_j}$, $\underset{\mathrm{d}}{\mu_j}$, and $\underset{\mathrm{nd}}{\mu_j}$:

$$\mu_j = \frac{\underset{\mathrm{v}}{\mu_j} m_{\mathrm{v}} - \underset{\mathrm{d}}{\mu_j} m_{\mathrm{d}} + \underset{\mathrm{nd}}{\mu_j} m_{\mathrm{nd}}}{m_{\mathrm{v}} + m_{\mathrm{d}} + m_{\mathrm{nd}}}. \tag{6.75}$$

The negative sign at the value of $\underset{d}{\mu_j}$ factor is associated with its somewhat different character of this factor. For $\underset{v}{\mu_j}$ and $\underset{nd}{\mu_j}$, the bigger the value of the factor measure, the better decision variant, and conversely in case of $\underset{d}{\mu_j}$, the smaller the factor's measure value, the better variant.

6.4.2.7 Stage IX. Ranking of Variants

Ranking of decision variants is made under the final value of importance factor μ_j. The bigger the value of the importance factor, the closer to decision-maker's preference the variant is.

6.4.2.8 Stage X. Calculation of the Importance Factor Including Subjective Criteria

The qualitative criteria can be described in words, for example, describing colors: red, green, and blue. Then, according to the decision-maker's preferences, colors will be assigned values. Various available methods can be used to do this. For example, in the AHP method, a pairwise comparing matrix is created for this purpose. Rows and columns of this matrix correspond to the compared aspects of decision variants. In this example, we will compare colors in respect of the decision-maker's preferences, who will determine how much more he prefers one color to another. When we have n colors, then the number of comparisons is $\frac{n^2-n}{2}$ (all which are compared to one another). In our case (at $n = 3$), this is $\frac{3^2-3}{2} = 3$. Much better solution is to compare specific decision variants of a given color with one another. However, in such a situation, the number of comparisons can increase significantly. For example, considering 100 variants in four colors, we have to perform 6 comparisons, while when we compare the decision variants in respect of color criterion there will be 4950 of comparisons. Apparently, this can be labor-intensive.

When making comparison, we construct the $n \times n$ matrix. The matrix is the same as pairwise comparing matrix in the AHP method. The only difference refers to the applied rating scale, which in our case is five-step not nine-step rating scale (Fig. 6.12).

When entering numbers the matrix we have to remember, that values in the matrix are interrelated. For each matrix entry, the following interdependence occurs:

$$c_{i,j,k} = \frac{1}{c_{i,k,j}}. \tag{6.76}$$

It means that if the entry in the first row of the second column is 3, then the entry in the second row of the first column must be 1/3. In the discussed case, this is

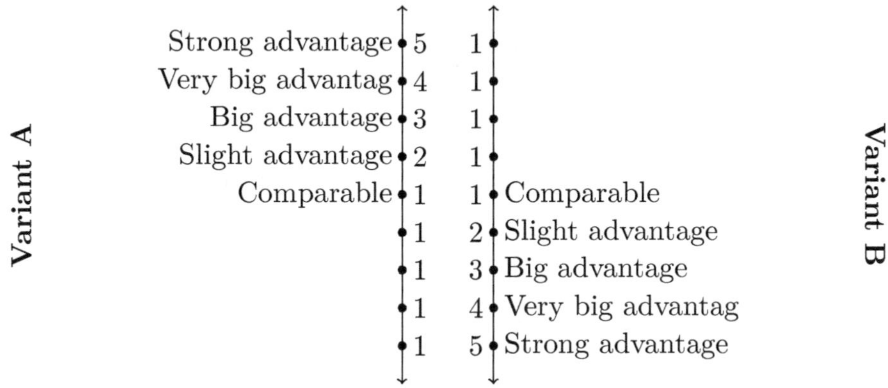

Fig. 6.12 Five-grade scale of criteria comparison

matrix. The main diagonal entries are all 1. Then we define how much the decision variant entered in a row is better than the variant in a column.

In such a way, the pairwise comparing matrix C_i is constructed:

A value greater than one means that the decision variant entered in the row has an advantage over the variant listed in the column against the selected criterion, a value less than one—the variant entered in the column has an advantage over the variant entered in the row, a value of one—the variants are comparable. Data in the pairwise comparing matrix is not always consistent. In the case under consideration, red has a big advantage over green and a very big advantage over blue, but blue is comparable to green, which indicates a certain inconsistency of a person comparing the decision variants. Like in the AHP method, in order to examine the cohesion of the pairwise comparison matrix, we must calculate the consistency ratio, and if its value is too big, eliminate such variable or verify answers given through pairwise comparing. Finally, indices should be calculated out of pairwise comparing matrix. To do so, eigenvectors are calculated whose values form the index used in further calculations. As shown above, with a larger number of objects, the pairwise comparison method is very tedious and requires a large number of comparisons. Therefore, it is recommended to divide the calculation into two stages. In the first stage, the importance coefficient should be determined without taking into account subjective criteria. In the second stage, all objects that have no chance of achieving the first rank should be discarded, and for other objects, set the values of subjective criteria and re-determine the importance coefficient. The procedure of discarding objects requires determining the threshold of the importance coefficient. Objects with an importance coefficient calculated for all criteria, which ignore subjective criteria with a value below the threshold, will not have a chance to move to the first position after taking into account subjective criteria. Due to the fact that the importance coefficient is calculated on the basis of three indicators, the threshold must be calculated on the basis of these indicators. The value of $\underset{v}{\mu_j}$ factor for all criteria including subjective ones can be calculated following the formula:

$$\underset{\mathrm{v}}{\mu_j} = \sum_{i=1}^{m_{\mathrm{v}}} \left(\underset{j}{x'_i} - \underset{\mathrm{v}}{\phi'_i} \right) \underset{\mathrm{v}}{\tau''_i} w'_i = \sum_{i=1}^{m_{\mathrm{v}}} \left(\underset{j}{x'_i} - \underset{\mathrm{v}}{\phi'_i} \right) \underset{\mathrm{v}}{\tau''_i} \frac{w_i}{\sum_{k=1}^{m} w_k}. \tag{6.77}$$

The value of $\underset{\mathrm{v}}{\mu_j}$ factor for subjective criteria only is determined by the formula:

$$\underset{\mathrm{v}}{\mu_j^{\mathrm{ns}}} = \sum_{i=1}^{m_{\mathrm{v}}-m_{\mathrm{vs}}} \left(\underset{j}{x'_i} - \underset{\mathrm{v}}{\phi'_i} \right) \underset{\mathrm{v}}{\tau''_i} \frac{w_i}{\sum_{k=1}^{m} w_k}. \tag{6.78}$$

The delta of $\underset{\mathrm{v}}{\mu_j}$ factor after adding the subjective criteria will be as follows:

$$\Delta \underset{\mathrm{v}}{\mu_j} = \underset{\mathrm{v}}{\mu_j} - \underset{\mathrm{v}}{\mu_j^{\mathrm{ns}}} = \sum_{i=m_{\mathrm{v}}-m_{\mathrm{vs}}+1}^{m_{\mathrm{v}}} \left(\underset{j}{x'_i} - \underset{\mathrm{v}}{\phi'_i} \right) \underset{\mathrm{v}}{\tau''_i} \frac{w_i}{\sum_{k=1}^{m} w_k}. \tag{6.79}$$

The maximum possible delta of $\underset{\mathrm{v}}{\mu_j}$ factor after subjective criteria are added is determined by the formula:

$$\underset{\mathrm{v}}{R} = \max_j \left[\Delta \underset{\mathrm{v}}{\mu_j} \right] = \max_j \left[\sum_{i=m_{\mathrm{v}}-m_{\mathrm{vs}}+1}^{m_{\mathrm{v}}} \left(\underset{j}{x'_i} - \underset{\mathrm{v}}{\phi'_i} \right) \underset{\mathrm{v}}{\tau''_i} \frac{w_i}{\sum_{k=1}^{m} w_k} \right]. \tag{6.80}$$

$\Delta \underset{\mathrm{v}}{\mu_j}$ factor will have the maximum value if for each criterion, a difference $\underset{j}{x'_i} - \underset{\mathrm{v}}{\phi'_i}$ will have maximum value for motivating criteria and minimum value for demotivating criteria. Provided that normalizing method ensures the criteria values within the range from zero to one, then $\underset{j}{x'_i} \in \langle 0; 1 \rangle$ and $\underset{\mathrm{v}}{\phi'_i} \in \langle 0; 1 \rangle$, so the maximum difference $\underset{j}{x'_i} - \underset{\mathrm{v}}{\phi'_i}$ for demotivating criteria will be one and for demotivating criteria will be zero, and thus

$$\underset{\mathrm{v}}{R} = \sum_{i=m_{\mathrm{v}}-m_{\mathrm{vs}}+1}^{m_{\mathrm{v}}} \begin{cases} \underset{\mathrm{v}}{\tau''}_i \dfrac{w_i}{\sum_{k=1}^{m} w_k} & \text{for } k_i \in \kappa_{\mathrm{m}} \\ -\underset{\mathrm{v}}{\tau''}_i \dfrac{w_i}{\sum_{k=1}^{m} w_k} & \text{for } k_i \in \kappa_{\mathrm{dm}}. \end{cases} \tag{6.81}$$

In case of $\underset{\mathrm{d}}{\mu}_j$ factor, the analogous derivation can be presented. The value of $\underset{\mathrm{d}}{\mu}_j^{\mathrm{ns}}$ factor for only subjective criteria is defined by the formula:

$$\underset{\mathrm{d}}{\mu}_j^{\mathrm{ns}} = \sqrt{\sum_{i=1}^{m_{\mathrm{d}}-m_{\mathrm{ds}}} \left(\underset{j}{x'_i} - \underset{\mathrm{d}}{\tau'_i} \right)^2 \left(\frac{w_i}{\sum_{k=1}^{m} w_k} \right)^2}. \tag{6.82}$$

$\Delta \underset{\mathrm{d}}{\mu}_j$ value will be as follows:

$$\Delta \underset{\mathrm{d}}{\mu}_j = \underset{\mathrm{d}}{\mu}_j - \underset{\mathrm{d}}{\mu}_j^{\mathrm{ns}} = \sqrt{\sum_{i=m_{\mathrm{d}}-m_{\mathrm{ds}}+1}^{m_{\mathrm{d}}} \left(\underset{j}{x'_i} - \underset{\mathrm{d}}{\tau'_i} \right)^2 \left(\frac{w_i}{\sum_{k=1}^{m} w_k} \right)^2}. \tag{6.83}$$

However, in this case, the minimal value is desired $\Delta \underset{\mathrm{d}}{\mu}_j$ because the smaller the value is $\underset{\mathrm{d}}{\mu}_j$, the higher the object's ranking:

$$\underset{\mathrm{d}}{R} = \min_j \left[\Delta \underset{\mathrm{d}}{\mu}_j \right] = \min_j \sqrt{\sum_{i=m_{\mathrm{d}}-m_{\mathrm{ds}}+1}^{m_{\mathrm{d}}} \left(\underset{j}{x'_i} - \underset{\mathrm{d}}{\tau'_i} \right)^2 \left(\frac{w_i}{\sum_{k=1}^{m} w_k} \right)^2}. \tag{6.84}$$

The $\underset{\mathrm{d}}{\mu}_j$ value will be minimal, when for each criterion $\left(\underset{j}{x'_i} - \underset{\mathrm{d}}{\tau'_i} \right)^2$ will be minimal. If the normalization method ensures criteria values within the range from zero to one, then minimal value $\left(\underset{j}{x'_i} - \underset{\mathrm{d}}{\tau'_i}\right)^2$ will be as follows:

$$\underset{\mathrm{d}}{R} = \sqrt{\sum_{i=m_{\mathrm{d}}-m_{\mathrm{ds}}+1}^{m_{\mathrm{d}}} \min\left\{\left(1-\underset{\mathrm{d}}{\tau'_i}\right)^2; \underset{\mathrm{d}}{\tau'^2_i}\right\}\left(\frac{w_i}{\sum_{k=1}^{m} w_k}\right)^2}. \tag{6.85}$$

The similar calculation can be made for $\Delta\underset{\mathrm{nd}}{\mu_j}$ with such a difference that for each criterion $\left(\underset{j}{x'_i} - \underset{\mathrm{d}}{\tau'_i}\right)^2$ must be maximal. Thus,

$$\underset{\mathrm{nd}}{R} = \sqrt{\sum_{i=m_{\mathrm{nd}}-m_{\mathrm{nds}}+1}^{m_{\mathrm{nd}}} \max\left\{\left(1-\underset{\mathrm{nd}}{\tau'_i}\right)^2; \underset{\mathrm{nd}}{\tau'^2_i}\right\}\left(\frac{w_i}{\sum_{k=1}^{m} w_k}\right)^2}. \tag{6.86}$$

Finally, the maximum increase of the importance factor of decision variants R will be as follows:

$$R = \frac{m_{\mathrm{v}}\underset{\mathrm{v}}{R} - m_{\mathrm{d}}\underset{\mathrm{d}}{R} + m_{\mathrm{nd}}\underset{\mathrm{nd}}{R}}{m_{\mathrm{v}} + m_{\mathrm{d}} + m_{\mathrm{nd}}}. \tag{6.87}$$

The threshold of the importance factor, below which all objects with value below, must be eliminated:

$$B = \max_j\left(\mu_j\right) - R. \tag{6.88}$$

6.4.3 PVM Method Calculation Example

The example is about selecting the preferred kabanos sausage. A few years ago, Mr. Kowalski used to buy a type of kabanos sausage called X. Unfortunately, the manufacturer withdrew this product from the market. Now, Mr. Kowalski is looking for a product that would be most similar to the X kabanos sausage. Mr. Kowalski, as a decision-maker, described the desired product with criteria in the form of a motivating and demotivating vector of preferences. Mr. Kowalski's preferences are provided in Table 6.11. Kryteria *Calorific value* and *price* are defined as demotivating criteria, *protein* and *fat* as desirable criteria, and *flavor* as motivating criteria.

Data about kabanos sausages most available in stores visited by Mr. Kowalski were collected. These data are provided in Table 6.12. Table does not include values for flavor criterion. They will be filled in for those kabanos sausages which get the best results in the initial ranking.

Mr. Kowalski assigned weights to individual criteria. They are presented in Table 6.13.

Weight values were normalized according to the formula (6.59). For example, for calorific value criterion, the result is

$$w_1' = \frac{w_1}{\sum_{i=1}^{5} w_i} = \frac{1}{1+1+2+2+0.5} = \frac{1}{6.5} = 0.1538. \tag{6.89}$$

As the result, normalized weight values were obtained, which are presented in Table 6.14.

The values of criteria were normalized according to the formula (6.60). For the calorific value criterion, the $\left\| \underset{1}{X} \right\|$ norm is

Table 6.11 Description of Mr. Kowalski preferences

Preference vector	Calorific value [kcal]	Protein [g]	Fat [g]	Price [zł/kg]	Flavor
$\vec{\Psi}$	300	21.5	18.3	41.5325	0.5
$\vec{\Phi}$	500	–	–	52.0925	0.2

Table 6.12 Criteria values for the example of kabanos sausages selection

Kabanos name	Calorific value [kcal]	Protein [g]	Fat [g]	Price [PLN/kg]	Flavor
Krakus	326	27.5	24.3	48.83	–
Chicken Konspol Natura	253	22.0	18.3	51.11	–
Gala Sokołów	561	26.0	50.0	52.42	–
Pork Delux	405	21.7	35.6	29.12	–
Preludium bekonowe Henryk Kania	479	18.0	41.0	64.08	–

Table 6.13 Weights assigned to criteria

Calorific value [kcal]	Protein [g]	Fat [g]	Price [PLN/kg]	Flavor
1	1	2	2	0.5

Table 6.14 Weights normalization

Calorific value [kcal]	Protein [g]	Fat [g]	Price [PLN/kg]	Flavor Flavor
0.1538	0.1538	0.3077	0.3077	0.0769

Table 6.15 Normalized criteria values for the example of kabanos sausages selection

Kabanos name	Calorific value [kcal]	Protein [g]	Fat [g]	Price [PLN/kg]	Flavor
Krakus	0.3478	0.5268	0.3044	0.4333	–
Chicken Konspol Natura	0.2699	0.4229	0.2292	0.4536	–
Gala Sokołów	0.5985	0.4998	0.6263	0.4652	–
Pork Delux	0.4321	0.4172	0.4459	0.2584	–
Preludium bekonowe Henryk Kania	0.5111	0.3460	0.5136	0.5686	–

$$\left\|\underset{1}{X}\right\| = \sqrt{\sum_{i=1}^{5} \underset{1}{x_i^2}} = \sqrt{326^2+253^2+561^2+405^2+479^2} = \sqrt{878472} = 937.2684. \tag{6.90}$$

The value of the calorific value criterion for Krakus kabanos sausage after normalization is

$$\underset{1}{x_1'} = \frac{\underset{1}{x_1}}{\left\|\underset{1}{X}\right\|} = \frac{326}{937.2684} = 0.3478. \tag{6.91}$$

All normalized values are presented in Table 6.15.

The values of the preference vectors $\overrightarrow{\Psi}$ and $\overrightarrow{\Phi}$ were also normalized. For example, the value of the normalized coordinate φ_1' associated with calorific value criterion of $\overrightarrow{\Psi}'$ vector is

$$\underset{1}{\varphi_1'} = \frac{\underset{1}{\varphi_1}}{\left\|\underset{1}{X}\right\|} = \frac{300}{937.2684} = 0.3201. \tag{6.92}$$

All normalized values for vectors $\overrightarrow{\Psi}$ and $\overrightarrow{\Phi}$ are presented in Table 6.16. Values for the flavor criterion were not normalized because of missing data.

In the next step, the vector $\overrightarrow{\mathrm{T}}'$ as a difference between $\overrightarrow{\Psi}'$ and $\overrightarrow{\Phi}'$ is determined. The difference is calculated for these coordinates, for which vector $\overrightarrow{\Phi}'$ has values. The value of the coordinate τ_1' of vector $\overrightarrow{\mathrm{T}}'$ linked to calorific value criterion will

Table 6.16 Normalized values of preference vectors

Preference vector	Calorific value [kcal]	Protein [g]	Fat [g]	Price [PLN/kg]	Flavor
$\overrightarrow{\Psi}'$	0.3201	0.4133	0.2292	0.3686	0.5
$\overrightarrow{\Phi}'$	0.5335	–	–	0.4623	0.2

Table 6.17 Normalized values of preference vector

Preference vector	Calorific value [kcal]	Protein [g]	Fat [g]	Price [PLN/kg]	Flavor
$\overrightarrow{\mathrm{T}}'$	−0.2134	0.4133	0.2292	−0.0937	0.3

Table 6.18 Values of normalized motivating and demotivating criteria, for the example of kabanos sausages selection

Kabanos name	Calorific value [kcal]	Price [PLN/kg]
Krakus	0.3478	0.4333
Chicken Konspol Natura	0.2699	0.4536
Gala Sokołów	0.5985	0.4652
Pork Delux	0.4321	0.2584
Preludium bekonowe Henryk Kania	0.5111	0.5686

be

$$\tau_1' = \phi_1' - \varphi_1' = 0.3201 - 0.5335 = -0.2134. \tag{6.93}$$

All values τ_i' are presented in Table 6.17.

Vectors $\overrightarrow{\mathrm{T}}'$ and $\overrightarrow{\Phi}'$ are divided into vectors related to motivating and demotivating criteria $\underset{\mathrm{v}}{\overrightarrow{\mathrm{T}}}'$, $\underset{\mathrm{v}}{\overrightarrow{\Phi}}'$ desirable $\underset{\mathrm{d}}{\overrightarrow{\mathrm{T}}}'$, and non-desirable criteria $\underset{\mathrm{nd}}{\overrightarrow{\mathrm{T}}}'$. Values with no data are rejected *Calorific value* and *Price* are demotivating criteria, and *Flavor* has no values, so $\underset{\mathrm{v}}{\overrightarrow{\mathrm{T}}}'$ will be

$$\underset{\mathrm{v}}{\overrightarrow{\mathrm{T}}}' = [-0.2134; -0.0937] \tag{6.94}$$

and vector $\underset{\mathrm{v}}{\overrightarrow{\Phi}}'$:

$$\underset{\mathrm{v}}{\overrightarrow{\Phi}}' = [-0.5335; -0.4623]\,. \tag{6.95}$$

Only the values for the motivating and demotivating criteria for which values are available are taken into account in the calculations related to these vectors (Table 6.18).

Table 6.19 Index values for the selection of kabanos sausages, as an example

Kabanos name	μ_j v	μ_j d	μ_j
Krakus	0.0182	0.0290	−0.0006
Chicken Konspol Natura	0.0234	0.0015	0.0135
Gala Sokołów	−0.0058	0.1229	−0.0527
Pork Delux	0.0242	0.0667	−0.0121
Preludium bekonowe Henryk Kania	−0.0061	0.0881	−0.0389

Vector $\underset{\mathrm{v}}{\vec{\mathrm{T}}}'$ is normalized by dividing by the sum of squares of the coordinates of vector $\vec{\mathrm{T}}'$ representing motivating and demotivating criteria (also those, for which no data is available). The normalizing coefficient is

$$\left\|\underset{\mathrm{v}}{\vec{\mathrm{T}}}'\right\| = \sqrt{(-0.2134)^2 + (-0.0937)^2 + 0.3^2} = \sqrt{0.1443} = 0.3799. \tag{6.96}$$

The vector $\underset{\mathrm{v}}{\vec{\mathrm{T}}}'$ after normalization will have the following values:

$$\underset{\mathrm{v}}{\vec{\mathrm{T}}}'' = \frac{\underset{\mathrm{v}}{\vec{\mathrm{T}}}'}{\left\|\underset{\mathrm{v}}{\vec{\mathrm{T}}}'\right\|} = \left[\frac{-0.2135}{0.3799}; \frac{-0.0937}{0.3799}\right] = [-0.5617; -0.2467]\,. \tag{6.97}$$

Then $\underset{\mathrm{v}}{\mu_j}$ values are calculated. The value of $\underset{\mathrm{v}}{\mu_1}$ will be

$$\underset{\mathrm{v}}{\mu_1} = \sum_{i=1}^{m_{\mathrm{v}}}\left(\underset{1}{x_i'} - \underset{\mathrm{v}}{\phi_i'}\right)\underset{\mathrm{v}}{\tau_i''}\mathrm{w}_i' = (0.3478 - 0.5335)\cdot(-0.5617)\cdot 0.1538$$
$$+ (0.4333 - 0.4623)\cdot(-0.2467)\cdot 0.3077 = 0.0160 + 0.0022 = 0.0182. \tag{6.98}$$

All calculated values are presented in Table 6.19.

Protein and fat are desirable criteria, and thus vector $\underset{\mathrm{d}}{\vec{\mathrm{T}}}'$ is

$$\underset{\mathrm{d}}{\vec{\mathrm{T}}}' = [0.4133; 0.2292]\,. \tag{6.99}$$

Only values for desirable criteria for which values are available are considered in calculations related to this vector (Table 6.20).

Next, values of $\underset{\mathrm{d}}{\mu_j}$ are calculated. The value of $\underset{\mathrm{d}}{\mu_1}$ will be

Table 6.20 Values of normalized criteria desirable for the example of kabanos sausages selection

Kabanos name	Protein [g]	Fat [g]
Krakus	0.5268	0.3044
Chicken Konspol Natura	0.4229	0.2292
Gala Sokołów	0.4998	0.6263
Pork Delux	0.4172	0.4459
Preludium bekonowe Henryk Kania	0.3460	0.5136

$$\underset{\text{d}}{\mu_1} = \sqrt{\sum_{i=1}^{m_\text{d}} \text{w}_i'^2 \left(\underset{1}{x_i'} - \underset{\text{d}}{\tau_i'}\right)^2} =$$
$$\sqrt{0.1538^2 \cdot (0.5268 - 0.4133)^2 + 0.3077^2 \cdot (0.3044 - 0.2292)^2} = 0.0290. \tag{6.100}$$

All calculated values are presented in Table 6.19. Non-desirable values are not present, and therefore in the next step values of μ_j are calculated. The value of μ_1 is

$$\mu_1 = \frac{\underset{\text{v}}{\mu_1} m_\text{v} - \underset{\text{d}}{\mu_1} m_\text{d}}{m_\text{v} + m_\text{d}} = \frac{0.0182 \cdot 3 - 0.0290 \cdot 2}{3 + 2} = -0.0006. \tag{6.101}$$

All calculated values are presented in Table 6.19. In the next step, kabanos sausages which will be taken into account in further studies are determined. For this purpose, R value was determined for the criterion not taking part in calculations that is *flavor* criterion. *Flavor* is the motivating criterion, so to determine R it was sufficient to determine $\underset{\text{v}}{R}$:

$$\underset{\text{v}}{R} = \sum_{i=m_\text{v}-m_\text{vs}+1}^{m_\text{v}} \underset{\text{v}}{\tau_i''} \text{w}_i' = \sum_{i=m_\text{v}-m_\text{vs}+1}^{m_\text{v}} \frac{\underset{\text{v}}{\tau_i'}}{\left\| \underset{\text{v}}{\vec{\text{T}}'} \right\|} \text{w}_i' = \frac{0.3}{0.3799} \cdot 0.0769 = 0.0607. \tag{6.102}$$

R will be

$$R = \frac{m_\text{v} \underset{\text{v}}{R}}{m_\text{v} + m_\text{d} + m_\text{nd}} = \frac{3 \cdot 0.0607}{3 + 2 + 0} = 0.0364. \tag{6.103}$$

Based on this, the threshold B is calculated:

$$B = \max_j \left(\mu_j\right) - R = 0.0135 - 0.0364 = -0.0230. \tag{6.104}$$

Values μ_j for Preludium bekonowe Henryk Kania and Gala Sokołów are below this threshold, and therefore they will not be included in further calculations. For

Table 6.21 The values of the normalized criteria for the selection of kabanos sausage as an example

Kabanos name	Calorific value [kcal]	Protein [g]	Fat [g]	Price [PLN/kg]	Flavor
Krakus	0.3478	0.5268	0.3044	0.4333	0.5703
Chicken Konspol Natura	0.2699	0.4229	0.2292	0.4536	0.2585
Pork Delux	0.4321	0.4172	0.4459	0.2584	0.1711

the rest of kabanos sausages, a comparison was made taking into account *flavor* criterion. In result, a comparison matrix was obtained:

$$C_5 = \begin{bmatrix} 1 & 5 & 2 \\ \frac{1}{5} & 1 & 3 \\ \frac{1}{2} & \frac{1}{3} & 1 \end{bmatrix}. \tag{6.105}$$

Under the comparison matrix, the eigenvector was determined:

$$C_5' = \begin{bmatrix} 0.5703 \\ 0.2582 \\ 0.1711 \end{bmatrix}, \tag{6.106}$$

which will then be the value of flavor criterion. Furthermore, these values should be normalized. The method that gives normalized values was applied for the calculations, and therefore normalization was not necessary. The values of the normalized criteria supplemented with the flavor criterion are presented in Table 6.21.

For kabanos sausages supplemented with *flavor* criterion $\underset{\mathrm{v}}{\mu_j}$, value was again determined. As an example, $\underset{\mathrm{v}}{\mu_1}$ value was calculated as follows:

$$\underset{\mathrm{v}}{\mu_1} = \sum_{i=1}^{m_{\mathrm{v}}} \left(\underset{1}{x_i'} - \underset{\mathrm{v}}{\phi_i'} \right) \underset{\mathrm{v}}{\tau_i''} \mathrm{w}_i' = (0.3478 - 0.5335) \cdot (-0.5617) \cdot 0.1538$$
$$+ (0.4333 - 0.4623) \cdot (-0.2467) \cdot 0.3077 + (0.5703 - 0.2) \cdot \frac{0,3}{0.3799} \cdot 0.0769$$
$$= 0.0160 + 0.0022 + 0.0225 = 0.0407. \tag{6.107}$$

All $\underset{\mathrm{v}}{\mu_j}$ values are entered in Table 6.22.

Values of $\underset{\mathrm{d}}{\mu_j}$ for kabanos sausages do not change. Therefore, μ_j values will be determined immediately in the next step. The value of μ_1 is

Table 6.22 Index values for the selection of kabanos sausages as an example

Kabanos name	$\underset{\text{v}}{\mu_j}$	$\underset{\text{d}}{\mu_j}$	μ_j
Krakus	0.0407	0.0290	0.0128
Chicken Konspol Natura	0.0328	0.0015	0.0191
Pork Delux	0.0261	0.0667	−0.0110

$$\mu_1 = \frac{\underset{\text{v}}{\mu_1} m_{\text{v}} - \underset{\text{d}}{\mu_1} m_{\text{d}}}{m_{\text{v}} + m_{\text{d}}} = \frac{0.0407 \cdot 3 - 0.0290 \cdot 2}{3 + 2} = 0.0128. \tag{6.108}$$

All μ_j values are presented in Table 6.22. The kabanos sausage most suited to Mr. Kowalski's preferences was the Chicken Konspol Natura sausage.

6.5 Comparison of the PVM Method with Selected Multi-criteria Methods

Table 6.23 provides a summary of different methods used in decision-making. For comparison, the PVM method has been attached to them. In terms of characteristics, it is the method most similar to TOPSIS. What distinguishes it from TOPSIS is that it applies a one-dimensional coordinate system in calculations. Contrary to other methods, it is not necessary to assess the relative significance of the criteria, as the method itself is able to evaluate them on the basis of determining a positive and negative pattern.

Table 6.24 provides a comparative overview of AHP, ELECTRE, PROMETHEE, TOPSIS, and PVM methods. The PVM method is distinguished primarily by its simplicity, which enables easy interpretation of the result and its operation. It uses a scalar product defined for the Euclidean space, but there are no methodological contraindications for using other scalar products. This allows for easy modification and adding to new elements, for example, multi-element numbers, describing the inaccuracy of the data, which would make it equivalent to methods using fuzzy numbers. Depending on the needs of a decision-maker, the PVM method can work in two versions. Can search for decision variants with criteria closest to the ones indicated by him or search for variants with criteria similar or better. A combination of both versions is also possible. None of the analyzed methods allows combining the two approaches. The calculation process of the PVM method is one of the simplest of the compared methods and is similar to the TOPSIS method. The number of steps is always constant and depends only on the character of criterion. The nature of the calculations allows easy presentation in the matrix form, which simplifies the parallelization of calculations and hardware implementation. This allows the method to be used where there is a need to quickly create a ranking for a large amount of data (for example, creating a ranking of all websites in a given language or all visitors to a given website).

Table 6.23 Characteristics of AHP, TOPSIS, ELECTRE and PVM methods (based on [227])

Characteristics	AHP	TOPSIS	ELECTRE I	ELECTRE II	ELECTRE III	PVM
Basic process	Create a hierarchical structure and pairwise comparison matrix	Calculating distances from positive and negative patterns	Defining concordance and discordance indexes	Defining concordance and discordance indexes	Defining concordance and discordance indexes with indifference and preference thresholds	Determining the projection length of a vector representing decision variant onto $\vec{T}$ vector and (or) distance from $\vec{\Psi}$
Need to assess relative significance criteria	Yes	Yes	Yes	Yes	Yes	No
Weights determination	Pairwise comparison matrices, scale 1–9	No specific method. Linear or vector normalization	No specific method. Depends on a decision-maker	No specific method. Depends on a decision-make	No specific method. Depends on a decision-maker decyzje	Dual weight system while calculating $\vec{T}$ and under the formula (6.59).
Number and type of outranking relation	$\frac{N(N-1)}{2}$	1	1	2	1 Fuzzy	1
Consistency check	Ensured	No	No	No	Ensured	No
Structure of a problem	Small number of alternatives and criteria, qualitative or quantitative data	Big number of alternatives and criteria, objective and quantitative data	Big number of alternatives and criteria, objective and quantitative data	Big number of alternatives and criteria, objective and quantitative data	Objective and quantitative data, use of fuzzy logic	Big number of criteria, quantitative data
Final result	Global ordering	Global ordering	Relevant content	Partial ordering	Partial ordering	Global ordering

Table 6.24 Comparison of AHP, ELECTRE, PROMETHEE, TOPSIS, and PVM methods (based on [208])

Method	Advantages	Disadvantages	Area of application
Analytical hierarchy process (AHP)	Easy to use, scalable, hierarchy structure can be customized to fit different size problems, not memory-consuming.	Problems resulting from the interdependence between alternatives and criteria; may lead to inconsistency between the decision and the ranking criteria; reverse ranking.	Performance Issues, Resource Management, Corporate Policy And Strategy, Public Policy, Political Strategies and Planning
ELECTRE	It takes into account the uncertainty	The process and results may be difficult to explain to a layperson, outranking relations make the strengths and weaknesses of individual solutions not easy to direct identification	Energy, Economy, Environment, Water Management, Transportation Issues.
PROMETHEE	Easy to use, it does not require the assumption that criteria are by percent (proportional).	It does not provide a clear method of weighting.	Environment, Hydrology, Water Management, Business And Finance, Chemicals, Logistics And Transport, Manufacturing And Assembly, Energy, Agriculture. .
TOPSIS	Simple process, easy to use and program, the number of steps is always the same regardless of the number of attributes	The use of the Euclidean distance does not take into account correlation between the attributes; it is difficult to determine the weights and keep the decisions consistent.	Supply Chain Management, Logistics, Engineering, Manufacturing Systems, Business and Marketing, Environment, Human Resources, Water Resource Management.
PVM	A very simple process, easy to use and program, the number of steps is always the same, regardless of the number of criteria and decision variants, the possibility of using any scalar product gives potentially great opportunities for further expansion of the method, for example with uncertainty.	Use of the Euclidean distance for the desirable and non-desirable criteria does not take into account the correlation between the criteria.	Environmental Protection, Economy, Consumer Decisions Making.

In order to compare the methods, the computation time was compared. ELECTRE I, ELECTRE Iv, ELECTRE II, ELECTRE III, PVM, AHP, PRTOMETHEE, MAUT, REMBRANDT, and DEMATEL methods were implemented into the Matlab environment. Where possible, the implementation included matrix operations that enable acceleration of computation by parallelizing them.

Research Experiment No. 1. Impact of the Number of Criteria on the Computation Time
In the first study, the number of variants was assumed to be constant and set at five. It was assumed that the number of criteria would change in the range from 2 to 50. The numerical values describing the decision variants and possibly other parameters were randomized. They had standard distribution. For each number of criteria between (2 and 50), numerical values were randomly generated on which calculations were performed. 100 such computations were made. The time was measured and then averaged. The result is presented in Fig. 6.13. The ELELCTRE II method is characterized by the longest computation time. The fastest methods are MAUT and DEMATEL.

Research Experiment No. 2. Impact of the Number of Decision Variants on the Computation Time
Similar studies were performed for a variable number of decision variants. The number of criteria was assumed to be five, while the number of decision variants was changed to the range from 3 to 50. As before, the values were randomized, and for each number of variants, 100 computations were made and the result was averaged. The results are shown in Fig. 6.14. For a larger number of variants, the ELECTRE methods and the AHP method performed weak, where the computation time grows non-linearly and very quickly with the increase in the number of decision variants. The MAUT method performed well, and for more decision variants also the PVM performed well in the study.

Research Experiment No. 3. Impact of Atypical Decision Variants on the Position of Other Variants in Ranking at Various Numbers of Criteria
The impact of atypical decision variants on the calculation result was analyzed. At the beginning, it was checked how atypical decision variants with a variable number of criteria affect the result. During the study, one of the decision variants was changed the value of one criterion so that it was equal to 10 standard deviations of the value of this criterion for all variants. The ranking before and after this operation was calculated and how many decision variants would change their position. The displacement of a decision variant which value was changed was not taken into account, and changes in the position of other variants resulting from the displacement of this variant were not taken into account. The other elements of the study were carried out in the same way as before. Only those methods that enable ranking were taken into account: ELECTRE II, ELECTRE III, PVM, AHP, PROMETHEE II, MAUT, and REMBRANDT. The result is presented in Fig. 6.15. It can be noticed that for a larger number of criteria, the ELECTRE, PROMETHEE

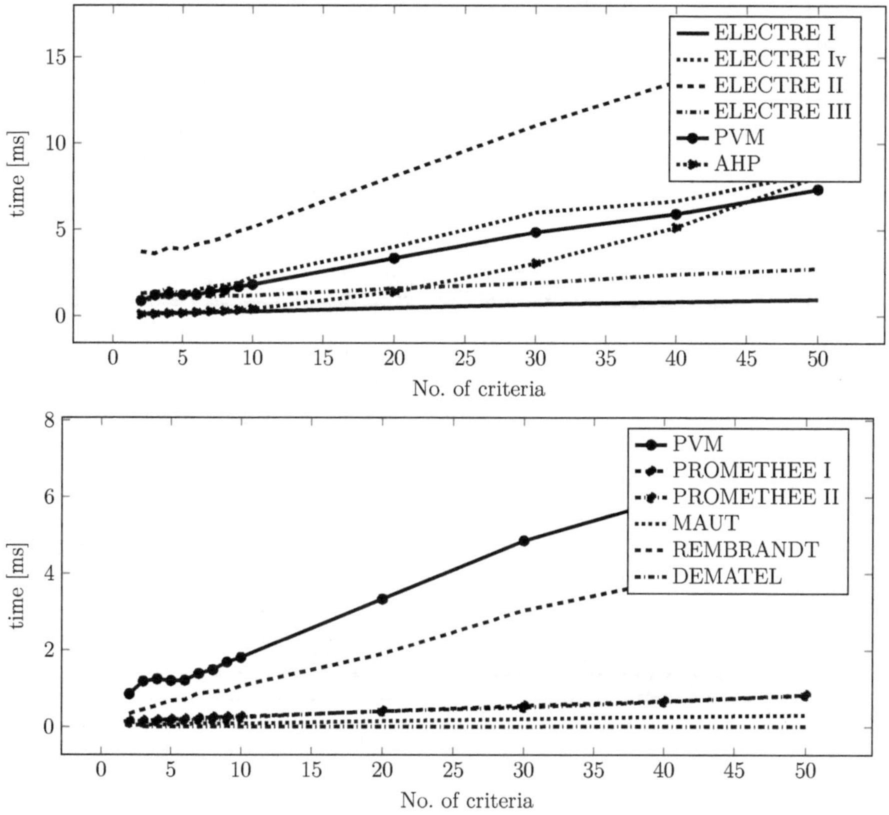

Fig. 6.13 Impact of the number of criteria on the computation time

II, and REMBRANDT methods perform quite well. For more than 20 criteria, ELECTRE methods are insensitive to atypical decision variants. With a smaller number, the PROMETHEE II and REMBRANDT methods work the best and the ELECTRE II the worst. For two, three, and four criteria, the ELECTRE II achieves a result close to 2.5. With 5 decision variants, this means that more than 50 percent of variants change their position in the ranking. The atypical decision variant is not taken into account, and the value of 2.5 should therefore be referred to the number 4 and not 5. Such a result disqualifies this method for use in the event of any atypical decision variants.

Research Experiment No. 4. Studying the Impact of Non-typical Decision Variants on the Place of Other Variants in the Ranking with a Different Number of Decision Variants

The research was carried out in a similar way for a variable number of decision variants (Fig. 6.16). As before, a very poor result can be observed for the ELECTRE II method. With a larger number of decision variants, the number of decision

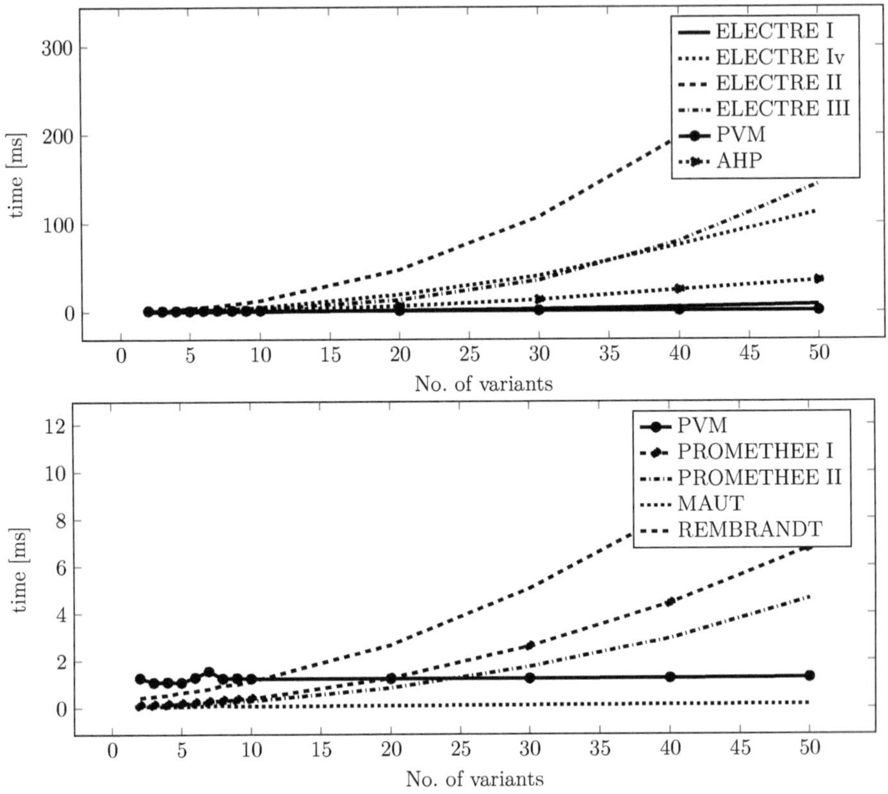

Fig. 6.14 Impact of the number of variants on computation time

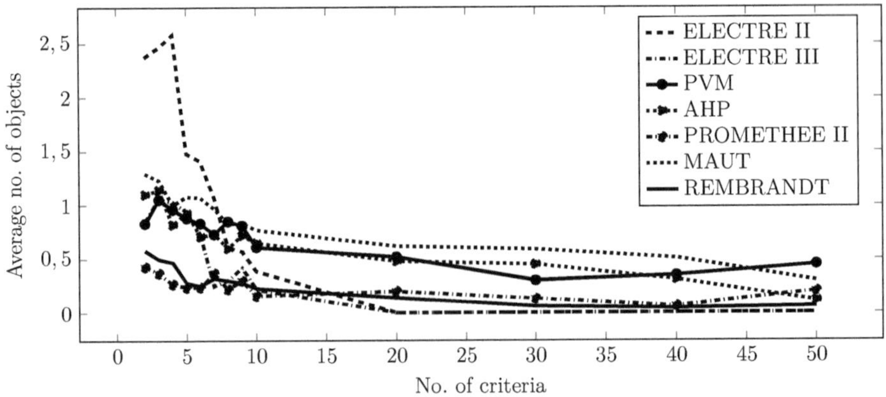

Fig. 6.15 Impact of atypical decision variants on the position of other variants in the ranking at various numbers of criteria

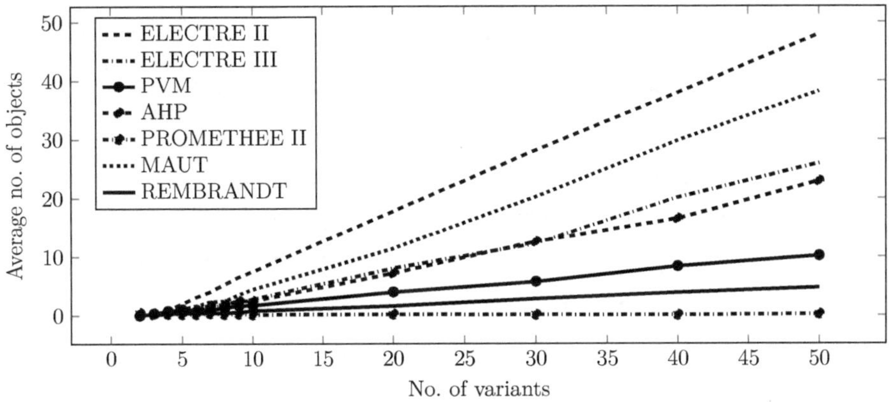

Fig. 6.16 Impact of atypical decision variants on the position of other variants in the ranking at various number of decision variants

variants that changed positions in the ranking reaches 100 percent. The MAUT method achieves a similarly poor result, with approximately 75 percent of variants. On the other hand, a very good result was achieved by the PROMETHEE II method, for which the level of change in the ranking is at about 1 percent. Taking into account the results of studies with a variable number of variants and criteria, the best method in the case of atypical decision variants turned out to be the PROMETHEE II method.

Research Experiment No. 5. Impact of Removing One Decision Variant on the Position of Other Variants in the Ranking at Various Numbers of Criteria
The impact of removing the decision variant on the ranking result was examined. The research was carried out in the same way as when examining the impact of atypical decision variants on the ranking. However, instead of changing the criterion value of the decision variant, it was removed from the set. The result of the experiment conducted for 5 decision variants for a variable number of criteria is shown in Fig. 6.17. The AHP method was the worst in this study. The ELECTRE methods worked the best for a large number of criteria and the MAUT method for a small number.

Research Experiment No. 6. Impact of Removing One Decision Variant on the Position of Other Variants in the Ranking at Various Number of Decision Variants
Figure 6.18 shows the results of studies on the impact of removing a decision variant on the ranking at the fixed number of criteria equal to 5 and a variable number of decision variants. It can be noticed that the methods are less sensitive to removing the decision variant than to atypical variants. The AHP method was the worst, and the MAUT method turned out to be the best. For a medium and large number of decision variants, it is best to use the MAUT method. With a large number of

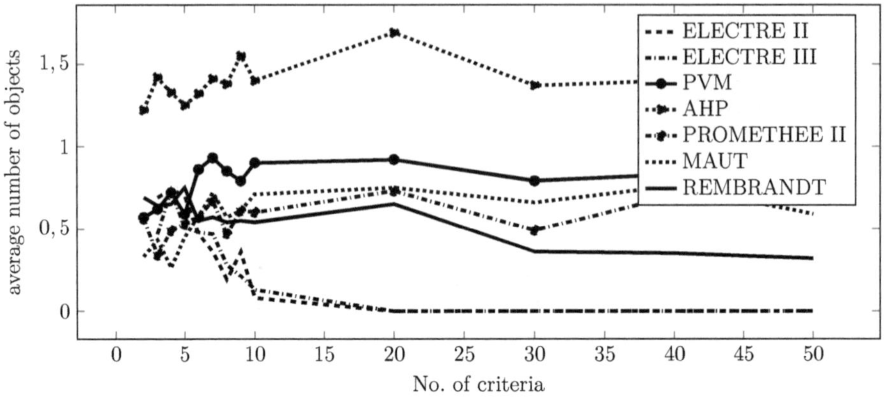

Fig. 6.17 Impact of removing one decision variant on the position of other variants in the ranking at various numbers of criteria

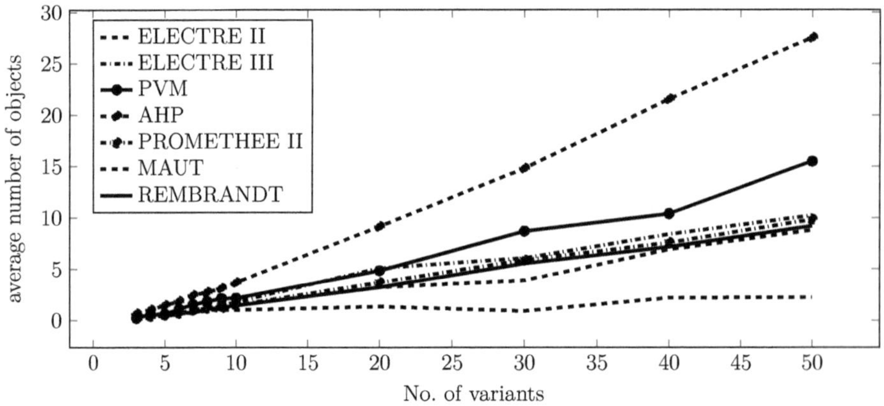

Fig. 6.18 Impact of removing one decision variant on the position of other variants in the ranking at various number of decision variants

criteria and a small number of decision variants, it is more advantageous to use the ELECTRE methods.

6.6 PVM Method in Decision-Making Support

6.6.1 Preference Vector Method in Decision-Making Support

The PVM method was used in research aimed at assessing the EU countries in terms of the quality of life of their inhabitants, disparities in the level of education

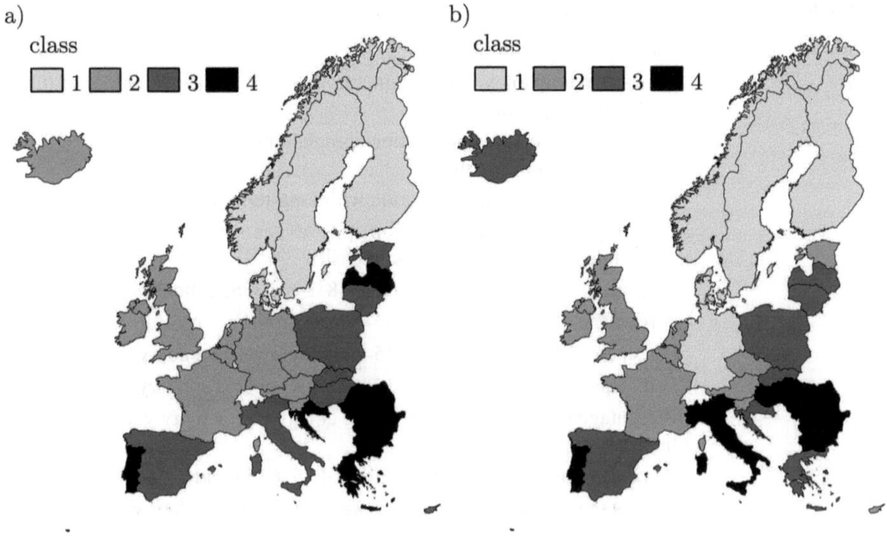

Fig. 6.19 Classification of countries according to (**a**) quality of life of residents and (**b**) disparities in the level of education

in individual countries, the situation on the labor market, living conditions for a retired person, the standard of living of the inhabitants, and friendliness of countries to newly emerging enterprises. For the purposes of the research, a database of 34 indicators was created. Variables X_1-X_{25}, i.e., 25, out of all variables referred to the year 2013 and were sourced from Eurostat database [34]. Other data referred to the year 2015 and were obtained from ESS reports [221] (Table 6.25).

6.6.2 Variant 1. Assessment of European Countries in Terms of the Quality of Life of Their Residents

This is a very important subject in terms of striving to reduce excessive differences in the material and social situation of the population, which is the goal of contemporary socio-economic development. Measuring quality of life is a multi-faceted issue, requiring the aggregation of many indicators. Therefore, 25 indexes have been taken into account (X_1–X_{25}). Only countries for which data were available from Eurostat were included. The countries were ranked according to the value of the μ_j index obtained. The result is presented in Table 6.26 and Fig. 6.19.

Table 6.25 Variables used in studies

Variable	Name
X_1	Long-term unemployment (12 months or more) as the percentage of the total unemployment
X_2	Percentage of the total population complaining about noise from neighbors or from the street
X_3	Percentage of the total population with long-term health problems
X_4	Percentage of the total population up to 60 years of age living in households with very low work intensity
X_5	Percentage of the population of age 18–24 leaving school prematurely
X_6	Percentage of population aged 25–64 with higher education
X_7	Percentage of population aged 15–64 with lower secondary education
X_8	Percentage of population aged 15–64 with upper secondary education
X_9	Percentage of population performing at least one activity via the Internet
X_{10}	Percentage of working population aged 15–64 in multi-shift work
X_{11}	Percentage of working population aged 15–64, sometimes working on Saturdays
X_{12}	Percentage of working population aged 15–64, sometimes working in the evening hours.
X_{13}	Percentage of working population aged 15–64, who sometimes work on Sundays
X_{14}	Percentage of working population aged 15–64 who sometimes perform night work
X_{15}	Percentage of population performing criminal activities, using violence or vandalism
X_{16}	Percentage of part-time working population aged 15–64
X_{17}	Percentage gender pay gap in industry, construction and services (except public administration, defense and compulsory social security)
X_{18}	Ratio of the top to bottom quintiles of population income
X_{19}	The unemployment rate of the population aged 15–74 as a percentage
X_{20}	The average life length
X_{21}	Median net income (in euro)
X_{22}	Percentage of the population having attended training in the last 4 weeks
X_{23}	Percentage of population at risk of poverty
X_{24}	Percentage of population in arrears since 2003 (mortgage, rent, utility bills or leasing)
X_{25}	Percentage of population reporting problems related to pollution, dirt or other environmental problems
X_{26}	Percentage of the population reporting not satisfied medical needs due to the high cost of service
X_{27}	The total number of procedures required to register a business activity
X_{28}	The total number of days required to register a business activity
X_{29}	Administrative costs of setting up a business as a percentage of national income per capita (as a percentage)

(continued)

Table 6.25 (continued)

Variable	Name
X_{30}	Financial collateral related to the registration of a business activity, which is brought to a bank or notary by a person starting business activity (before registration or within 3 months of registration) (defined as a percentage of income per capita)
X_{31}	Total amount of taxes paid by companies in the second year of operation (as a percentage of profit)
X_{32}	Percentage of population who rated the state of health care at the time of the study at 5 or more (on a scale of 0–10)
X_{33}	Percentage of population who rated the state of education at the time of the survey at 5 or more (on a scale of 0–10)
X_{34}	Percentage of emigrants who rated a given country as better to live in at 5 or more (on a scale of 0–10)
X_{35}	Percentage of population who rated the impact of emigration on the country's economy at 5 or more (on a scale of 0–10)
X_{36}	Percentage of population that said there was discrimination based on nationality (on a scale of 0–10)

Table 6.26 The values of the μ_j index are used to assess the EU countries in terms of the quality of life of their residents

Country	μ_j	Class	Country	μ_j	Class
Norway	1.00	1	Cyprus	0.44	3
Luxembourg	0.94	1	Malta	0.41	3
Sweden	0.87	1	Estonia	0.41	3
Denmark	0.84	1	Slovakia	0.41	3
Finland	0.79	1	Italy	0.41	3
France	0.76	2	Lithuania	0.32	3
The Netherlands	0.74	2	Poland	0.32	3
Austria	0.72	2	Spain	0.30	3
Belgium	0.66	2	Hungary	0.22	3
Great Britain	0.63	2	Portugal	0.15	4
Germany	0.61	2	Latvia	0.14	4
Slovenia	0.59	2	Romania	0.11	4
Czech Republic	0.59	2	Croatia	0.10	4
Island	0.54	2	Bulgaria	−0.02	4
Ireland	0.53	2	Greece	−0.17	4

6.6.3 *Variant 2. Assessment of Education Disparities in European Countries*

The second variant of the study compared countries in terms of educational disparities of education. The level of education is reflected in the role that a given country will play on the European market. A well-educated population provides the basis for the development of the high-tech enterprise sector and increases the state revenues related to taxation of these enterprises. Indicators X_5–X_9 and X_{21}

Table 6.27 Values of μ_j index used to assess the EU countries in terms of disparities in the level of education

Country	μ_j	Class	Country	μ_j	Class
Norway	0.90	1	Cyprus	0.54	2
Sweden	0.88	1	Croatia	0.47	3
Luxembourg	0.87	1	Latvia	0.46	3
Finland	0.87	1	Poland	0.46	3
Germany	0.86	1	Slovakia	0.42	3
Denmark	0.83	1	Island	0.41	3
France	0.80	2	Lithuania	0.37	3
Ireland	0.79	2	Spain	0.31	3
Great Britain	0.78	2	Greece	0.27	3
The Netherlands	0.75	2	Bulgaria	0.25	4
Slovenia	0.70	2	Hungary	0.21	4
Austria	0.68	2	Romania	0.16	4
Estonia	0.65	2	Malta	0.08	4
Czech Republic	0.65	2	Portugal	0.04	4
Belgium	0.56	2	Italy	0.01	4

were taken into account during the survey. The ranking shows that people living in rich countries pay great attention to education and further training (Table 6.27 and Fig. 6.19b). The greatest disparities are associated with indicator X_{21}: *the percentage of the population having attended training in the last 4 weeks*. The coefficient of variation for this indicator was 0.73 with the top-ranked countries having a coefficient of variation exceeding 20% and the bottom-ranked countries below 10%. In addition, the coefficient was high for indicator X_5: *percentage of the population of age 18–24 leaving school prematurely* (0.48) and X_7: *percentage of the population of age 15–64 with lower secondary education* (0.43). The coefficients of variation for the remaining indexes did not exceed 0.3. This means that the decisive influence on the position in the ranking was exerted by indicators X_5, X_9, and X_{21}. The results indicate a lower awareness of the need for further education and training in poorer countries, which have fewer financial resources. A certain role may also be played here by the high technology industry, which is well developed in rich countries.

6.6.4 *Variant 3. Assessment of EU Countries' Friendliness Toward Business Start-Ups*

The study made an assessment to find among the European countries the one that is the friendliest to business start-ups in terms of both the listed economic and social conditions. Ten decision criteria were selected for study: five economic and five social (X_{26}–X_{35}). Four of the analyzed criteria for making decisions to locate a business in a particular country were

Table 6.28 Values of the μ_j indicator used to assess countries in terms of their friendliness to business start-ups

Country	μ_j	Class	Country	μ_j	Class
Finland	1.13	1	France	0.47	3
Ireland	1.11	1	Portugal	0.44	3
Denmark	1.04	1	Island	0.39	3
Norway	0.83	1	Kosovo	0.38	3
Luxembourg	0.82	1	Slovenia	0.32	3
Great Britain	0.76	2	Croatia	0.31	3
Israel	0.76	2	Spain	0.31	3
Sweden	0.73	2	Russia	0.28	3
Lithuania	0.72	2	Latvia	0.26	3
The Netherlands	0.70	2	Poland	0.20	3
Austria	0.69	2	Cyprus	0.12	4
Belgium	0.61	2	Ukraine	0.11	4
Switzerland	0.59	2	Czech Republic	0.10	4
Albania	0.53	2	Greece	0.06	4
Bulgaria	0.53	2	Slovakia	0.05	4
Estonia	0.50	2	Italy	−0.03	4
Germany	0.50	2	Hungary	−0.04	4

found to be stimulants (X_{31}–X_{34}), and six were found to be destimulants (X_{26}–X_{30} i X_{35}).

Table 6.28 presents the obtained values of the μ_j index evaluating the contextual conditions for choosing country for business location. These results allow ranking the analyzed countries from the least to the most friendly to new entrepreneurship and dividing these countries into four classes. Finland is the best country to start a business and Hungary the worst. Finland is a country where an entrepreneur starting a business is subject to only 3 procedures (fewer only in Slovenia, ranked in the third tier of countries analyzed), and Hungary has 4 business registration procedures. In Finland, however, the time to register a new business is almost 3 times longer (14 days) than in Hungary (5 days). Finland has one of the lowest start-up costs (1.1% of income, the lowest is in Slovenia), while a person who decides to start a business in Hungary has to pay more than seven times higher costs. There are similar discrepancies regarding the level of financial security required to register a business. The overall tax rate in Finland, although 8% point lower than in Hungary, is not among the lowest among the analyzed countries. It is 8% point higher than in Slovenia and is more than 2.5 times the tax rate in Kosovo, where it is the lowest. However, what most differentiates the countries at the beginning and the end of the ranking in Table 6.28 is the social conditionality of economic activity. In Finland, more than 4 times as many people rate the state of education and health services highly, more than 2 times as many people point to the positive impact of immigration on the state of the economy, and the country is a better place to live and has more than 6 times fewer xenophobes compared to Hungary.

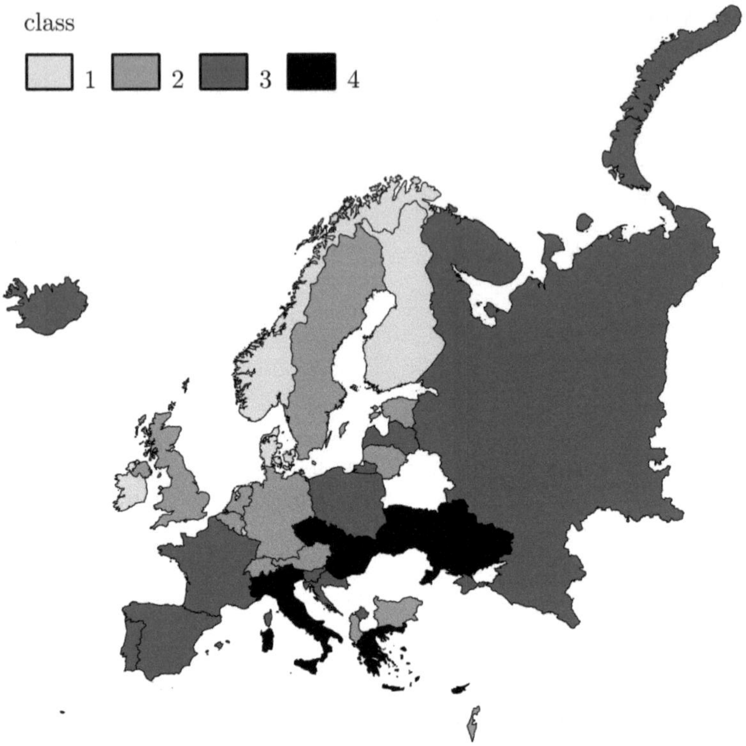

Fig. 6.20 Ranking of countries in terms of their friendliness to business start-ups

Apart from Finland, the first group of the most entrepreneur-friendly countries includes four countries classified as the most developed and also characterized by a high standard of living (Fig. 6.20). Thus, the analysis carried out shows that not only, as shown by other studies, the level of GDP is positively correlated with entrepreneurship but also these countries, by creating friendly formal and informal conditions conducive to running a business, can attract enterprising people from other countries.

The most numerous group is the countries included in the second class. At the same time, this group of countries is the most diverse in terms of both GDP per capita and the level of human development measured by HDI [222]. It consists of countries which, due to the level of development, are classified both as highly developed countries (7 countries) and those at the medium (Estonia and Lithuania) or lower development level (Albania). However, the assessment of other conditions, which are the analyzed decision criteria, classified these countries in the same class.

Poland is one of the third-class countries, and its inclusion in this group is determined primarily by the long duration of business registration (6 times longer than in Hungary), one of the highest levels of costs of its registration (higher costs should be borne only in Italy) and a low rating of the state of education and health services (half and twice as low as in Finland, respectively), despite a relatively high percentage of people positively evaluating the effects of immigration and the lack of nationality discrimination (in the opinion of the Poles surveyed).

6.6.5 Variant 4. Assessment of the Labor Market Situation

The first survey assessed the labor market situation. The following indexes were taken into consideration: X_1, X_4, X_{10}–X_{14}, X_{16}, X_{17}, X_{19}, and X_{20}. The obtained ranking (Table 6.29, Fig. 6.21) indicates better situation of employees in the developed countries. The value of the coefficient of variation for all indicators ranges from 0.38 to 0.66. Only X_1: long-term unemployment (12 months or more) as a percentage of the total unemployment is lower. The highest values of the coefficient of variation are achieved by indexes X_{20}: median net income in euro (0.66) and X_{16}: percentage of the working population of age 15–64 forced to work part-time (0.58). One can conclude from the above that the problem of long-term unemployment is fairly uniform in all European countries. However, thanks to better salaries in the developed countries, work comfort is much higher. Employers do not force employees to work overtime, it is voluntary. Working non-standard hours is less common.

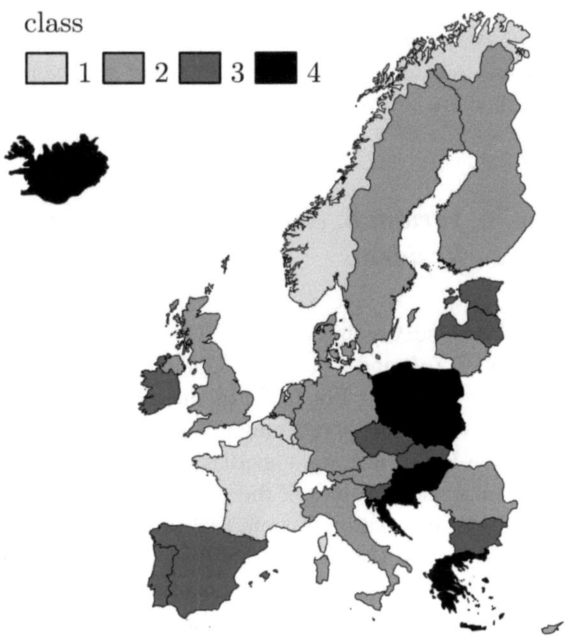

Fig. 6.21 Classification of EU countries by labor market situation

Table 6.29 Values of μ_j used to assess the EU countries in terms of the labor market situation

Country	μ_j	Class	Country	μ_j	Class
Luxembourg	1.19	1	Lithuania	0.49	2
Norway	0.93	1	Estonia	0.43	3
France	0.87	1	Slovenia	0.41	3
Belgium	0.85	1	Czech Republic	0.36	3
The Netherlands	0.84	2	Latvia	0.34	3
Sweden	0.81	2	Spain	0.17	3
Denmark	0.79	2	Portugal	0.17	3
Malta	0.76	2	Bulgaria	0.14	3
Italy	0.75	2	Ireland	0.12	3
Austria	0.75	2	Slovakia	0.12	3
Finland	0.73	2	Hungary	0.07	4
Germany	0.69	2	Poland	0.07	4
Cyprus	0.61	2	Island	0.06	4
Great Britain	0.55	2	Greece	−0.28	4
Romania	0.50	2	Croatia	−0.45	4

6.6.6 Variant 5. Assessment of Countries in Terms of Housing Conditions for Retired Persons

In study two, an assessment was made in terms of housing conditions for a retired person. Indexes: X_2, X_3, X_{15}, X_{24}, and X_{25} were taken into account. The results obtained are shown in Table 6.30 and Fig. 6.22.

6.6.7 Variant 6. Assessment of Living Standards of EU Residents

The fourth survey assessed the living conditions of EU residents. Indexes X_2, X_5, X_{17}–X_{20}, X_{22}, and X_{23} were taken into account. The results obtained are presented in Table 6.31 and Fig. 6.23. In this study, the indicators that most differentiate countries are X_{23}—percentage of population in arrears since 2003 (coefficient of variation 0.71) and X_{20}—median net income in Euro (0.66). The least influential indicators on the values of the μ_j index were X_{18}—ratio of upper quintile to lower quintile of population income (0.23) and X_{22}—percentage of population at risk of poverty (0.24). This means that the problem of poverty in Europe and the income stratification between rich and poor are similar. Countries differ mainly in terms of repayment problems and citizens' income.

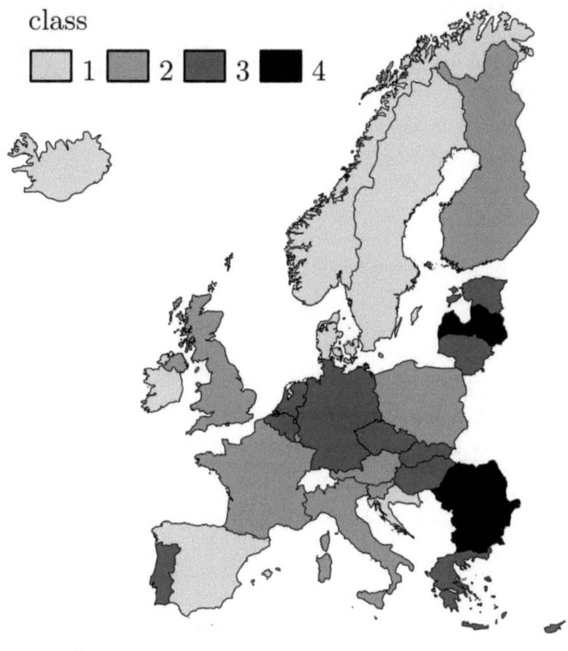

Fig. 6.22 Classification of EU countries in terms of housing conditions for a retired person

Table 6.30 Values of μ_j index for rating EU countries in terms of housing conditions for a retired person, na emeryturze

Country	μ_j	Class	Country	μ_j	Class
Island	1.14	1	Slovakia	0.41	3
Norway	1.03	1	Czech Republic	0.30	3
Ireland	0.98	1	Portugal	0.26	3
Sweden	0.88	1	Hungary	0.24	3
Denmark	0.86	1	Lithuania	0.23	3
Croatia	0.83	1	Belgium	0.21	3
Spain	0.81	1	Estonia	0.20	3
Luxembourg	0.75	2	Cyprus	0.18	3
Slovenia	0.69	2	The Netherlands	0.13	3
Austria	0.56	2	Greece	0.04	3
Finland	0.56	2	Germany	0.03	3
Poland	0.53	2	Malta	−0.08	4
Great Britain	0.51	2	Romania	−0.12	4
Italy	0.50	2	Bulgaria	−0.24	4
France	0.48	2	Latvia	−0.42	4

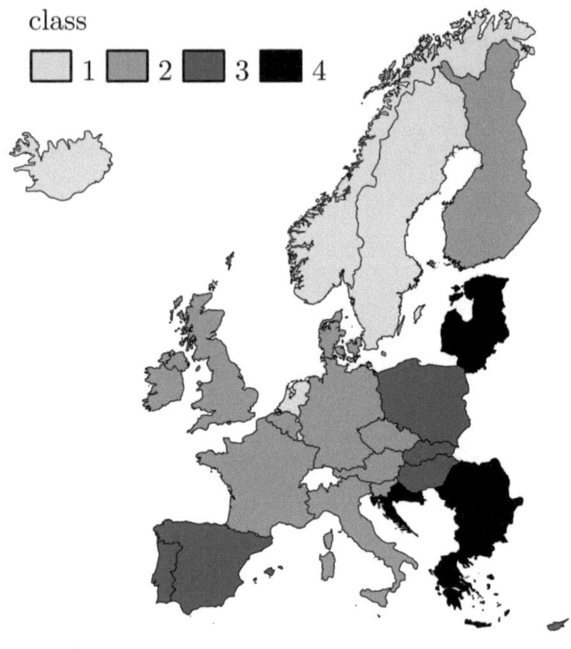

Fig. 6.23 Classification of EU countries according to the standard of living of their inhabitants

Table 6.31 Values of μ_j to assess EU countries in terms of living standards of its population

Country	μ_j	Class	Country	μ_j	Class
Norway	1.30	1	Ireland	0.51	2
Luxembourg	1.03	1	Italy	0.50	2
Sweden	1.01	1	Poland	0.42	3
The Netherlands	0.97	1	Cyprus	0.41	3
Island	0.96	1	Slovakia	0.32	3
Finland	0.92	2	Portugal	0.23	3
Denmark	0.91	2	Hungary	0.20	3
Belgium	0.86	2	Spain	0.12	3
Malta	0.84	2	Croatia	0.04	4
Austria	0.79	2	Estonia	0.02	4
France	0.78	2	Lithuania	0.00	4
Slovenia	0.74	2	Romania	−0.08	4
Czech Republic	0.68	2	Latvia	−0.09	4
Great Britain	0.67	2	Bulgaria	−0.28	4
Germany	0.62	2	Greece	−0.36	4

6.6.8 Application of the PVM Method in Consumer Decision Support

In everyday life, every consumer is faced with decisions related to the choice of different types of sales offers. They experience problems and dilemmas which concern their expectations, the size of the budget allocated to purchase the product, or the quality offered. The buyer would like to receive a high-quality product, which at the same time meets their expectations and has the best price. When making any decision, the consumer considers various criteria, both objective and subjective.

Subjective criteria are usually secondary ones. They are taken into account only after the decision options have been pre-selected according to the most important objective criteria. For example, nobody will buy a car just because it is pretty. It must first of all meet the basic objectives, such as size relevant to the intended use, maximum price, minimum equipment, etc. These objectives determine a certain group of decision options which are acceptable. For these decision options, other criteria, including subjective criteria, are used.

Subjective criteria depend on the influence of the environment on the consumer, which is often used by producers in product promotion. This means that we do not always buy what we want and need, but what the manufacturer wants to sell us. This applies above all to cheap items that we do not have time to think about when purchasing. In the case of cheaper items, people do not spend as much time for the decision itself. This is related to the lack of time to analyze each purchase decision. In the case of cheaper items, people do not spend as much time for the decision itself. This is related to the lack of time to analyze each purchase decision.

Modern technology can support consumers in their decisions by providing necessary information related to a given product during purchase. The use of a computerized system in the decision-making process makes the consumer less susceptible to be influenced by producers when promoting a product. The computer system together with an appropriate set of input and output devices can act as an assistant to consumer by gathering information and providing it to the consumer at the right moment.

A consumer assistant may consist of a computer and a camera with an IMU (*Inertial Measurement Unit*), which collects information about everything in the vicinity of the shopper. The IMU is an Inertial Measurement Unit used to determine the position of the camera in relation to the ground. It allows you to eliminate frames of film that are not useable due to motion blur, correction of the image due to incorrect orientation of the camera in relation to the ground, and determination of the state in which consumer has stopped while viewing the product. The role of the IMU is auxiliary, but very important, as it allows to simplify the algorithms used in product identification, which translates into less computer processing power required. The next component of the system is the handset, which purpose is to provide information to the buyer (Fig. 6.24a).

The consumer assistant can collect data and retrieve it or send it to a system for the exchange of information between consumers and institutions and social organizations (Fig. 6.25). The concept of such a system could be based on a central database collecting data from various sources, such as testing institutions and centers controlling the quality of food products. Any information about a penalty and the results of tests and analyses can be entered into the database. In this way, the terminal that the consumer has will be able to connect to the database, in order to immediately obtain information on a given producer and possibly his product.

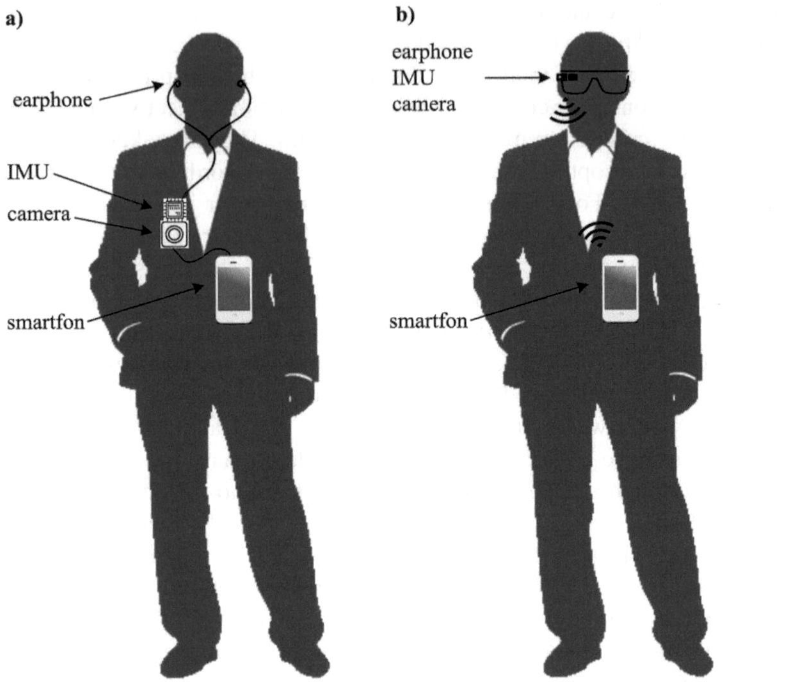

Fig. 6.24 The consumer assistant: (**a**) camera placed in a suit and (**b**) a camera placed in glasses

Consumers can report their dissatisfaction and suspicions even in the shop. The system can also evaluate the product itself and automatically transmit the information to the database. Out-of-date products, missing price tags, strange color, or stains on the product can be registered and sent to the database straight away. Such information can be forwarded to control institutions, which will be able to easily track down dishonest sellers. On the basis of the frequency of irregularities at various manufacturers and sellers, the system, using the implemented penalty grid, may itself propose a penalty for a given act. It is possible to create databases of prices suggested by producers for the turnover of their products. Such a database can prevent the consumer from falling victim to unfair promotions.

Ranking methods in the consumer assistant software can be used primarily to compare goods of a similar nature or equivalents suggested by the consumer. The right choice of criteria had an important influence on the outcome of the ranking. In the case of a consumer assistant, the criteria should be related to customer preferences, which depend on the type of goods. For example, in some cases, aesthetics is very important, and in some cases it is not important at all. There are many properties which only goods of a certain type have. An appropriate set of criteria should be selected for each of them. For example, the following relevant criteria can be identified for food products:

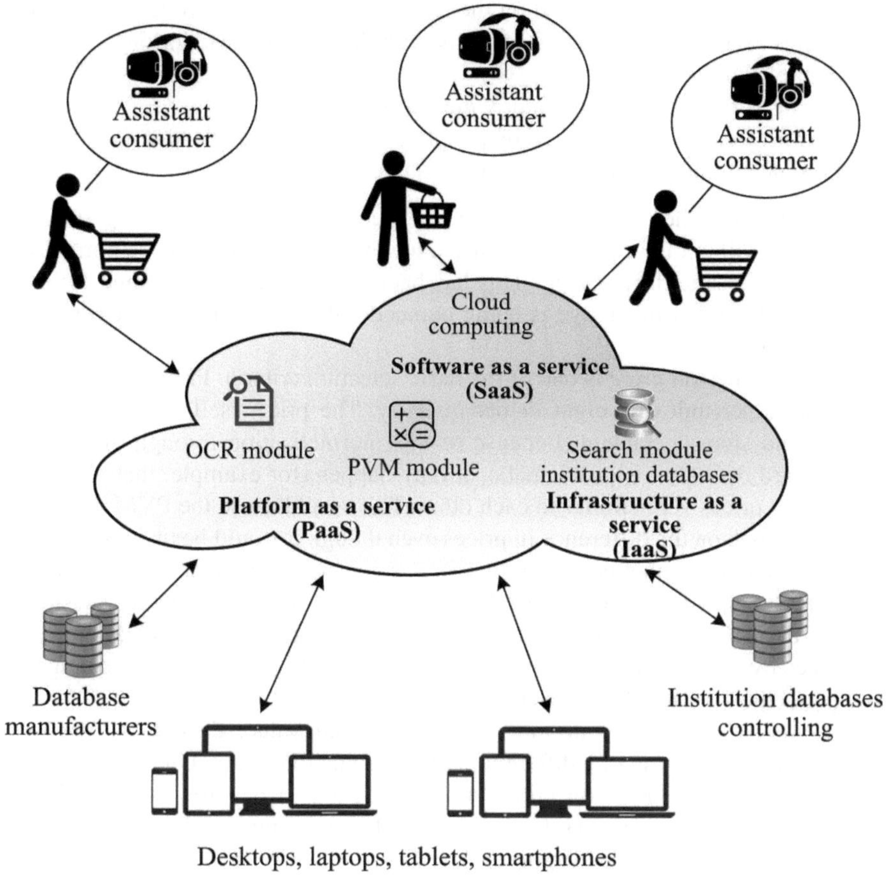

Fig. 6.25 Exchange of information system

1. Price per weight unit or the price per number of pieces or the price per content of certain components.
2. Weight of the good or the number of units.
3. Percentage of the essential ingredient or ingredients in the product, for example the meat in the product.
4. Content of undesirable substances, for example, preservatives.
5. Conformity to nutrient profile.
6. Production process, by which is meant the way the product is made, e.g., in case of eggs, this may be free range farming.
7. Appearance of the goods, which is not a visual effect but an assessment of the quality and freshness of the product based on color, discoloration, etc.
8. History of penalties imposed on the manufacturer by courts and control bodies, related to purity and exceeding permitted standards of substances.

9. History of penalties imposed on the manufacturer by courts of law and control bodies as a result of failure to comply with the product description as declared by the manufacturer.
10. Flavor as rated by self and family members.
11. Flavor of the product as rated by people who claim to be friends.
12. Presence of the producer on the social share list.

The validity of the criteria depends on the specific product. For some goods, certain criteria will not have any importance. However, all criteria must be normalized to a more or less uniform range. This has been assumed to be the range $\langle 0; 1 \rangle$. It is assumed here that this range is being pursued rather than strictly adhering to its extreme values.

The first criterion *price* is one of the basic selection criteria. Primarily important is the price per unit of weight or per quantity. The price itself is strongly time-varying and store-dependent. Because of this, normalization through dividing by the standard deviation is problematic. It may happen, for example, that all ranked goods have prices very similar to each other. This would cause the PVM method to focus too much on the difference in prices even though it would be insignificant. On the other hand, in another period of time, goods may have a large price spread due to, for example, a promotion of one of them. This would result in an under-sensitivity to the price difference this time. It was therefore assumed that normalization would take place by means of dividing by the average, which is less sensitive to changes in the spread than the standard deviation.

Price is not a linear criterion. Below a certain value, differences are very insignificant and criteria of a different nature become important. On the other hand, above a certain amount, consumers are not willing to pay for a good, even if compensated by other criteria. Consequently, the price must undergo a non-linear transformation during normalization:

$$f(x) = 2 - \mathrm{e}^{x}. \tag{6.109}$$

The graph of this function is shown in Fig. 6.26. It pursues the value of 2. At low prices, their differences are reduced, so that they are not so important for ranking. In the vicinity of the zero value, near which there is a place corresponding to the value of the average price, the relationship between the value of the function and its argument is linear. At high prices, the differences between them are magnified and the course of the function is almost vertical, which means price values unacceptable for the consumer. To make proper use of the function, the values of its arguments must take the appropriate range:

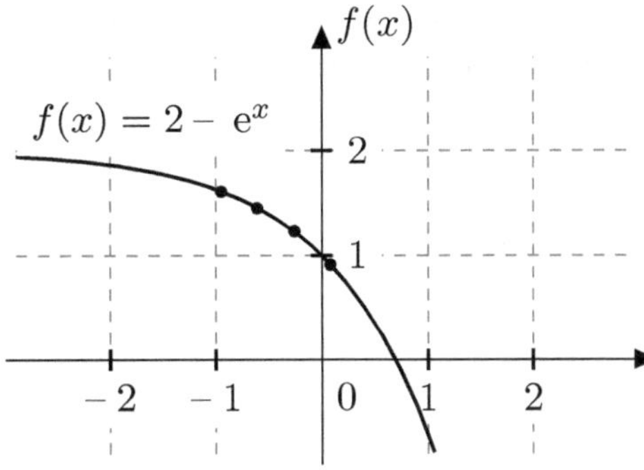

Fig. 6.26 Price value transforming function

$$x''_{\substack{i\\j}} = f\left(\frac{\dfrac{x'_{\substack{i\\j}}}{\mathrm{w_p}} - 1.1}{\dfrac{\mathrm{w_r}}{100}}\right), \tag{6.110}$$

where

$\mathrm{w_p}$—average value,
$\mathrm{w_r}$—the range of values in %.

The $\mathrm{w_p}$ value is the average price for which a consumer would be willing to purchase the good and $\mathrm{w_r}$ is the possible deviation from the price expressed as a percentage. The $\mathrm{w_p}$ and $\mathrm{w_r}$ values can be given directly by the consumer or calculated from the consumer's purchase history. The $\mathrm{w_r}$ parameter brings the range of acceptable prices to the range where the function $f(x) = 2 - \mathrm{e}^x$ gives similar values to the function $f(x) = -x + 1$. For example, five possible prices for similar goods have been identified: 10 PLN, 11 PLN, 12 PLN, 12 PLN, and 13 PLN. In order to determine the average price, the average value was determined, which amounted to 11 PLN 60 gr, and hence $\mathrm{w_p} = 11.6$. The value $\mathrm{w_r}$ was taken as 25% of the determined amount. The values of the variable after normalization were 1.61, 1.23, 1.46, 1.23, and 0.91, respectively, and are marked with dots in Fig. 6.26. You can see that they are more or less in the range of function $f(x) = 2 - \mathrm{e}^x$, where it resembles $f(x) = -x + 1$.

Of slightly different character is the variable related to weight and the number of pieces. In a certain weight (or quantity) range, the greater the weight at the same price, the better. In the case of food products, however, over-buying does not make sense. We cannot consume the excess goods before the end of their shelf life. Although theoretically we pay less per unit of goods (kilogram, piece), in reality we may pay more, because we use only part of the goods and the rest is thrown away. Thus, the more of a good we buy over the assumed level, the less profitable it is for us. The consumer assistant takes from the consumer the assumed quantity of the good w_{wp} and the percentage tolerance for the increase in quantity w_{wr}. Based on this, the variable is normalized:

$$x''_{\substack{i\\j}} = \begin{cases} 1 & \text{For } \begin{matrix} w_{wp} - \frac{w_{wp}w_{wr}}{100} \leq x'_{\substack{i\\j}} \\ w_{wp} + \frac{w_{wp}w_{wr}}{100} > x'_{\substack{i\\j}}, \end{matrix} \\ 1 - \frac{\left\lceil \frac{w_{wp} + \frac{w_{wp}w_{wr}}{100}}{x'_{\substack{i\\j}}} \right\rceil x'_{\substack{i\\j}} - w_{wp}}{w_{wp}} & \text{For othercases.} \end{cases} \tag{6.111}$$

The variable *percentage of the essential ingredient(s) in the product* may be present on its own or combined with the *price* variable, depending on its importance. If it is a very important parameter, the *price* variable should be calculated not per unit of the good but per content of essential ingredient in a unit of the good. This can be done, for example, in case of certain meat products. Due to the non-linear nature of price, this will result in very low rankings for products that are strongly outliers in meat content. If the content of the ingredients is not highly significant, then it can be treated as a separate variable of a linear nature. In this case, it should be expressed as a percentage, and therefore the normalization will simplify to the following form:

$$x''_{\substack{i\\j}} = \frac{x'_{\substack{i\\j}}}{100}. \tag{6.112}$$

The content of essential ingredients may or may not be stated on the product. Where information is provided, the source of information is the product label, possibly verified by reports from control bodies. In the absence of information on the label, the only source of information is the reports of control bodies.

The content of non-desirable substances is a very important variable, but unfortunately their quantitative content is very rarely stated, most often the manufacturer only informs about its use. The list of non-desirable substances is well known. Scientists have carried out various studies to determine their effects on the human body. Experts in medicine, chemistry, and nutrition technology can be involved in the construction of the customer assistant in order to determine the harmfulness of individual substances. They can rank the harmfulness on a scale from 0 to 10, where 0 is no harmfulness and 10 is the most harmful substance. The variable will be created by adding up the scores of all the harmful ingredients contained in the product.

An important problem is the normalization of the variable determining the content of non-desirable substances. The normalization should be done for each of them separately according to the following formula :

$$x''_{\substack{i\\j}} = 1 - \frac{\sum_{k=1}^{N_{sn}} \mathrm{w}_{sn} x'_{\substack{i,k\\j}}}{10N_{sn}}, \tag{6.113}$$

where

$x'_{\substack{i,k\\j}}$—k-th non-desirable substance included in the i-th variable,
N_{sn}—the number of non-desirable substances,
w_{sn}—weight of non-desirable substance value.

The weights of the non-desirable substance values will initially be one, but after a longer action of the consumer assistant, they should be related to the amount of goods bought. The more goods containing a harmful ingredient are bought, the higher the weight should be, so as to limit the amount of consumption of the substance.

The nutrient profile compliance variable is a variable which value should be determined by the consumer assistant module which examines the composition of the consumer's diet on the basis of the food products purchased. This module should evaluate the products consumed in terms of vitamins, micronutrients, calories, etc. On this basis it can propose a shopping list. In addition, it should determine the value of this variable in order to influence, for example, the reduction of the calorie content of the products purchased. It is assumed that the value of the variable obtained from this module is already normalized in a way suitable for ranking construction.

The goods appearance variable concerns goods that can be assessed visually. Evaluation is carried out by a consumer assistant while viewing the goods. For this purpose, a camera will be used and image processing and recognition methods based on expert knowledge will be applied. The evaluation is a variable ranging from 0 to 1 (so it is not subject to normalization), where 1 means the best good and 0 the worst one. The production process is a variable related to the customer's preference for specific ways of producing a good. The consumer can give certain production processes a score from 0 to 10, where 0 means least desirable and 10 means most desirable. In addition, the consumer assistant can propose its own scores based on the opinion of experts evaluating the process in terms of its impact on health. The normalization of the variable is done according to the following formula:

$$x''_{\substack{i\\j}} = \frac{x'_{\substack{i\\j}}}{10}. \tag{6.114}$$

History of penalties related to both cleanliness and non-conformity of goods with the description is a point value ranging from 0 to 10, allocated by the information exchange system. It is the higher the higher the number of penalties imposed on the manufacturer. It should be calculated according to the time when these penalties were imposed. The more distant in time, the impact on the variable should be smaller. Also, the seriousness of the penalty should be reflected in the point value charged. The distinction between two types of penalties is due to the possibility of different treatment of them by the consumer. The normalization of the variable is done according to the following formula:

$$x''_{i_j} = 1 - \frac{x'_{i_j}}{10}. \tag{6.115}$$

Flavor is a variable expressed in points ranging from 0 to 10. The higher the score, the better the flavor. Normalization is done according to the formula (6.114). For certain goods, this variable can be replaced by a variable indicating suitability for preparing, for example, cakes or other home-made products. Its point value depends on the intended use of the product, so the consumer should determine the intended use before buying the good.

The variable presence of a manufacturer on the social share list is related to the possible adherence to this type of action. The action may consist in not buying the products of a specific producer/producers. Such actions may be aimed at forcing a manufacturer to behave in a certain way by refraining from purchasing their products. In the case of food products, such action can be very burdensome due to their limited shelf life. A value of zero for this variable indicates a neutral attitude and a value of one indicates a sanction against the producer. In the case of ranking construction, all products with a value of this variable equal to one will be moved to the end of the ranking, and the display of the results will indicate this.

Not all variables have to take part in the construction of the ranking. The consumer assistant will select the variables depending on the type of commodity. The values of the weights when building the PVM on the basis of the average value will depend not only on the type of product but also on its intended use. For example, a product intended for direct use will have different weights for price and flavor and even the same product intended for processing. The weight should be chosen by the consumer, but this will not be easy for everyone. Therefore, the consumer assistant can first observe the activities and on this basis determine the purchasing patterns for the products concerned. These will be used to calculate the weights which can be presented to the consumer for correction. These patterns can be evaluated in terms of the health impact of the goods and, on this basis, the consumer assistant can propose adjustments to the weights.

An example of a ranking that the consumer assistant could perform is the ranking of salt. The most important variable determining salt is the price per unit of weight. The basic additive to salt is potassium iodide called iodine, which is obligatorily added to salt. In the past, this was regulated by specific Polish regulations, today by EU regulations.

Salt that does not contain potassium iodide is artificially iodized in a suitable production process and is called iodized salt. Therefore, a variable can be introduced to specify the production process, taking, for example, the value 2 for ordinary salt and 0 for iodized salt. Furthermore, salt can be rock salt or sea salt. This also implies a production process. Rock salt is mined from great depths and sea salt is made from sea water. Both these types of salt are not subjected to purification and therefore contain many trace elements. Therefore, the variable for these types of salt can be assigned a value of 10 as the most desirable. Some of these types of salt may be artificially iodized, so a value of 8 can be taken for the variable.

Potassium ferrocyanide may be added to the salt as an anti-caking agent. It may be added to food in certain quantities. Information about this addition must be included on the packaging of the salt. From the point of view of the consumer, it is a non-desirable substance. It can be taken to form the *non-desirable substance variable*. This substance is approved for use, so a small point value can be given, for example, 2 points for a quantity corresponding to the limit value of $3\frac{\text{mg}}{\text{kg}}$. If the packaging indicates a lower content, fewer points may be awarded: $\frac{2}{3}x$, where x means the content of potassium ferrocyanide. If no information is available on the amount of potassium ferrocyanide, it may be assumed that this is the maximum permitted amount.

The limits for potassium ferrocyanide and potassium iodide may be exceeded in salt. It is also possible that the minimum standard for the latter substance is not met. In the salt iodization process, potassium iodide is often added in an uncontrolled manner. As a result, the standard is exceeded or not met. This results in numerous penalties from the State Trade Inspection. This variable can be assigned a value of 10 points for the penalty imposed during the last inspection, 5 points for each penalty of the current year, 2 points for each penalty imposed during the previous year, and 1 point for each penalty imposed two years ago.

A variable related to flavor needs to be assigned a score for flavor. This poses a problem, as salt is purchased quite infrequently, so most of the range cannot be assigned any variable value. To solve this problem, it is possible to assign by default to each product a value of 3, which we consider to be neutral. Anything below 3 means the product flavors unacceptable, and anything above 3 means it tasted to the customer. After buying the product, the customer can rate it and update the information.

When calculating μ_j at the beginning, the consumer assistant can identify the range of prices of interest to the consumer by analyzing historical data. For example, such a graph could look like the one presented in Fig. 6.27. It shows that consumers buy goods in two price ranges: around one zloty and around six zloty. In the latter range, however, price may be less important due to high price dispersion. The consumer assistant can take note of the intended use of the goods, since depending on the intended use, different characteristics of the good may be important to the consumer. In this case, two intended uses can be distinguished: salt used for home-made preparations, for which price is mainly important, and salt intended for daily addition of salt to food (e.g., sandwiches). In the case of this salt, flavor is also important.

Taking into account the different purposes of the product, two rankings should be made. For the first ranking, the average price at which a consumer purchases can be determined on the basis of historical data. It amounts to $\mathrm{w_p} = 0.79$ PLN. The

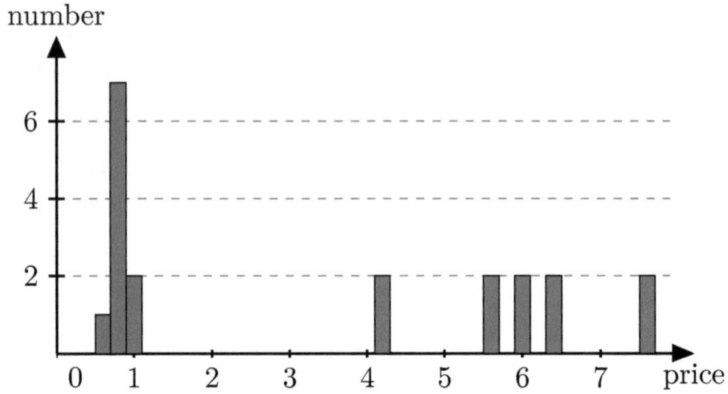

Fig. 6.27 The amount of goods purchased depending on the price

standard deviation of the price at which the consumer bought the salt was 0.08 PLN. Assuming that the price distribution is normal more than 90% of the prices of interest to the customer fall within the range $\pm 2\sigma$. Hence, it can be assumed that $w_r = \frac{4\times 0.08}{0.79} \times 100\% = 40.5\%$. For the second ranking, the average price amount to $w_p = 5.98$ PLN. The standard deviation of the price at which the consumer bought the salt was PLN 1.25. Hence $w_r = \frac{4\times 1.25}{5.98} \times 100\% = 83.6\%$. The consumer most often bought salt in 1 kg packs, and hence $w_{wp} = 1$. Salt is a non-perishable product, and hence the tolerance on packaging size can be assumed to be very high. There is no danger of it becoming out of date and having to be thrown away, and therefore $w_{wr} = 50\%$.

After determining the normalization coefficients, the next step is to determine the weights of individual variables. In the first ranking for salt for processing *price* is the most important variable. The weight for this variable can be taken as 4. Flavor is not very important and can therefore have a very low value of 1. The weight of non-desirable substances depends on individual consumer preferences. For ranking purposes, this can be taken as 4. Producer penalties and the food profile can be identified as significant variables, so the weights for these can be set at 8. Once the weights have been determined, they need to be normalized:

$$w_i = \frac{wn_i}{\sum_{j=1}^{m} wn_j}, \tag{6.116}$$

wn_i—i-th normalized weight,
w_i—i-th not normalized weight.

Table 6.32 provides specific values for the variables that are to be normalized according to the formulae presented earlier. Result of the rankings is discussed

Table 6.32 Variable values for different types of salt

	Salt nr								
Variable	1	2	3	4	5	6	7	8	9
Price [PLN]	0.69	7.00	3.80	5.49	10.90	3.00	4.99	3.90	5.99
Weight [kg]	1	1	1	0.5	1.2	0.25	1	0.3	0.5
Manuf. process [scores]	8	8	8	10	10	10	10	10	10
Non-desirable subst. [scores]	1	0	0	0	0	0	0	0	0
Penalties [scores]	1	0	0	0	0	5	0	1	0
Flavor [scores]	4	5	5	7	8	7	7	7	9
Nutr. profile	0	0.2	0	0	0.4	0	0	0	0
Ranking 1	0.72	–	–	–	–	–	–	–	–
Ranking 2	0.64	0.68	0.68	0.62	0.78	0.49	0.72	0.54	0.64

below the table. For the former, values less than -1000 have been replaced by $-$. Such a low value of the measure results from non-linear normalization of the criteria. It is recommended that objects having values well below zero should be treated as not matching the preferences of the decision-maker. It is clear that only one good meets the consumer's criteria. It has the lowest price significantly different from the others. The use of non-linear normalization eliminated from the ranking all goods more expensive than assumed. The number 1 product can only be competed with by a product in a similar price range.

For the second ranking the weight values have been changed. Price is not as important here so it has been assigned a weight 2. As salt is a non-perishable good and weight is not important here, it has been assigned the weight of 1. The weights related to undesirable substances, penalties and food profile have been left unchanged. With a ranking of 2, flavor is of great importance, and therefore the weight for flavor has been increased to a value of 8. The flavor is also influenced by the production process and has a bearing on the appearance of the goods, which is important in this application. Therefore, its weight was increased to 8. The results of the rankings for the second case are shown at the bottom of Table 6.32. The best result was obtained for product number 5. The price per unit of the product here is attractive, plus it has good taste and is in line with the food profile. Admittedly, it comes in a large package, but the weighting of this variable was low.

Conclusion

The essence of the monograph was to gather in one place the methodical apparatus used to support multi-criteria decision-making. Due to the fact that all methods are based on data (of various types), the issue related to the initial data analysis has been reflected in theoretical considerations and has been practically verified on numerous examples. The detailed principles of selecting variables, assigning weights to them, as well as the presented guidelines for determining the importance of criteria and the use of methods of variable normalization, should be an issue that should be explored by each decision-maker. The final result of the entire decision-making process may depend on the proper acquisition and preparation of data, as proved in the second chapter. Also the choice of a decision support method with many evaluation criteria should be determined by the knowledge of these methods, their advantages, limitations, and practical application possibilities.

This monograph is a summary of many years of research on decision support issues, concerning, in particular, the areas of multi-criteria decision analysis and multidimensional comparative analysis. In the case of the first of these areas, multi-criteria methods of supporting decisions were discussed, American schools (e.g., AHP, ANP) and European schools (e.g., ELECTRE, PROMETHEE). Each of the discussed methods has been thoroughly analyzed and tested in various conditions, with different parameters and for various variables, types of criteria, etc. Such a detailed approach to the analysis of commonly known methods is certainly an added value in relation to many other publications available on the Polish market, and what is associated, this enables a better understanding of the algorithms of these methods and areas of their use.

The second area, concerning multidimensional comparative analysis, has been characterized in the context of the procedure and methods originating from the so-called Polish school (Czekanowski, Hellwig), focusing on taxonomic methods. These methods are mainly used for the linear ordering of objects (rankings) and are used in practice, e.g., to study the socio-economic development of regions or individual countries. Since their inception, various developments and new areas

K. Nermend, *Multi-Criteria and Multi-Dimensional Analysis in Decisions*, Vector Optimization, https://doi.org/10.1007/978-3-031-40538-9

of application have appeared. As one example, the author's VMCM method is presented, which applies the properties of vector calculus to build a vector aggregate measure. This approach eliminates the limitations known from the HELLWIG's method, regarding, e.g., the possibility of taking into account objects better than the defined pattern. It also allows you to add objects outside the sample without the need to rebuild the pattern and is more sensitive to the dynamics of the changes taking place.

Against the background of many existing methods of supporting decision-making, including the so-called Polish school with which the author identifies himself, the author's multi-criteria method of the vector of preferences PVM was presented. This method can be classified as a group of methods (e.g., TOPSIS, VIKOR, TMAI) that have common features of methods from the area of multidimensional comparative analysis and multi-criteria decision analysis. They are characterized by the fact that the participation of the decision-maker is limited to the necessary minimum, and thus, it is possible to automate the decision-making process to a large extent. There is also a proposal to name this new area as *Multidimensional Comparative Analysis Decision-Making* (MCADM). Due to its relative simplicity, the PVM method can be used as an alternative to generally known decision support methods. Its advantage is that the participation of the decision-maker is reduced to the prior specification and expression of one's preferences in the form of two vectors: motivating and demotivating. This approach allows solving decision problems with virtually any number of criteria and decision variants, which is not possible in the case of methods such as AHP, ANP, or some versions of the ELECTRE method. The PVM method is also relatively easy to implement in programming languages supporting matrix operations, thanks to which the decision support process can be relatively easily automated. This method is used wherever the ranking process should be carried out and wherever we are dealing with the selection of one decision variant from among many others. The applicability of the PVM method was confirmed by the implementation of several practical case studies, covering various aspects of its application, in various areas of the economy.

Moreover, in the book, it is demonstrated that some solutions developed for the PVM method can be effectively used in other multi-criteria methods, but also vice versa. And so, the ELECTRE and PROMETHEE methods have been extended with new types of criteria derived from the PVM method: motivating, demotivating, desirable, and non-desirable. On the other hand, the possibility of operating on qualitative data was added to the PVM method, using the pairwise comparison matrices utilized in the AHP method. The comparison of the author's PVM method with several others (AHP, ELECTRE, PROMETHEE, TOPSIS) made it possible to point at their advantages and disadvantages, as well as the practical application possibilities of individual methods.

Bibliography

1. Kodikara, P. N. (2008). *Multi-objective optimal operation of urban water supply systems*. Victoria University, Melbourne, Australia. Thesis (Ph.D.)? Victoria University, Melbourne, VIC.
2. Ait Younes, A., Azibi, R., & Roy, B. (2000). ELECTRE IS : Manuel d'utilisation. Document du LAMSADE No. 118, Université Paris-Dauphine, France.
3. Anderson, D. R., Sweeney, D. J., Williams, T. A., & Martin, R. K. (2007). *An introduction to management science: a quantitative approach to decision making*. South-Western College Publishing House.
4. Aronsona, E., Wilsona, T., & Alert R. (2007). *Psychologia społeczna* (2 ed.). Poznań: Zysk i S-ka.
5. Azadi, H., Berg, J. v. d., Peter, H., & Hosseininia, G. (2009). Sustainability in rangeland systems: Introduction of fuzzy multi objective decision making. *International Research Journal of Environmental Science, 4*(1), 19–32.
6. Bąk, I., Markowicz, I., Mojsiewicz, M., & Wawrzyniak, K. (2015). Wzory i tablice. Metody statystyczne i ekonometryczne, CeDeWu.
7. Bana e Costa, C. A., & Vansnick, J.-C. (1997). A theoretical framework for measuring attractiveness by a categorical based evaluation technique (MACBETH). In J. Clímaco, editor, *Multicriteria Analysis: Proceedings of the XIth International Conference on MCDM, 1–6 August 1994, Coimbra, Portugal* (pp. 15–24). Berlin, Heidelberg: Springer.
8. Banaszyk, P., Fimińska-Banaszyk, R., & Stańda, A. (1997). *Zasady zarządzania w przedsiębiorstwie*. Poznań: Wyższej Szkoły Bankowej.
9. Barron, F. H., & Barrett, B. E. (1996). Decision quality using ranked attribute weights. *Management Science, 42*(11), 1515–1523.
10. Bartosiewicz, S. (1984). Zmienne syntetyczne w modelowaniu ekonometrycznym. In *Prace naukowe Akademii Ekonomicznej we Wrocławiu*, number 262 in Monografie i Opracowania (pp. 5–8). Wrocław: Wydawnictwo Uczelniane Akademii Ekonomicznej we Wrocławiu.
11. Bartosiewicz, S. (1989). *Ekonometria. Technologia ekonometrycznego przetwarzania informacji* (2nd ed.). Warszawa: PWE.
12. Baryłko-Pikielna, N. (1975). *Zarys analizy sensorycznej żywności*. Warszawa: Wydawnictwa Naukowo-Techniczne.
13. Benayoun, R., Roy, B., & Sussman, B. (1966). *ELECTRE: Une méthode pour guider le choix en presence de points de vue multiples*. Direction Scientifique.
14. Berger, J. (1990). *Statistical decision theory. Foundations, concepts, and methods*. Springer-Verlag GmbH.

K. Nermend, *Multi-Criteria and Multi-Dimensional Analysis in Decisions*, Vector Optimization, https://doi.org/10.1007/978-3-031-40538-9

15. Bertolini, M., & Bevilacqua, M. (2006). A combined goal programming? AHP approach to maintenance selection problem. *Reliability Engineering & System Safety, 91*(7), 839–848.
16. Binderman, A. (2011). Wielokryterialne metody analizy zróżnicowania polskiego rolnictwa w 2009 roku. *Metody ilościowe w badaniach ekonomicznych, 12*(2), 58–68.
17. Binderman, Z., Borkowski, B., & Szczęsny, W. (2008). O pewnej metodzie porządkowania obiektów na przykładzie regionalnego zróżnicowania rolnictwa. In Z. Binderman (Ed.), *Metody ilościowe w badaniach ekonomicznych: Wielowymiarowa analiza danych*. Warszawa: Wydawnictwo Szkoły Głównej Gospodarstwa Wiejskiego.
18. Borawski, M. (2007). *Rachunek wektorowy w przetwarzaniu obrazów*. Szczecin: Wydawnictwo Uczelniane Politechniki Szczecińskiej.
19. Borawski, M. (2012). *Rachunek wektorowy z arytmetyką przyrostów w przetwarzaniu obrazów*. Warszawa: Wydawnictwo Naukowe PWN.
20. Borys, T. (1978). Metody normowania cech w statystycznych badaniach porównawczych. *Przegląd Statystyczny, 2*, 227–239.
21. Borys, T. (1984). *Kategoria jakości w statystycznej analize porównawczej*, vol. 284 of *Prace naukowe Akademii Ekonomicznej imienia Oskara Langego we Wrocławiu*. Wrocław: Wydawnictwo Uczelniane Akademii Ekonomicznej we Wrocławiu.
22. Boudon, R. (1979). Effets pervers et ordre social. *Revue française de pédagogie, 47*(1), 68–72.
23. Bozóki, S., & Lewis, R. H. (2005). Solving the least squares method problem in the ahp for 3x3 and 4x4 matrices. *Central European Journal of Operations Research, 13*, 255–270.
24. Brans, J.-P. (1982). L'ingénierie de la décision: élaboration d'instruments d'aide a la décision. La méthode PROMETHEE. In R. Nadeau, & M. Landry, (Eds.), *L'aide a la décision: Nature, Instruments et Perspectives d'Avenir* (pp. 183–214). Quebec: Presses de l'Université Laval.
25. Brans, J.-P., & Mareschal, B. (2005). *Promethee methods* (pp. 163–186). New York, NY: Springer New York.
26. Brans, J. P., & Vincke, P. (1985). A preference ranking organisation method: (The PROMETHEE method for multiple criteria decision-making). *Management Science, 31*(6), 647–656.
27. Bronsztejn, I., & Siemiendiajew, K. (2000). *Matematyka, Poradnik encyklopedyczny*. Warszawa: PWN.
28. Candidate Support Pack. (2009). Decision Making for Managers. Technical Report F5GG 36, Scottish Qualifications Authority, Glasgow, Midlothian.
29. Całczyński, A., Kędzierska-Stróż, D., Orzechowska, D., & Śleszy nski, Z. (2000). *Elementy badań operacyjnych w zarządzaniu* (vol. I). Radom: Politechniki Radomskiej.
30. Ching-Lai, H., & Kwangsun, Y. (1981). *Multiple attribute decision making methods and aplications, a state-of-the-art survey*. Berlin, Heidelberg, New York: Springer-Verlag.
31. Choo, E. U., & Wedley, W. (2004). A common framework for deriving preference values from pairwise comparison matrices. *Computers & Operations Research, 31*(6), 893–908.
32. Cieślak, M. (1974). Taksonomiczna procedura programowania rozwoju i określania zapotrzebowania na kadry kwalifikowane. *Przegląd Statystyczny, 21*(1), 29–39.
33. Cieślak, M. (1976). *Modele zapotrzebowania na kadry kwalifikowane*. Biblioteka ekonometryczna. Państwowe Wydawnictwo Naukowe.
34. European Commission. (2015) Eurostat databse.
35. Craig, A. (1996). Wprowadzenie do analizy decyzyjnej i jej zastosowanie w farmakoekonomii. *Pharmacotherapy in Psychiatry and Neurology, 12*(1).
36. Czermiński, A., & Czapiewski, M. (1995). *Organizacja procesów decyzyjnych*. Gdańsk: Wydawnictwo Uniwersytetu Gdańskiego.
37. Czermiński, A., & Trzcieniecki, J. (1969). *Elementy teorii i zarządzania*. PWN.
38. Czermiński, J. (2002). *Systemy wspomagania decyzji w zarządzaniu przedsiębiorstwem*. Toruń, Gdańsk: Wydawnictwo Dom Organizatora.
39. Kahneman, D. (2012). *Pułapki myślenia. O myśleniu szybkim i wolnym*. Poznań: Media Rodzina.

40. Diakoulaki, D., Antunes, C. H., & Martins, A. G. (2005. MCDA and energy planning. In S. Greco, (Ed.), *Multiple criteria decision analysis: state of the art surveys*, number 78 in *International series in operations research & management science* (pp. 859–890). New York: Springer.
41. Dittman, P., & Pisz, Z. (1975). Metoda dynamicznego badania zróżnicowania przestrzennego zjawisk społeczno-ekonomicznych. *Wiadomości Statystyczne, 20*(11), 27–28.
42. Domański, C., & Pruska, K. (2000). *Nieklasyczne metody statystyczne*. Warszawa: PWE.
43. Duckstein, L., & Gershon, M. (1983). Multicriterion analysis of a vegetation manage- ment problem using ELECTRE II. *Applied Mathematical Modelling, 4*(6), 254–261 (1983)
44. Konarzewska-Gubała, E. (1991). *Wielokryterialne wspomaganie decyzji: system BIPO-LAR*. Number 551 in Monografie i Opracowania. Wrocław: Prace Naukowe Akademii Ekonomicznej we Wrocławiu.
45. Edwards, W., & Fasolo, B. (2001). Decision technology. *Annual Review of Psychology, 52*, 581–606.
46. Evangelos, T. (2000). *Multi-criteria decision making metods: A comparative study* (vol. 44). Springer-Science+Buzness Media, B.V.
47. Fierich, J. (1957). Próba zastosowania metod taksonomicznych do rejonizacji systemów rolniczych w województwie krakowskim. *Myśl Gospodarcza, 3*.
48. Figueira, J., Greco, S., & Ehrgott, M. (2005). Introduction. In J. Figueira, S. Greco, & M. Ehrgott, (Eds.), *Multiple criteria decision analysis: state of the art surveys*, number 78 in *International series in operations research & management science* (pp. 22–37, 1 ed.). New York: Springer-Verlag.
49. Figueira, J., Mousseau, V., & Bernard, R. (2005). Electre methods. In S. Greco, (Ed.), *Multiple criteria decision analysis: state of the art surveys*, number 78 in *International series in operations research & management science* (p. 1048). New York: Springer-Verlag.
50. Figueira, J., Greco, S., & Słwiński, R. (2009) Building a set of additive value functions representing a reference preorder and intensities of preference: GRIP method. *European Journal of Operational Research, 195*(2), 460–486.
51. Findeisen, W., Szymanowski, J., & Wierzbicki A. (1980). *Teoria i metody obliczeniowe optymalizacji, PWN, Warszawa, 1980*. Warszawa: PWN.
52. Flakiewicz, W. (1976). Semantyczne aspekty opisu procesu informacyjno-decyzyjnego. *Prakseologia*.
53. Flakiewicz, W., & Wawrzyniak, B. (1975). *Techniki podejmowania decyzji*. Warszawa: TNOiK.
54. Florek, K., Ł ukaszewicz, J., Perkal, J., Steinhaus, H., & Zubrzycki, S. (1951). Taksonomia wrocĹ'awska. *PrzeglÄ'd Antropologiczny, XVIII*(17).
55. Gabus, A., & Fontela, E. (1972). *World problems, an invitation to further thought within the framework of DEMATEL*. Geneva, Switzerland: Batelle Institute, Geneva Research Centre.
56. Gatnar, E., & Walesiak, M. (Eds.). (2004). *Metody statystycznej analizy wielowymiarowej w badaniach marketingowych*. Wrocław: Wydawnictwo Akademii Ekonomicznej im. Oskara Langego we Wrocławiu.
57. Ginda, G., & Maślak, M. (2012). Ekspercka analiza relacji pomiędzy różnoźródłowymi ryzykami w kontekście wymagań zrównoważonego budownictwa. *Czasopismo techniczne Politechniki Krakowskiej, 21*(4-B), 51–74.
58. Gliński, B., & Kuc, B. R. (1990). *Podstawy zarządzania organizacjami*. Warszawa: PWE.
59. Goicoechea, A., Hansen, D. R., & Duckstein, L. (1983). Multiobjective decision analysis with engineering and business applications. *The Engineering Economist, 29*(1), 76–77.
60. Grabiński, T. (1984). *Wielowymiarowa analiza porównawcza w badaniach dynamiki zjawisk ekonomicznych*, vol. 61 of *Monografie*. Kraków: AE w Krakowie.
61. Grabiński, T. (1985). Wybrane problemy dynamicznej wielowymiarowej analizy porównawczej. In *Ruch Prawniczy, Ekonomiczny i Socjologiczny* (vol. 2).
62. Grabiński, T. (1995). Informacyjne aspekty statystyki międzynarodowej. *Wiadomości Statystyczne, 9*, 32–36.

63. Grabiński, T., Wydymus, S., & Zeliaś, A. (1989). *Metody taksonomii numerycznej w modelowaniu zjawisk społeczno-gospodarczych*. Warszawa: Państwowe Wydawnictwo Naukowe.
64. Grabiński, T. (1984). *Wielowymiarowa analiza porównawcza w badaniach dynamiki zjawisk ekonomicznych*. Number 61 in seria specjalna: monografie (p. 256). Kraków: AE w Krakowie.
65. Grabiński, T., Wydymus, S., & Zaliaś, A. (1989). *Metody taksonomii numerycznej w modelowaniu zjawisk społeczno-gospodarczych*. Warszawa: PWN.
66. Grolleau, J., & Tergny, J. (1971). Manuel de reference du programme ELECTRE II. Technical report, Document de travail 24, SEMA-METRA International.
67. Grünig, R., & Kühn, R. (2013). *Successful decision-making. A systematic approach to complex problems* (3rd ed.). Berlin, Heidelberg: Springer-Verlag.
68. Guitouni, A., & Martel, J.-M. (1998). Tentative guidelines to help choosing an appropriate mcda method. *European Journal of Operational Research, 109*(2), 501–521.
69. Gwo-Hshiung, T., & Jih-Jeng, H. (2011). *Multiple attribute decision making*. New York: Taylor & Francis Group. Chapman & Hall Book Edition.
70. Hammond, J. S., Keeney, R. L., & Raiffa, H. (2002). Smart choices: A practical guide to making better life decisions.
71. Hastie, R. (2001). Problems for judgment and decision making. *Annual Review of Psychology, 52*, 653–683.
72. Hazen, A. (1914). Storage to be provided in impounding reservoirs for municipal water supply, (with discussion). *Transactions of the American Society of Civil Engineers, 77*, 1539–1669.
73. Hellwig, Z. (1968). Zastosowanie metody taksonomicznej do typologicznego podziału krajów ze względu na poziom ich rozwoju oraz zasoby i strukturę wykwalifikowanych kadr. *Przegląd Statystyczny, 15*(4), 307–326.
74. Hellwig, Z. (1968). Zastosowanie metody taksonomicznej do typologicznego podziału krajów ze względu na poziom ich rozwoju oraz zasoby i strukturę wykwalifikowanych kadr. *Przegląd Statystyczny, 4*.
75. Hellwig, Z. (1969). Problem optymalnego doboru predykant. *Przegląd Statystyczny*, (3–4).
76. Hellwig, Z. (1972). The selection of a Set of "core" indicators of socio-economic development. Technical Report SHC/WS/274, United Nations Educationals Scientific and Curtural Organization, Paris.
77. Hellwig, Z. (1981). *Wielowymiarowa analiza porównawcza i jej zastosowanie w badaniach wielocechowych obiektów gospodarczych*. Warszawa: PWE.
78. Heurgon, E. (1982). Relationships between decision-making process and study process in OR intervention. *European Journal of Operational Research, 10*(3), 230–236.
79. Hinloopen, E., Nijkamp, P., & Rietveld, P. (1983). The regime method: a new multicriteria technique. In P. Hansen, (ed.), *Essays and Surveys on Multiple Criteria Decision Making: Proceedings of the Fifth International Conference on Multiple Criteria Decision Making, Mons, Belgium, August 9–13, 1982* (pp. 146–155). Berlin, Heidelberg: Springer.
80. Hwang, C.-L., & Yoon, K. (1981). *Multiple attribute decision making*. Number 186 in *Lecture notes in economics and mathematical systems*. Berlin Heidelberg: Springer-Verlag.
81. International Society on MCDM. (2015). Multiple Criteria Decision Making.
82. Ishizaka, A., & Labib, A. (2011). Review of the main developments in the analytic hierarchy process. *Expert Systems with Applications, 38*(11), 14336–14345.
83. Jacquet-Lagreze, E., & Siskos, J. (1982). Assessing a set of additive utility functions for multicriteria decision-making, the UTA method. *European Journal of Operational Research, 10*(2), 151–164.
84. Jahanshahloo, G. R., Lotfi, F. H., & Davoodi, A. R. (2009). Extension of {TOPSIS} for decision-making problems with interval data: Interval efficiency. *Mathematical and Computer Modelling, 49*(5-6), 1137–1142.
85. Jahanshahloo, G. R., Lotfi, F. H., & Izadikhah, M. (2006). An algorithmic method to extend {TOPSIS} for decision-making problems with interval data. *Applied Mathematics and Computation, 175*(2), 1375–1384.
86. Jajuga, K. (1990). *Statystyczna teoria rozpoznawania obrazów*. Warszawa: PWN.

87. Jajuga, K. (1984). Zbiory rozmyte w zagadnieniu klasyfikacji. *Przegląd Statystyczny, 3/4*, 237–249.
88. Jihong, P. (2011). Electre i decision model of reliabilty design scheme for computer numerical control machine. *Journal of Software, 6*, 894–900.
89. JRC - Ispra site. (1996). NAIADE. Manual & tutorial.
90. Kaliszewski, I. (2008). *Wielokryterialne podejmowanie decyzji. Obliczenia miękkie dla złożonych problemów decyzyjnych*. Warszawa: WNT.
91. Karagiannidis, A., & Moussiopoulos, N. (1997). Application of ELECTRE III for the integrated management of municipal solid wastes in the greater Athens area. *European Journal of Operational Research, 97*, 439–449.
92. Karami, A. (2011). *Utilization and comparison of multi attribute decision making techniques to rank Bayesian network options*. Master Thesis, Department of Humanities and Informatics, University of Skövde, Skövde Sweden.
93. Keeney, R., & Raiffa, H. (1993). *Decisions with multiple objectives: preferences and value trade-offs*. Wiley series in probability and mathematical statistics. Applied probability and statistics. Cambridge: Cambridge University Press.
94. Kendall, M. G. (1970). *Rank correlation methods*. Griffin's Statistical Monographs and Courscs (iv edn.). London: Griffin.
95. Kieżun, W. (1998). *Sprawne zarządzanie organizacją*. Warszawa: SGH.
96. Kirch, W., (ed.). (2008). *Level of measurementLevel of measurement* (pp. 851–852). Dordrecht: Springer Netherlands.
97. Kobryń, A. (2014). *Wielokryterialne wspomaganie decyzji w gospodarowaniu przestrzenią*. Warszawa: Difin SA.
98. Kolenda, M. (2006). *Taksonomia numeryczna. Klasyfikacja, porządkowanie i analiza obiektów wielocechowych*. Number 170 in Monografie i opracowania. Wydawnictwo Akademii Ekonomicznej im. Wrocław: Oskara Langego we Wrocławiu.
99. Kompa, K. (2014). Zastosowanie mierników taksonomicznych do oceny efektywności finansowej giełd europejskich w latach 2002–2011. *Metody Ilościowe w Badaniach Ekonomicznych, 15*(4), 52–61.
100. Kompa, K., & Witkowska, D. (2010). Zastosowanie wybranych mierników syntetycznych do porównań poziomu rozwoju społeczno-gospodarczego w krajach Unii Europejskiej. In K. Jajuga, & M. Walesiak, (eds.), *Klasyfikacja i analiza danych - teoria i zastosowania*, number 17 in Taksonomia (pp. 71–80). Wrocław: Wydawnictwo Uniwersytetu Ekonomicznego we Wrocławiu.
101. Koopmans, T. C. (1951). An analysis of production as an efficient combination of activities. In Koopmans T.C., (ed.), *Activity analysis of production and allocation*. Cowles Commission for Research in Economics (p. 404). New York: John-Wiley and Sons.
102. Kordos, J. (1988). *Jakość danych statystycznych*. Warszawa: PWE.
103. Kostrikin, A. (2004). *Wstęp do algebry. Podstawy algebry*. Warszawa: PWN.
104. Kozak, R., Staudhammer, C., & Watts, S. (2007). *Introductory probability and statistics: applications for forestry and natural sciences*. CABI.
105. Koźmiński, A. K., & Piotrowski, W. (2002). *Zarządzanie. Teoria i praktyka*. Warszawa: PWN.
106. Kożuch, B. (1999). *Wstęp do teorii zarządzania, Warszawa, 1999*. Warszawa: Wydawnictwo Nauka-Edukacja.
107. Kukuła, K. (2000). *Metoda unitaryzacji zerowanej*. Warszawa: PWN.
108. Kukuła, K. (2000). *Metoda unitaryzacji zerowanej*. Biblioteka ekonometryczna. Warszawa: Wydawnictwo Naukowe PWN.
109. Kurnal, J. (1978). *Zarys teorii organizacji i zarządzania*. Warszawa: PWE.
110. Lang, S. (1984). *Algebra*. Warszawa: PWN.
111. Langford, E. (2006). Quartiles in elementary statistics. *Journal of Statistics Education, 14*(3).
112. Leclercq, J. P. (1984). Propositions d'extension de la notion de dominance en presence de relations d'ordre sur les pseudo-criteres: MELCHIOR. *Revue Belge de Recherche Operationelle, de Statistique et d'Informatique, 24*(1), 32–46.

113. Levin, R. I., Kirkpatrick, C. A., & Rubin, D. S. (1982). *Quantitative approaches to management*. McGraw-Hill Education.
114. Lima, A.,& Soares, V. S. (2011). Multi criteria decision making models: an overview on electre methods. *Documentos de Trabalho Working Papers, 21*, 3–41.
115. Lin, C.-C. (2007). A revised framework for deriving preference values from pairwise comparison matrices. *European Journal of Operational Research, 176*(2), 1145–1150.
116. Lis, Ch. (2013). *Wartość dodana brutto i jej znaczenie w procesie akumulacji kapitału w świetle teorii wzrostu i konwergencji. Podejście taksonomiczne* (i edn.). Volumina.pl. Szczecin: Daniel Krzanowski.
117. Lootsma, F. A. (2000). The REMBRANDT system for multi-criteria decision analysis via pairwise comparisons or direct rating. Technical Report 92-05, Faculty of Technical Mathematics and Informatics, Delft University of Technology, Delft, Netherlands.
118. Lunenburg, F. C. (2010). Group decision making. *National Forum of Teacher Education Journal, 20*(3), 1–6.
119. Länger, H. (2001). Matrices with a strictly dominant eigenvalue. *Elemente der Mathematik, 56*(2), 55–61.
120. Matlin, M. W. (2005). *Cognition* (6th edn.). Orlando, FL: John Wiley & Sons.
121. Maystre, L., Pictet, J., & Simos, J. (1994). *Les methodes multicriteres ELECTRE*. Lausanne: Presses Polytechniques et Universitaires Romandes.
122. Michnik, J. (2013). Weighted influence non-linear gauge system (wings)? An analysis method for the systems of interrelated components. *European Journal of Operational Research, 228*(3).
123. Mota, P., Campos, A., & Neves-Silva, R. (2013). First look at MCDM: choosing a decision method. *Advances in Smart Systems Research, 3*(1), 25–30.
124. Mousseau, V., Figueira, J., & Naux, J.-P. (2001). Using assignment examples to infer weights for ELECTRE TRI method: Some experimental results. *European Journal of Operational Research, 130*(2), 263–275.
125. Moy, J. W., Fung Lam, K., & Ung Choo, E. (1997). Deriving the partial values in MCDM by goal programming. *Annals of Operations Research, 74*(0), 277–288.
126. Munda, G. (1995). *Multicriteria evaluation in a fuzzy environment*. Contributions to economics. Berlin, Heidelberg: Physica-Verlag Heidelberg.
127. Młodak, A. (2006). *Analiza taksonomiczna w statystyce regionalnej*. Warszawa: Difin.
128. Nermend, K. (2006). A synthetic measure of sea environment pollution. *Polish Journal of Environmental Studies, 15*(4b), 127–130.
129. Nermend, K. (2007). Taxonomic vector measure of region development (TWMRR). *Polish Journal of Environmental Studies, 16*(4A), 195–198.
130. Nermend, K. (2008). Employing similarity measures to examine the development of technical infrastructure in Polish counties. *Folia Oeconomica Stetinensia, 15*(7), 87–97.
131. Nermend, K. (2008). *Rachunek wektorowy w analizie rozwoju regionalnego*. Szczecin: Wydawnictwo Naukowe Uniwersytetu Szczecińskiego.
132. Nermend, K. (2008). Zastosowanie rzutu wektora do budowy miernika syntetycznego. *Przegląd Statystyczny, 55*(3), 10–21.
133. Nermend, K. (2009). *Vector calculus in regional development analysis. comarative regional analysis using the example of Poland*. Contributions to Economics. Berlin, Heidelberg: Springer.
134. Nermend, K. (2013). Badanie własności metod normowania wykorzystywanych w rangowaniu obiektów społeczno-gospodarczych. *Problemy Ekonomiki Uslug, Zeszyty Naukowe Uniwersytetu Szczecińskiego, 781*(103), 171–186.
135. Nermend, K. (2013). Properties of normalization methods used in the construction of aggregate measures. *Folia Oeconomica Stetinensia, 12*(2), 31–45.
136. Nermend, K. (2015). Wielokryterialna metoda wektora preferencji jako narzędzie wspomagające proces decyzyjny. *Przegląd statystyczny, 62*(1), 71–92.
137. Nermend, K., & Borawski, M. (2014). Modeling users? Preferences in the decision support system. *Indian Journal of Fundamental and Applied Life Sciences, 4*(S1), 1480–1491.

138. Nermend, K., & Tarczyńska-Łuniewska, M. (2013). Badanie jednorodności przestrzennej i czasowej rozwoju obiektów społeczno-gospodarczych. *Przegląd Statystyczny, 60*(1), 85–100.
139. Nowak, E. (1984). *Problemy doboru zmiennych do modelu ekonometrycznego*. Warszawa: PWN.
140. Nowak, E. (2009). *Metody taksonomiczne w klasyfikacji obiektów społeczno-gospodarczych*. Warszawa: PWE.
141. Nowak, E. (1990) *Metody taksonomiczne w klasyfikacji obiektów społeczno-ekonomicznych*. Warszawa: PWE.
142. Nowak, M. (2004) Metody electre w deterministycznych i stochastycznych problemach decyzyjnych. *Decyzje, 2*, 35–65.
143. Nowak, M. (2006) INSDECM? An interactive procedure for stochastic multicriteria decision problems. *European Journal of Operational Research, 175*, 1413–1430.
144. Opricovic, S. (1998). Multicriteria optimization of civil engineering systems. Technical report, Faculty of Civil Engineering, Belgrade.
145. Opricovic, S., & Tzeng, G.-H. (2004). Compromise solution by {MCDM} methods: A comparative analysis of {VIKOR} and {TOPSIS}. *European Journal of Operational Research, 156*(2), 445–455.
146. Panek, T., & Zwierzchowski, J. (2013). *Statystyczne metody wielowymiarowej analizy porównawczej. Teoria i zastosowania*. Warszawa: Oficyna Wydawnicza SGH.
147. Pawłowicz, L. (1988). *Wybrane metody taksonomii numerycznej i ich zastosowanie w badaniach ekonomicznych* (vol. 1). Gdańsk: Wydawnictwo Uniwersytetu Gdańskiego.
148. Pei, Z. (2013). Rational decision making models with incomplete weight information for production line assessment *Information Sciences: An International Journal, 222*, 296–716.
149. Pirdashti, M., Ghadi, A., Mohammadi, M., & Shojatalab, G. (2009). Multi-criteria decision-making selection model with application to chemical engineering management decisions. *International Journal of Chemical, Molecular, Nuclear, Materials and Metallurgical Engineering, 3*(1), 1–6.
150. Pluta, W. (1977). *Wielowymiarowa analiza porównawcza w badaniach ekonomicznych*. Warszawa: PWE.
151. Pluta, W. (1977). *Wielowymiarowa analiza porównawcza w badaniach ekonomicznych: metody taksonomiczne i analizy czynnikowej*. Warszawa: Państwowe Wydawnictwo Ekonomiczne.
152. Pociecha, J., Podolec, B., Sokłowski, A., & Zając, K. (1988). *Metody taksonomiczne w badaniach społeczno-ekonomicznych*. Warszawa: PWN.
153. Pociecha, J. (1984). Taksonomia zgodności w badaniach rynkowych,. *Folia Oeconomica Cracoviensia, XXVII*, 85–96.
154. Pociecha, J. (2008). Rozwój metod taksonomicznych i ich zastosowań w badaniach społeczno-ekonomicznych.
155. Pomerol, J.-C., & Barba-Romero, S. (2000). *Multicriterion decision in management: principles and practice*. International series in operations research & management. Boston, London: Kluwer Academic Publishers.
156. Pringle, C. D., Jennings, D. F., & Longnecker, J. G. (1988). *Managing organizations: functions and behaviors, Columbus*. Merrill Publishing Company.
157. Prusak, A., & Stefanów, P. (2014). *AHP - analityczny proces hierarchiczny. Budowa i analiza modeli decyzyjnych krok po kroku*. Ekonomia Zarządzanie. Warszawa: C.H.Beck.
158. Robbins, S. P. (2005). *Skuteczne podejmowanie decyzji*. Warszawa: PWE.
159. Rogers, M. G., Bruen, M., & Maystre, L.-Y. (2000). *ELECTRE and decision support. Methods and applications in engineering and infrastructure investment* (1st edn.). New York: Springer US.
160. Roszkowska, E., & Wachowicz, T. (2016). *Negocjacje. Analiza i wspomaganie decyzji*. Wolters Kluwer SA.
161. Roubens, M. (1982). Preference relations on actions and criteria in multicriteria decision making. *European Journal of Operational Research, 10*(1), 51–55. Cited By 73.

162. Roy, B. (1968). Classement et choix en pr´esence de points de vue multiples (la methode ELECTRE). In *La Revue d'Informatique et de Recherche Opérationelle* (vol. 8, pp. 57–75).
163. Roy, B. (1978). ELECTRE III: Un algorithme de rangement fonde sur une representation floue des preferences en presence de criteres multiples. *Cahiers du Centre d'etudes de recherche operationnelle, 20*, 3–24.
164. Roy, B. (1990). *Wielokryterialne wspomaganie decyzji*. Warszawa: WNT.
165. Roy, B. (1996). *Multicriteria methodology for decision aiding*. Number 12 in Nonconvex optimization and its applications. Springer US, Springer-Verlag US.
166. Roy, B. (2016). Paradigms and challenges. In S. Greco, M. Ehrgott, & J. R. Figueira, (eds.), *Multiple criteria decision analysis. State of the art surveys*. Number 233 in International Series in Operations Research & Management Science (pp. 19–39). New York: Springer-Verlag.
167. Roy, B., & Bertier, B. (1971). La Méthode ELECTRE II: Une méthode de classement en presence de crit'res multiples. *Note de travail, 142*.
168. Roy, B., & Bertier, B. (1973). La méthode ELECTRE. In M. Ross, (ed.), *Operational research* (vol. 72, pp. 291–302). Amsterdam: North-Holland.
169. Roy, B., & Bouyssou, D. (1993). *Aide multicrit're' la décision : méthodes et cas*. Production et techniques quantitatives appliquées' la gestion. Paris: Economica.
170. Roy, B., & Hugonnard, J. C. 1982. Ranking of suburban line extension projects on the Paris metro system by a multicriteria method, transportation research. *Elsevier, 16A*(4), 301–312.
171. Roy, B., & Skalka, J. M. (1984). ELECTRE IS : Aspects méthodologiques et guide d'utilisation. *Document du Lamsade, Université Paris Dauphine, France*, 30.
172. Runiański, J. (1965). *Przed decyzją*. Warszawa: PWE.
173. Saaty, T. (1980). *The analytical hierarchy process*. New York: McGraw-Hill.
174. Saaty, T. (2000). *Fundamentals of decision making and priority theory with the analytic hierarchy process*. AHP Series. RWS Publications.
175. Saaty, T. (2005). The analytic hierarchy and analytic network processes for the measurement of intangible criteria and for decision-making. In *Multiple criteria decision analysis: state of the art surveys*, vol. 78 of *International Series in Operations Research & Management Science* (pp. 345–405). New York: Springer.
176. Saaty, T. (2005). *Theory and applications of the analytic network process: decision making with benefits, opportunities, costs and risks*. Pittsburgh, Pennsylvania: RWS Publications.
177. Saaty, T. L. (1987). Rank according to perron: A new insight. *Mathematics Magazine, 60*(4), 211–213.
178. Saaty, T. L. (1990). How to make a decision: The analytic hierarchy process. *European Journal of Operational Research, 48*(1), 9–26. Desicion making by the analytic hierarchy process: Theory and applications.
179. Saaty, T. L. (1996). *Decision making with dependence and feedback: the analytic network process*. Pittsburg: RWS Publications.
180. Saaty, T. L. (2012). *Decision making for leaders: the analytic hierarchy process for decisions in a complex world*. Analytic hierarcy process series. Pittsburg: RWS Publications.
181. Saaty, T. L., & Hu, G. (1998). Ranking by Eigenvector versus other methods in the Analytic Hierarchy Process. *Applied Mathematics Letters, 11*(4), 121–125.
182. Saaty, T. L., & Ozdemir, M. S. (2003). Why the magic number seven plus or minus two. *Mathematical and Computer Modelling, 38*(3), 233–244.
183. Scharlig, A. (1996). *Pratiquer ELECTRE et PROMETHEE : Un Complement'a Decider sur Plusieurs Crit'eres*. Lausanne: Polytechniques et Universitaires Romandes.
184. Schniederjans, M. J., Hoffman, J. J., & Sirmans, G. S. (1995). Using Goal Programming and the analytic hierarchy process in house selection. *The Journal of Real Estate Finance and Economics, 11*(2), 167–176.
185. Sikora, W. (2008) *Badania operacyjne* (i edn.), Warszawa: PWE.
186. Simon, H. (1982). *Podejmowanie decyzji kierowniczych. Nowe nurty*. Warszawa: PWE.

187. Siskos, Y., Grigoroudis, E., & Matsatsinis, N. (2005). Uta methods. In J. Figueira, S. Greco, & M. Ehrgott, (eds.), *Multiple criteria decision analysis: state of the art surveys* (pp. 297–344). Boston, Dordrecht, London: Springer Verlag.
188. Sobczyk, M. (1977). Analiza porównawcza produkcji rolniczej w województwie lubelskim. *Wiadomości Statystyczne, 2*, 677–680.
189. Stanek, S., & Wachowicz, T. (2013) Negocjacje w dobie Internetu. In *Autonomiczne systemy w negocjacjach, Monograph 13*, number 138 in Studia Ekonomiczne (pp. 9–30). zeszyty naukowe wydziałowe: Wydawnictwo Uniwersytetu Ekonomicznego w Katowicach.
190. Steczkowski, J. (1966). *Zasady i metody rejonizacji produkcji rolniczej.* Warszawa: PWRiL.
191. Stevens, S. S. (1946). On the theory of scales of measurement. *Science, 103*(2684), 677–680.
192. Strahl, D., (ed.). *Metody oceny rozwoju regionalnego.* Wydawnictwo Akademii Ekonomicznej im. Wrocław: Oskara Langego we Wrocławiu.
193. Szarfenberg, R. (2007). Paradoks nieuchronnej niesprawiedliwości w polityce społecznej. In M. Karwata, (ed.), *Paradoksy polityki.* Warszawa: Dom Wydawniczy Elipsa.
194. Słowiński, R. (2007). Podejście regresji porządkowej do wielokryterialnego porządkowania wariantów decyzyjnych. In P. Kulczycki, O. Hryniewicz, & J. Kacprzyk, (eds.), *Techniki informacyjne w badaniach systemowych* (pp. 315–338). Warszawa: WNT.
195. Tarczyński, W. (1996). Analiza dyskryminacyjna na giełdzie papierów wartościowych. *Przegląd statystyczny, 1-2*(XLIII).
196. Tarczyński, W. (2002). *Fundamentalny portfel papierów wartościowych.* Warszawa: PWE.
197. Tarczyński, W. (2004). Dynamiczne ujęcie taksonomicznej miary atrakcyjności inwestycji na przykładzie wybranych spółek notowanych na giełdzie papierów wartościowych w Warszawie. *Zeszyty Naukowe Uniwersytetu Szczecińskiego, 394*(15), 299–322.
198. Tarczyński, W., & Mojsiewicz, M. (2001). *Zarządzanie ryzykiem.* Warszawa: PWE.
199. Tarczyński, W., & Łuniewska, M. (2006). *Metody wielowymiarowej analizy porównawczej.* Inwestycje. Wydawnictwo Naukowe PWN.
200. Triantaphyllou, E., & Mann, S. H. (1989). An examination of the effectiveness of multi-dimensional decision-making methods: a decision-making paradox. *Decission Support Systems, 5*(3), 303–312.
201. Trzaskalik, T. (ed.). (2006). *Metody wielokryterialne na polskim rynku finansowym.* Warszawa: Polskie Wydawnictwo Ekonomiczne.
202. Trzaskalik, T. (2008). *Wprowadzenie do badań operacyjnych z komputerem* (2nd edn.). Warszawa: Polskie Towarzystwo Ekonomiczne.
203. Trzaskalik, T. (2014). *Wielokryterialne wspomaganie decyzji. Metody i zastosowania* (1st edn.). Warszawa: Polskie Towarzystwo Ekonomiczne.
204. Tsyganok, V. (2010). Investigation of the aggregation effectiveness of expert estimates obtained by the pairwise comparison method. *Mathematical and Computer Modelling, 52*(3-4), 538–544.
205. Vagias, W. M. (2006). Likert-type scale response anchors. *Clemson International Institute for Tourism & Research Development, Department of Parks, Recreation and Tourism Management. Clemson University.*
206. Vallée, D., & Zielniewicz, P. (1994). Electre III-IV, version 3. x. Guide d'utilisation (tome 2). Document du LAMSADE No. 85 et 85 bis, Université de Paris Dauphine, France.
207. Vansnick, J. C. (1986). On the problem of weights in multiple criteria decision making (the non-compensatory approach). *European Journal of Operational Research, 24*, 288–294.
208. Velasquez, M., & Hester, P. T. (2013). An analysis of multi-criteria decision making methods. *International Journal of Operations Research, 10*(2), 56–66.
209. Vincke, P. (1992). *Multicriteria decision-aid.* New York: John Wiley & Sons.
210. von Winterfeldt, D., & Edwards, W. (1986). *Decision analysis and behavioral research.* Cambridge University Press.
211. Walesiak, M. (2002). *Uogólniona miara odległości w statystycznej analizie wielowymiarowej.* Wydawnictwo Akademii Ekonomicznej im. Oskara Langego we Wrocławiu, Wrocław.
212. Walesiak, M. (2003). Miara odległości obiektów opisanych zmiennymi mierzonymi na skalach pomiaru. *Prace Naukowe AE we Wrocławiu, 1006*, 261–267.

213. Walesiak, M. (2011). *Uogólniona miara odległości GDM w statystycznej analizie wielowymiarowej z wykorzystaniem programu R.* Wydawnictwo Uniwersytetu Ekonomicznego. Wrocław: Wrocław.
214. Walesiak, M. (1990). Syntetyczne badania porównawcze w świetle teorii pomiaru. *Przegląd Statystyczny, 1–2*, 37–46.
215. Wang, Y. (2007). The theoretical framework of cognitive informatics. *The International Journal of Cognitive Informatics and Natural Intelligence (IJCINI), 1*(1), 1–27.
216. Wang, Y., & Wang, Y. (2006). Cognitive informatics models of the brain. *IEEE Transactions on Systems, Man, and Cybernetics, 36*(2).
217. Wang, Y., Wang, Y., Patel, S., & Patel, D. (2004). A layered reference model of the brain (LRMB). *IEEE Transactions on Systems, Man, and Cybernetics (C), 36*(2).
218. Wawrzyniak, B. (1977). *Decyzje kierownicze w teorii i praktyce zarządzania.* Warszawa: PWE.
219. Wilson, R. A., & Keil, F. C. (2001). *The MIT encyclopedia of the cognitive sciences.* London: MIT Press.
220. Witkowska, D. (2010). Zastosowanie syntetycznych mierników taksonomicznych do pomiaru efektywności Chińskich banków. *Metody Ilościowe w Badaniach Ekonomicznych, 11*(2), 281–292.
221. World Bank Group. (2015) Doing Business.
222. World Bank Group. (2016) World Development Indicators.
223. Wydymus, S. (1984) Metody wielowymiarowej analizy rozwoju społeczno-gospodarczego. Number 62 in seria specjalna: monografie. Kraków: AE w Krakowie.
224. Zając, K. (1971). *Zarys metod statystycznych.* Warszawa: Państwowe Wydawnictwo Ekonomiczne.
225. Zdyb, M. (1993). *Istota decyzji.* Lublin: Wydawnictwo UMCS.
226. Zeliaś, A. (2000). *Metody statystyczne.* Warszawa: PWE.
227. Özcan, T., Çelebi, N., & Esnaf, Ş. (2011). Comparative analysis of multi-criteria decision making methodologies and implementation of a warehouse location selection problem. *Expert Systems with Applications, 38*(8), 9773–9779.
228. Żak, J. (2005). *Wielokryterialne wspomaganie decyzji w transporcie drogowym.* Poznań: Wydawnictwo Politechniki Poznańskiej.

Index

K. Nermend, *Multi-Criteria and Multi-Dimensional Analysis in Decisions*, Vector Optimization, https://doi.org/10.1007/978-3-031-40538-9

MIX
Papier aus verantwortungsvollen Quellen
Paper from responsible sources
FSC® C105338

If you have any concerns about our products,
you can contact us on
ProductSafety@springernature.com

In case Publisher is established outside the EU,
the EU authorized representative is:
Springer Nature Customer Service Center GmbH
Europaplatz 3, 69115 Heidelberg, Germany

Printed by Libri Plureos GmbH
in Hamburg, Germany